# African Philosophy and the Marginalization of Women

This book examines the underexplored notion of epistemic marginalization of women in the African intellectual place. Women's issues are still very much neglected by governments, corporate bodies and academics in sub-Saharan Africa. The entrenched traditional world-views which privilege men over women make it difficult for the modern day challenges posed by the neglect of the feminine epistemic perspective, to become obvious.

Contributors address these issues from both theoretical and practical perspectives, demonstrating what philosophy could do to ameliorate the epistemic marginalization of women, as well as ways in which African philosophy exacerbates this marginalization. Philosophy is supposed to teach us how to lead the good life in all its ramifications; why is it failing in this duty in Africa where the issue of women's epistemic vision is concerned? The chapters raise feminist agitations to a new level; beginning from the regular campaigns for various women's rights and reaching a climax in an epistemic struggle in which the knowledge-controlling power to create, acquire, evaluate, regulate and disseminate is proposed as the last frontier of feminism.

**Jonathan O. Chimakonam**, Ph.D., is a Senior Lecturer at the University of Calabar, Nigeria and a Research Fellow, Department of Philosophy, University of Pretoria, South Africa.

**Louise du Toit**, Ph.D., is Associate Professor in the Department of Philosophy at Stellenbosch University, South Africa.

# Routledge African Studies

# African Philosophy and the Epistemic Marginalization of Women

Edited by
Jonathan O. Chimakonam and
Louise du Toit

LONDON AND NEW YORK

First published 2018
by Routledge

2 Park Square, Milton Park, Abingdon, Oxfordshire OX14 4RN
52 Vanderbilt Avenue, New York, NY 10017

*Routledge is an imprint of the Taylor & Francis Group, an informa business*

First issued in paperback 2020

*British Library Cataloguing in Publication Data*
A catalogue record for this book is available from the British Library

*Library of Congress Cataloging in Publication Data*
Names: Chimakonam, Jonathan O., editor.
Title: African philosophy and the marginalization of women / edited by Jonathan O. Chimakonam and Louise du Toit.
Description: New York : Routledge, 2018. | Series: Routledge African studies; 27
Identifiers: LCCN 2017053638| ISBN 9780815359647 (hardback) | ISBN 9781351120104 (ebook) | ISBN 9781351120074 (mobipocket)
Subjects: LCSH: Philosophy, African–History–21st century. | Philosophy–Africa–History–21st century. | Feminist theory–Africa. | Women philosophers–Africa. | Women–Africa–Social conditions.
Classification: LCC B5321 .A37 2018 | DDC 199/.6082–dc23
LC record available at https://lccn.loc.gov/2017053638

ISBN: 978-0-8153-5964-7 (hbk)
ISBN: 978-0-367-59116-8 (pbk)

Typeset in Times New Roman
by Taylor & Francis Books

To Aisha Buhari and other women in the sub-Saharan Africa who daily bear the brunt of male chauvinism in the form of 'October 14, 2016 comment'.

# Contents

# Tables

# Acknowledgements

This book is the outcome of an International Colloquium on 'Marginalization in African Philosophy: Women and the Environment' which we hosted in September of 2016 at the University of Calabar, Nigeria. This is the second instalment of the proceedings of that great conference. The first, which focuses on the theme of environment, was released by the same publisher in the last quarter of 2017. This volume collects papers on the second theme of the colloquium, which is women. We thank the Vice Chancellor of the University of Calabar, Professor Zana Akpagu, for the part funding the University provided for the International Colloquium at which most of the papers in this volume were presented. We owe a basket of gratitude to Distinguished Professor Thaddeus Metz of the University of Johannesburg, who assisted greatly in organising the colloquium and reviewing the essays in this volume. We thank Professor Metz specifically for providing financial support which enabled some of the delegates to attend the colloquium. Our special appreciations go to members of the Conversational School of Philosophy – The Elite African Philosophy Circle, who worked tirelessly with us to organize and host the International Colloquium. Mention must be made of Dr Mesembe Edet, Victor Nweke, Segun Samuel, Aribiah Attoe, Eloka Uduagwu, L. Uchenna Ogbonnaya, Umezurike Ezugwu, Amadioha Egwu, Charles Onyeanwuna and others. We thank also the undergraduate African philosophy students of University of Calabar, who lightened up the colloquium with their participation. We cannot forget the Head of Department, Professor K. A. Ojong and colleagues in the Department of Philosophy at the University of Calabar, as well as the Dean of Faculty of Arts, Professor Dorothy Oluwagbemi-Jacob, for their support during the colloquium. We thank in a special way the Director (Professor Chris Nwamuo) and Staff of Bassey Andah Institute for African and Asian Studies, and the Director and Staff of the Directorate of Research and Quality Assurance, both of University of Calabar for providing us with venues, support and facilities during the colloquium. Perhaps, the best part of our appreciations should go to colleagues who honoured our invitation to come to Calabar from different countries and make their presentations, without which we would not have this volume on African Philosophy and the Epistemic Marginalization of Women. Finally, we thank some friends that assisted in one way or the other either during the colloquium or in the preparation of this volume, including: Professor Oladele Balogun, Professor Eno Nta, Professor Chris Ijiomah, Dr Angela Ajimase, Mr Arinze U. Chizube, Mr Ayi Okon, Mrs Victoria Anna, Mr Douglas Afu and a host of others. Finally, this volume contains one previously published article and we here heartily acknowledge the author and the original source of the essay: Louise du Toit, 'Human Rights Discourse: Friend or Foe of African Women's Sexual Freedoms?', first published in *Acta Academica* (2014), vol. 46, no. 4, pp. 49–70, © UV/UFS ISSN 0587–2405, www.ufs.ac.za/ActaAcademica, and reprinted here with permission of the author and publishers.

# Contributors

**Olajumoke Akiode** has a doctoral degree in applied ethics from the University of Lagos, Nigeria. Her research interests include ethics, African philosophy, postmodernism, feminism and gender studies. She has attended and presented papers at international conferences.

**Oladele Abiodun Balogun** received his Ph.D. in Philosophy from the University of Ibadan. He is a Professor of Philosophy at Olabisi Onabanjo University, Ogun State, Nigeria, where he currently serves as Dean of the Faculty of Arts. His papers have appeared in international journals such as: *African Identities* 3(2) (2005), *Nordic Journal of African Studies* 16(1) (2007), The *Journal of Pan African Studies* 2(3) (2008), *Philosophia: International Journal of Philosophy* 38(1) (2009), and *Thought and Practice: A Journal of the Philosophical Association of Kenya* 1(2) (2009) among other numerous scholarly journals. His research interests are in African Philosophy, Philosophy of Education, and Philosophy of Law. Balogun has attended international philosophical conferences in Ghana, Leicester (UK), South Africa, Korea, Singapore, Texas and Minnesota in America. When not engaged in deep thought and writing, he enjoys hanging out with his marvellous children, and lovely wife, Temitope. He is a member of the Conversational School of Philosophy (CSP).

**Jonathan O. Chimakonam**, Ph.D. is a Senior Lecturer at the University of Calabar, Nigeria and a Research Fellow at the University of Pretoria, South Africa. His teaching and research interests include: African Philosophy, Logic, Women Studies, Environmental Ethics and Postcolonial thought. He is the editor of *Atuolu Omalu: Some Unanswered Questions in Contemporary African Philosophy* (University Press of America, 2015); and *African Philosophy and Environmental Conservation* (Routledge, 2018). He aims to break new ground in African Philosophy and Systems of Thought. He is the convener of the African Philosophy Circle, the Conversational School of Philosophy (CSP) and a winner of the Jens Jacobsen Research Award for Outstanding Research in Philosophy presented by the International Society for Universal Dialogue and conferred at the Polish Academy of Sciences, University of Warsaw (July 2016). He is African philosophy Area

Editor for the *Internet Encyclopedia of Philosophy.* He propounded the theories of Conversational Thinking and Ezumezu Logic. Chimakonam has published widely in learned international journals, has organized a good number of international conferences, and has also given several international conference lectures.

**Louise du Toit**, Ph.D. is Associate Professor in the Department of Philosophy at Stellenbosch University, South Africa. Her main research interests include a wide range of themes within feminist philosophy, especially in the European and African traditions. She is interested in sexual violence, critical theory, political philosophy, African feminism, hermeneutics, philosophy and literature, phenomenology, legal philosophy, environmental philosophy and feminist philosophy of religion. She is the author of *A Philosophical Investigation of Rape: The Making and Unmaking of the Feminine Self* (Routledge, 2009) and is currently working on a second monograph with the title *Sexual Violence and Political Transition.* She was also guest editor of 'Rape and Its Meaning/s', a special edition of *Philosophical Papers,* November 2009. She is on the editorial board of the *Indo-Pacific Journal of Phenomenology, De Uil van Minerva* and of *Gender Questions.* She is also part of the Sexual Violence in Armed Conflict (SVAC) research group based in Hamburg, Germany. She is a member of the following international research projects: 'Women, Rights and Religion' (based in Calgary, Canada), 'Boundaries and Legal Authority in a Global Context' (based in Tilburg, The Netherlands and at the Stellenbosch Institute for Advanced Study), 'Towards a Political Ontology of Violence: Reality, Image and Perception' (based in Leiden, The Netherlands) and 'Governing Intimacies' (based at the Stellenbosch Institute for Advanced Study).

**Mesembe I. Edet**, Ph.D. is a Senior Lecturer in the Department of Philosophy at the University of Calabar and a Visiting Scholar in the Department of Philosophy at the Federal University, Wukari, Nigeria. He specializes in African philosophy, comparative philosophy, inter-cultural philosophy, axiology and philosophy of law. His research efforts have been published widely in reputable national and international journals and he has made presentations at various national and international professional conferences, including the 23rd World Congress of Philosophy (WCP) which was hosted by the International Federation of Philosophical Societies (FISP) at the National and Kapodistrian University of Athens, Greece in 2013. His specific contributions to knowledge (theory) in African philosophy include his theory of 'Afroxiology'; his theory of 'Conceptual Mandelanization', his theory of personhood as 'Autonomy-in-community' and his theory of 'the Principle of Regeneration' proposed as explanation to resolve the paradox generated by the belief in reincarnation in African culture. He is the propounder of the 'Philosophy of Mandelanism' developed from his 'Conceptual Mandelanization' as an African socio-political developmental philosophy. He has also developed a 'Theory of virtue-holism in African moral philosophy'. Mesembe Edet is the Associate Editor of *Filosofia Theoretica: Journal of African Philosophy, Culture and Religions*, and the Scribe of the Conversational School of Philosophy (CSP).

**Anke Graness**, Ph.D. is Assistant Professor at the chair of Philosophy in a Global World/Intercultural Philosophy, Department of Philosophy, University of Vienna (Austria). She studied philosophy and African Studies at the University of Leipzig (Germany) and the University of Vienna, where she obtained her M.A. and Ph.D. She is the project leader of a FWF-funded research project on the 'History of Philosophy in Africa' at the University of Vienna. Graness is the author of *Das menschliche Minimum. Globale Gerechtigkeit aus afrikanischer Sicht: Henry Odera Oruka.* (Frankfurt/New York: Campus, 2011). She has also co-edited an anthology on the Kenyan philosopher Henry Odera Oruka: *Sagacious Reasoning: H. Odera Oruka in Memoriam* (Frankfurt/M.: Peter Lang, 1997, with K. Kresse), and a book on intercultural philosophy: *Perspektiven interkulturellen Philosophierens. Beiträge zur Geschichte und Methodik von Polylogen* (Vienna: Facultas/WUV 2012, with F. Gmainer-Pranzl). Graness has published a number of articles in peer reviewed journals in the area of African philosophy, intercultural philosophy, and global justice. Her research interests include history of philosophy, ethics, political philosophy, and feminist theory.

**Elvis Imafidon**, Ph.D. teaches in the Department of Philosophy, Ambrose Alli University, Ekpoma, Nigeria. He is a 2017 Writing Fellow of the Johannesburg Institute of Advanced Study (JIAS), University of Johannesburg, South Africa. His research centers on African ontology and ethics. He is concerned with the extent to which African concepts of reality affect the African idea of the good, and the implications of African ontology for concepts such as corruption, otherness, disability, difference, personhood and gender. He has published several essays in these areas. He is the editor of *Ontologized Ethics: New Essays in African Meta-ethics* (Lexington Books, 2013); *The Ethics of Subjectivity: Perspectives since the Dawn of Modernity* (Palgrave Macmillan, 2015); author of *The Question of the Rationality of African Traditional Thought: An Introduction* (CreateSpace, 2013); and *White Skin, Black Race: The Philosophical Discourse of Albinism in Africa* (forthcoming).

**Bernard Matolino**, Ph.D. is an Associate Professor in Philosophy at the University of KwaZulu-Natal, Pietermaritzburg. His interests are in African philosophy and race and racism. He has published several book chapters and articles in journals such as *Acta Academica, Alternation, Theoria* (SA), *African Studies Quarterly, South African Journal of Philosophy, African Studies, Phronimon, Quest, Philosophia Africana,* and *Social Dynamics.* He is author of the monograph *Personhood in African Philosophy* (2014) and he has just completed another monograph on consensual democracy in Africa, to be published by NISC in 2018.

**Pius M. Mosima**, Ph.D. teaches Philosophy at the Higher Teachers' Training College, University of Bamenda; and is vice Country Director in charge of Research and Programs at the Benchmark Institute for Research and Development (BIRD) Yaoundé, Cameroon; and Executive Board Member of the African Centre for Research, Innovation and Development (ACRID) Limbe/Buea; Cameroon. He is also Assistant Chief Examiner for Philosophy at the Cameroon General Certificate of Education Board (CGCEB) and Fellow at the African Studies Center, Leiden; the Netherlands. His research interests include African/intercultural philosophy, moral and political philosophy, gender studies and bioethics, etc. He has presented papers in different conferences.

**Rianna Oelofsen**, Ph.D. has been a Senior Lecturer at the University of Fort Hare, South Africa since April 2012. She was the secretary of International Society for African Philosophy and Studies (ISAPS) 2013–2016, and organized the ISAPS conference hosted by Fort Hare in May 2014. She is also secretary for the South African Centre of Phenomenology, launched in 2012. Oelofsen completed her Ph.D. dissertation, entitled 'Afro-Communitarianism and the Nature of Reconciliation' with Rhodes University. Oelofsen's areas of interest include: African philosophy; Race and gender theory; Existentialism and phenomenology, and Feminist philosophy. She has published articles in the South African Journal of Philosophy, and has co-edited a book entitled *An African Path to a Global Future*, due to be published in 2018.

**Egbai Uti Ojah**, Ph.D. is a Senior Lecturer in the Department of Philosophy, University of Calabar. His teaching and research interests include Philosophy of Science, African Postcolonial Thought, and Feminism. Currently, he is Director of the Centre for General Studies, University of Calabar. Egbai has published in learned journals and has given some conference lectures.

**Renate Schepen**, is working on her PhD research in intercultural philosophy at the University of Vienna. She studied philosophy at the Vrije Universiteit, Amsterdam, Universidad de la Republica, Montevideo and the University of Legon in Ghana. She is co-author of *Filosofie van het verstaan, een dialoog* (*Philosophy of Understanding, a Dialogue*) (Garant, 2014) and co-editor of *Doordenken, Doorwerken, intercultureel en ecosociaal denken en doen* (*Reflections, intercultural and ecosocial thinking and acting*) (Garant, 2016). She has published a number of articles in the area of intercultural philosophy and dialogue and developed an 'intercultural philosophy' curriculum For the International School of Philosophy (ISVW) in Leusden, The Netherlands.

**Uduma Oji Uduma**, Ph.D. until recently, was a Professor in the Department of Philosophy, Ebonyi State University, Abakaliki, Nigeria. Currently, he is Professor of Philosophy and Director of Abakaliki Center of the National

Open University of Nigeria. He has also taught at the University of Lagos, University of Port Harcourt, Kogi State University and University of Uyo as well as the University of Cape Coast Ghana. His areas of research interest include African philosophy, logic, philosophy of law and metaphysics. He has authored a number of books in these areas and is widely published in learned journals. Uduma is also a solicitor and Advocate of the Supreme Court of Nigeria as well as a chartered manager.

**Betty Wambui**, Ph.D. is Associate Professor and current chair of the Africana and Latino Studies at the State University of New York - Oneonta. A UUP/SUNY Drescher Awardee (2014/15), she received her Ph.D. in Philosophy from Binghamton University (SUNY), USA; and her M.A. in Philosophy from the University of Nairobi, Kenya. Her areas of specialization within social and political philosophy include African Philosophies, Feminist Philosophies, Critical Race Theories and Critical Legal Studies. She has a particular interest in social contract theory, discrimination and morality. She is a member of the Women's Caucus of the African Studies Association and former co-convenor of the Caucus. She has also served as President of the New York Africana Studies Association. Her most recent publication is 'Arrow of God: An Exploration of Psycho-Social and Political Health' in *Illuminations on Chinua Achebe: The Art of Resistance* edited by Michere Githae Mugo and Herbert G. Ruffin II (2017).

# Preface

Once 'the question of women in African philosophy' starts to receive some focused attention, as in this volume, it quickly becomes apparent that the matter is complex, multifaceted and multilayered, and what had seemed to be a singular question inexorably breaks up into a multitude of questions. Among these questions we find the following. What is the place of women and women's issues, experiences and concerns as *themes* for philosophical deliberation, and what should it be? Apart from the question of themes, do *women* currently feature as equal participants in the philosophical discussion, discipline, canon and institutions and if not, what are the contributing causes? What, if anything, do *key concepts* in African philosophy such as Ubuntu and sagacity say or imply about women's status? Is gender equity and women's full humanity first and foremost an ancient African principle that was destroyed and perverted by colonialism, or is it instead an alien imposition on African world-sense? Should we speak about epistemic (both testimonial and hermeneutic) injustices – in Fricker's vocabulary – perpetrated against African women when they are systematically excluded from the African philosophical canon? What are the implications of an answer in the affirmative? What distortions, systemic failures and impoverishments of African philosophy arguably result from the omission of women's voices? Thus, not only does the question arise what injustice is done to women when women are excluded from philosophy, but also what 'injustice' or violence is done to (the promise of) philosophy when women are thus excluded? Has the exclusion of women from (African) philosophy (but also from philosophy more broadly understood) to do with the traditional style of philosophy, or rather with its traditional themes, with institutionalization or maybe with all of these? In other words, if women are to be fully included in philosophical practice, what changes are likely to occur in terms of topics and style of conversation, in matters of institutionalization of the discipline? What are the historic and contemporary causes of women's exclusion from African philosophy? Here we might want to include considerations of the colonial inferiorization and domestication of African women, coupled with colonial exclusion of colonized women from formal educational systems; the collusion of indigenous or pre-colonial African patriarchal tendencies with colonial patriarchies in subjugating African women politically, economically, academically and epistemologically; and the neglect of existing female philosophers' voices and contributions in African philosophical places and publications. Finally, there are all the 'normal', everyday trappings of patriarchy that cast pervasive doubt on women's intellectual abilities, such as education for girls geared toward their sexualization and domestication, rather than toward developing their intellectual excellence. All of these questions and more are raised by this collection of essays. As editors, we are very excited about the range of questions opened up here and the scope of future investigation suggested.

One of the main questions that emerges from this set of essays is the question of women philosophers and its relation to the decolonization of African philosophy. This question is likely to appear strange from more than one perspective. Some might think that what goes under the name of African philosophy is per definition always already decolonized. Others might grant that African philosophy has followed Western philosophy too closely in some respects – such as in its masculine bias – and should use the question of women to reconsider the extent of this imitation, i.e. to become more authentically African. Some may object that the question of women philosophers has nothing to do with the question of decolonization. Still others may argue that the question of women philosophers is 'feminist' and thereby alien to the African continent, and is therefore an indication of (neo-)colonization rather than decolonization. Clearly, these issues need time and space to be more thoroughly investigated. One's response to the question is likely to be strongly informed by one's understanding of pre-colonial African societies, and as this volume also shows, the empirical question about sex and gender arrangements in traditional societies on the continent, is far from becoming resolved. Clearly there is scope for much more dedicated research. Yet at the very least, we must by now acknowledge that pre-colonial Africa was a large, dynamic and diverse place with very different gender arrangements spread across the continent. Moreover, what counted as custom was always temporary and local, and never timeless, universal or unchallenged. As some authors imply here, what makes African philosophy African is that it can never move too far away from local understandings, context, world sense, material arrangements, power distributions and frames of reference, while what makes it philosophy is that it will forever critically interrogate whatever is presumed to be 'given'.

Yet, the debate on women and African philosophy runs the risk of remaining a speculative exercise in an ivory tower with which a largely masculine constituency may well while away their hours and advance their careers unless the actual inclusion of many more women into the philosophical conversation is actively and concretely pursued. It is to be expected that once women enter the philosophical enterprise in greater numbers, their interests will be varied and their contributions multiple, at every level and on every philosophical topic. Thus, there can be no simple answer to the question 'what do women (in Africa) want (from philosophy)?' Tackling institutional philosophical sexism head on like this will teach the African philosophical community much about the nature of the beast called (African) philosophy – aspects that remain hidden and unquestioned and become naturalized and finally rationalized if the material distortion which is women's exclusion remains in place for a long time. One of the questions that will emerge clearly should this agenda be pursued, is precisely the status and image of philosophy on the continent. What is the role of philosophy in both maintaining and rationalizing systems of domination and implied superiority? How does it go about its excluding business, in terms of topics, programs, calls for papers, style of conversation and organization, etc.? Philosophy, popularly under-stood as highly prestigious and as supreme hallmark of intellectual endeavor, may be said to implicitly justify larger social exclusions and hierarchies through its own exclusions and hierarchies. There are clear parallels between the institutionalized racism in philosophy globally and its institutionalized sexism on the African continent and elsewhere.

Clearly then, there is an enormous practical, concrete and symbolically powerful gap between on the one hand, the promise of philosophy as guar-dian of an egalitarian, open, and free-flowing conversation of all with all, driven only by the love of wisdom in whatever form and shape it may be encountered, giving birth to new insights collectively, in the between of ques-tion and answer, and the reality of a highly stratified and jealously guarded privileged space closely following the global patterns of domination in terms of sex, race and class. Insofar then as African philosophy remains true to its own origins in the collaborative reflective practices of pre-colonial societies and to its stated interests in inclusiveness, community, conversation, relationality, and dynamism (as argued by many within the discipline), then it will always retain a revolutionary, egalitarian and emancipatory impulse. It will (should) in other words get activated wherever there is systemic injustice perpetrated in the name of thoughtless rationalizations and uncritically pandered 'givens', whether proclaimed by tradition, custom, religion, peddlers of human rights, global corporate interests, big media, politicians or other parties with vested interests in African communities.

The concrete effort to bring women into this pivotal conversation on the continent is likely to elevate women's status and have a spill-over effect on the larger social inequalities, it will start to do epistemic justice to women and women's typical concerns, and it will irrevocably change the character and quality of philosophy on the continent for the better. When Chimakonam says in his contribution that currently African philosophy tries to sell off half a cake as a full cake, we could add, and the cake is also half-baked. The absence of women's voices cannot but affect the quality and veracity of the 'male half' of reality as expressed in philosophical works. The exclusion of women is not only bad for women; it is bad for philosophy and bad for the world as a whole. This insight is to my mind best expressed in the contribu-tions to this volume (Wambui and Graness) that suggest that one of the most peculiar and damaging distortions of (both western and African) philosophy is its privileging of metaphysical and abstract constructs and its resulting blind spot regarding material conditions of life and existence, including the fragility of the environment. Because of how especially poor and rural women are socially and materially positioned on the continent, they may be in the best position to teach the current practitioners of African philosophy about a dynamically evolving indigenous African environmental philosophy. The renewal of the discipline which may flow from these women's philosophical voices is potentially enormous. It will most certainly serve the agenda of decolonization because including rural women's voices in the philosophical conversation as equal partners will run counter to the most revered and exclusionary cultures of philosophy both Western and more globally. It will thus contribute to the Africanness of African philosophy by more strongly anchoring the conversation in the material conditions of life on the continent and it will contribute to its philosophical nature by radically opening up the conversation driven by the love of wisdom.

On the whole, it is our hope that this volume will stimulate a new and vibrant line of discussion on the subject of women's subordination in African thought. We have benefitted from the help of many people in putting this volume together and here thank them all. We have labored to weed out errors from this volume but as it is a human creation, we humbly take responsibility for any errors that may have escaped us. Our contributors deserve high praise for their efforts at making this project a reality. They are however, finally responsible for the views they expressed in their individual contributions. We have laid down an outline for renewed feminist discussions in African philosophy, so, as the scholars in the Conversational School of Philosophy, an African Philosophy Circle say, 'let the conversation begin!'

J. O. Chimakonam,
University of Pretoria

Louise du Toit,
Stellenbosch University

October 30, 2017

# Introduction

*Jonathan O. Chimakonam and Louise du Toit*

A good number of works have been published on the topic of women's sub-ordination in Africa, especially in the postcolonial era. Most of these works have tended to be advocacies for the release of one right or the other. Others, quite at the extreme, have pursued the opprobrious goal of turning women into men when they make demands that castigate the spaces women occupy in terms of careers, family and society in general. To the latter, it must be emphasized here that there is nothing bad about being a woman, nor is there anything particularly bad about some of the spaces women are known to occupy traditionally. What should be at issue is twofold: 1. The disrespectful way some chauvinists legislate that women *must* be confined to specific spaces which they also caricature as spaces for weaklings. 2. The acceptance of women's freedom not only to venture into other spaces as they please but specifically, the freedom to think for themselves and reach informed decisions on matters that concern them and the society. These serious issues, rather than the radical call for the abandonment of the existing spaces in order to compete for spaces in the presumed masculine territory, should occupy the feminist or the womanist or the femalist in Africa today. There are two things that happen as a result of this spatial abandonment: 1. Those women demonstrate lack of pride in womanhood, 2. As a result, they unwittingly seek release from it in order to become men. But womanhood is a powerful thing, if not the most powerful, and one can share spaces with men without losing her womanhood.

This collection is not about the release of one right or the other for the women in Africa, nor is it about pitting womanhood against masculine chauvinism; it is rather about reasonably expanding the spaces of women, and specifically their intellectual spaces, because we believe that what is happening in all sectors where women are marginalized has its roots in the mind. Human society and civilization have progressed over time due mainly to ideas or knowledges; and ideas or knowledges are products of the human mind. To control the workings of the society, one must first control its knowledges. The idea of women's marginalization we address in this book has to do with the wilful or accidental, cultural or institutional deprivation of knowledge pro-duction, evaluation, regulation and dissemination opportunities to women in the sub-Saharan Africa. The African philosopher must therefore call this problem by its true name – epistemic marginalization!

Thus it is the goal of this collection to confront this epistemic marginalization and prevent reason from derailing in the African place. In the end, this work will offer a proposal for building a conversational culture in which every human being in a society, irrespective of gender, is a citizen philosopher and has a voice in the public arena which should only be challenged objectively. This work is not calling for the overthrow of African cultural framework, nor is it calling for the *masculinization* of women, no! What this work is about is the modernization of some aspects of the African cultural world-views which have proven dangerously archaic. No culture is able to enhance the well-being of a people which does not undergo regular evolution. Much of Africa's cultural heritage, especially that which legislates on women, is at the point where necessary adjustments have become imperative. This collection goes beyond re-hashing what African women have suffered, to point out what they can contribute and help make right in a part of the world that has been the subject of degrading case studies in different fronts, if epistemic power is equitably redistributed and the woman is free to operate from her own entitled space.

Jonathan O. Chimakonam in Chapter 1 makes a claim that the theme of women is being marginalized in discourses in African philosophy. He argues that it is only when African philosophers discuss women as a theme that they would be able to address some of the challenges women face as a group. He observes that there is fear that because women were neglected in Western philosophy for years until recent times, with some dire consequences for civilization, that the case of African philosophy might be worse. He argues that African philosophers have an intellectual duty to end the marginalization imposed on the female mind and allow a space for the voice of the woman. He categorizes this form of discrimination as an epistemic marginalization of women in the African place. This is an exciting piece that ushers in other discourses in this volume on the epistemic marginalization of women in sub-Saharan Africa.

In Chapter 2, Pius Mosima attempts to show how Odera Oruka's conception of sage philosophy/philosophic sagacity is enmeshed in a patriarchal culture. He argues that the position Oruka gives to the female sage needs serious rethinking. The author claims that Oruka's sage philosophy which is centered on indigenous thinkers and the *modern* debate on African philosophy delicately sidelines women. He critically examines Oruka's vision of sagacity from a different philosophic position and aesthetic style; namely, *post-modernism*. The author concludes that this critical endeavor will enable us to see if Oruka's tendentious exclusion of women is still valid in our search for African traditional wisdom in contemporary times. This is an insightful and pro-women re-thinking of Oruka's project of philosophic sagacity that recommends the expansion of the intellectual spaces for women which Oruka's program contrasted.

Rianna Oelofsen in Chapter 3 discusses the theme of women and *ubuntu*. She attempts to answer the pregnant question: 'Does *Ubuntu* Condone the Subordination of Women?' She argues that the world-view of *ubuntu* has been interpreted as giving the highest regard to relationships. On this basis, she claims that a relational ethic such as *ubuntu* is egalitarian at its core. She argues that the reason that *ubuntu* is egalitarian, is as a result of what a good relationship entails. Accordingly, the author concludes, once we understand that a good relationship requires equality, it follows that African societies which condone the subordination of women are acting against the spirit of *ubuntu*. This is an audacious piece that attempts to question African culture's solidarity with women concerns and recommends that a proper interpretation of *ubuntu* would endorse the balancing of epistemic spaces for men and women.

In Chapter 4, Olajumoke Akiode writes on the topic 'African Philosophy: Its Questions, the Place and the Role of Women and Its Disconnect with Its World'. This chapter questions the communitarian orientation as the specificity of African world-view and challenges the assumption that it allocates fair epistemic spaces to men and women. The author asks: Why, despite these inclusive, communalist, being-with, interconnectedness and interdependent traditional/cultural world-views, women are still marginalized in contemporary Africa? Why is there disconnect between what these Afro-communitarian philosophers claim was an essential DNA of the African traditional communities and the actions of contemporary African communities? Again, we have a chapter by an African woman philosopher that radically speaks to the epistemic marginalization of African women. This chapter is a must-read for all those hooting for a new radical idea in defense of women's epistemic perspective.

The title of Chapter 5 by Renate Schepen is 'Dialogues and Alliances: Positions of Women in African Philosophy'. This chapter follows Heinz Kimmerle's interpretation of Irigaray to argue that African philosophy also has an affinity with the way women experience the world: first, the author argues that an alliance between feminist and non-Western philosophies is possible and will strengthen each other's position in the dominant philosophical discourses. Second, she reveals the necessity on the part of the Western philosophical practice to engage with this alliance. This would mean including philosophies from different parts of the world as well as philosophies that represent both men and women. This is an important aspect of the needed worldwide process of democratization of knowledge and socio-political strategies and praxis. Third, she argues that African philosophy also has an affinity with the way women experience the world and see different world-views as complementary. Therefore, it could help both to solve the marginalization of women in philosophy and the marginalization of non-Western philosophies. This is an interesting chapter that speaks to the value of intercultural engagement in the battle against the marginalization of women in African philosophy.

Elvis Imafidon in Chapter 6 discusses the problems associated with how African women deal with the trauma of loss in a culture that subordinates women. He investigates the feminine experience of coping with the death of a spouse. The author draws evidence from, and critically interrogates, rich cultural heritages in Africa such as those of Southern and Eastern Nigeria. He shows that in the feminine existential experience of coping with a spouse's death, there is clearly a tension between individual expectations and communal expectations. He argues that there is the difficulty of rationalizing the ideologies of mourning rites for women in African traditions, particularly when viewed against the background of an epistemology of ignorance. Further, he shows that there is the challenge of understanding the paradox inherent in the sexist treatment of women as perpetuated by women in conformity with societal expectations for mourning. The author concludes from these analyses that a philosopher in Africa researching African thoughts and traditions is saddled with the crucial responsibility of critiquing cultures and traditions within African communities of dwelling, with the primary goal of liberating persons from indefensible ideologies. This is a rich and critical onslaught on fragments of African traditional culture and its policy issues that are now inimical to modern life and deny women respectable epistemic spaces to make their own decisions.

Chapter 7, entitled 'Human Rights Discourse: Friend or Foe of African Women's Sexual Freedoms?' by Louise du Toit, concerns the serious issue of sexual violence against women in the South African postcolony. The author argues that at least one of the reasons for the fundamental *unfreedom* of women in contemporary South Africa, is the clash between two dominant but opposing paradigms that tend to quash the radical potential that a claim to the fundamental right to bodily integrity holds for women. Strategically, the author argues, it is vitally important that human rights activism be used to bolster this cause in the South African context. This is an exciting analytic engagement with the issue of sexual violence that seeks to expand the epistemic spaces of women in policies concerning their sexual health within the South African context.

In Chapter 8, Bernard Matolino writes on the topic 'African Philosophy's Injustice against Women'. The author argues that despite decades of political independence enjoyed by African states, the presence and influence of African women in the intellectual sphere, particularly in philosophy, is truly marginal. He argues further that African male philosophers share a dishonorable characteristic with their European male counterparts. Both sets of males, in the pursuit of philosophy, do not only dominate philosophy but surreptitiously make both the environment in which philosophy is done and the philosophy itself, a male venture. The exclusion of women has greatly impoverished philosophy everywhere, but specifically on the African continent, where women suffer the double tragedy of oppression and burdens of ordinary existence. With a philosophy that actively seeks to invite women's views and style of philosophizing, the continent's philosophy will be diverse and accommodating. By showing that the replication by African males of Western males' styles of philosophizing has done a disservice to philosophy, the author calls for an inclusive mode of philosophizing that takes all inhabitants of this continent seriously as potential philosophers. This is a brilliant piece that touches not only on the epistemic marginalization of women in African philosophy but also on the cost of such marginalization to Africa's intellectual history.

In Chapter 9, Oladele Balogun attempts to conceptually decolonize the concept of 'women' in African thought using the Yoruba as a case study. He argues that such an exercise in conceptual decolonization will assist in getting rid of various distortions and misinterpretations revolving around the conception and roles of women in contemporary Africa, and disrobe contemporary African women from an alien accretion that has always relegated them to the background in contemporary Africa. The author submits that such an exercise in conceptual decolonization from a feminine perspective will reveal the original and undiluted views of traditional Africa on women, which will serve as reference for future generations. This is an interesting piece that attempts to present the traditional African view on women and their epistemic ability in a charitable light.

Chapter 10 by Mesembe Ita Edet is titled 'Women in the His-story of African Philosophy and the Imperative for a "Her-Storical" Perspective in Contemporary African Philosophy'. It seeks to inaugurate a movement or trend in the history of African philosophy that it designates as 'Afro-herstoricism'. The author argues that the 'problem of women and African philosophy' which comes across as 'the absence of strong women's and feminist voices within the discipline of African philosophy' is an epistemic question which contemporary African philosophy ought to address. As the project of writing or (re)writing the history of African philosophy is only recently ongoing, the author argues that the absence of women in historical texts needs to be addressed so that African philosophy does not, like Western philosophy, commit the same historical injustices against half of humanity which is the consequence of a 'gender-blind his-toric deterministic conception of history of philosophy'. The author goes on to say that such an approach would constitute an attempt at 'her-storycide' – the killing (neglect) of women's perspective of knowledge and history. This is a fine piece that speaks directly to the notions of history, epistemic injustice and marginalization of African women in the history of African philosophy.

Betty Wambui in Chapter 11 attempts to develop an Afro-feminist response to some of the environmental questions that confront our world. She makes the case that serious questions raised by the increasingly tragic impact of human interactions within our ecology, are in part answered by an exploration of indigenous and post/decolonial knowledges that find solutions to what is in contemporary times generally recognized as an unfolding environmental crisis. She employs the thoughts of feminist scholars such as Wangari Maathai, Pala Achola, Vandana Shiva, Maria Mies, Ariel Sallah, Mary Mellor and others to explore the place of women in the debates that characterize environmentalism. She presents a post/decolonial feminist take on the problem. She argues that there is a real need to tap into the epistemic resources of women and even recover the relationship of certain special populations (such as women) with our environment if we are to begin to understand and address the issues raised by our environmental crisis. She claims that this is especially important on the African continent, where women's voices continue to require amplification as well as locational empathy and ingress due to systemic epistemic marginalization. This is a brilliant piece on what the African women can contribute in dealing with the environmental crisis if allocated fair intellectual spaces.

Anke Graness in Chapter 12 discusses the intersection of feminist theory and environmental protection reflected in the theoretical and practical work of the Kenyan feminist and ecological activist Wangari Maathai (1940–2011), winner of the Nobel Prize in 2004. In her political and environmental activism, especially in the Green Belt Movement, as well as in her theoretical work, Maathai showed that environmental conservation and women's rights are two sides of the same coin. The author discusses the approach she employs in her books *Replenishing the Earth: Spiritual Values for Healing Ourselves and the World* and *the Challenge for Africa*, and compares her thought with the eco-feminist thought of the Indian scholar and environmental activist Vandana Shiva. The comparison shows that Maathai's conceptualization of the relationship between women and nature follows a historical approach which takes economic, political, and power relations into account and avoids any kind of essentialism. In this, the author claims, Maathai avoids certain pitfalls of eco-feminism, including the perpetuation of a dualistic perspective. In considering the relevance of her work for philosophy, the author points out issues which deserve further philosophical exploration, including the relationship between the renewal of values and the need for structural changes, and the inter-cultural dimension of Maathai's work. This is a fine piece that deals with women's place in environmental conservation as well as intercultural discourse.

In Chapter 13, Egbai Uti Ojah advocates for the re-asking of the questions of African philosophy, especially regarding those issues that concern women. He employs the powerful analogy of 'women in the kitchen of African phi-losophy' to argue that women are being marginalized in African philosophy. The author investigates two questions, namely: In general, what has been the place of women philosophers in Africa? And what exactly should be the place of women philosophers in Africa? He claims that these questions are inspired by the popular African cultural world-view that perceives the place of women at home to be in the kitchen and not in the sitting room where ideas are dis-cussed and decisions are made. Adopting this analogy, the author argues that there is a correlation between the cultural subjugation of women and what obtains in philosophy education in Africa, and specifically in the practice of philosophy in Africa. He submits that the intellectual dangers of this pattern are enormous and recommends an African philosophy-driven solution to integrate the concerns and the voice of women in the framing of its questions. This piece is a must-read, especially for all those who long to see the intellectual consequences of women's subordination made clear.

Uduma O. Uduma in Chapter 14, like Balogun, questions the claim that women are marginalized in Africa and in African philosophy. He re-examines the role and status of women in traditional African society vis-à-vis that of traditional Western societies, with the aim of canvassing that the epistemic validity of today's orchestration of the marginalization of women in traditional Africa is utterly misplaced, wrongheaded and ill-informed. He contends that there is need to distinguish between women's marginalization in postcolonial Africa and women's marginalization in traditional African societies. In the light of this distinction, the author emphasizes that because of the etched distortions introduced into African culture and values by a rather seamless, Westernized African thought process, a distortion which in importing and universalizing the status of women in traditional Western societies enables a dysfunctional distinction between the precolonial, colonial and postcolonial African woman, there are indeed structural difficulties in deconstructing Western historiography in the attempt to identify an authentic, nay, archetypical traditional African milieu or female persona. The author, while lauding the various strands of African feminism – motherism, womanism, femaleism, etc. – as attempts to rein in the misguided orchestrations and emphasize complementarity over inequality, concludes by calling for a robust and holistic rethinking and epistemic reconstruction of feminist African philosophy by situating it in a system of African cultural values, and furthermore making it globally relevant and honed for intercultural engagement. This is a revolutionary piece that attempts to disrupt popular orientation in the women discourse in African philosophy.

On the whole, the idea of this volume is to rethink women discourses in Africa, in African philosophy and in Africa's intellectual history, with the aim of ridding Africa's intellectual history of distortions and misinterpretations on the subject of women. The collection addresses themes cutting across the roles of African women in combatting environmental crisis, cultural subordinations, rights and sexual freedom, sexual difference, epistemic marginalization, gendered estrangement, ubuntu, intercultural discourses, power relations, gender imbalance and injustice, history and gender perspectives, postcolonial, decolonial and postmodern strategies, and so on. Contributors, both women and men, question the conventional discourses and unveil new perspectives on our understanding of women and their contributions in Africa. We heartily recommend this volume to researchers, to philosophers, and to all those interested in the question of women in the African place.

# 1 Addressing the epistemic marginalization of women in African philosophy and building a culture of conversations

*Jonathan O. Chimakonam*

## Introduction

My understanding is that one is a philosopher if one has learned to employ the tool of reason to engage rigorously with questions of life. One is an African philosopher if one can manage to do this not only at the individual level but in engaging those problems facing the African peoples. In Africa, we have many problems that trouble people daily. Some of these problems are social and political; others are economic and psychological. In this work, I want to focus on one quite different problem that is most times less honed in academia, namely the epistemic marginalization of women in the African place. In a world where the epistemic perspective of the opposite sex is trivialized, epistemic lop-sidedness is inevitable.

The concerns of women generally are still very much neglected by governments, corporate bodies, academics and philosophers in sub-Saharan Africa. The entrenched, traditional world-views which privilege men over women make it difficult for the modern day challenges posed by the neglect of women's epistemic perspective to become obvious. Although some efforts are now being made at the global level to address this and all forms of marginalization against women, the impact is yet to be felt at local levels. For example, the United Nations General Assembly in 1996 adopted the Beijing Declaration and Platform for Action (BPfA) articulated in 1995 as a program of action against gender inequality (United Nations, 1995). The 20-year assessment of the BPfA implementation does not show much progress, especially in places like sub-Saharan Africa (UN Women, 2015).

Though it is no longer in doubt how women's subordination affects the economic and socio-political development of a society; and it has also been echoed that women can play pivotal economic, social, political, educational and technological roles for the growth of a state, most societies, particularly those in sub-Saharan Africa, continue to marginalize women. This line of argument has been made in the literature by Lydia Makhubu (1993), Idah Sithole (1993) and Rose Eholie (1993). But my inquiry here will be focused on the epistemic marginalization of women as opposed to other forms of marginalization. I will attempt to trace all the subjugations which women suffer to one source, namely epistemic marginalization. I will then reach out to examine the extent to which African philosophy has become complicit or otherwise in this marginalization. My investigations will, therefore, be guided by the following questions: How has African philosophy marginalized women in its questions? What roles has philosophical education played to ameliorate or exacerbate this epistemic marginalization? Before I wade into these fundamental questions, let me briefly explain what African philosophy is, as well as what it is not.

## African philosophy in brief: what it is, what it is not

Let me begin with what African philosophy is not. African philosophy is not the description of an African world-view or an account of African cultures or histories. These come short of fulfilling the basic properties of philosophical language, namely: rigor, criticism, creativity and systematicity. Against this backdrop, let me turn to what African philosophy is.

African philosophy is the location of wonder in the African place; it is the rigorous and critical application of the tool of reason such that a culturally-inspired methodic ambience accounts for the systematicity of its discourses. Needless to point out that this is my own conviction and may not represent the views of some other actors who are bent on conceiving African philosophy as a reactionary or as a retrospective project of cultural excavations. Granted the foregoing, I will sketch a brief history of African philosophy that aligns with my understanding of the discipline.

African philosophy as a systematic study dates back to the beginning of the twentieth century (Chimakonam, 2014). Some of the factors that stimulated it, according to Ruch and Anyanwu (1981) include racialism, history of slavery and colonialism. During colonial times, the identity of the African was European, so also was their thought system and even their perception of reality structured by the colonial shadow which stood towering behind them. So, to discover or rediscover the lost African identity in order to initiate a non-colonial or original history for Africa in the global matrix, and thereby begin a course of viable economic, political and social progress that is entirely African, became the focal point of African philosophy. Frustrated with the colonial system, the newly trained Africans returning from European and American universities stimulated the journey of philosophical reason in the African place by creating nationalist and ideological discourses later to be elevated into a school of thought in African philosophy. By the time philosophy moved into the universities, a curious brand of theoretical philosophy, later to be christened ethnophilosophy, emerged from the African place. Leading the advocates of this new school was the Belgian priest, Placid Tempels (1959).

Tempels, the European missionary, in his controversial book *Bantu Philosophy*, constructed African philosophy and sought to create Africa's own philosophy as proof that Africa has its own peculiar identity and thought system. Tempels argues that the African is not a nobody but somebody, that s/he is not unintelligent or even less than human (Chimakonam, 2014). Unfortunately, Tempels' efforts were later rejected and criticized by the mainstream African intelligentsia for promoting the Eurocentric vision and for making inaccurate claims about African ontology and thought systems (Hountondji, 1996; Asouzu, 2007). However, it was George James (1954), another concerned European, who attempted a much more ambitious project in his work, *Stolen Legacy*. In this work, there were strong suggestions not only that Africa has philosophy but that so-called Western philosophy, the very bastion of European identity, was stolen from Africa. This claim was intended to make the proud European colonialists feel indebted to the humiliated Africans, but it was unsuccessful (Chimakonam, 2014). That Greek philosophy had roots in Egypt does not imply, as some claim, that Egyptians were dark skinned people, nor that dark skinned Africans authored that philosophy. The use of the term 'Africans' in this present work is in keeping with George James' demarcation, which precludes the light-skinned people of North Africa and refers to what is generally known as sub-Saharan Africa.

Following the efforts of those two Europeans, Africans began to attain maturation. John Mbiti, Odera Oruka, Julius Nyerere, Leopold Senghor, Nnamdi Azikiwe, Kwame Nkrumah, Obafemi Awolowo, Alexis Kegame, Uzodinma Nwala, Emmanuel Edeh, Innocent Onyewuenyi and Henry Olela, to name just a few, opened the doors of ideas. A few of their works sought to prove and establish the philosophical basis of a unique African identity in the history of humankind, while others sought to chart a course of Africa's true identity through unique political and economic ideologies. Elsewhere, I have demarcated the history of African philosophy into two broad epochs, namely pre-systematic and systematic. While the pre-systematic epoch refers to the period from 1900 back to the beginning of time, the systematic epoch begins in the 1900s and runs to date (Chimakonam, 2015a). The systematic epoch is further divided into four periods, namely:

1   Early period: 1920s–1960s
2   Middle period: 1960s–1980s
3   Later period: 1980s–1990s
4   New (contemporary) era: post-1990s.

I will not discuss these periods here as they lie outside the scope of the present research. I must, however, clarify that to state that African philosophy can only be dated back to the twentieth century does not commit us to saying that, in the pre-systematic epoch, people in Africa never philosophized – they did. But one fact that must not be denied is that they did not document their thoughts and, as such, scholars cannot attest to their systematicity or sources. In other words, what this periodization shows is that African philosophy as an academic system first began in the late 1920s; the first period being the early period.

The early period was an era of nationalisms and struggles for political independence. It also witnessed the development of ethnophilosophy by the

academic African philosophers as a theoretical response to the Eurocent.
attack on the African identity and intellectual standing. The middle period
of African philosophy is characterized by the great debate between those who
sought to clarify and justify the position held in the early period (traditionalists
or particularists) and those who sought to criticize and deny the viability of
such position (modernists or professional/universalists).

The middle period eventually gave way to the later period, which had as its
focus the construction of an African episteme. Two camps rivaled each other,
namely the Critical Reconstructionists, who were the evolved Universalists,
and the Eclectics, who were the evolved Traditionalists. The former sought to
build an African episteme untainted by ethnophilosophy; whereas the latter
sought to do the same by a delicate fusion of relevant ideas from the two
camps. In the end, Critical Reconstructionism ran into a brick wall when it
became clear that whatever it produced could not truly be called African
philosophy if it was all Western without African marks. The mere claim that
it would be African philosophy simply because it would be produced by
Africans, as Hountondji (1996) and Oruka (1975) argued, would collapse
under any argument. Due to this great failure, the influence of Critical
Reconstructionism in the later period was whittled down and later absorbed
by its rival – Eclecticism.

The works of the Eclectics heralded the emergence of the New Era in
African philosophy. The focus becomes Conversational philosophizing,
in which the production of philosophically rigorous and formidable African
episteme, an improvement on that produced by the Eclectics, occupied center
stage. It is eclectic in that the ideas in traditional and universal African
philosophy are combined. But above all, it is conversational, eschewing perverse dialogues and concentrating on individual creativity, originality and
system building. I will explain conversational philosophy in more detail in a
later section.

With this brief on African philosophy, one can now seek to know whether
or not there is a nexus between African philosophy and the epistemic
marginalization of women. Does this nexus ameliorate or escalate the problem?

Coming to African philosophy's roles in either ameliorating or escalating
the epistemic marginalization of women, one can argue that where African
philosophers have done nothing to stop it, they have done a lot to encourage
it. Philosophers do owe some obligations to women, as Nkiru Nzegwu explains
(1996). It is perhaps the philosopher who understands the enormous influence
on the affairs of humans of the power to control knowledge. Epistemology
and all of its social, political, economic and psychological appurtenances are
well within the philosopher's domain. Challenging this old order that has kept
women down through epistemic marginalization should be his or her concern
and responsibility. By epistemic marginalization I mean all measures spoken,
written or gestured by men which seek to convey the impression that women
are incapable of, or at least, not sufficiently capable of intellectual rigor or
cognitive enterprise in general. It is the responsibility of African philosophers

to overcome epistemic marginalization of women in all of its ramifications. The fact that African philosophers have continued to neglect this responsibility is one that can no longer be denied. Those who proclaim themselves feminist scholars merely indulge in campaigns for this or that women's right, whereas the kernel of the matter, which is epistemological power, is left untouched. It is my conviction in this work that all the denials women suffer in the society have a common source, namely the power to control knowledge creation, acquisition, evaluation, regulation and dissemination in the society. It is their failure to attack and break this masculine hegemony over knowledge-controlling power that characterizes African philosophers' complicity in the epistemic marginalization of women. Discussions surrounding this subject shall be the concern of the next section.

## How African philosophy marginalizes women: epistemic necessity as the last frontier

Quite a good number of African philosophers/thinkers (Odi, 2010; Uchem, 2001; Chuku, 2013; Chimakonam and Agu, 2013) today agree that women are being short-changed in the intellectual space, but exactly how this is done has not been fully clarified. The likely views you will find out there are about men entertaining poor opinions about women's rigor and men not encouraging women philosophers to aspire. Needless to point out that culture, in the midst of all this failures, drives in the final nails. As correct as these may be, it is hard to believe that they are the main challenges, let alone the only ones, that African philosophy should confront. What about the structure and scope of the questions of African philosophy? One way of scheming women out of the equation has been by excluding them from its questions. When wonder strikes, what follows inevitably is a question. Wonder and questioning are thus the lightning and thunder of philosophy. It is wonder that inspires the questions of philosophy. The framing of questions not only marks the beginning of philosophizing, it determines most importantly, the nature of philosophy that takes place in a given tradition. So, if the opposite sex is not accommodated in the questions of, say, African philosophy, such a philosophy becomes a 'genderized' philosophy. And a gendered philosophy is not only lopsided, it is deformed. Epistemology is not complete if it is built on the foundation of injustice.

Interestingly, this is the problem that Miranda Fricker (2007) attempts to tackle in her book, *Epistemic Injustice: Power and the Ethics of Knowing.* Fricker sheds light on the lopsidedness of epistemology which sidelines the perspective of otherness. She argues that epistemology is undergirded by an ethical rule that necessitates the balancing of perspectives, the violation of which will amount to a form of injustice. As she puts it:

> the project of this book is to home in on two forms of epistemic injustice that are distinctively epistemic in kind, theorizing them as consisting,

most fundamentally, in a wrong done to someone specifically in their capacity as a knower. I call them *testimonial injustice* and *hermeneutical injustice*. Testimonial injustice occurs when prejudice causes a hearer to give a deflated level of credibility to a speaker's word; hermeneutical injustice occurs at a prior stage, when a gap in collective interpretive resources puts someone at an unfair disadvantage when it comes to making sense of their social experiences.

(2007, p. 1)

The point highlighted in the book is that it is not enough to talk about knowing, that process must, in our context, observe gender balance without which the process might be deemed unjust (Fricker, 2007). Knowing and constructing knowledge structures thus become a right, but like all rights, one's right ends where another's begins. When we take a handful of epistemological theories, what do we observe? We observe that they are masculine narratives representing masculine perspectives. One is bound to ask: what about the feminine perspective? We can no longer deny that despite our shared human perceptions and values, men and women have some epistemological differences. I make this claim without wishing to be sexist. But the fact is that psychologists and sociologists who study the depths of human mind, desires and social relations have established that what men basically want out of life is not completely the same as what women want. And these differences in desire and social interaction often manifest in the different shades of emotional strengths they have. While men hurry in life, women tend to be more patient with life. Also, while men manifest high level of courage with their eyes fixed on an immediate result, women tend to manifest the virtue of endurance with their eyes fixed on hope. While men are easily undone by mental stress and trauma, women have a great capacity to absorb mental stress and pressure.[1]

Certainly, all these emotional dispositions count immensely in the way men and women perceive and relate to reality, and should be taken seriously. The problem I wish to highlight is that this important epistemological layer (that is, the feminine perspective) is not considered as having any worthwhile consequence in our knowledge acquisition processes and endeavors. Without serious attention to the women perspective, our knowledge acquisition process is like cutting a cake in half and selling one half as though it was a full cake. Indeed, our epistemological edifice becomes a half-cut cake. Denying or ignoring the feminine epistemological perspective thus becomes one great source of the marginalization of women in African philosophy.

Again, African philosophers have imbibed the attitude of generalizing masculine concerns and experiences. I think this is erroneous. Men and women may have shared values, needs and problems as humans but there are still some peculiar experiences. How do some masculine life experiences contrast with the feminine life experiences? We know of course, that some challenges which women face are not problems for men, for example, pregnancy and childbirth. Many of us might consider this a little trivial and of no importance for the day-to-day philosophical concern, but when we realize that procreation stands at the center of human existence, then we might be able to grasp the ontological, epistemological and ethical import of the question of pregnancy and childbirth. Nzegwu (2003) in her paper, 'Epistemological Challenge of Motherhood to Patriliny', hints this point; but a detailed discussion of the substance of her position is not my focus here. What is highlighted in the above is the possible epistemic cost of marginalizing the female experience of reality in African philosophy. I will make this argument more pungent later in this section.

Also, what is shown here in analyzing the value of the female perspective is that epistemology could have normative concerns. I have explained this process in 'The Knowledge Question in African Philosophy: A Case for Cogno-Normative (Complementary) Epistemology'. I argued that we cannot claim to possess knowledge as something of value if that piece of knowledge does not have a human face – the so-called principle of human interest – and if it does not balance the perspectives of the cognitive and the normative (Chimakonam, 2015b). On the first point, an epistemological edifice loses normative content if it marginalizes or devalues some voices or if it becomes impossible to evaluate it. And it becomes lopsided or non-complementary if it trims off other relevant perspectives like the female gender.

I now turn to what I will call the last frontier of feminism – epistemic necessity. 'Epistemic necessity' for me states that granting women power over knowledge is not a favor but a necessity, because; epistemic marginalization is not only bad for women, it is also bad for men, for philosophy and for knowledge as a whole. The whole of women's agitation and indeed, all of the feminist struggles can be summed up as an advocacy for epistemic inclusion/balance. Knowledge is everything. Its creation, acquisition, evaluation, regulation and dissemination (the five strands of epistemology) collectively represent the genesis of all the problems/discriminations women face in the world. All manner of discriminations and subjugations of women can be traced to these five strands of epistemology. Whether it is labor rights, equal pay, birth control, political office, the right to drive a car, voting rights, economic/business rights, freedom of expression, fair treatment, equal opportunity, etc., insofar as men are the ones who make decisions on the evaluation and regulation of knowledge created or that to be acquired or disseminated, women will always come out short-changed. Think about it, every society has agencies that evaluate any newly created knowledge and regulate the dissemination of knowledge in general. Somehow, the society uses its machinery to decide what people read by deciding well ahead what is printed and how it is disseminated. It is this powerful machinery which is a subliminal strategy that the society uses to control our thinking.

Today everyone, including most women, somehow has this ridiculous idea that women are physically weak and should not work in certain sectors or be in certain professions. And this subliminal messaging somehow influences and determines decisions until it becomes enshrined in the labor laws of different countries. Again, we read books, journals, magazines and watch TV shows or listen to radio programs that associate feminine virtue with home care and project men as family breadwinners. Somehow, when the majority of the people have internalized this falsehood you see countries enacting minimum wage laws with the concept of men rather than humans. And when a woman who should be at home goes looking for a job, she is expected to be grateful for a wage cut. This is also what happens in all areas of feminine agitation today. Men who control knowledge creation, acquisition, evaluation, regulation and dissemination use this powerful position to control what the society thinks and when they finally have the people thinking the way they want them to think, then, they put it in the law books so that no one will be able to think and do otherwise tomorrow.

My point in the above is clear. Labor rights, equal pay, birth control, political office, the right to drive a car, voting rights, economic/business rights, freedom of expression, fair treatment, equal opportunity, etc., are all important for today's woman but above all else, it is the power to create, acquire, evaluate, regulate and disseminate knowledge that women's groups and movements should seek to share with men, and this sharing has to be equitable. It is not something they have to spend eternity campaigning for, it is something they must fight and wrestle out of men. Power is never given or shared by those who control it; it is wrestled and struggled for. Campaigning for women's epistemological entitlements can only hope for Fricker's epistemic justice which will never completely be realized. What is required is epistemic necessity, which can be speedily achieved through a struggle of some sort. What is at stake is 'power over knowledge'. All the sundry rights which women campaign for are determined by 'power over knowledge'. Women can very easily obtain these rights by first laying their hands on the cradle of this power that controls knowledge. The ultimate battle women face in our world today is an epistemological one. It is the last frontier of feminist struggles.

Thus, the concern of this work is the epistemic liberation of women. Knowledge creation, acquisition, regulation, evaluation and dissemination in parts of sub-Saharan Africa are viewed almost like men's rights or a domain which women are not qualified to enter. But this is incorrect. No one has a patriarchal right to wield absolute epistemic power. Power is not synonymous with right, either. It is something which people strategically gain control of in order to control others. This is what Lynne Spender ridicules when she talks of women in knowledge as 'intruders on the rights of men' (1983). She laments the gate keeping strategy which society employs to prevent women from getting a hold on the processes of knowledge acquisition, evaluation and dissemination (1983). This power argument is further sustained by Spender when she explains:

> The values which a society holds and the institutions it creates are not an accident. They reflect the conscious and unconscious choices made by people in power and positions of authority. The way of life – and the quality of life – is directly or indirectly determined by the decisions which

are made within the circles of the powerful. So it would be reassuring to know that those who enjoy the privilege of decision-making were a 'representative' group ... but this is not the case. There is no reassurance. Since we have been keeping records we know that only half of humanity (and a segment of that half) has had any influence in the decision-making circles. The only values and priorities that have been reflected are those of the male.

(Spender, 1983, pp. 1–2)

Spender's position above strengthens my call for epistemic necessity and the hoisting of female epistemology as the last frontier of feminism. What is truly at stake is power to control knowledge. This is what women do not yet have and it is what men use to wreck the feminine folk. The world has been under the control of men all along because they have been able to completely control power over knowledge from generation to generation. In this connection Spender, again, writes:

In each generation, a group of privileged men, on the basis of their own experience and with the endorsement of other men, has had the right to decree the social values. It is not just a matter of whether there will be peace or war, mines or conservation areas, football pitches or child-minding facilities, that has been decided by men, but the more subtle – and some would say more insidious ... What is considered significant, sane and suitable at the most basic level in our ordering of experience, has been decreed – and built upon – for centuries by a small band of men who have found it easy to accept that their ways are the right ways. From government to education, from science to religion, from medicine to media, it has been men who have been in command and given the orders; they have made the policy decisions and put them into practice through the organization and institutions which they, as the dominant group control.

(1983, p. 2)

Regardless of what people thought is going on in the family units or in the villages without electricity or contact with the rest of the world, the foregoing explains the type of power play that has kept women from reaching their full potential for ages. On the whole, the question that looms large is: to what extent can African philosophy help in solving this problem?

In sub-Saharan Africa particularly, it can be argued that African philosophers on average do not see why the subject of women should be given some intellectual space. As a result, their epistemological undertakings are chauvinistic and straight-jacketed by the male perspective. So far, I have been able to explain, however briefly, how women are being marginalized in African philosophy. This is a call for a reconsideration of the questions of African philosophy. There is a need to accommodate the subject and perspective of women in the field of African philosophy. This call, it must be stressed, is not just about gender parity; it is about epistemic balance. African philosophy, no doubt, has been on trial of viability all along; we cannot afford to go on constructing a lopsided epistemology. In the next section, I will outline my proposal for a conversational turn.

## Building a culture of conversations

Do African philosophers owe a duty to African women? There are two ways one might look at this question. First would be to point at its implication that women need men's approval to philosophize, which I believe will not sound so pleasing to feminist thinkers who do not look to the future as one that men will create for women. Second would be to understand the matter as a possible scenario of intellectual marginalization by one gender against the other in which case there is room for admission of crime and for atonement. It is in the sense of the second that I ask this question here. And this also was the burden of Nkiru Nzegwu (1996) in her paper 'Philosophers' Intellectual Responsibility to African Females'. She suggests that a moral society is that in which everyone has the right to be human and engage in the exercise of his or her abilities irrespective of gender. Being human entails among other things, being able to live freely and exercise rights and privileges which others enjoy in the society; and without prejudice or discrimination of any type, being judged by the veracity of one's claims and by the viability of one's accomplishments.

In any society like most sub-Saharan African societies, where men conspire to build an intellectual dichotomy between males and females, of which the one is superior and the other is treated as inferior, there the philosopher has a responsibility to wade in. In the African place, that responsibility falls squarely on the shoulders of the African philosopher. So, yes, African philosophers owe a duty to African women and that duty is to (a) pronounce the epistemic marginalization of women an intellectual wrong; (b) counter the marginalization; and (c) atone for the crime by leveling the ground between men and women such that the epistemic power to create, acquire, evaluate, regulate and disseminate knowledge in the society is equitably distributed between men and women in the African place.

One way of doing this is to propose an intellectual culture of conversations. Philosophical conversation is not like any other informal exchange. It is what happens when actors irrespective of gender, race or other dichotomizing factors engage their faculties of reason in a rigorous, systematic encounter that is successively disjunctive and conjunctive in motion. Disjunctively, this encounter breaks at dialectic concession and turns into dialectic complementarity, while conjunctively, it breaks at *benoke* point and turns into tension of incommensurables.

This can be called a relationship of some sort. The conversational relationship primarily upholds and respects the right of any individual to reflect and come up with their own views on issues of concern and to go on to express such views. Those engaging in a conversation of this kind are agents or actors who enjoy the freedom to think and express their thoughts, as well as own up to the responsibility such philosophical activities demand. In this sort of equation of freedom and responsibility, there is no room for gender, race, or indeed any form of clannish mindset. The focus is not on the standing of who says what but on the rigor of what is said. Criticisms are directed at the expressed thoughts rather than at the person. I think it is safe to say that conversational thinking makes the most of the rule that banishes the *ad hominem* attack.

Following the above, when one rejects the conclusion of an argument simply because it was thought out or expressed by a woman, there and then that person commits a version of the *ad hominem* attack. Regrettably, the condition of 'reason's' journey in the African place is such that some object to a woman's ability to reflect rigorously, creatively and systematically. So, it does not really matter what she says; she cannot possibly do philosophy. All this might be thought too trivial to occupy a philosopher, but many of the big lessons which humankind has had to learn the hard way, have come from things once thought trivial. A certain American puppet by name Osama Bin Laden turned out at the dusk of the twentieth century and the dawn of the twenty-first to become America's worst nightmare in living memory. Similarly, a series of aviation stunts by the Wright brothers then thought to be trivial eventually gave birth to a complex aeronautical history that has now changed our thinking about time and space. Philosophy, more than any other discipline, can open the doorway into a woman's mind. The female perspective is still very much missing at the hub of epistemology. The project of epistemology stands tallest in all human activity. Yet, it remains lopsided without the female perspective; unravelling the female perspective is the last frontier of epistemology.

Fricker builds up her argument of the need for epistemic justice which tends to gesture toward duties. I think what is at stake is more than that. It is not just a question of moral duties and commitments that male philosophers are obligated to keep to their female counterparts. What is at stake is beyond good and evil. It is a power which has to do with the survival of the species. Without the knowledge-controlling power equitably shared regardless of gender, the most comprehensive and accurate knowledge of reality cannot be reached. Whatever epistemic fragment that is required to complete the equation cannot be left to obligation; it is a necessity that cannot be compromised. As attractive as duties and moral obligation might be, and I have tried to highlight this in the previous section where I discussed epistemic *normativity*, the superiority of what I would like to call 'epistemic necessity' over 'epistemic justice' is not in doubt.

Recognizing and investigating the female perspective in our knowledge equation is an epistemic necessity. The method of conversation appears to be one of the viable ways to balance the power equation between the two sexes. In a conversation, gender, race and all other discriminating identities disappear. What is left are individuals or citizen philosophers who must think on their own, converse their thoughts, create new knowledge, acquire some, revise old knowledge, evaluate new thoughts, regulate old and new and disseminate knowledge with others. Conversational strategy is something that can give women this power.

In conversational thinking, there are two principal actors involved, namely *nwa-nju* who raises the critical questions and *nwa-nsa* who attempts to answer them. These two are engaged in what I call contestation and protestation, which is about doubting the viability of thoughts and defending such thoughts against such doubts, and where the defence could involve a measure of creativity (2015c). I have explained this process and concepts in more detail elsewhere (2015d) as involving a complex string of conceptual schemes from relational equilibrium to tension of incommensurables. Relational equilibrium is the point at which *nwa-nju* and *nwa-nsa* meet to converse on an equitable platform. When this conversation occurs, it is possible for the opposing actors to sometimes agree. This is called dialogical equilibrium. But as soon as dialogical equilibrium occurs, a new vista is opened in thought which again sustains the conversation. However, when the programs of contestation and protestation reach a deadlock where the contestant is unable to further doubt or the protestant is unable to sustain her defence, it is called logical equilibrium. At such a point, *nwa-nju* and *nwa-nsa* appropriate the principles of arumaristic concession and arumaristic complementarity to reinvent the conversation following two types of conversational motions, namely the disjunctive and the conjunctive. Arumaristics is a type of dialectical relationship without a synthesis. Arumaristic concession is when actors in a disjunctive motion concede ground to each other while arumaristic complementarity is when they enter a conjunctive motion and complement each other's position. This reinvention is called for in order to avoid the compromise of philosophical reason in which doubt is annihilated and conversations permanently stalled. This scenario which is referred to as *conversationund* replaces philosophical thinking with emotional pronouncements and promises final answers in the absence of sustained conversation. Rather than *conversationund*, conversationalists in a conjunctive motion usually end up creating what is called the Tension of Incommensurables (TI) (2015d) once the *benoke* point – a point beyond which two variables cannot further their relationship – is reached. Similarly, their disagreement or disjunctive motion, whenever it reaches a critical level, inaugurates a conjunctive motion yet again.

This tension of incommensurables calls for a new vista that will ultimately reinvent the discourse and sustain the conversation through the readjustment of knowledge formations characterized by the theme of *unfoldment* (2015e). *Unfoldment* is a creative program of conversational thinking which unveils new thoughts and concepts from critical encounters between actors in a philosophical village and between philosophical places.

It is this culture of conversations that we must institute in African philosophy to allow a level playing field for both men and women in order to create a comprehensive episteme for Africa. It is a necessity for African male philosophers, who maintain a firm grip on the reins of African epistemology, to loosen their grip and allow equitable space for females to join the epistemic conversation. Conversation is power if without it, one cannot create her own, acquire, or regulate and evaluate the knowledge dissemination in any society. The strategy of conversation therefore holds the promise to reorder the knowledge-controlling power, and quash, in due course, the epistemic marginalization women suffer in Africa.

## Conclusion

The main argument of this chapter was to show that women have been epistemologically marginalized and are still being marginalized in and by African philosophy and African philosophers. I argued that very little space is allocated to discourses on women in the African philosophy literature. I associated this with the mentality of male chauvinism which doubts the ability of women to engage in intellectual exercises, as well as with the moribund aspects of the traditional African world-view which empower the male gender not only to dominate women but to deny their epistemic vision. My goal was to arouse the consciousness of African philosophers to realize their responsibilities to the opening of epistemic space to accommodate the women's perspective. I proposed a culture of conversation following the principles of conversational philosophy as a ground leveller that can balance the knowledge-controlling power between men and women in African philosophy.

## Note

1   For some discussions on this see for example: M. Farouk Radwan, www.2knowm yself.com/psychological_differences_between_men_and_women.

## References

Asouzu, I. I. (2007). *Ibuanyidanda: New Complementary Ontology Beyond World-Immanentism, Ethnocentric Reduction and Impositions.* Zurich/ Münster: Litverlag.

Chimakonam, J. O. (2014). African Philosophy, History of. *Internet Encyclopedia of Philosophy: A Peer Reviewed Internet Resource.* www.iep.utm.edu/afric-hi. Retrieved 15/06/16.

Chimakonam, J. O. (2015a). Dating and Periodization Questions in African Philosophy. In Chimakonam, J. O. (Ed.), *Atuolu Omalu: Some Unanswered Questions in Contemporary African Philosophy* (pp. 9–34). Lanham, MD: University Press of America.

Chimakonam, J. O. (2015b). The Knowledge Question in African Philosophy: A Case for Cogno-Normative (Complementary) Epistemology. In Chimakonam, J. O. (Ed.), *Atuolu Omalu: Some Unanswered Questions in Contemporary African Philosophy* (pp. 67–81). Lanham, MD: University Press of America.

Chimakonam, J. O. (2015c). Conversational Philosophy as a New School of Thought in African Philosophy: A Conversation with Bruce Janz on the Concept of 'Philosophical Space'. *Confluence: Journal of World Philosophies*, 3: 9–40.

Chimakonam, J. O. (2015d). Transforming the African Philosophical Place through Conversations: An Inquiry into the Global Expansion of Thought (GET). *South African Journal of Philosophy*, 34(4): 462–479.

Chimakonam, J. O. (2015e). The 'Demise' of Philosophical Universalism and the Rise of Conversational Thinking in Contemporary African Philosophy. International

Conference on African Philosophy, Past, Present and Future, Department of Philosophy, University of the Witwatersrand, South Africa, 9–11 September.

Chimakonam, J. O. and Agu, S. N. (2013). The Epistemology of Womanhood: Ignored Contentions among Igbo Women of Eastern Nigeria. *Thought and Practice: A Journal of the Philosophical Association of Kenya (PAK) New Series*, 5(2): 57–79.

Chuku, G. (2013). Nwanyibuife Flora Nwapa, Igbo Culture and Women's Studies. In Chuku, G. (Ed.), *The Igbo Intellectual Tradition: Creative Conflict in African and African Diasporic Thought* (pp. 267–293). New York: Palgrave Macmillan.

Eholie, R. (1993). The Ivorian Woman: Training and Involvement in the process of Economic Development in Cote d'Ivoire. In American Association for the Advancement of Science (Ed.), *Science in Africa: Women Leading from Strength* (pp. 37–71). Washington, DC: AAAS.

Fricker, M. (2007). *Epistemic Injustice: Power and the Ethics of Knowing*. Oxford: Oxford University Press.

Hountondji, P. (1996). *African Philosophy: Myth and Reality*. 2nd rev. edn. Bloomington, IN: Indiana University Press.

James, G. (1954). *Stolen Legacy: Greek Philosophy Is Stolen Egyptian Philosophy*. New York: Philosophical Library.

Lynne, S. (1983). *Intruders on the Rights of Men: Women's Unpublished Heritage*. London: Pandora Press.

Makhubu, L. P. (1993). The Potential Strength of African Women in Building Africa's Scientific and Technological Capacity. In American Association for the Advancement of Science (Ed.), *Science in Africa: Women Leading from Strength* (pp. 1–17). Washington, DC: AAAS.

Nzegwu, N. (1996). Philosophers' Intellectual Responsibility to African Females. *American Philosophical Association's (APA Newsletter)*, 90(1): 130–135.

Nzegwu, N. (2003). Epistemological Challenge of Motherhood to Patriliny. *Jenda: A Journal of Culture and African Women Studies*, 5. www.jendajournal.com/issue5/nzegwu.html.

Odi, M. (2010). *The Power of Women's Collective Action*. Lagos: Ruwen.

Oruka, O. (1975). The Fundamental Principles in the Question of African Philosophy. *Second Order*, 4(1): 44–55.

Radwan, F. M. (n.d). Psychological Differences between Men and Women. www.2knowmyself.com/psychological_differences_between_men_and_women.

Ruch, E. A. and Anyanwu, K. C. (1981). *African Philosophy: An Introduction to the Main Philosophical Trends in Contemporary Africa*. Rome: Catholic Book Agency.

Sithole, I. (1993). Women and Science in Zimbabwe: Some Issues That Still Persist. In American Association for the Advancement of Science (Ed.), *Science in Africa: Women Leading from Strength* (pp. 27–36). Washington, DC: AAAS.

Spender, L. (1983). *Intruders on the Rights of Men: Women's Unpublished Heritage*. London: Pandora Press.

Tempels, P. (1959). *Bantu Philosophy*. Paris: Présence Africaine.

Uchem, R. (2001). *Overcoming Women's Subordination: An Igbo African and Christian Perspective: Envisioning an Inclusive Theology with Reference to Women*. Enugu: Snaap Press.

United Nations. (1995). *Beijing Declaration and Platform for Action (BPfA)*. Paris: UN Women.

UN Women. (2015). *Summary Report: The Beijing Declaration and Platform for Action turns 20*. Virginia: Colorcraft.

# 2 Henry Odera Oruka and the female sage

## Re-evaluating the nature of sagacity

*Pius M. Mosima*

### Introduction: philosophic sagacity and the marginalization of the African female

Over the years, much extensive attention has been paid to philosophic sagacity/sage philosophy as conceived by the late and much lamented Kenyan philosopher, Henry Odera Oruka (1944–1995).[1] Even though he died at just 51, his contributions to academic African philosophy have made a remarkable difference – being original, imaginative, rich, indispensable, decisive, and bent on situating the validity and relevance of indigenous African knowledge systems. His contributions, especially his conception of philosophic sagacity, remain among the most important trends in African philosophy, have attracted quite a good number of scholars, and continue to play a leading role in contemporary African philosophical discourses. They have also made significant contributions to the search for wisdom in oral sources.

One area has been conspicuously absent in interpreting Oruka: the place he gives to the female sages. Even though Oruka raised questions on the equality of the sexes in his interviews with some of his sages, the female sage is still marginalized and the male sage takes pride of place in a predominantly male-dominated African philosophy.[2] Oruka's project is surviving and flourishing after his premature death, but the position he gives to the female sage needs serious rethinking. Oruka's tendentious marginalization of women is not just limited to African philosophy. Many scholars have expressed regrets at the marginalization and lack of academic recognition and respectability of African women's history and to the social sciences in general.[3] In this work, I attempt to answer two main questions: What is philosophic sagacity or sage philosophy and how does it marginalize the contribution of African women?

How can we broaden Oruka's conception of philosophic sagacity in a bid to contribute to solving the problem of the marginalization of women in African philosophy?

### Oruka on the nature and possibility of an African philosophy

Since its very inception more than half a century ago, philosophy in African academic circles has been dominated by the discussion of one compound question: Is there an African philosophy? (Bodunrin, 1981, p. 163; Onyewuenyi, 1991, p. 29). And if there is, what is it? (Bodunrin, 1981, p. 163). How can we retrieve it? What are the conditions of its possibility? (Mudimbe, 1988, p. ix).

The first inspiration to the debate was provided by Placide Tempels' *La Philosophie Bantoue*, which was published in Dutch in 1945, later in French in 1949 and in English in 1959. This debate about the nature and existence of African philosophy was largely sustained by the first generation of university-trained African philosophers.[4] Academic African philosophy in the 1970s and 1980s was dominated by the heated ideological debate between defenders and critics of ethnophilosophy. Oruka (1990) contributes to this debate by identifying four trends in current African philosophy. They are ethnophilosophy, professional philosophy, nationalist-ideological philosophy and philosophic sagacity. They were presented to the debate on African philosophy in Oruka's *Trends in Contemporary African Philosophy* (Oruka 1990).[5] He also classifies African philosophy into 'schools' of African thought.[6]

The fourth trend in this list, and which is the focus of Oruka's own distinguished work and this chapter, is 'sage philosophy' or 'philosophic sagacity'. It was introduced to the debate on African philosophy during the Dr Anthony William Amo Conference in Accra, July 1978.[7]

According to Odera Oruka:

> Sage philosophy consists of the expressed thoughts of wise men and *women* in any given community and is a way of thinking and explaining the world that fluctuates between popular wisdom (well-known communal maxims, aphorisms and general common sense truths) and didactic wisdom (an expounded wisdom and a rational thought of some given individuals within a community). While popular wisdom is conformist, didactic wisdom is at times critical of the communal setup and popular wisdom. Thoughts can be expressed in writing or as unwritten sayings and arguments associated with some individual(s).
>
> (Oruka, 1991, pp. 33–34; italics mine)

Even though Oruka claims that sage philosophy consists in expressing the thoughts of wise men and women in any given community, in this paper I demonstrate the inadequate representation of women by looking at the treatment he gives to the female sage. Second, I attempt to broaden Oruka's conception of sagacity by advocating for the inclusion of more women in the interviews, and advocate for a practical sagacity in which the role of women is much more visible.

## Odera Oruka's method

According to Oruka, ethnophilosophy is based on the assumption that traditional Africa is a place of philosophical unanimity, steeped in anonymity and myths. To solve this apparent misconception, he decides to interview individual thinkers who are knowledgeable of their customs and traditional beliefs. The method used in researching sage philosophy may be called philosophical anthropology. Ethnophilosophers, according to Oruka, used this method but were unable to go beyond anthropology, which they accepted as the definition of African philosophy (Oruka, 1991, p. 5). Traditional individual African sages are identified and dialogue is carried out with them. Traditional Africa here refers to an era when the dominance of beliefs and practices in an African setting, as shown by the sages who represent a domain, a sphere of life, was constituted prior to the penetration of the North Atlantic and/or global post seventeenth-century technology, and has managed to more or less survive as a relatively autonomous, relatively intact domain of thought and action ever since. The discourses were held in the native language of the presumptive wise men or women. Such selected persons are capable of giving detailed explanations concerning the beliefs and practices of their community. They are also at times capable of offering reasonable criticism of some such beliefs and practices. They go beyond the mere systematization of communal wisdom and give relevant explanations and background to popular wisdom. Therefore, one major task of the professional philosopher becomes to identify the sages in a culture and then record their potentially unique insights on certain themes of fundamental importance to human life such as the existence of God, the nature of time, the nature of freedom, the nature of death, the nature of education, etc. The insights of some of the sages could be termed unique because they may very well differ from conventional beliefs in their societies. By this method, it was believed, true philosophy could be separated from popular wisdom.

## Distinguishing the philosophic sage from the folk sage

Another important element in Oruka's technique in searching for wisdom among his Kenyan sages is to distinguish the philosophic sage from the folk sage. Findings in Kenya show that there are two main divisions of sage philosophy (Oruka, 1991).

(1) First of all, there is the sage who is well versed in the popular wisdom, culture and beliefs of his people. He is essentially a conformist within the communal set-up. He is a folk-sage because he does not transcend the celebrated folk wisdom of his people. He remains at the first order of sage philosophy, which is popular wisdom, as opposed to another type of sage, the philosophic sage.

(2) The philosophic sage individually unfolds rational thoughts and didactic wisdom. He is at times critical of the communal set-up and popular wisdom. He is able to reflect and evaluate what is given in the first order. What is given in the first order is a mixture of conventional-cum-customary beliefs and practices. He is an exponent of second-order philosophy,[8] which is didactic wisdom. Second-order philosophy is what is referred to as philosophic sagacity.

Philosophic sagacity is the reflection of a person who is a sage and a thinker. As a sage a person is, as already pointed out, well versed in the wisdoms and traditions of his people. As a thinker, he is critical and transcends the communal wisdom. Philosophic sagacity, therefore, is the expounded and well-reasoned thought of some individuals in a given culture. To make the distinction between the folk sage and the philosophic sage Oruka (1991, p. 36) asserts that:

The folk sage is versed in the commonplace culture, customs and beliefs of his people. He can recite or describe them with much competence. However, he is neither able to raise any critical question about them, nor is he able to observe the inherent contradictions. The philosophic sage, like the folk sage, may equally be versed in the beliefs and values of his society. His main task is to make a critical assessment of them and recommend them as far as the communal pressure allows only those beliefs and values that pass his rational scrutiny. The folk sage is identifiable by his consistent inability to isolate his own opinions from the beliefs of the community and his ready inclination to take refuge behind the popular unexamined wisdom wherever he is intellectually challenged. The philosophic sage, on the other hand, is clearly able to isolate the given beliefs of the community from his own evaluation, rationalization, and even criticism of those beliefs. He is also able to enjoy a dialectical or intellectual game with the interviewer, as opposed to the folk sage. It is against this background that Oruka postulates the main argument for philosophic sagacity.

Philosophic sagacity maintains that African philosophy in its pure traditional form does not begin and end in a folk talk and consensus. It maintains that Africans, even without outside influence, are no strangers to logical and dialectical, critical inquiry. Philosophic sagacity proceeds on the supposition that the ability to read and write is not a necessary condition for philosophical reflection and exposition. Oruka's project demonstrates that one is likely to find thoroughly indigenous thinkers who are illiterate. They are critical, independent thinkers who oversee their thoughts and opinions by the power of reason and innate ingenuity rather than by the influence of community wisdom. They are capable of taking a problem or concept, and offering a more or less rigorous philosophical explanation of it, thereby making clear rationally where they accept or reject the communal judgment on the matter. Dialogue with these sages enables Oruka (1991, pp. 1–2) to counter three negative claims pertaining to the status of indigenous African thought: first, the claims of ethnophilosophy that traditional Africa is a place of philosophical unanimity with no individuals with the frame of mind to detach himself (herself) from the prevailing established beliefs and offer a critical assessment or rational rejection of such beliefs; second, that writing is a precondition for philosophy; and third, the Eurocentric claim that Greek sages such as Thales, Anaximander, Heraclitus, Parmenides and Socrates are 'philosophers' while African sages are not. His rebuttal of these negative claims enables Oruka to show an African system of thought which he considers indigenous and philosophical.

## The invisible and inferior female sage

In this section I argue that the female sage is largely invisible, or rather presented as naturally inferior and subordinate as an eternal victim of male oppression. Even though Oruka posits that sage philosophy consists of the expressed thoughts of wise men and women, and that neither age nor gender is a necessary condition for one to become a sage, in his *Sage Philosophy* (1991, pp. 87–160), Oruka interviews twelve sages, yet only one is a woman. Oruka quotes extensively from the eleven men, while the lone female is a folk sage. In the book's acknowledgements section Oruka mentions only male students as research assistants while the females are appreciated for typing and reorganizing manuscripts and helping with data analysis (Oruka, 1991, Acknowledgements). Little wonder that Stephen M'Mukindia Kithanje, one of Oruka's philosophic sages, in assigning the role of a man and a woman in marriage, equates the man to a chairman and the woman to a secretary, as we see in any organization (Oruka 1991, pp. 132–133). When Oruka gets to the subject matter (Oruka 1991, p. 4) of the views of the sages, he presents the views of eight, who are all men, and he asks nine sages (men) on the equality of the sexes. Gail Presbey adds that Oruka also interviewed two other women: 'a wise lady, Abiero Nyar Miyere, a wife of Owidh Kohene and another lady, Randiga Nyar Ogut, wife of Ohomo of Ndere Clan, East Ugenya (Oruka, 1993, p. 83)'. However, transcripts of these interviews have been lost (Presbey 2012). In a dissertation titled 'Sagacious Reasoning in African Philosophy' by Nigerian philosopher Anthony Oseghare, supervised by Oruka at the University of Nairobi 1985, two male sages (Paul Mbuya Akoko and Oruka Rang'inya) and no female texts are used as part of the study.[9] Nevertheless, Oseghare endorses Mbuya's thesis of 'balance of forces' between man and woman as original and cogent (Oruka, 1991, p. 157). In another dissertation written by Frederick Ochieng' – Odhiambo and supervised by Oruka in 1994 there are five sages interviewed; only two of them, men, were asked the question of the equality of men and women and the one woman sage was not asked the question (Presbey, 2012, p. 117).

Oruka's position on the equality of the sexes is quite ambiguous. He is pleased with his philosophic sages who express the equality of the sexes and thinks that culture influences the way some of the sages conceive female inferiority. As Oruka put it:

> On the subject of man and woman, most folk sages are convinced of the superiority of man. This is a repetition of the belief of the cultural mass from which the sages hail. The philosophic sages, however, make a qualification even where some of them are of the view of the inequality between man and woman. Mbuya Akoko sees no inequality between the genders and offers proof to discount any thesis for inequality. Oruka Ranginya finds no inequality except for the use of the intellect. Stephen Kithanje sees inequality only as a division of functions and the prevention of

conflict between two people (man and woman) who are to live together. He thus assigns the husband the role of 'chairman' and the wife the role of 'secretary'. Culture often has a profound influence on people whether or not they are sages or philosophers. Influenced by ancient Greek culture, Plato and Aristotle did not see slaves as having the worth of human beings. In this book, C.M. Neugebauer (Chapter 13) explains the racist, anti-black attitudes of two of the most famous philosophers, Emmanuel Kant and Friedrich Hegel. Besides such prejudices, the anti-feminist philosophies of Arthur Schopenhauer and Friedrich Nietzsche are well known. The seeming man-superior-to-woman attitude found in some of the sages in this book should be seen for what it is – a judgment dominated by the cultural mythos of the surrounding culture. But this aside, the objective, reflective views of some of the sages on the subject command reasonable acceptance or appreciation.

(Oruka, 1991, pp. 4–5)

From the quotation above, Oruka, following his philosophic sages, castigates those who think that women are inferior. He insinuates that even though major philosophers like Plato and Aristotle justified slavery, Kant and Hegel were racist and anti-black, while Schopenhauer and Nietzsche were anti-feminists; these negative traits in their philosophies should not make us totally dismiss their thoughts. Even though Oruka praises the philosophic sages for their ability to transcend the common views held by their community on the equality of the sexes, the answers of some of his sages do not clearly reflect the distinction he makes between the folk sage and the philosophic sage. For example, of the seven folk sages in *Sage Philosophy*, three think women are inferior, two think they are equal to men and two were not asked the question. Of the five philosophic sages, three of those interviewed argued that women were inferior to men; only one thought they were equal and one was not asked. Hence, we cannot clearly see the differences between the folk sages and philosophic sages on the basis of going beyond communal consensus on the subject of the equality of man and woman.

Oruka's sages also give the impression that men are superior to women, thereby reinforcing the predominantly male and sexist underestimation of women. Women are discussed in their stereotypical reproductive roles as wives and mothers. Hence the value attached to women is linked to their fertility. One of his folk sages, Ali Mwitano Masero, thinks that man and woman have the same rational capacity, yet 'the woman – since the days of our ancestors is below a man. Even if she is a district officer or president, she is below a man.' Even when provoked by the interviewer that this could be a misconception, he asserts that 'Women are inferior to men because a woman leaves her place of birth, like a bird of the bush, to go to a man's home. She is a migrant. How can she be equal to the host, the man?' He also reinforces the patriarchal culture when he provokes women with this highly androcentric statement: 'If a man wants us to be partners, let him come to my father's home and I will build him a house there' (Oruka, 1991, pp. 94–95). Another reason he gives for female inferiority is that 'women reveal their feelings too easily'. Another folk sage, Josiah Osuru, when asked the broader question on equality, thinks that people are never equal. Equality is only in the eyes of God, since all of them are His creatures. He also thinks the Europeans could be superior to the Africans in some respects. For example, the Europeans have superior weapons to those of the Africans but the Africans showed greater superiority to them in magic and herbs (Oruka, 1991, p. 103). He opines that the woman ranks below the man as the relationship between man and woman is even more unequal. For him, the woman is skilful at home but on the battlefield the man displays courage and superior nature. The wife, he asserts, is the property of the husband, who buys her with bride price from other people and brings her into his house. Another sage interviewed by Ochieng'-Odhiambo (1994) also asserts women's inferiority and he states that even though God treats people equally it does not necessarily mean that they are really equal. He explains that:

> The women are fighting a battle they cannot win. No individual in his proper and sane senses can accord women equal status and opportunities to men. Women are inferior to men in both physical and mental strength.
> (Ochieng'-Odhiambo, 1994, p. 240)

Nevertheless, these views are contrasted with another folk sage, Abel M'Nkabui, who thinks that all human beings are equal and terms any apparent inequalities as historical accidents (Oruka 1991, pp. 100–101). This folk sage is able to reject the prevailing societal tendency to regard men as being superior to women. This contrast also seriously questions Oruka's distinction between the folk sage and the philosophic sage. M'Nkabui's opinion on this topic is also different from some philosophic sages like Okemba Simiyu Chaungo, Stephen Kithanje and Oruka Rang'inya.

When asked about the relationship between man and woman concerning marriage, a philosophic sage like Stephen Kithanje has this to say:

> As for the role of a man and a woman in marriage, I would equate the man to a chairman and the woman to a secretary, as we have in any organization. This is because a man will always be occupied with the different things outside the home. When he comes back home, the woman should give him a detailed report of what has been happening around home for the time he was away. This situation as it is happening today – women equating themselves to men – is very sad. This is something I believe can never be possible. Men are superior to women. This can be seen very clearly from such physical signs such as beards, bald, etc., which are only found in men. They are signs of superiority. In a family, there can be harmony only if a man is the leader. A man has a direct relationship with God, the same way a woman has a direct relationship with man. If a woman wants to be leader, maybe because she is learned,

and yet the husband is naturally endowed with qualities of leadership, surely there will be problems. There cannot be two equals in a situation where important decisions are to be made. Such a family will obviously fail. Again, women are inferior to men because, as is the case with the whole of Africa, it is the man who chooses the woman he wants to marry. There is no time when the woman proposes marriage to the man.

(Oruka, 1991, pp. 132–133)

As we can see above, Kithanje's argument can be summarised into four categories (Presbey, 2012, p. 122):

1   The importance of public duties over private duties. In this case, the man is linked to the public duties while the woman is relegated to the private sphere.
2   Physical basis of superiority.
3   Harmony in the home is based on the rule of one partner, in this case the man, while the woman is the ruled.
4   Social customs surrounding marriage give a clear advantage to the man over the woman in terms of autonomy and choice.

Stephen Kithanje's arguments above only reflect the patriarchal culture in which sage philosophy is steeped. He warns us in his interview:

First, I think that people should be very careful as to whom they marry or get married to. They should strictly follow the society's rules pertaining to marriage in order to avoid problems ... According to Meru traditional thought, the purpose of marriage is procreation.

(Oruka, 1991, p. 132)

What he does above is recite the culture and commonplace beliefs of his people on marriage with much competence. Yet, he is not able to clearly go beyond them or isolate himself from these beliefs. In reinforcing this male hegemony, he remains, following Oruka's categorization, a folk sage and not a philosophic sage.

Another philosophic sage, Paul Mbuya Akoko, goes beyond his societal beliefs in the rapport between man and woman. He distances himself from the traditional Luo belief and argues for the correlation between man and woman, contrary to what Stephen Kithanje does with Meru traditional thought above, when he states that:

There is a popular Luo belief that the man is owner and master of the homestead, the whole homestead, but I think this belief is wrong. For, when we come to the house, the woman is in control there. In the house, the man can only ask for things. He cannot do as he pleases without any restraints. However, the woman too cannot do anything without asking her husband. Thus, husband and wife help each other. Where peace is desired, each person tries not to over step the boundary which common sense determines in relationships.

(Oruka, 1991, pp. 139–140)

Mbuya goes further to explain the question of equality of the sexes in political and social terms. This is because if it is not properly handled, unnecessary problems may crop up. He argues that equality could be sought after several years of education and orientation. If this is hastily done, there could be chaos. He argues that 'Education will in time help to redress this imbalance since men and women are inherently equal. We see that woman can be more intelligent than man just as man can also be more intelligent than woman' (Oruka, 1991, p. 140).

He castigates traditions in which women are portrayed as inferior to men. This makes women feel they are so, which Mbuya labels laziness. Mbuya's view on the question relating to the relations between men and women is convincing and original. He goes against normal Luo beliefs and proposes the thesis of 'balance of forces'. Mbuya sees no inequality between the genders and so offers proof to discount the thesis. He lashes out at traditions that say that women are inferior to men. This thesis invalidates male chauvinism and is a downright call for female emancipation. Let us now turn to the interview with Oruka's lone female sage.

## Peris Njuhi Muthoni: Oruka's lone female sage

This is the lone female sage and the last of the folk sages to be interviewed (Oruka, 1991, pp. 105–108). Like all the other sages Oruka gives a brief biography with a picture before describing her in very peripheral and unchanging terms. She is presented mostly in connection with her failed marriages, infertility, and poverty and after futile visits to a medicine man; she retreats to her brothers and lives with them in her quest for fraternal love and acceptance in a society that puts great value on fertility and children. She also finds solace in Christianity as an escape from her embittered life, and like many women of her generation, Muthoni never went to any formal school. The first day she ever heard of philosophy was when the researcher was introducing the subject matter of his visit. In this presentation, Oruka does not mention her economic and political potentials as he does of most of the male sages. The patriarchal conception of a woman in that society is conspicuous in his presentation as she is underestimated in stereotypical and even limited reproductive roles as a wife and mother. The language Oruka uses in this presentation of the female sage underestimates her painful experiences, which are considered static with words like 'permanent childlessness' which has caused 'three failed marriages' and her retreat to her brothers or Christ for a solution. It is in her brothers' house that she 'can listen to the pleasant cries and chatters of her brothers' children while worshipping her savior, the Lord Jesus Christ' (Oruka, 1991, p. 106). This woman is seen as a timeless victim of a ferocious patriarchal order that Oruka does not explicitly interrogate.

The answers she gives to the interviewer are also of great philosophical value, and this raises the question of why Oruka, following his categorization, would think she was a folk sage and not a philosophic sage. On the nature and existence of God, she opines that God is an invisible force that moves the world. This force is called *Roho* (spirit), which is one for all people and is revealed through faith (*witikio*). This God is believed by every member of traditional Kikuyu society to live in Kirinyaga (Mount Kenya). This view is similar to Aristotle's and Aquinas' Unmoved Mover/God. She affirms the existence of Kikuyu traditional religion and is able to make an important difference in the manner of praying between Christianity and traditional Kikuyu worship in these words: 'Whereas the Christian keeps going to church to offer prayers to God, the traditional Kikuyu prays too and offers sacrifices to God only when the need arises' (Oruka, 1991, pp. 106–107).

She decries the loss of faith in these words:

> people do not have as much faith in their God as they used to have in the old days. You see faith is very important. If you believe in something strongly, it happens. And this is because you become completely insensitive to factors which lie outside your faith.
>
> (Oruka, 1991, p. 107)

On the subject of God's nature and existence, she expresses the indigenous community's beliefs and religious allegiance, but she is able to make an important distinction between these beliefs and the Christian ones. Her views are very similar to Oruka's philosophic sages like Paul Mbuya Akoko (Oruka, 1991, pp. 136–138), Stephen Kithanje (Oruka, 1991, p. 134), Oruka Ranginya (Oruka, 1991, p. 119) and Okemba Simiyu (Oruka, 1991, pp. 115–116). Oruka argues that:

> Views of the sages on God oscillate between three parameters: the Christian conception of God, the common cultural idea of God and personal reflective sagacious thought. Thus when Mbuya Akoko stipulates that God is a Supreme Being who is One for all races and cultures, it is clear that this is not a common Luo view of God. But it is not clear whether Mbuya's view is a re-echoing of the Christian concept of God. Or it is his own sagacious postulate of God. Stephen Kithanje is not comfortable talking about God. He is not happy either with the traditional Meru idea of God or with the conventional Christian concept. But he takes it that God is the ultimate explanation behind things that are really true, genuine or great. Okemba Simiyu's view of God as the Sun is a typical Luhyia concept.
>
> (Oruka, 1991, p. 4)

Peris Muthoni's answer to the question on God clearly reflects these parameters Oruka highlights above. Yet, curiously Oruka makes no mention of her views in 'The subject matter of *Sage Philosophy*' (Oruka, 1991, p. 4), and even when she is asked the question on God's existence, she is 'warned' to give her individual view, not the orthodox Christian belief. This suggests that while male sages are free to oscillate between the three parameters mentioned above, a particular one is imposed on the female sage. Does this not suggest an ideological construct in which Oruka deliberately wants to project the hegemonic structure of patriarchal culture or male domination? When Oruka qualifies Peris Muthoni as a folk sage is this not a subtle way of strengthening the very hegemony he sets out to challenge?

Moreover, the quotation above implicitly gives us some argument to undermine Oruka's claim that these sages have not benefitted from Western education or values, or on whom these had not made an impact. In fact, Oruka compliments one of the philosophic sages – Paul Mbuya Akoko – when he goes against the common Luo beliefs in their god and other gods, as Akoko claims that all these gods are one and that there is only one God (*Nyasaye*) (Oruka, 1991, p. 137). Nevertheless, this must show the influence of European missionaries on indigenous Luo concepts of religion and God. Gail Presbey (2007) argues that the idea of one God was what the missionaries taught the Luo when they entered Luoland. Oruka does not permit Peris Muthoni to express the views of the European missionaries and if Akoko, Oruka's sage *par excellence*, had said he had learned from foreign missionaries, moreover, it would have undercut the evidence put forward in the study.

Muthoni expresses her personal views in her answers to the next two questions on the concepts of culture and freedom. On the concept of culture, she opines that culture is the way of life of a people, the organized means through which they realize their lives. Yet, she asserts that the notion of a national or universal culture is a dream. She cites some examples of ceremonies through which people express their culture, such as circumcision, marriage and funeral rites. When asked about her personal thoughts on circumcision and marriage, she expounds her community's (Kikuyu)[10] conception of circumcision: a way of initiating a young man or woman in a bid to make him or her behave maturely and respectfully in society. However, she argues that circumcision is not the only way of initiation for all cultures, as different societies have different methods of initiation. She cites the case of another community, the Luos, who remove their teeth to mark initiation. Yet, she appreciates the fact that female circumcision is dying out and highlights some of the dangers of female circumcision such as 'problems at childbirth' and 'difficulty appreciating the pleasure of contact with men'. She also castigates the Luos for removing their teeth as a mark of initiation as 'It causes loss. They need their teeth' (Oruka, 1991, p. 107).

On the concept of freedom, she argues that freedom is a thought. It exists in the mind, even if physical conditions may try to suppress the person. She asserts that it is the duty of every person to reject force imposed by the other.

She also defends the equality of woman and man and castigates her community (the Kikuyu) that treats women as unequal to men. She thinks it is only a matter of division of duties/responsibilities.

As earlier mentioned, Muthoni, the one female sage, is not given enough space in the interview. She is the last of the folk sages to be interviewed and the length of the interview gives the impression that she is the least of them and we may not expect much from her. Moreover, the tone Oruka uses in the interview may be read as justifying this claim, and suggesting that Oruka does not enjoy a 'dialectical game' with her or they are not involved in 'sagacious didactics'. Let me substantiate.

Of all the sages interviewed Oruka does not ask a question twice or specify what kind of answer he would expect to have, which he does, however, in Muthoni's case. He also insists that he wants her individual views. Take a look at these questions to Peris Njuhi Muthoni:

1 'Does God exist? And what is his nature? *I want your individual view, not the orthodox Christian belief*' (Oruka, 1991, p. 106; my italics).

Oruka does not ask any question like this to any of the other sages. It gives the impression that the female sage would not know how to go about the answer and so she needs direction.

1 'What do you understand by culture (*mila* in Kishahili)? What are your thoughts on circumcision? Is circumcision the only way of initiation for all cultures? And what do you think of inter-tribal marriage?'

Second, if Oruka has accepted this answer as her individual view could we not, rather, qualify her as a philosophic sage and not a folk sage? Does the individual view here mean the Kikuyu point of view? Moreover, Oruka claims that folk sages are identifiable by their consistent inability to isolate their own opinions from the beliefs of their community and their ready inclination to take refuge behind the popular unexamined wisdom whenever they are intellectually challenged (Oruka, 1991, p. 36). Yet in her answers seen above, Peris Muthoni does not just recite the common, dogmatic and unchanging Kikuyu and Luo world-views, but offers her personal appraisal of those beliefs. Oruka himself notes that the distinction between popular (folk) wisdom and didactic (philosophic) wisdom is not cast iron but plastic, as it *fluctuates* between the two poles. This suggests that there are folk sages who can also be philosophic sages. However, Oruka does not respect this qualification in his categorization of sagacity. This explains why Jay van Hook's (1995) proposal that Oruka's categorization of sages into 'folk' and 'philosophic' be more *flexible* than Oruka advocates. Gail Presbey thinks that the folk sages even show a talent that is more philosophical than Oruka's description of them would have us believe. She thinks the folk sages should be included as philosophic sages because some of the sages distinguish their views from those of their communities on at least one topic (Presbey, 2007, pp. 142–143). Instead of distinguishing folk sages from philosophic sages, she thinks that the distinction often occurs within the same individual sage, who is even an 'active interpreter of tradition' (Presbey 2007). And even if the distinction between the folk and philosophic sage is a matter of degree (Presbey, 2007), I still think Peris Muthoni qualifies as a philosophic sage. Hence Oruka's criteria for distinguishing a philosophic sage from a folk sage need further clarification.

## The way forward: beyond male/female identity

Oruka's treatment of the female sage falls in line with his modernist conception of philosophy. In fact, the book *Sage Philosophy* conspicuously has as its subtitle *Indigenous Thinkers and Modern Debate on African Philosophy*. His conception of sage philosophy/philosophic sagacity is enmeshed in a patriarchal culture which gives a single identity to man/woman (sexism). However, the modernist position in itself is severely in doubt from the postmodern standpoint and from existential critiques. Postmodernism represents a new opportunity to break away from old patriarchal views, standards and perspectives to a liberating position which questions the dominant patriarchal modes of thinking. Postmodernism has developed since the 1950s, and embraces the relativism of a sophist like Protagoras and even Aristotle. For the postmodernist, knowledge claims are not absolute or universal, but they exist in relation to specific discourses. For the French postmodern philosopher Lyotard (1984), knowledge claims can only be legitimated by reference to the scientific language game *à la* Wittgenstein in which they are made. Postmodernist criticisms of a single identity of man/woman and the conception of a bounded culture could help us go beyond Oruka's tendentious marginalization of the female sage. The meaning Oruka gives to man/woman does not fit with the philosophy of French philosopher Jacques Derrida, for example. According to Derrida (1976) meaning is a process that is always relational and fluctuating. Given that meaning can occur only as experience, our experiences are constantly overriding ('overwriting') the lexical definitions of words, effacing those definitions, which in turn are constantly changing. Moreover, Oruka's search for the sagacity of the sages by using oral sources, and his claim to final interpretation, sounds hegemonic and ridiculous in light of Derrida's philosophy. It gives us the impression that Kenyan culture is fixed, unique and self-evident. We have argued above that Oruka cannot claim that these sages have not been influenced by foreign cultural values. Yet Oruka claims that their opinions are 'indigenous'.

Derrida's deconstructive method aims at breaking down the binary system that privileges terms that are implicit in assumptions embedded within language systems. Derrida suggests that in the use of language, the first term in a group of two is given pride of place. In distinctions like male/female, public/private, white/black, mind/body, master/slave, sign/signified, the first term is always privileged. This is what Michel Foucault debunks as the power/knowledge system, which in this context, illustrates male prejudices about the female in a bid to construct cultural paradigms of the other. In the mind of Derrida, this is not correct because the first term has meaning only in relation to, and only because of, the second term. A man can only be a man if there is a woman. A man's existence depends on that of a woman and vice versa. It suggests that existence is depicted as the dynamic interactivity of its manifestations. In other words, one cannot perceive of a man unless one thinks of him in terms of his determining relationship with a woman. That is to say the existence of male is intelligible only by affirming the existence of female. It suggests that meaning is relational and always fluctuating. This implies that we do not need to settle on binary opposites or establish axiological hierarchies, but think them together or approach them in a creative, reconfiguring manner. Given the male/female interactions evident in the world today, language ought to be open-minded, changeable, incomplete and not contain radically opposed entities or be couched in such fixed categories as Oruka endorses, with his tendentious marginalization of the female sage. Summarily, Derrida asserts that the binary vision contained in these dualisms misrepresents the inter-dependence and interconnectedness of social reality and processes. These dichotomies, be they conceptual categories or empirical realities, are derived from Enlightenment thought. This dichotomy is what Oruka exploits rather than attempts to solve!

According to existentialist philosophy, the use of fixed and stable categories gives the mistaken impression that male/female identity is stable. Sartre (1943) argues that existence comes before essence. I exist before I define my identity and no specific essence defines what it is to be human. This means that a person is what he/she makes of him/herself. Cultural identity is one of the identities a person may have. They are important to that person but they do not define her/his total being. A single conception of identity of male/female could also promote stereotypes, prejudices and give the impression that human life is reduced to an immobile essence. Simone de Beauvoir (1974) sees identity as a product of daily life. It is one that is not fixed but changes. We cannot today claim that a person's identity is predetermined by her or his 'culture', and that the human person cannot choose freely or make decisions.

## Broadening our sources of sagacity: *sophia* and *phronesis*

I agree with Gail Presbey that Oruka could have gone beyond the margin-alization of the female sage by including many more women in his interviews. This is alright, given Oruka's fascination for the search for oral wisdom in the sages and his modernist tendencies. Nevertheless, Oruka is limiting himself to *sophia*. We could add *phronesis*, the practical side of sagacity. These two terms are associated with Aristotle in his attempt to classify intellectual virtue. *Sophia* pertains to the intellectual ability to theorize the nature of the world and also to find out a causal explanation of its existence. *Sophia* takes into consideration a deliberation concerning a universal truth. It is specialist theoretical knowledge within the competence of the philosopher. This is what Oruka is looking for when he interviews his sages, and this is what leads him to divide them into folk and philosophic sages. *Phronesis* or wisdom, on the other hand, is ingenious practical knowledge. This form of wisdom is more pragmatic as it is linked to action and enables one to decide on a mode of life based on daily experiences. Oruka does not categorize sagacity into *sophia* and *phronesis* like Aristotle does. He rather makes two divisions, namely the folk sage and her/his popular wisdom on the one hand, and the philosophic sage and her/ his didactic wisdom on the other. Oruka's conception of wisdom/sagacity as abstract thinking, limited to the mind, and which could only be retrieved via interviews needs serious rethinking. Wisdom is not just theoretical or abstract thought (*sophia*) as Oruka makes us understand when he interviews his sages. A richer approach to African traditional wisdom would be to explore both *sophia* and *phronesis* in African traditional society, and not focus exclusively on one, as Oruka does in his sage philosophy. We may go ahead and cite some examples of such viable African traditional wisdom as we find in rituals concerning healing or initiation, naming those in which women are at the fore. Such examples of traditional African wisdom drive home the message that African sagacity should not be conceived as an abstract and academic undertaking removed from the multifarious and excessive problems of African life today (as we note in Oruka's interviews and articulations of philosophic sagacity), but as a way of contributing to the practical dilemmas of individual and collective life.

We could broaden sagacity to include symbols, rituals in the African contexts. Richard Werbner (1989) describes divination among the Tswapong peoples of modern Botswana; Walter van Beek and M. Peek (2012) give fascinating accounts of crab divination among the Kapsiki/Higi of Northern Cameroon and Nigeria; while Wim van Binsbergen (2003) is involved in *sangoma* healing in southern Africa, or Hallen and Sodipo (1986) with the *onisegun* among the Yoruba in Nigeria. In these examples we find women very active in many of the rituals and we find them helping to negotiate the practical dilemmas of individual and collective life. These examples of traditional healing, ritual, and so forth, go beyond the body/mind distinction and relate to a more holistic natural-spiritual conception of being.

Finally, we could also look at the active role women have played in the history of Africa. In their search for independence, women have been very active. Consider, for example, the Aba women's riots in 1929 in Aba-Nigeria; the Anlu women's resistance in Cameroon; the South African women's fight against apartheid in South Africa in the 1950s; and women's contribution to resistance in the National Liberation Movement in Algeria, the Mau-Mau in Kenya, and other significant movements all over Africa. These examples show that women have been very active in state politics in the independence struggles. Their experiences could be highlighted as forming part of sage philosophy and even as nationalist ideological philosophy. Moreover, we could also include women philosophers like Sophie

Oluwole, Anke Graness and Gail Presbey and their respective contributions to African philosophy.[11]

## Conclusion

Oruka's contributions, especially his conception of philosophic sagacity, remain among the most important trends in African philosophy and have attracted a good number of scholars while continuing to play a leading role in contemporary African philosophical discourses. Nevertheless, his conception of philosophic sagacity, and much of mainstream philosophy, need to be broadened to include more female sages. It is time to proceed with a new vision of African philosophy that deconstructs the dualistic analytical categories male/female, public/private, and move on to an inclusive, gendered philosophy. If we expand African philosophy to a model that runs from abstract thinking to negotiating the practical dilemmas that affect our individual and collective existence, then we will be able to see the profound roles women have played in these. This will provide enough justification for us to include and celebrate our female sages. The reconsideration of the practical side of sagacity will not just concern women; it will also lead to the re-evaluation of men, as many rituals, are done by men. But it may also re-evaluate the many philosophic female sages who may have been forgotten or marginalized, as our analysis of Oruka in this chapter has shown.

## Notes

1 For more critical perspectives on Oruka's philosophic sagacity, see, for example; Azenabor, 2009; Graness and Kresse, 1997; Janz, 2009; Kalumba, 2002, 2004; Kresse, 1993, 2007; Masolo, 1994, 1997, 2005; Mosima, 2016; Ndaba, 1996; Ochieng'-Odhiambo, 1994, 1996, 1997, 1999, 2002a, 2002b, 2006, 2007; Ogutu, 1995/1996; Oseghare, 1985; Presbey, 1996, 1997, 1999, 2000, 2002, 2007, 2012; Tangwa, 1997; Van Hook, 1995.

2 For more on Oruka's inclusion and treatment of female sages, see Presbey, 1997, 2012.

3 See, for example, 'Gender Analysis and African Social Science', CODESRIA Workshop, Dakar, September 1991. It was reported in *CODESRIA Bulletin* no. 4, 1991; Amadiume, 1987, 1997; Nzegwu, 2006; Oyewumi, 1997, 2003, 2005.

4 For more on the history of this debate see, for example, Bodunrin, 1981; Oruka, 1975, 1990.

5 Oruka (1991, p. 5) later added two other approaches to African philosophy, namely the hermeneutic and the artistic or literary trends. The hermeneutic trend more specifically accommodates those who choose a linguistic approach. Oruka understands the hermeneutic trend as involving 'the philosophical analysis of concepts in a given African language to help clarify meaning and logical implications arising from the use of such concepts' (Oruka, 1991, p. 11). The main proponents of this school include Wiredu, 1987; Gyekye, 1987; Hallen and Sodipo 1986. The artistic or literary trend applies to African intellectual figures in the humanities who address themselves to themes basic to Africa's cultural identity. The main proponents include Okotp'Bitek, Ngugi wa Thiong'o, and Wole Soyinka.

6 Oruka mentions the ethnographical school which he subdivides into the 'ethno-graphical descriptivist' (Placide Tempels, John Mbiti) and 'ethnographical ration-alists' (Robin Horton, E. A Ruch, Innocent Onyewuenyi and K. C. Anyanwu); the rationalist school (Kwasi Wiredu, Bodunrin, Paulin Hountondji and Campbell Momoh) and the historical school (Claude Sumner, Valentin Yves Mudimbe, Dismas Masolo and Lucius Outlaw). For more description of these 'schools' see Oruka (1991, pp. 15–31).

7 This conference was held in commemoration of the intellectual achievements of Ghanaian philosopher Anthony William Amo/Anton Wilhelm Amo. He was born in Ghana around 1704, moved to Germany where he studied and taught philoso-phy in German universities such as Halle, Wittenberg and Jena in the first half of the eighteenth century, before returning to his home country where he died around 1759. For more on Amo, see Abraham, 1996, 2004; Hountondji, 1996.

8 This categorization should not be confused with the philosophy journal of that name.

9 Part of the study is published in Oruka, 1991: 156–160.

10 The Kikuyu and the Luo are among two of the largest ethnic groups in Kenya.

11 I am limiting myself to these three African/Africanist women philosophers who have, paradoxically, explicitly defended the contribution and philosophy of Oruka Oluwole (1992a, 1992b); Graness and Kresse, 1997; Presbey, 1996, 1997, 1999, 2000, 2002, 2007, 2012).

# References

Abraham, W. E. (1996). 'The Life and Times of Anton Wilhelm Amo, the First Afri-can (Black) Philosopher in Europe', in Molefi K. Asante and Abu S. Abarry, (eds), *African Intellectual Heritage: A Book of Sources*, Philadelphia, PA: Temple Uni-versity Press, pp. 424–440. (First published in *Transactions of the Historical Society of Ghana*, 2(1) (1963).)

Abraham, W. E. (2004). 'Anton Wilhelm Amo', in Kwasi Wiredu (ed.), *A Companion to African Philosophy*, Malden, MA: Blackwell, pp. 191–199.

Amadiume, I. (1987). *Male Daughters, Female Husbands: Gender and Sex in and African Society*, Atlantic Highlands, NJ: Zed Books.

Amadiume, I. (1997). *Reinventing Africa: Matriarchy, Religion and Culture*, London: Zed Books.

Azenabor, G. (2009). 'Odera Oruka's Philosophic Sagacity', *Thought and Practice* (New Series), 1 (June): 69–86.

Bodunrin, P. O. (1981). 'The Question of African Philosophy', *Philosophy*, 56(216): 161–179.

Ceton, C. (2005). 'Identity as Evolutive: An Intercultural Approach Based on an Examination of Mudimbe, de Beauvoir, Taylor, and Mbembe', *Quest: An African Journal of Philosophy/ Revue Africaine de Philosophie*, XIX(1–2): 109–128.

de Beauvoir, S. (1974). *The Second Sex*, H. M. Parshley, trans. New York: Vintage Books.

Derrida, J. (1976). *Of Grammatology*. Baltimore, MD: Johns Hopkins University Press.

Graness, A. and Kresse, K. (eds) (1997). *Sagacious Reasoning: H. Odera Oruka in Memoriam*, Frankfurt: Peter Lang.

Gyekye, K. (1995). *An Essay on African Philosophical Thought: The Akan Conceptual Scheme*. Revised edn. Philadelphia, PA: Temple University Press. First published 1987, Cambridge: Cambridge University Press.

Hallen, B. and Sodipo, J. O. (1986). *Knowledge, Belief and Witchcraft: Analytical Experiments in African Philosophy*, London: Ethnographica.

Hountondji, P. J. (1996). *African Philosophy: Myth and Reality*, 2nd edn, Bloomington and Indianapolis: Indiana University Press. English translation first published 1983; first French edition published 1976.

Janz, B. B. (2009). *Philosophy in an African Place*, Lanham, MD: Lexington Books.

Kalumba, K. (2002) 'A Critique of Odera Oruka's Philosophic Sagacity', *Philosophia Africana*, 5(1).

Kalumba, K. (2004) 'Sage Philosophy: Its Methodology, Results, Significance, and Future', in: Kwasi Wiredu (ed.), *A Companion to African Philosophy*, Malden, MA: Blackwell, pp. 274–282.

Kresse, K. (1993). 'Interview with Professor Henry Odera Oruka', *Quest – Philosophical Discussions: An International African Journal of Philosophy/ Revue Africaine Internationale de Philosophie*, IX(2)/X(1): 22–31.

Kresse, K. (2007). *Philosophising in Mombasa: Knowledge, Islam and Intellectual Practice on the Swahili Coast*, Edinburgh: Edinburgh University Press.

Lyotard, J. F. (1984). *The Postmodern Condition: A Report on Knowledge*, trans. Geoff Benington and Brian Massouri, Minneapolis, MN: University of Minnesota Press.

Masolo, D. A. (1994). *African Philosophy in Search of Identity*, Bloomington, IN: Indiana University Press/ Edinburgh: Edinburgh University Press.

Masolo, D. A. (1997). 'Decentering the Academy: In Memory of a Friend', in Anke Graness and Kai Kresse (eds), *Sagacious Reasoning: Henry Odera Oruka in Memoriam*, New York: Peter Lang.

Masolo, D. A. (2005) 'Lessons from African Sage Philosophy', *Africa e Mediterraneo*, 53 (December): 46–53.

Mosima, P. M. (2016). *Philosophic Sagacity and Intercultural Philosophy: Beyond Henry Odera Oruka*, African Studies Collection 62, Leiden/Tilburg: Tilburg University.

Mudimbe, V. Y. (1988). *The Invention of Africa: Gnosis, Philosophy, and the Order of Knowledge*, Bloomington, IN and London: Indiana University Press/Currey.

Ndaba, W. J. (1996). 'Odera Oruka's Sage Philosophy: Individualistic vs. Communal Philosophy', in, A. P. J. Roux and P. H. Coetze (eds), *Beyond the Question of African Philosophy: A Selection of Papers Presented at the International Colloquia, UNISA, 1994–1996*, Pretoria: University of South Africa (UNISA) Press.

Nzegwu, N. (2006). *Family Matters: Feminist Concepts in African Philosophy of Culture*, Albany, NY: State University of New York Press.

Ochieng'-Odhiambo, F. (1994). 'The Significance of Philosophic Sagacity in African Philosophy,' *Ph.D. Thesis*, University of Nairobi.

Ochieng'-Odhiambo, F. (1996). 'An African Savant: Henry Odera Oruka', *Quest: An African Journal of Philosophy/ Revue Africaine de Philosophie*, IX(2)/X(1) (December 1995/June 1996): 12–15.

Ochieng'-Odhiambo, F. (1997). 'Philosophic Sagacity Revisited', in Anke Graness and Kai Kresse (eds), *Sagacious Reasoning: Henry Odera Oruka in Memoriam*, New York: Peter Lang.

Ochieng'-Odhiambo, F. (2002). 'The Evolution of Sagacity: The Three Stages of Odera Oruka's Philosophy', *Philosophia Africana*, 5(1): 19–32.

Ochieng'-Odhiambo, F. (2002). 'Some Basic Issues about Philosophic Sagacity: Twenty Years Later', in Claude Sumner and Samuel Wolde Yohannes (eds),

*Perspectives in African Philosophy: An Anthology on 'Problematics of an African Philosophy: Twenty Years Later'*, Ethiopia: Addis Ababa University Press.

Ochieng'-Odhiambo, F. (2006). 'The Tripartite in Philosophic Sagacity', *Philosophia Africana*, 9(1): 17–34.

Ochieng'-Odhiambo, F. (2007). 'Philosophic Sagacity: A Classical Comprehension and Relevance to Post-colonial Social Spaces in Africa', *Quest: An African Journal of Philosophy/ Revue Africaine de Philosophie*, XXI(1–2).

Ogutu, G. E. M. (1995/1996). 'Weep not ... Philosophers Never Die', *Quest – An African Journal of Philosophy/ Revue Africaine de Philosophie*, IX(2)/X(1) (December 1995/June 1996): 5–11.

Oluwole, S. B. (1992a). 'The Africanness of a Philosophy', in H. Nagl-Docekal and F. M. Wimmer (eds), *Postkoloniales Philosophieren: Afrika*, Vienna: Oldenbourg, pp. 101–124.

Oluwole, S. B. (1992b). *Witchcraft, Reincarnation and the God-Head: Issues in African Philosophy*, Ikeja, Lagos, Nigeria: Excel Publishers.

Onyewueni, I. C. (1991). 'Is There an African Philosophy?' in T. Serequeberhan (ed.), *African Philosophy: The Essential Readings*, New York: Paragon House. First published in Claude Sumner (ed.), *African Philosophy*, Addis Ababa, 1980.

Oruka, H. O. (1975). 'The Fundamental Principles in the Question of African philosophy', *Second Order: An African Journal of Philosophy*, 4(1): 44–55.

Oruka, H. O. (1990). *Trends in Contemporary African Philosophy*, Nairobi: Shirikon.

Oruka, H. O. (1991). *Sage Philosophy*, Nairobi: Acts Press.

Oseghare, A. S. (1985). 'Relevance of Sagacious Reasoning in African Philosophy', *Doctoral dissertation*, University of Nairobi.

Oyewumi, O. (1997). *The Invention of Women: Making an African Sense of Western Gender Discourses*, Minneapolis, MN: University of Minnesota Press.

Oyewumi, O. (ed.) (2003). *African Women and Feminism: Reflecting on the Politics of Sisterhood*, Trenton, NJ: Africa World Press.

Oyewumi, O. (ed.) (2005). *African Gender Studies: A Reader*, New York: Palgrave Macmillan.

Presbey, G. M. (1996). 'African Sage-Philosophers in Action: H. Odera Oruka's Challenges to the Narrowly Academic Role of the Philosopher', *Essence: An International Journal of Philosophy* (Nigeria), 1(1): 29–41.

Presbey, G. M. (1997). 'Who Counts as a Sage? Problems in the Future Implementation of Sage Philosophy', *Quest – Philosophical Discussions: An International African Journal of Philosophy / Revue Africaine Internationale de Philosophie*, XI(1–2): 52–66.

Presbey, G. M. (1999). 'The Wisdom of African Sages', *New Political Science*, 21(1): 89–102.

Presbey, G. M. (2000). 'On a Mission to Morally Improve Society: Odera Oruka's African Sages and the Socratic Paradigm', *International Journal of Applied Philosophy*, 14(2): 225–240.

Presbey, G. M. (2002). 'African Sage Philosophy and Socrates: Midwifery and Method', *International Philosophical Quarterly*, 42(2): 166.

Presbey, G. M. (2007). 'Sage Philosophy: Criteria That Distinguish It from Ethnophilosophy and Make It a Unique Approach within African Philosophy', *Philosophia Africana*, 10(2): 127–160.

Presbey, G. M. (2012). 'Kenyan Sages on Equality of the Sexes', *Thought and Practice: A Journal of the Philosophical Association of Kenya (PAK)* (New Series), 4(2): 111–145.

Sartre, J.-P. (1943). *L'Etre et le néant: Essai d'ontologie phénoménologique*, Paris: Gallimard.

Tangwa, G. B. (1997). '*Sagacious Reasoning: Henry Odera Oruka in Memoriam*. Anke Graness and Kai Kresse (eds), Frankfurt am Main: Peter Lang (Review)', *Quest – Philosophical Discussions: An International African Journal of Philosophy/ Revue Africaine Internationale de Philosophie*, XI(1–2): 175–182.

Tempels, P. (1959). *Bantu Philosophy*, Paris: Présence Africaine. First published as Tempels, P. (1955). *Bantoe-filosofie*, Antwerp: De Sikkel.

Van Beek, W. E. A. and Peek, Ph. M. (eds) (2012). *Reviewing Reality: Dynamics of African Divination*, Berlin: LIT Verlag.

Van Binsbergen, W. M. J. (2003). *Intercultural Encounters: African and Anthropological Lessons Towards a Philosophy of Interculturality*, Berlin/Boston/Münster: LIT Verlag.

Van Hook, J. (1995). 'Kenyan Sage Philosophy: A Review and a Critique', *Philosophical Forum*, XXVII(1): 54–65.

Werbner, R. P. (1989). 'Making the Hidden Seen: Tswapong Wisdom Divination', in R. P. Werbner, *Ritual Passage, Sacred Journey: The Process and Organization of Religious Movement*, Washington, DC and Manchester: Smithsonian Institution Press and Manchester University Press, 19–60.

Wiredu, K. (1987). 'The Concept of Mind with Particular Reference to the Language and Thought of the Akans', in G. Floistad (ed.), *Contemporary Philosophy, Volume 5: African Philosophy*. The Netherlands: Martinus Nijhoff.

# 3 Women and *ubuntu*

## Does *ubuntu* condone the subordination of women?

*Rianna Oelofsen*

## Introduction

The world-view of *ubuntu* has been interpreted as giving the highest regard to relationships (Metz, 2007). This chapter will argue that a relational ethic such as *ubuntu* is in its essence egalitarian. The reason that *ubuntu* is egalitarian, it will be argued, is as a result of what a good relationship entails. Once we understand that a good relationship requires equality, it follows that African societies which condone the subordination of women are acting against the essence of *ubuntu* and similar Afro-communitarian ideals.

A contrary view, argued for by Oritsegbubemi Oyowe and Olga Yurkivska (2014) in their paper 'Can a Communitarian Concept of African Personhood Be both Relational and Gender-Neutral?' is that Afro-communitarianism reproduces and perpetuates gender inequality. They believe this is as a result of the reproduction of traditional norms (that discriminate against women), being incorporated into the creation of personhood and identity of women and men in these communities.

However, contrary to Oyowe and Yurkivska's view, I will argue that an ethic of *ubuntu* is in essence egalitarian. This is for the reason that the value of *ubuntu* can fundamentally be explained in terms of the high value it ascribes to the goal of community building. Human fellowship is ascribed the status of the highest of human needs (once basic physical needs are met), and from this it follows that building a healthy community in which such fellowship is fostered has great value. However, it will be argued that the understanding of *ubuntu* (which can be translated as 'a person is a person through other persons' or 'humanity') as *simunye* (which can be translated as 'we are one' or 'united') is problematic, and thus *ubuntu* need not be interpreted as undermining individuality and critical engagement. As I aim to show, this also means that *ubuntu* does not undermine egalitarian ideals. Instead, individual and *different* subjectivities need to be equally fostered and nurtured, in order to create well-developed individual characters. Relationships mature and become richer and deeper as a result of the different parties having well developed individual characters, allowing for harmonious relationships between people. The converse is also true – the less developed an individual is, the less chance there is for a deep and meaningful relationship with her. For example, in an unequal romantic relationship, it is probable that the person who sees themselves as *only* in a supporting role to the other, does not add as much value to the relationship. This relates to the salience of mutual aid and reciprocity in the African communitarian tradition. It means that a partner with their own interests, who challenges the other, can be argued to foster growth, and allows a critical reflection on the values that are important in the relationship, as well as for the individuals.

The claim that *ubuntu* requires equality between the sexes will be supported and analyzed in light of Nkiru Nzegwu's (1994) understanding of a dual-sex system in some traditional African societies.

## What is *ubuntu*?

From engaging with some theorists in African thought, it becomes clear that many have argued for a different (normative) metaphysical conception of the self from what is prevalent in most Western philosophy. These theorists all try to interpret the concept of *ubuntu*, utilizing different methodological approaches. While the theorists I focus on here do not have a background in a lived reality in which *ubuntu* is a linguistic and social reality, this should not undermine the academic discourse, understanding and interpretation of the concept as I aim to utilize it in this chapter. In terms of academic discourse, it does not imply that sub-Saharan Africans just are, or live, this way, as this project is not essentialist in this manner. The project does not claim that there is an 'ideal African past' in which this was instantiated, just as there is no 'ideal European past' in which Kantian ethics was adhered to by all.

Michael Onyebuchi Eze (2008) explains in his paper 'What Is African Communitarianism? Against Consensus as Regulative Ideal' how *ubuntu* allows for and values individual subjectivity as well as community. To understand the person as subsumed and utterly constituted by community (as is the case when consensus is the regulative ideal of society) is to utilize the 'false metaphor of *simunye* as descriptive of *ubuntu*' (2008, p. 387). *Ubuntu* has mistakenly, Eze claims, been understood to have only a collective meaning – that I am a person *only* through other people. Eze argues, however, that this is a better rendition of *simunye* – which means 'we are one'. It is important not to confuse the two concepts, as *ubuntu* does not deny the importance of individuals and their rights, but merely places a heavy emphasis on the importance of community. *Simunye* is a Zulu word with the meaning 'we are one', and, according to Eze, 'feature[s] prominently as a politicized rendition of *ubuntu* in the socio-political discourse of post-apartheid South Africa' (2008, p. 387). The fact that *ubuntu* is not equal to *simunye*, is an important and under-emphasized aspect of *ubuntu*, which values unity in diversity, and can be successfully related to Tutu's metaphor of the rainbow nation. Therefore, the valuing of 'otherness', of diversity, is inherent in an ethics based on *ubuntu*, as there have to be different persons in order for relationships between them to be valuable and valued.

Antjie Krog, a South African thinker who has reflected on the Truth and Reconciliation Commission and the subsequent journey towards reconciliation in South Africa, explains the difference between the notions of moral personhood prevalent in Western and African thought as captured in the concept of *ubuntu*. Krog attempts to 'understand how this interconnected moral self [as prescribed by *ubuntu*] is formed' (2008, p. 353). She draws the distinction between the constitution of the self through either becoming 'two-in-one', or, 'one-in-many'. Constituting the self through becoming 'two-in-one' is exemplified in Hannah Arendt's thought (during her reflections on some insights by 'the father of Western philosophy', Socrates). Arendt claims that splitting the self into two, such that the self comes into conversation with itself, is the 'beginning of thinking and knowing which would make a moral entity possible' (Krog, 2008, p. 363, citing Arendt, 2003). However, for Krog,

> The fundamental point of departure between an African and Western world-view, could be … in the place and the way the moral compass is formed: for Arendt it is formed in the *self* through conversations with the *self*. For African awareness it would be formed in the *self*, but through conversations with *those around one*.
>
> (2008, p. 363)

In other words, in the African world-view which subscribes to *ubuntu*, 'one's self-awareness is not formed by splitting oneself in two, but by becoming one-in-many – dispersed as it were among those around one' (2008, p. 363). Moral reflections then happen in communities, and not in isolated individuals, and this would mean that the 'moral compass' (to be understood as what gives an individual direction in moral decision making) is formed by the community, and not within the individual. When someone adopting what I understand to be a Western individualistic view of personhood, forms a moral compass through forming a 'conscience' or splitting the self into two in order to have a dialogue about the morality of a certain course of action, she might think that it is her own voice with whom she is holding the conversation. Alternatively, it is possible (and, many would say, highly likely), that she simply does not recognize that it is the voice of society that she has integrated, internalized and incorporated into herself.[1] In this way, the Afro-communitarian understanding of the formation of the moral compass is more accurate, in that it recognizes the centrality of our community in what we see as 'moral'. In order for this Afro-communitarian moral compass to work, however, it is necessary for individuals in the community to engage with views that diverge from their own; otherwise there can be no *proper* dialogue with regards to the issue in question. This requirement of dialogue requires the fostering of tolerance for and engaging with difference. As such, Krog's take on *ubuntu* is one that does not entail the unanimity and homogeneity that Eze feared some versions of Afro-communitarianism would be committed to.

I intend to utilize the term 'Afro-communitarianism' as an umbrella term to include core aspects of various accounts of communitarian personhood put forward by numerous African philosophers.[2] (While it is true that 'the West' vs. 'Africa' is always a reduction of the plurality of both entities, I still find it useful to draw on some general features of each part of the binary. However, that these are generalizations and simplifications should be borne in mind.) In utilizing the term Afro-communitarianism, the aim is to distinguish this understanding of personhood and community from the communitarian tradition in the Western philosophical tradition.[3] Afro-communitarianism does not *only* emphasize, as does Western communitarianism,[4] the importance of cultural groups in identity formation, and therefore a focus on group rights. Nor is it a focus on individual human rights as is the convention in the Western liberal tradition. Afro-communitarianism, I maintain, is not trapped in the false dichotomy posed between individualism and communitarianism.[5] Rather Afro-communitarianism emphasizes the importance of *relationships* between people, their interdependence, and the duty to maintain flourishing relationships of a particular kind.[6] An Afro-communitarian understanding of personhood recognizes the importance of history, context and community in the formation of one's identity, and emphasizes the interdependent relations between individuals and collectives. Recognizing interdependence and the importance of interpersonal relations for the self, this world-view sees the individual as necessarily socially embedded, and affected by her context in a very deep way. However, it still acknowledges that there *are* individuals, and that these individuals need to be well developed in order for there to be the possibility of healthy relationships.

By considering the above authors, we see that, from within the Afro-communitarian world-view, it is still necessary to focus on individuals in order to understand the particular context and society. However, such a focus is always against the background assumption and understanding that we can speak of the individual as separate from her community only in very abstract terms, that it is only for reasons of simplification and discussion, and that it is not possible to separate these in reality. This is similar to the way in which Martin Heidegger speaks of 'being-in-the-world', and emphasizes that we cannot understand 'being' without 'world' or *vice versa*, and yet it is possible to focus on one or the other.[7] When speaking of individual and community in terms of Afro-communitarianism, it is not possible to see the one as isolated from the other. Rather, the necessary relationship between the two needs to be kept in mind at all times – one cannot understand the individual without reference to the community, but one also cannot understand the community without reference to the individual. It is, however, possible to focus on one or the other, as long as the necessary relationship between the two is always kept in mind.

From an appreciation of this metaphysical account of personhood, it becomes clear that the concept of a person in Afro-communitarianism also expresses a moral claim (Menkiti, 2004; Metz, 2010, p. 51; Wiredu, 1992). To be human and to perceive someone else as being human encapsulates a moral response to the other, a belief in their equal claim on respectful treatment and protection from harm. This means that this metaphysical conception of the self necessarily has implications for ethical theory. With this in mind, let us investigate the notion of *ubuntu* as an ethical theory.

Under an Afro-communitarian account, personhood comprises the creation of the person through her community, and a central aspect of personhood is understood to be being ethical and accepting the resulting moral duties and responsibilities. This means that the Afro-communitarian understanding of the person *entails* a particular kind of ethic.[8] In other words, the metaphysical understanding of Afro-communitarianism has specific implications for ethical theory. I will concentrate here on *ubuntu* as an instantiation of the general Afro-communitarian focus on the normativity of personhood. 'Human being' is therefore a normative, and not a merely descriptive concept. 'Human,' as normative, prescribes standards in terms of how one ought to act toward others designated as 'human', but also prescribes certain standards to the actor designated as human, in terms of actions and behavior befitting a human. It is then in the recognition[9] of the other as human, that I have an obligation to treat her ethically. Acting in a way which does not recognize this obligation subverts her humanity (Bell, 2002, p. 12).

This way of speaking about the 'human' is at the core of the concept of personhood in Afro-communitarianism, and it emphasizes being and becoming human *through* others (or, 'humanization'). If it is possible to 'humanize' the self and others in this way, it is, however also possible that this project (of becoming human) will fail or be thwarted. And yet, if it was thwarted, that humanity might still be restored after such a failure. As a result, in this conceptual framework de- and re-humanization refers to recognizing a person's moral agency, including or excluding someone from the moral community, and a person's capacity and ability to behave as a moral agent.[10] I use the language of de- and re-humanization with the *caveat* that I do not believe it is possible to dehumanize people, if by that is meant that they become beings that do not deserve equal respect. Instead, dehumanization occurs through the processes of exclusion or maltreatment which result in the *perception* that the other (or oneself) is less (or more) worthy of moral consideration. This means that I am using 'human' as a normative term, not as a merely descriptive term – I do not mean 'member of the species *homo sapiens*'. Instead, when using the terms 'human' and 'humanizing' these refer to a prescribed standard of treatment which befits this type of being. I will argue later in the chapter that this normative understanding of 'human' does not exclude women, but requires that women are also understood to be deserving of the prescribed standard of treatment that befits the type of creature we call 'human'.

This normative understanding of the person is central to Afro-communitarianism. For someone to be a person, in this Afro-communitarian sense, is for them to have *ubuntu*.[11] *Ubuntu* is often explained through the maxim '*umntu ngumntu ngabanye abantu*' (Liwane, n.d., n.p.) which can be translated as 'I am a person because of other people', or that a person can only be a person through the help of others. This means that the values of community and solidarity are integral to *ubuntu*, and it also has connotations of the importance of human dignity. Nombeko Liwane claims that

> This fundamental concept stands for personhood and morality. The important values of *Ubuntu* are group solidarity, conformity, compassion, respect, human dignity and collective unity … Respect is reciprocal irrespective of race, ethnicity, class, age, and gender. *Ubuntu* requires one to respect others if one is to respect him or herself.
>
> (n.d., n.p.)

This means that a good relationship between people, which includes mutual respect for human dignity, is seen as a fundamental moral goal. Desmond Tutu, in line with this support for human dignity and respect, famously explains the value of *ubuntu* in society as the fact that

> Harmony, friendliness, community are great goods. Social harmony is for us … the greatest good. Anything that subverts or undermines this sought after good is to be avoided like the plague. Anger, resentment, lust for revenge, even success through aggressive competitiveness are corrosive of this good.
>
> (2000, p. 35)

The world-view of *ubuntu* has, in line with this understanding, been interpreted as giving the highest regard to relationships (Metz, 2007). The value of *ubuntu* can, I contend, fundamentally be explained in terms of the high value it ascribes to the goal of community building. Human fellowship is ascribed the status of the highest of human needs (once basic physical needs are met), and from this it follows that building a healthy community in which such fellowship is fostered has great value. As we have seen, the understanding of *ubuntu* as *simunye* is problematic, and thus *ubuntu* need not be interpreted as undermining individuality and critical engagement. Instead, as Eze writes,

> The pursuit of the common good need not undermine individual subjectivity nor yield to univocal unanimity insofar as the good of the community is dependent on an intersubjective affirmation and unique subjectivities. In fact, the common good flourishes where individual subjectivities are fostered.
>
> (2008, p. 389)

In other words, individual and *different* subjectivities need to be fostered and nurtured, in order to create well-developed individual characters. Relationships mature and become richer and deeper as a result of the different parties having well developed individual characters, allowing for harmonious relationships between people. The converse is also true – the less developed an individual's character is, the less developed her own views, projects and interests are, the less chance there is for a deep and meaningful relationship with her. It is not possible to engage in deep and meaningful discussion with someone who simply repeats the views of others, and/or who does not really understand what these views entail and what their implications are. Someone who simply reflects the views of the other person in a conversation does not challenge that person to justify her views, and as a result both parties lack the ability to enable the discussion to result in change, or an experience of growth in either person's world-view. In an unequal romantic relationship, for example, it is probable that the person who sees themselves as *only* in a supporting role to the other does not add as much value to the relationship. Instead, a partner with their own interests, who challenges the other, can be argued to foster growth, and allow a critical reflection on the values that are important in the relationship, as well as for the individuals.[12]

This can be further clarified through a particular interpretation of Tutu's metaphor of the rainbow nation. Instead of a homogeneous society, the rainbow nation ideal is meant to capture that we ought to strive for an affirmation of difference and celebration of diversity. It is when there is a diversity of opinion (as long as these opinions are respectful of others' humanity), a diversity of culture and interests, that a community is able to develop and grow through expanding its horizons and thus grow as a community and as individuals. However, the celebration and dialogue of difference necessary for such an ideal 'rainbow nation' requires at least some form of egalitarianism. This is because all opinions (as long as they respect others' humanity) ought to be taken as important in the conversation, and so all voices need to be heard equally. In order to recognize the other's views and contributions to the conversation, she needs to be recognized as equal. This conversation is meant to lead to a heterogeneous, pluralistic society in which the human rights of all are respected and allowed to materialize within the context of different cultures, perspectives and world-views.

Within this possibility for ethical interplay between universality and difference, we see that 'in advancing the good of the community, the individual's good is concomitantly advanced precisely because the community's and individual's goods are not radically opposed, but interwoven' (Eze, 2008, p. 388). It is still important to note that it is relationships that are deemed to be of moral importance, and that relationships require different parties in the relationship to be distinct in some sense, even though they are related, and even though their relationship constitutes their identity in some way. Thus moral value can be seen as fundamentally residing in relationships between individuals, rather than in individuals themselves, as Thaddeus Metz has argued (2007).

## *Ubuntu* as oppressive to women?

So, from the above section, it is clear why, on my interpretation of *ubuntu*, it would not be an oppressive ethic for women. However, Oyowe and Yurkivska

(2014) argue in their article 'Can a Communitarian Concept of African Personhood Be both Relational and Gender-Neutral?' that African communitarianism is in fact oppressive to women. In this section I will analyze their argument and show why I do not think it is successful.

In their article, Oyowe and Yurkivska argue that defenders of an African communitarian conception of personhood ignore the role gender plays in such a conception of personhood. Oyowe and Yurkivska claim that feminist issues such as gender based violence are routinely and systematically ignored in African philosophy, and that this is as a result of a supposed gender-neutrality. So, an African communitarian understanding of personhood is meant, and understood to be, gender-neutral. However, they argue that as a matter of necessity, the 'relational and community-based nature of the communitarian idea of personhood indicates that it is in fact a gendered notion' (2014, p. 85). In fact, however, they argue that most African philosophy, and thus most African communitarianism, have the male of the species in mind when they discuss the 'human'.

Oyowe and Yurkivska see themselves as engaging with 'those African philosophers who subscribe to the concept of person as relational and at the same time argue for its egalitarian nature' (2014, p. 87). They describe this position in particular in relation to *ubuntu*, of which they write:

> All proponents of Ubuntu are unanimous in the view that the communitarian ethics of Ubuntu is founded in the traditional African worldview based on a core principle that affirms one's humanity through recognition of an 'other' in his or her uniqueness and difference.
>
> (2014, p. 86)

In other words, according to Oyowe and Yurkivska, an ethics of *ubuntu* understands the person to be 'essentially relational and normative'. They also argue that *ubuntu* is always presented as what they call 'gender-neutral', in that it is understood to embrace all community members equally, 'irrespective of their gender, in a network of mutual moral obligations associated with the Ubuntu values of respect, solidarity, cooperation, loyalty, empathy, collective responsibility and consensual democracy' (2014, p. 86). This gender-neutrality, they believe, is a result of African communitarian philosophers having lost touch with the 'actual, embodied, inhabited, real persons because those are positioned and constructed in a fundamentally historical, culturally diversified, and gender-specific social realm' (2014, p. 87). So, in essence they argue that a philosophical position which understands the person to be created by the community, yet does not recognize gender as an important aspect in the creation of personhood, 'is inherently contradictory' (2014, p. 87).

However, even if all traditional African societies were patriarchal and subjugated women, why would this undermine the egalitarian principles of *ubuntu*? The fact that African societies did (or do) not live up to certain ethical implications of *ubuntu* does not mean that *ubuntu* does not have these implications. To understand the self as essentially relational and normative means that the self is constituted by her relations with others – it does not say that these relations are necessarily egalitarian, but it *prescribes* that they ought to be, through recognition of 'uniqueness and difference'. In other words, it seems that the whole argument relies on the fallacy that in African society you can derive an 'ought' from an 'is'. Even though Oyowe and Yurkivska make this mistake in their reasoning, I believe that they do point toward an important aspect of African philosophy when they point out that women's issues and feminist issues have not been adequately represented or explored in most of the literature. While I agree that it is true that

> the African communitarian concept of personhood as it is envisioned by African communitarian philosophers speaks neither of women nor for them and as 'gender-blind' intellectual and analytical perspectives, continue to hold central stage the impact of persisting male domination on all aspects of social and political life remains unproblematized and normative.
> (Mama, 2005, p. 105, cited in Oyowe and Yurkivska, 2014, p. 87)

But this does not mean that we cannot utilize the principles of *ubuntu* and African communitarianism and use them to critique some of the ways in which the philosophy has excluded women (for example in using 'man' and 'he' to denote all persons). This is true in the same way as we can argue that Kant's categorical imperative can be used to argue against his racist views, and that if he applied the categorical imperative consistently he should have seen that. In the same way we can show that even though it might be the case that women are not necessarily explicitly understood as equal in African communities and in how their personhood is formed, if the principles of *ubuntu* are applied consistently, we will see that it is prescribed that women ought to be treated as equal.

In fact, it is possible, as this quotation in Oyowe and Yurkivska's paper notes, that

> gender expresses the idea that otherness – and so difference – is a feature of the very human nature of human (which is to say bodily) persons. The fullness of human nature is not realized in any single human individual but only in the male and female couple.
> (Shutte, 1993, p. 144, quoted in Mama, 2005, p. 105, cited in Oyowe and Yurkivska, 2014, p. 87)

To say that we are essentially gendered as Oyowe and Yurkivska argue, is not yet to say that there is or ought to be a hierarchy between the two genders. Even if it is the case that all traditional African societies were oppressive to women, this is still not enough to say that gender differences must connote gender inequality. This can be seen if we look at the importance of relationships in the *ubuntu* ethics (as discussed earlier in the chapter) – good relationships in essence need to be egalitarian, otherwise they are not good relationships. In other words, in contrast to what Oyowe and Yurkivska argue, we can use the very notion of the importance of relationships and see that this principle of *ubuntu* implies equality, even if this equality is not necessarily seen in actual communities in practice.

## Response to Oyowe and Yurkivska: gender complementarity according to Nkiru Nzegwu

What is necessary in order for the argument I am putting forward to work, is that it is possible to have gender differences in a society without that necessarily leading to gender hierarchy. In other words, there needs to be the possibility of 'gender complementarity'.

Oyowe and Yurkivska, however, argue against the idea of such gender complementarity (namely that gender difference does not need to equal gender hierarchy) in their paper. Their argument relies on engaging with claims made by Ifi Amadiume (1987) in her book *Male Daughters, Female Husbands*. In this part of the chapter I will claim that their argument against the possibility of complementarity fails, by referring to Nkiru Nzegwu's (1994) paper 'Gender Equality in a Dual-Sex System: The Case of Onitsha'.

Oyowe and Yurkivska argue against the claim that the 'African notion of personhood connotes equality among persons and that consequently, traditional African societies were egalitarian, since gendered differences evince complementarity rather than a hierarchical social power distribution along gender lines' (2014, p. 88). In order to support their conclusion that it is a mistake to suppose that traditional African societies were egalitarian as gender differences were understood to be complementary rather than hierarchical, they turn to some claims by Amadiume, who they claim argues that 'these asymmetries indicate complementarity between the genders, i.e. it does not necessarily signify discrimination or oppression of women' (2014, p. 95). Oyowe and Yurkivska claim that Amadiume does not see women as oppressed in the particular traditional African society that she analyzes, as a result of the fact that gender is understood to be flexible in this society. In support of this claim of flexible gender systems, Amadiume describes the customs of 'male daughters' and 'female husbands'. However, as Oyowe and Yurkivska rightly point out, the mere fact that some women are able to take on male roles in ritual and political aspects of society would not undermine the fact that women *in general* in the society have less power and ability to run their own affairs. In fact, that these women have to take on these male roles simply highlights that power in the society lies with men. I agree with this observation on the part of Oyowe and Yurkivska. However, in engaging with their argument, it is not clear how they see Amadiume's account as meant to support an understanding of gender complementarity. In fact, Amadiume sets out to record some traditional Igbo practices which highlight that gender was (is?) not a static category among the Nnobi people, and that it is not always closely linked to sex. This seems like a very different claim from the one about complementarity which Oyowe and Yurkivska ascribe to her. While the understanding of gender complementarity is certainly in evidence in Amadiume's book, I believe that it does not rest on the flexibility of gender and the fact that some women take on ritual and politically 'masculine' roles. Instead, gender complementarity is based on the fact that women are in charge of certain spheres of life, and this is not properly recognized by Oyowe and Yurkivska.

Instead of utilizing an account such as Amadiume's, I believe that the argument for complementarity by Nkiru Nzegwu in her article 'Gender Equality in a Dual-Sex System: The Case of Onitsha' is a better account of what we could mean by gender complementarity in a traditional African society. However, I would like to make clear that even if it was not the case that any traditional African societies did in fact ascribe to such gender complementarity, this would not undermine the fact that, conceptually speaking, such a society would fulfill the criteria for equality in difference which many African communitarian philosophers subscribe to. In other words, Nzegwu's account shows us that there is the potential for a society in which this kind of communitarian personhood is possible without the subjection of women. And, as *ubuntu* and other African communitarian ethics have prescribed such equality, it would therefore be disingenuous to argue that these communalist ethics are not able to prescribe equality between the sexes. In the rest of this section I will therefore give a description of Nzegwu's argument for a dual-sex system, which is what Oyowe and Yurkivska call 'gender complementarity'.

Nzegwu's paper asks the following question about white people:

> Why do they think equality necessarily begins with individual autonomy and sameness? We begin life and form our relational identity in the nexus of a caring, sharing family and society. Yet, they insist our conception of equality must begin with antagonistic, solitary individuals who lack social and family histories.
>
> (1994, p. 73)

From this question, it is clear that she subscribes to the type of communal understanding of personhood which Oyowe and Yurkivska discuss in their paper. But Nzegwu's aim is to explain to white feminists what equality would look like when men and women are not seen as the same, but are conceived of as 'social complements, and gender identity is defined by social roles and responsibilities' (1994, p. 74). Nzegwu makes clear that if men and women were seen as complementary, they would stand in an equal power relationship to each other, even if (or rather, because) their social roles and responsibilities differ.

An objection she considers with regards to this view, is that according to the gender complementarity that she describes, these are 'stereotypical things that women normally do: marriage, motherhood, procreation, reproduction, nurturing ...' (1994, p. 81). According to this objection, it is necessary that women be able to assume some of the social and political roles that are seen as within the domain of men, in order to be sure that there is indeed equality between the sexes. However, the response to this objection that Nzegwu puts forward, is that in the traditional African society she is referring to, women 'assign value to what we do and we make sure that the whole community sees it as such' (1994, p. 81). In accordance with this type of difference feminism, then, Nzegwu's point is that it is counterproductive, as feminism in the West has done, to 'seek equality as individuals in spaces and with concepts that were created with the devaluation of women in mind ... What white women seem to miss is that their prevailing conception of equality as sameness is a sexist notion of equality that is already stacked against them' (1994, p. 85). So, in accordance with this view, Western feminism which seeks to overcome patriarchy by advocating that women take on roles usually set aside for men, are going about the project of overthrowing patriarchy in the wrong way. Instead, Nzegwu argues, in Western culture,

> since women are undervalued by the asymmetry and assumptions of the socio-political structure, equality cannot be established simply by extending to women the 'privileges' of the male-privileging notion of equality. A radical restructuring of all the ground rules of the socio-political system is required if the structural inadequacies that treat women as immature and less than equal are to be corrected.
>
> (1994, p. 86)

Instead of this socio-political structure, it is, however, possible to imagine a complementary gender system in which

> individuals are valued for the skills they bring to community-building, and the role they play developing the culture ... Identity is not abstractly constructed in terms of sameness, but concretely defined in terms of equal worth of social duties and responsibilities. Because gender equality implies comparable worth, women and men are complements, whose duties, though different, are socially comparable.
>
> (1994, p. 85)

As a result of the possibility of this different kind of socio-political structure, Nzegwu argues that we ought to recontextualize and reinterpret the mainstream Western feminist understanding of equality. Instead of this reconceptualization, Nzegwu, however, claims that many African women scholars have simply imported the Western concepts and categories they encountered in their Western education, and applied these concepts and categories to traditional African societies without due consideration as to whether they applied in the same ways.

In particular, Nzegwu accuses Amadiume of doing this in her analysis of Igbo women. Nzegwu writes that Amadiume portrays Igbo society as patriarchal, even as she claims to challenge the patriarchal values that were imposed during colonialism and Christianization. Employing a problematic proprietal language of ownership, she recovers Nnobi society into a framework that portrays women as objects and properties rather than as subjects.

(1994, p. 89)

Instead of imposing these categories of understanding, Nzegwu recommends that traditional African societies ought to be investigated with a different frame of reference. In light of this, she argues that it is possible to see men and women as of comparable worth in some traditional African societies, even as it is recognized that such societies may also have a hierarchical structure with regards to 'age, experience, marital status, and rites of initiation' (1994, p. 94). In light of this, it is therefore possible for a society to subscribe to gender equality while still being a hierarchical society with regards to other social factors. However, as social divisions are achieved through one's social accomplishments, these hierarchies do not prevent men or women from attaining positions of power, though they would be different positions of power.

## Conclusion: some remaining issues with the *ubuntu* view

In conclusion, I have argued that Afro-communitarian understandings of personhood and ethics, in principle, would not condone the subordination and oppression of women. I have shown how, in spite of the fact that gender differences would be central to personhood under an African communitarian understanding of personhood, it is possible for this not to result in the oppression of women. This is possible through an understanding of gender complementarity.

While this argument shows how it is possible for Afro-communitarianism to be egalitarian when it comes to gender relations, there are, however, still some issues that the kind of gender complementarity described here would have to deal with. For example, we might question the reverence of motherhood, and the possibly problematic results this might have for women, such that we are judged by our reproductive capacities, and that it does not allow for women to make the choice to be childless without some societal judgment.

Also important, is that this kind of dual-sex system and gender complementarity seems to leave us with some problematic issues of heteronormativity and heterosexism. If women (and men) are defined by their biological sex, and expected to live up to these socially and biologically constructed roles, this seems unnecessarily restrictive. However, it is possible to see that it is here that Amadiume's description of the flexibility of gender present in some traditional African societies might not make this as constraining as it would be in a society where sex and gender seem to coincide by prescription.

## Notes

1 This is, of course, the insight that Freud expresses through the formation of the superego as the internalization of authority figures.
2 For the purposes of this chapter I focus on only a couple, but other notable examples include Emmanuel Eze, Mogobe B. Ramose, Kwame Nkrumah, Augustine Shutte, John and Jean Comaroff, and others.
3 For an excellent comparison between the Western and African conceptions of communitarianism, see Masolo, Dismas, 'Western and African Communitarianism: A Comparison', in *A Companion to African Philosophy*, Kwasi Wiredu (ed.), 2005; and chapter 6 of his *Self and Community in a Changing World*, Indiana University Press, 2010.
4 For examples, see political philosophers such as Alasdair MacIntyre, Michael Sandel, Charles Taylor and Michael Walzer.
5 See David Morrice, 'The Liberal-Communitarian Debate in Contemporary Political Philosophy and Its Significance for International Relations', *Review of International Studies*, vol. 26, 2000; and Charles Taylor's seminal paper, 'Cross-Purposes: The Liberal-Communitarian Debate', in *Debates in Contemporary Political Philosophy: An Anthology*, Derek Matravers and Jonathan E. Pike (eds), Routledge, 2003, p. 195.
6 For the kind of relationship that is the focus, see Thaddeus Metz, 'Toward an African Moral Theory', *Journal of Political Philosophy*, vol. 15, no. 3, 2007, pp. 321–341. The kind of relationship involved is the ethic which flows from an Afro-communitarian understanding of personhood.
7 See his *Being and Time*.
8 The development of personhood as a moral goal has some possibly disconcerting effects in terms of seeing people as 'more' or 'less' of a person, and consequent 'grades' of personhood which translate into more or less human rights being accorded to individuals and/or groups. I recognize this issue, and yet I do not want to engage with this at present.
9 My current project is amenable to being referred to in terms of recognition in the 'politics of recognition' tradition, but for simplicity's sake I will not refer to this literature for the purposes of this project. This would hopefully be a future project.
10 In this normative sense, to perceive someone as being human encapsulates a moral response toward the other, a belief in their equal claim on respectful treatment and protection from harm. In other words, when referring to the humanizing of the other or the opponent, I employ humanity in a similar fashion to Emmanuel Lévinas, who claims that an encounter with the other's genuine alterity entails a responsibility to the other. He writes, 'The Other becomes my neighbor precisely through the way the face summons me, calls for me, begs for me, and in so doing recalls my responsibility, and calls me into question' (Lévinas, Emmanuel and Hand, Seán (eds), *The Levinas Reader*, 1989, Blackwell Publishing, p. 84).
11 I am here using *ubuntu* as an example of the central importance of the normativity of personhood from an Afro-communitarian ethical position.
12 This is in line with the proposition that feminism has resulted in richer and deeper romantic heterosexual relationships within the context of a patriarchal society, as equal partnerships hold more possibility for growth, development and support for both parties.

## References

Amadiume, I. (1987). *Male Daughters, Female Husbands*, Basingstoke: Palgrave Macmillan.

Bell, R. (2002). *Understanding African Philosophy: A Cross Cultural Approach to Classical and Contemporary Issues*, New York and London: Routledge.

Eze, M. O. (2008). 'What Is African Communitarianism? Against Consensus as Regulative Ideal', *South African Journal of Philosophy*, 27 (4).

Heidegger, M. (1996). *Being and Time*, translated by Joan Stambaugh, Albany, NY: SUNY Press.

Krog, A. (2008). 'This Thing Called Reconciliation … Forgiveness as Part of an Interconnectedness-Towards-Wholeness', *South African Journal of Philosophy*, 27 (4).

Lévinas, E. and Hand, S. (1989). *The Levinas Reader*, Malden, MA: Blackwell Publishing.

Liwane, N. (n.d.). 'The Significance of Ubuntu in the Development of an ANC Cadre'. www.anc.org.za/ancdocs/pubs/umrabulo/umrabulo13v.html, accessed 9 July 2009.

Menkiti, I. (2004). 'On the Normative Conception of a Person', in Wiredu, K. (ed.), *A Companion to African Philosophy*, Malden, MA: Blackwell Publishing.

Metz, T. (2007). 'Towards an African Moral Theory', *Journal of Political Philosophy*, 15 (3), 321–341. doi:10.1111/j.1467–9760.2007.00280.x.

Metz, T. (2010). 'African and Western Moral Theories in a Bioethical Context', *Developing World Bioethics*, 10 (1), 49–58. doi:10.1111/j.1471–8847.2009.00273.x.

Nzegwu, N. (1994). 'Gender Equality in a Dual-Sex System: The Case of Onitsha', *Canadian Journal of Law and Jurisprudence*, VII (1).

Oyowe, O. A. and Yurkivska, O. (2014). 'Can a Communitarian Concept of African Personhood Be both Relational and Gender-neutral?' *South African Journal of Philosophy*, 33 (1), 85–99.

Tutu, D. (2000). *No Future without Forgiveness*, New York: Doubleday.

Wiredu, K. (1992). 'The African Concept of Personhood', in Harley, E. and Pellegrino, Edmund D. (eds), *African-American Perspectives on Biomedical Ethics*, Washington, DC: Georgetown University Press.

# 4 African philosophy, its questions, the place and the role of women and its disconnect with its world

*Olajumoke Akiode*

## Introduction

African philosophy, comprising of ethno-philosophy, professional philosophy, nationalist-ideological philosophy, philosophic sagacity and their contemporary variants, is said to have begun as an account of contradiction and denial of Western-imposed identity. Through its journey to date, it tackled the questions of identity, its authenticity, and thoroughly debated the ideal logical, ontological and epistemic framework that will underpin it. Given that every philosophy is a product of its environment and culture, most of the account is replete with ingeniously proposed cultural world-views such as 'Communal Thought', 'Negritude' 'Life/Vital force', 'Ujaama', 'Uwa', 'Ibuanyidanda' and so on, most of which implicitly accommodated women, defined their place and roles. But a pertinent question this generates is this: Why despite these inclusive, communalist, being-with, interconnectedness and interdependence in traditional/ cultural world-views, are women marginalized in contemporary Africa? Why is there disconnect between what these philosophers claim was in the very DNA of traditional African communities and the actions of contemporary African communities, which is its world? Besides, why is there scant representation of women in the whole African philosophic enterprise? Could it be because excavating or reconstructing the African identity was done as a holistic block project and not demographically disaggregated to include issues of concern to women, children, the environment and the future generations? Furthermore, looking closely at the inclusive and communal world-views, how thoroughly inclusive are they?

This chapter attempts to resolve the paradox of the overarching disconnect between the tenets of African philosophy and the practice of marginalization of women in contemporary Africa and within African philosophy. This entails the questioning of seemingly tenable assumptions about the process of the evolution of African philosophy as well as tracing the roots of these tenets to analyze epochal influences that gave birth to them and the contemporary practice of marginalization of women. This paper will also analyze gender consciousness and inclusion vis-à-vis the pre-colonial Yoruba African world-view.

African philosophy evolved from the quest to forge an African identity to contest Africans' derogatory exclusion from rational thought by Western scholars (Ruch and Anyawnu, 1981). This work describes and questions a fundamental assumption that a historical perspective of the evolution of African philosophy, with its anti-imperialist genesis, may largely account for the scant representation of women in African philosophy. Noting the complementarity that characterizes African world-views, the marginalization of women according to this assumption, arises essentially as a consequence of the process of the unraveling of the African personality or identity by African thinkers over the decades. That is, this unraveling occurred in a blanket and absolute manner that left no room for the disaggregation of the African project, which was necessary to highlight the interests of women, children, and the environment.

## Debunking the assumption of the blanket process of evolution of African philosophy

An attempt to resolve the paradox of African philosophy's disconnecting with its origin and practice threw up the assumption that the marginalization of women is a consequence of the process of the unraveling of the African personality or identity by African thinkers over the decades. That is, this unraveling occurred in a blanket and absolute manner that left no room for the disaggregation of the African project, which was necessary to highlight the interests of women, children, and the environment.

It would seem that given the urgency and desperation of the African philosophy project, it is possible to overlook and distort the African reality, to reconfigure the African DNA to be able to exclude women, to ignore and silence women's voices in almost ten decades of its philosophic enterprise. At least a Yoruba saying could be proffered to support this anomaly as follows: '*Bi ina ba n joni, ti onjo omo eni, ti ara eni ni a ma koko gbon*'. Meaning literally – if your body catches fire at the same time as your child's body, you put out your own first, after which you can help the child to put out its own fire too.

But the import of this proverb does not support the assumption that justifies women's marginalization; it simply prioritizes the order for an effective rescue effort. And by implication for the philosophic enterprise, it spells out the order of its unraveling and evolution rather than condone gender blindness. Also, ten decades is enough time to get round to including women's issues and voice.

Furthermore, the African philosophic quest was about African identity: such answers ought to begin from the existential reality of relatedness, 'We are who we are because of these others – women, children, future generations and the environment'. Therefore, this assumption is neither tenable nor valid. It reeks of a colonial mentality that is yet to be expunged from the African mind-set and thought system.

To further corroborate this argument, I will employ the logical tool of hypothetical syllogism as follows:

i   If African philosophy is based on African world-views of com-
    plementarity, inclusion, interrelatedness, and being-with-others, then the
    scant representation of women in African philosophy is due to the pro-
    cess of unraveling which occurred in a blanket and absolute manner that
    left no room for the disaggregation of the African project.
ii  If the scant representation of women in African philosophy is due to the
    process of unraveling which occurred in a blanket and absolute manner
    that left no room for the disaggregation of the African project, then
    external (colonial) influence on the thought and socialization process is
    responsible for the contemporary marginalization of women.

Therefore, if African philosophy is based on African world-views of complementarity, inclusion, being-with-others; then external (colonial) influence
on the thought and socialization process is responsible for contemporary
marginalization of women.

The rest of this chapter is devoted to analyzing the validity, truth and
soundness of each premise of the hypothetical syllogism argument through
the hermeneutic analysis of the pre-colonial Yoruba African world-view.

## African philosophy and African world-view

African philosophy evolved as a reaction to Africans' peculiar experience
of slavery, colonialism, racism and derogatory exclusion from the realm of
rationality and intellectual vibrancy by Western scholars like Hegel, Kant and
Levy-Bruhl (Chimakonam, 2014a). And its main focus is on answering the
question – who am I? Embedded in this question are the issues of identity,
capability, reconstruction and futurity. Chimakonam (2014b), in his very illumi-
nating encyclopedia entry on the history of African philosophy, delineates the
history of African philosophy into two main epochs – the pre-systematic and the
systematic. According to him (Chimakonam 2014b), the pre-systematic is the era
before colonization in which largely undocumented world-views and cultural
ideas propagated by the anonymous thinkers were dominant. It is also known as
the pre-literate period, which could be said to encompass the acclaimed era of
interaction and intellectual flight or exportation between Greece, the architect of
Western philosophy, and Egypt, presumed to be a representative of Black Africa
as depicted in George James' *Stolen Legacy* (James, 1954). Chimakonam (2015)
goes on to divide the systematic epoch into the following four periods:

1   Early period: 1920s–1960s
2   Middle period: 1960s–1980s
3   Later period: 1980s–1990s
4   New (contemporary) era: post-1990s.

In their search for African identity, African philosophers spanning the early
to the later periods engaged in 'an essentialist interpretation of African

culture' (Hallen, 2002). While some of them claimed that the lost African identity could only be found in the depths of African indigenous culture, others coined economic and socio-political ideologies within an indigenous African cultural framework. Hence, from Bantu Philosophy to Ujamaa, from the Eclectic School to the contemporary era, African philosophy evolved on the foundation of an African cultural system comprising of religion, economics, a socio-political structure and language.

The defining trait of this African philosophy is its cultural hue, the connectivity and interconnectedness of all beings, the essential 'being-with-others', the inclusivity and overarching complementarity. These are traits distilled from communities within the African geographical space. Most importantly, they are traits traced to an epoch before colonization, along with the claim that its fragments survived the experiences of slavery and colonization and are manifest in contemporary times. What is the empirical evidence and episteme of these traits on which African philosophy is based? The focus of this work is on the Yoruba African world-view.

## The Yoruba African world-view: a hermeneutic analysis

In the traditional societies within the African geographical space, most accounts of creation, such as that of the Yoruba, are based on their conceptual scheme, which evolved from a binary understanding of reality, where every unit of existence is made up of two complementary and inseparable elements. Therefore, their creation account concerns Osun and Orunmila, female goddesses and male gods whose roles and functionality were complementary (Oluwole, 2014, p. 7). There are accounts of male and female progenitors, gods such as Sango, Ogun and goddesses such as Oya and Osun; as well as male and female founders of kingdoms, warriors and people versed in statecraft.

Of all the essential elements of the Yoruba African world-view, I will focus mainly on the concept of being (the self), eldership, and economic and socio-political structure. I will also differentiate between the experiences of pre-colonial, colonial and post-colonial epochs. This will help to drive home the point that African philosophy based on the African world-view that excluded and marginalized women is an aberration; that it can only be a consequence of colonial influence on Africans' thought processes.

### The Yoruba concept of 'being'

The Yoruba culture is replete with rigor, depth, structure and representation, and its language is a well-crafted, efficient conceptualization and communication mechanism. Its intellectual content is excellent and the narratives are evidence of people who are accustomed to thinking (Odejobi, 2013).

The concept of being or the Self in Yoruba cosmology recognizes three states of existence and two states of being, as follows:

*Table 4.1* How 'being' is defined in relation to others

| S/N | Yoruba terms | Meaning | English use | Meaning |
|-----|-------------|---------|-------------|---------|
| 1 | Ebi | A group defined by common-birth (Ajobı) relations. Ancestors and future generation. | Family | Blood relation, usually nuclear but may be extended. Limited to the living. |
| 2 | Iyawo | A woman married into the family – 'ebi' | Wife | A woman married to a man |
| 3 | Baba | All male parents in the 'Ajobı' relation | Father | A male biological parent |

*Source*: Odejobi, 2013.

Three states: (i) the ancestors, (ii) the living, and (iii) future generations (yet to be born).
Two forms: (i) the tangible (physical), and (ii) the intangible (spiritual).

Being, or the Self, is usually defined in the context of others, its relation to others such as the family, the clan and the community. A person is described not just as an individual, but as a member of a certain family, clan, community and sometimes a profession. For example, Efunsetan, omo aniwura, iyalode Ibadan; Efunsetan is described in terms of her parentage, her occupation and position in the society. The importance of this relatedness is highlighted by the following popular admonition: '*Ranti omo eni ti iwo nse.*' Meaning, 'Remember the family, its values and good name, to which you belong.'

It is argued that the concept of the knowledge of 'self' in the Yoruba cosmology subsumes the knowledge of others. This is demonstrated in the following communal concepts as differentiated from individualized ones below:

*Table 4.2* 'Ajo' (communal) in contrast to 'ada' (individualism) concepts

| S/N | Communal | Meaning | Individualism | Meaning |
|-----|----------|---------|---------------|---------|
| 1 | Ajobı | Communal birth | Adabı' | Individualistic birth |
| 2 | Ajogbe | Communal living | Adagbe | Individualized living |
| 3 | Ajomo | Communal knowledge | Adamo' | Individualized knowledge |
| 4 | Ajose | Cooperation | Adase | Individual effort |
| 5 | Ajoro | Communal brainstorming | Adaro | Individual thinking |
| 6 | Ajoje | Communal eating | Adaje | Individualized eating |

*Source*: Odejobi, 2013.

Furthermore, the Yoruba concept of being or the Self shares some semblance with the 'Ubuntu' – 'I am who I am because of whom you are' – concept among the Bantu people of southern Africa. A person with Ubuntu is said to be open and available to others, affirming of others, does not feel threatened that others are able and good, for he or she has a proper self-assurance that comes from knowing that he or she belongs in a greater whole and is diminished when others are humiliated or diminished, when others are tortured or oppressed (Desmond Tutu, 1999).

Ubuntu is further explained as follows:

> 'A person is a person through other people', this strikes an affirmation of one's humanity through recognition of an 'other' in his or her uniqueness and difference. It is a demand for a creative inter-subjective formation in which the 'other' becomes a mirror (but only a mirror) for my subjectivity. This idealism suggests to us that humanity is not embedded in my person solely as an individual; my humanity is co-substantively bestowed upon the other and me. Humanity is a quality we owe to each other. We create each other and need to sustain this otherness creation. And if we belong to each other, we participate in our creations: we are because you are, and since you are, definitely I am. The 'I am' is not a rigid subject, but a dynamic self-constitution dependent on this otherness creation of relation and distance.
>
> (Eze, 2007)

In the Yoruba world-view, a person is identified by his or her relations, the family tree, the community, the community's language, customs, and differentiating signs such as tribal marks and tattoos. This idea of relatedness and interconnectedness ensures complementarity and inclusion. The communality it gives rise to creates a win–win interaction among men and women, elders and the young. Most people undertake activities for the common good. This assertion is supported by axioms like:

i   *Bi okunrin ri ejo, bi obirin ba pa, ki ejo saa ti ku.* Meaning: If a man sees a snake and a woman kills it, the important thing is for the snake to be dead/killed.
ii  *Owo omode ko to pepe, ti agbalagba ko wo akengbe.* Meaning: A child's hand may not be able to reach the ceiling, but the adult's hand cannot enter the gourd. That is, everyone has his or her usefulness and limitations, which ensures that we complement one another.

### Governance and decision making

Governance in pre-colonial Yoruba society is consensual rather than autocratic or dictatorial and has an integral and elaborate series of checks and balances to ensure an essentially egalitarian system (Drewal and Schildkrout, 2010).

An integral part of governance and communal decision making is the concept of eldership. 'Being' is a force in the universe of forces that fits into an hierarchy that starts from God ('Olodumare') and descends through the ancestors, the living human beings, animals, and down to the least force in the inorganic world (Tempels, 1954). This intermingling, interdependent hierarchy of forces is the basis of eldership. It informs the ranking by age, which gave birth to the structure of the traditional system that defines the role and relevance of elders in promoting stability to the economic and socio-political structure of the traditional societies. The Yoruba cosmology has both an existential and functional hierarchy which are interdependent and complementary (Okoro, 2011). The Yoruba world-view holds the position of elders sacrosanct and their role is to steer society on the right course. This is backed by adages like *Agba ki I wa l'oja ki ori omo tuntun wo*. Meaning: Where there is an elder, the young cannot go astray.

Oyeronke Oyewumi defines eldership as seniority, 'which is the primary social categorization that is immediately apparent in Yoruba language. It is the ranking of persons based on their chronological ages, the prevalence of age categorization in Yoruba language is the pivotal principle of social organization'(Oyewumi, 1997). That is, the language of identification and interaction is defined basically by eldership/seniority – I (*emi*), You (*iwo, o*) – for one's contemporaries, You (*eyin, e*), they/them (*awon*) for elders/seniors. Also, hierarchy within a lineage is structured on eldership or seniority, defined on a first-come-first-served basis. Entrance into a lineage is either through birth or through marriage, and a person's place in the existing hierarchy is fixed by the time of arrival. For example, in the case of birth, it is *egbon, agba* for those who were born first; *aburo, omode* for those born later. While in the case of marriage, *iyawo agba, iyawo ile* is used for elder wives or women who got married into the family first, and *iyawo kekere* for wives that arrived later.

According to C. S. Momoh, eldership is the basis from which authority, discipline and respect flows; eldership is leadership, it is authority (Momoh, 2000). The implication of this is that the elders have legitimate authority that demands subservence, obedience and deference. With this authority comes power, and it lays the foundation for inequality of authority and power in the society and in any relationship involving elders and young ones. This also influences power relations both in the private and public spheres.

However, in the public sphere, that is in communal space, eldership is not essentially age-based or seniority-based; there are other factors such as maturity, virtuous living, character, pedigree and so on that can qualify a person for eldership. This is corroborated by the following proverbs:

i   *Ti omode ba mo owo we, a ba agba jeun.* Meaning: If a child comports himself properly in the society, he or she will be called upon to sit and commune with the elders.

ii   *Agba merin ni o n se ilu, agba okunrin, agba obirin, agba omode ati agba alejo.* Meaning: Four experienced or mature groups of people manage the affairs of a community, mature men, mature women, mature youth and mature foreigners.

These components of inclusion, interconnectedness, complementarity and eldership can be said to be responsible for the remarkable fluidity and dynamism of decision making in Yoruba society. According to Sophie Oluwole, there is abundant historical evidence to show that no specific public sphere was institutionally closed to women (Oluwole 2014).

This discourse on the Yoruba African world-view or any African world-view will not be complete without the inclusion of Africa's colonial experience. This is essential in the sense that it locates the African world-view in the reality of its era or epoch. It is classified into pre-colonial, colonial and post-colonial epochs. The African world-view and reality was transformed by the emergence of these epochs.

It is important to declare here and now that this epochal classification transformed the Yoruba reality as well as other African world-views. This implies that the preceding discourse about the African and Yoruba world-view describes a pre-colonial reality. Given that world-views and culture encompass the social structures and political economy of a people, situating these within a specific epoch ensures a deeper understanding that will help resolve our paradox. Furthermore, this epochal delineation helps to answer questions about patriarchy, about the marginalization of women, and about feminism in Yoruba society.

### The Yoruba African world-view in the pre-colonial epoch

The prevailing features of this era are communality, interconnectedness, interrelatedness due to the universe of interconnected forces, and eldership with its attendant respect, obedience, deference and complementarity.

Was it a patriarchal society? Yes. But a broader definition of patriarchy that is not necessarily oppressive to women is evident here. Communality, inclusion, interconnectedness and interdependence preclude a perception of females/women as the 'other' that is inferior, unequal, that should be suppressed, manipulated, subjugated and silenced. From their accounts of creation, their religious worship, their governance and decision making process, their social institutions and their political economy, a complementarity of men and women is prevalent. Analyzing this within the spectrum of eldership sheds more light on this particular version of patriarchy. In both private and public spaces, complementarity and inclusion is evident.

For instance, as mentioned earlier, both men and women played significant roles in their account of creation, as their objects of worship, as the custodians of knowledge and culture. Their governance and consensual decision making implies inclusion of both men and women. Women not only groom kings and princes, they are involved in the coronation rites and even stand as transitional kings (*adele oba*) pending the coronation of a new king. They play a substantive role in their political economy and have a representative in the government as *iyaloja* or *iyaláje* (women in charge of economic affairs) and *iyalode* (women in charge of socio-political affairs).

A typical example is Efunsetan Aniwura. A native of Abeokuta, Egbaland, she was married to a warrior from Ibadan and so settled down in Ibadan even after her husband's demise. Because of her intelligence, business acumen, wealth and influence, she became the Iyalode of Ibadan around 1870. She became extremely powerful during the reign of King Oluyole in Ibadan because of her peculiar business of war promotion, the leasing of slaves as soldiers and supplying ammunition for the Oyo war crusade. She was a business tycoon who traded in gold, jewelry, war horses, guns and ammunition, and was involved in the local and transatlantic slave trade (Akinwumi, 2010; Lebu, 2006; Olukoju, 2010; Soetan, 2001; Osewa, 2005).

Furthermore, Yoruba education was divided into two, namely *eko-ile* and *eko-ode*, which entails *eko-ise* or *eko-owo sise*. This literarily means home training, socialization and skills acquisition. The home training, as well as the socialization process, was left in the hands of women. The implication of this is that women were considered moral agents capable of moral agency.

Therefore, the variant of patriarchy in pre-colonial Yoruba society was not oppressive to women. Bearing in mind the place of eldership that commands respect, subservience and deference, the existing power relations may be due to seniority. According to Momoh, because marriage was between men who were older than women, the power relation was age-based and not necessarily due to a notion of subjugating and suppressive patriarchy (Momoh, 2002). Also, the eldership concept allows older married women or women who have been married for a long time – matriarchs – to wield enormous power in their families. This is corroborated by the following adage: *Bi obinrin ba ti pe ni ile oko, aje ni won ma n da*. Meaning: When a woman has been married into a family for a long time, she becomes very powerful or she is invested with great authority. Their patriarchy could be defined as a social system in which the father, being the eldest, is the head of the household, and has authority over women and children.

To this end, I argue that feminism as defined as an intellectual commitment and political movement that seeks justice for women and the end of sexism in all forms (*Stanford Encyclopedia*, 2004), and as a theory, a social and political movement that focuses on women's experiences and highlights various forms of oppression which the female gender is subjected to in the society (Sotunsa, 2008), had no place in pre-colonial Yoruba society. According to Oyewumi Oyeronke, gender was not an organizing principle prior to colonization by the West (Oyewumi, 1997).

### An anti- ethno-philosophic inclusion

It is important to note however, that for this discourse to avoid being tainted with the brush of ethno-philosophy, I have included a skeptical canon that portrays an imperfect African Yoruba past. That is, the admission and inclusion of the possibility or instances that could be argued to reflect discrimination against women evident in some Yoruba proverbs.

According to Oladele Balogun,

> non-genderization in the Yoruba thought system does not logically entail non-oppression of women. The Yoruba proverbial linguistic resources can be used to substantiate this position. Proverbial oppression here is construed as cruel and unfair pithy sayings that derogate the dignity, integrity, rights and freedom of the women folk.
>
> (Balogun, 2010)

Balogun (2010) provides a list of some of such proverbs as follows:

> Some of the proverbs that capture this negative perception of women in Yoruba culture are: (i) kaka ko san lara iya aje, ofi gbogbo omo re b'obinrin, eye wan yi lu eye ('Instead of it getting better for the witch, all her children are girls, the birds are thus multiplying') (Bello-Olowookere 2005, p. 44).
>
> (ii) Eni ti ofe arewa fe iyonu, eni gbogbo ni i ba won tan (Delano 1976, p. 134) ('He who marries beauty marries trouble; everybody claims relationship with her'). This is an unfair indictment of the beautiful feminine folk. There is no established causal connection between physical beauty and faults in character. This proverb confuses, perhaps even equates, elegance and admiration with a promiscuous lifestyle.
>
> (iii) Obinrin ko se finu han ('Secrets should not be revealed to a woman') (Ajibola 2005, p. 26). This proverb implies that women naturally have the tendency to divulge secrets. It explains, partly or wholly, why women are not always involved in decision making, despite their indispensable contribution to society.

These proverbial resources provide proof that the pre-colonial Yoruba society was not entirely free from discrimination against women and negative perception. This admission, however, does not detract from the overwhelming fact that their society was a non-subjugating patriarchal society. Theirs was not a saintly paradise but there were no laws, policies, or culture that silenced the voice of women, denied them basic human rights, or kept them out of their social, economic and political spheres. Most importantly, the existence of proverbial oppression of women does not negate the intrinsic existential realities of complementarity, inclusion, being-with-others, interconnectedness and interdependence of pre-colonial Yoruba society. In fact, fragments of this existential reality survived the colonial influence and are still evident in twenty-first-century Yoruba communities.

### The colonial and post-colonial epoch in the Yoruba world-view

After the conquest of most kingdoms in Africa and the launch of colonialism, the existing world-views were attacked and through a program of gradual but consistent deconstruction. British colonial rule overwhelmingly replaced the traditional world-views with its own. The British imported suppressive and subjugating patriarchy, and changed the power dynamics from eldership to male dominance, in the guise of benevolent sexism.

English the colonial language, entails the generalization of certain linguistic items in support of men over women that differentiates and stratifies between men and women, powerful and weak, etc. Given the affinity between language and thought, it easily led to linguistic oppression that fostered male domination and women's subjugation (Akinola, 2012). Through the linguistic conquest came thought conquest and the subjugation of women to the lower rung of society.

The women that wielded economic and socio-political power, who had a significant share in political power, ritual leadership, and the transmission of oral history and traditions, had their powers withdrawn, and rights to property and resources significantly limited.

The collusion of colonial Western values with the pre-colonial Yoruba world-view gave birth to the distortion of thought, identity and perception; the fragmentation of communal attitude, complementarity and inclusion. It led to the exclusion of women from participation in meaningful production and it undermined the economic and political power of Yoruba women. Such colonial policies have had far-reaching consequences on women's present position; consequences which the male bias in post-colonial policy-making has done little to correct (Afsar, 1987).

Women's exclusion from the formal economy was mirrored in their exclusion from the colonial political administration. Colonial states generally developed strong relationships with men as workers, administrators and officials, while women were confined to positions of domesticity which entirely distorted the women's pre-colonial place and role. According to Musafare (2007),

> I therefore think that the cult of domesticity imposed through colonial rule and ideology has had enormous practical and ideological implications for many African women. It can also be noted that from an ideological perspective, it has been central to ways in which nationalism – articulated by male elites schooled in the colonial educational system – defined decorous roles for women as mothers of the nation or the handmaidens of anti-colonial struggles. Overall, the cult of domesticity shaped by colonialism set major ideological constrains [sic] for conceptualizing powerful roles for women. Rooted in colonial prescriptions for 'civilized' and 'feminine' positions for African women, the view that women's legitimate duties were to their immediate families and homes has been all pervasive.

The pervasiveness of this ideological perspective is felt even in this twenty-first-century. In political organizations women are better suited as campaign managers and deputies than as governors and presidents. There is an overwhelming bias against women in the public space as a result of the mental captivity orchestrated by the colonial conquest.

It was in the colonial and post-colonial epoch that the real African feminist struggle began in protest of oppressive policies and economic and socio-political structures. Some of the colonial and post-colonial feminist struggles include various women's guilds, professional associations, political movements such as the Abeokuta Ladies Club, and women activists like Funmilayo Ransome Kuti who led protests against the British in 1947, Omu Okwei who led the Aba riot in 1929, and Yaa Asantewa of Ghana who led an Ashanti rebellion against the British between 1900 and 1901 (Oluwole, 2014).

### *The fallout of colonial influence*

Unfortunately, the new thought process, perception and attitude have become difficult to overturn. Even after independence, the identity of the African remained European, her language, thought system, standards and even her perceptions have an indelible colonial underpinning. Or perhaps, the African mind is an unconscious prisoner of colonial influence.

Furthermore, the attempt to forge an African identity and claim to rationality through the documentation of African philosophy was flawed by the colonial consciousness, thought process and language template. Even the Western philosophic heritage, is not only essentially 'male-centric', its contemplation of humanity and 'metaphysical mores' substantially excluded women. In instances where women were remembered, some referred to women in passing and in a condescending manner. Examples that readily come to mind are especially those of Aristotle's view of women as less rational than men. Kant claims that women are 'too lazy to dare', an attribute that confines them to a state of immaturity whereby they do not have the civil nature to enable them participate in the public sphere. Machiavelli also compared women to Fortune, who ought to be controlled and ill-treated to enable her smile on the audacious, and so on. Unfortunately, African philosophers are consciously and unconsciously aligned with this heritage.

This can be said to account for the exclusion of women from African philosophy, or as implied by Odera Oruka, as less philosophically minded than men. Gail Presbey criticized his labeling of women sages as folk sages; she believed that they exhibited sound philosophic temperament in their contemplation and answered questions better than those males he labeled as philosophic (Presbey, 2007).

It can also be the reason behind the under-representation of female philosophers and their views and philosophy, and even for the very low number of women philosophers in philosophy departments in various universities in Africa. It is not that philosophy departments in the West have equal number of men and women, but that the imbalance is ridiculously high for a culture that claims to define itself by the existence of others. In African philosophy departments where African philosophy is said to be practiced, men and women experience different realities. And these realities are not considered or even contemplated. Unfortunately, this could be described as a form of micro-inequality that is not entirely or immediately visible but contributes to the marginalization of women. This could be better explained with reference to women's experiences such as not being recommended for assignments that could expose their capabilities and potentials as often as men, not being regularly involved in tasks that could bring extra income as often as men, having fewer publications than men, and not being promoted at the same pace as men, to mention but a few.

I argue therefore, that the exclusion of women from African philosophy is a flaw caused by the colonial conquest of thought and language. That is, according to Dennis Ekpo, the influence of 'logo-centric' rationality on African minds, such as, discourse formations in European languages that are elaborated and structured, using European procedures and models of rationality, by African intellectuals in order to conceptualize and define African realities and problems (Ekpo, 2006).

It is also the reason for their assumption of gender neutrality in their African philosophical enterprise. Nancy Tuana argues that traditional claim of gender neutrality in philosophy is merely a socially reinforced delusion and deception (Tuana, 1992); a reflection of incomplete weaning from colonial ties.

All of these assumptions point to the fact that the marginalization of women or exclusion of women in African philosophy from the early era to the contemporary era is a result of the process of philosophizing from a mind that is not completely free from colonial influence. It is the probable reason why philosophers who claim to be forging an African identity from resources distilled from a pre-colonial African past will assume that women can be excluded. Or it could be a blanket process that cannot accommodate disaggregation into its component reality. Or philosophize with a gender blind-spot.

## Roadmap for inclusion

To begin with, concerted effort has to be made to remove the gender blind-spot that may have caused women's exclusion from African philosophy. This has to begin with a realistic project of decolonization of the African thought system or mental decolonization. It will entail creating awareness of the incompleteness of an African philosophy that excludes or marginalizes women. This should be followed by a deconstruction of imported Euro-centric paradigms of sexism and the oppressive fallout of colonial and post-colonial institutionalized designs originating from male chauvinism and women-subjugating patriarchy. Philosophy departments in universities in Africa should shift from lip-service commitment to gender issues, overcome their gender bias, proactively contemplate an inclusive African reality, and advocate it.

Gender-inclusive initiatives should transcend pursuit of the feminist cause to a 'more comprehensive integration of women into political parties' hierarchy and policy making cadre complemented with sustainable socio-economic mobilization for both rural and urban women' (Oluwole, 2014).

African feminism, especially its philosophic element, should incorporate the translation and implementation of the emancipation and liberation drives of colonial and post-colonial Nigeria, for example. They should build upon the pre-colonial cultural complementarities of male and female roles in state management.

Female philosophers should work together to propose alternative moral theories birthed by their peculiar experiences and concerns; as well as rationality that portrays complementarity, inclusion and sustainable stakeholder management.

They should set goals for African philosophy to promote gender inclusion by doing the following:

i   Creating awareness about existing gender blind-spots in both public and private spaces of interaction;
ii  Deconstructing oppressive social structures in collaboration with the men;
iii Addressing moral issues in both private and public spaces that subjugated and silenced women;
iv  Pursuing gender and feminist initiatives in African philosophy in a way that will promote economic and socio-political development in sub-Saharan Africa.

## Conclusion

An African philosophy that excludes women despite its African cultural origin and DNA of complementarity, inclusion, interrelatedness and interconnectedness as highlighted by concepts like 'Ubuntu' is indeed an aberration. The excuse that the process of forging the African identity in an era of exclusion from rationality called for a blanket or block procedure that could not accommodate demographic disaggregation, is untenable. Also, the assumption of gender neutrality is a farce. This African philosophic enterprise is essentially an exhibition of a colonized mentality.

The hermeneutic analysis of the pre-colonial Yoruba African world-view, its concept of existence, being/self, governance and eldership, has offered proof that ideas of interconnectedness, interrelatedness, being-with-others, inclusion and complementarity are entrenched and inseparable from the African world-view.

In conclusion, it is therefore a valid argument and conclusion that if African philosophy is based on African world-views of complementarity, inclusion and being-with-others, then external (colonial) influence on thought and socialization process is responsible for the contemporary marginalization of women. When a correct diagnosis has been made, a prescription can be made accurately and the cure is at hand.

# References

Afsar, H. (1987). *Women, State and Ideology: Studies from Africa and Asia.* London: Macmillan.

Akinola, A. A. A. (2012). 'Linguistic Oppression on The Female Race: Revisiting Some English Lexical and Structural Items', *Gender Issues: International Journal of the Feminist/Womanist Theorists*, 4 (March).

Ajayi, S. (2015). 'Story Behind Efunsetan Aniwura'. The Sun Publishing Ltd. www.sunnewspaper.com. Retrieved 26/01/2010.

Akinwunmi, I. (2010). *Efunsetan Aniwura.* Ibadan: Ibadan University Press.

Akinwunmi, I. (2014). 'I Misrepresented Efunsetan Aniwura In My Book'. *The Punch*, 20 September. www.punchng.com. Retrieved 6/08/2014.

Ayinla, F. O. (2011). 'Traditional Institutions in Omu-Aran, during the Colonial Era'. B.Sc. Project Submitted to the Department of History and International Studies, Faculty of Arts University of Ilorin, Ilorin, Nigeria.

Balogun, O. A. (2010). 'Proverbial Oppression of Women in Yoruba African Culture: A Philosophical Overview', *Thought and Practice: A Journal of the Philosophical Association of Kenya (PAK)*, New Series, 2 (1), 21–36. http://ajol.info/index.php/tp/index. Retrieved 25/08/16.

Chimakonam, J. O. (2014a). 'Ezumezu: A Variant of Three-valued Logic – Insights and Controversies'. Paper presented at the Annual Conference of the Philosophical Society of Southern Africa. Free State University, Bloemfontein, South Africa. 20–22 January.

Chimakonam, J. O. (2014b). 'African Philosophy, History of', *Internet Encyclopedia of Philosophy: A Peer Reviewed Internet Resource.* www.iep.utm.edu/afric-hi/. Retrieved 15/06/16.

Chimakonam, J. O. (2015). 'Dating and Periodization Questions in African Philosophy', in J. O. Chimakonam (ed.), *Atuolu Omalu: Some Unanswered Questions in Contemporary African Philosophy* (pp. 9–34). Lanham, MD: University Press of America.

Drewal, J. and Schildkrout, E. (2010). *Dynasty and Divinity: Ife Art in Ancient Nigeria.* Washington, DC: University of Washington Press.

Ekpo, D. (2006). 'Towards a Post-Africanism: Contemporary African Thought and Postmodernism'. *Textual Practice*, 9 (1), 121–135.

Eze, M. O. (2007). 'Intellectual History in Contemporary South Africa'. *Anglia – Zeitschrift für Englische Philologie*, 129 (3–4), 190–191.

Hallen, B. (2002). *A Short History of African Philosophy.* Bloomington, IN: Indiana University Press.

Ilesanmi, O. O. (2010). 'Bridging Gender Inequity Gap in Africa: A Psycho-Historical Exposition of Efunsetan Aniwura', *International Journal of Psychology and Counselling*, 2 (3), 33–43.

James, G. (1954). *Stolen Legacy: Greek Philosophy Is Stolen Egyptian Philosophy.* New York: Philosophical Library.

Kolawole, M. (1997). *Womanism and African Consciousness.* Trenton, NJ: Africa World Press.

Lebu, A. Y. (2006). 'Nigerian Women in Politics: A Study of the Role of Women in President Obasanjo's Adminisration 1999–2003', in T. Folola and S. U. Fwatshak (eds), *Beyond Tradition: African Women and Cultural Spaces.* Trenton, NJ: Africa World Press.

Levy-Bruhl, L. (1947). *Primitive Mentality.* Paris: University of France Press.

Momoh, C. S. (2000). 'The Function of Eldership in African Marital Relations', in C. S. Momoh (ed.), *The Substance of African Philosophy*. 2nd edn. Lagos: First Academic Publishers.

Momoh, C. S. (2002). 'Eldership in Traditional African Society'. Lecture delivered in a philosophy master class at the Philosophy Department, University of Lagos.

Musafare, M. (2007). 'African Women under Pre-Colonial, Colonial and Post-Colonial Rule'. http://politicaleconomicandsocialissues.blogspot.com.ng/2007/09/african-women-under-pre-colonial.html. Retrieved 07/08/16.

Nkrumah, K. (1961). *I Speak of Freedom: A Statement of African Ideology*. London: Mercury Books.

Nkrumah, K. (1962). *Towards Colonial Freedom*. London: Heinemann (First published 1945).

Nyerere, J. (1986a). *Freedom and Unity*. Dar-es-Salaam: Oxford University Press.

Nyerere, J. (1986b). *Freedom and Socialism*. Dar-es-Salaam: Oxford University Press.

Nyerere, J. (1986c). *Ujamaa: Essays on Socialism*. Dar-es-Salaam: Oxford University Press.

Odejobi, O. A. (2013). 'Self Knowledge and Intellectualism: A Perspective from the Yoruba Cosmology'. International Conference in honour of Dr. Oladipo Fashina, Department of Philosophy, Obafemi Awolowo University, 7–8 May.

Oruka, H. O. (1990). *Trends in Contemporary African Philosophy*. Nairobi: Shirikon.

Oruka, H. O. (1991). 'Sage Philosophy: The Basic Question', in H. Odera Oruka (ed.), *Sage Philosophy: Indigenous Thinkers and Modern Debate on African Philosophy*. Nairobi: Acts Press.

Ogunleye, F. (2004). 'A Male-Centric Modification of History 'Efunsetan Aniwura' revisited', *History in Africa*, 31, 303–318.

Okoro, C. (2011). 'The Notion of Integrative Metaphysics and Its Relevance to Contemporary World Order', *Integrative Humanism Journal – Ghana*, 1 (2). Accra: Emmpong Press.

Olukoju, A. (2010). 'Entrepreneurship, Accumulation, and Consumption and Societal Under Development: Western Nigeria in Historical and Comparative Perspective'. Paper Presented at the WCFIA/IIAS Conference on Understanding African Poverty over the Longue Durée. Accra, 15–17 July.

Olutoye, O. (1995). 'Leadership and Discipline in Yoruba Palaces', *Obitun: Journal of Humanities* 1 (1). Ibadan: JBS Forward Ever Printing & Publishing Company.

Oluwole, S. B. (2007). 'African Philosophy on the Threshold of Modernization'. *A Valedictory Lecture*, 15 February. Lagos: First Academic Publishers.

Oluwole, S. B. and Sofoluwe, A. J. O. (2014). *African Myths and Legends of Gender*. Lagos: Ark Publishers.

Osewa, O. (2005). 'Great Leaders in Nigeria's History before Total Colonization: Efunsetan (1800–1874)'. www.nairaland.com. Retrieved 26/01/2012.

Onuegbu, M. C. (2004). 'Transcending Patriarchal Subjugation: The Female in J. C. Maduekwe's *Uru Nwa*', in O. Ndimele (ed.), *Language and Culture in Nigeria: A Festschrift for Okon Essien* (pp. 313–323). Port Harcourt: Emhai Printing and Publishing.

Oyewumi, O. (1997). *The Invention of Women: Making an African sense of Western Gender Discourses*. Minneapolis, MN: University of Minnesota Press.

Presbey, G. M. (2007). 'Sage Philosophy: Criteria That Distinguish It from Ethno-philosophy and Make It a Unique Approach within African Philosophy', *Philosophia Africana*, 10 (2), 127–160.

Ruch, E. A. and Anyawnu, K. C. (1981). *African Philosophy: An Introduction to the Main Philosophical Trends in Contemporary Africa.* Rome: Catholic Book Agency.

Sen, G. and Grown, C. (1987). *Development Crisis and Alternative Visions: Third World Women's Perspectives.* New York: Monthly Review Press.

Soetan, R. O. (2001). 'Culture, Gender and Development'. *Report Submitted to the African Institute for Economic Development and Planning (IDEP)* Dakar, October.

Sofola, Z. (1996). 'Women and Literature', in A. Odejide (ed.), *Women and the Media in Nigeria.* Ibadan: WODOC.

Sotunsa, M. (2008). *Feminism and Gender Discourse: The African Experience.* Sagamu: Asaba Publications.

Tempels, P. (1954). *Bantu Philosophy.* Paris: Présence Africaine.

Tuana, N. (1992). *Woman and the History of Philosophy.* New York: Paragon House.

Tutu, D. (1999). *No Future Without Forgiveness.* New York: Random House.

# 5    Dialogues and alliances

## Positions of women in African philosophy

*Renate Schepen*

## Introduction

In the debate about the lack of diversity in philosophy, there is either a focus on the dominant masculine character or on the dominant Western character. Non-Western philosophies and feminist philosophies are often repeating systems of marginalization: the canon of African philosophy is, for example, mostly male and the canon of feminist philosophy is mostly white and Western. The use of the terms 'Western' and 'non-Western' is problematic as it in itself places the West as a center of reference and constitutes a binary, oppositional way of thinking. I still choose to use these terms as it is still the case that a Eurocentric perspective dominates the academic discipline of philosophy, and the use of these terms helps expose the problem. The term 'African philosophy' is also contested, and philosophers differ in positions as wide as restricting it to African-born philosophers to applying it to all philosophers taking responsibility and caring about Africa's daily problems (Mosima, 2016). Women in African philosophy are marginalized in both domains. In *African Philosophy: An Anthology* (1998), out of the forty-eight philosophers listed, only five are female and only one is African-born. In the book, great care has been taken to include gender discourse, which is also the part of the book where the five female philosophers are located.

In this work, I will explore whether alliances, and which ones, could help address the marginalization of women in African philosophy more adequately. For intercultural philosophy the method is dialogue. I will explore whether this can also benefit the position of women in African philosophy, and what needs to be taken into account if different parties enter into dialogue in their explorations to form alliances.

Sandra Harding (2015) indicates a weak complementarity between post-colonial studies that have been dominated by the South and feminist studies that have been dominated by the North. There is also an affinity and possibly an alliance between philosophy of sexual difference and intercultural philosophy, as proposed by Luce Irigaray and Heinz Kimmerle's response to Irigaray. Irigaray considers philosophy of sexual difference a way to rethink and re-establish the relations between genders as different, but equivalent, and considers this a way to attain the respect of other differences, such as race and culture (Irigaray, 2002). Thus, combining expertise from post-colonial and feminist studies, philosophy of sexual difference and intercultural philosophy could lead to reciprocal enrichment of different disciplines and better insight in the possibilities of such alliances.

Intercultural philosophy aims to take as equal contributions philosophical traditions and discourses from different regions and cultures of the world. Dialogues in intercultural philosophy are treating topics which are of common interest and/or exceed the problems of one specific culture (Kimmerle, 2011). However, we are limited if we only focus on the goal of intercultural philosophy to take contributions from philosophical traditions and discourses from different cultures as equal, and leave out specific attention to women philosophers. Dialogue is aimed at mutual understanding and reciprocal enrichment, and is a way to establish possible alliances, but therefore, the setting of dialogue, power structures, and historical experiences need to be taken into account.

Throughout this chapter, I will also explore my own position as a white Western woman. I feel honored to be invited to contribute to this volume, and at the same time I realize that in the intersection between non-Western philosophies and feminist studies which I explore, I am located in a privileged position in both domains. In her essay 'Can the Subaltern Speak?' G. C. Spivak (1988) cautions the intellectual elite working in the area of post-colonial studies, and emphasizes the importance of questioning the position of the researcher, as they might unintentionally contribute to the continuing construction of the subaltern (Spivak, 1988). Therefore, I also question my own position in this work. In an intercultural world, the issue of 'marginalization of women in African philosophy' cannot be isolated as a purely African affair. In this chapter I will show that Western colonization contributed to the marginalization of women in Africa and the effects of this are still being felt today in the global academic discourse and beyond. Universities across the world where philosophy is taught are often located in places marked by a great diversity of culture, and yet the philosophical curriculum is dominated by Western philosophy. A 2016 article in the *New York Times* states that 'of the top 50 philosophy doctoral programs in the English-speaking world, only 15 percent have *any* regular faculty members who teach *any* non-Western philosophy'. The authors, both American, address the persistent exclusion of philosophies from other cultures and call for the inclusion of African philosophers in the philosophical curriculum (Garfield and van Norden, 2016). Yet, there are no women among their suggested alternative philosophers. This not only perpetuates women's invisibility, but also that of epistemologies, which are necessary for a better comprehension of the world, as this work will show.

In this chapter, I will first explore the expressed need of African philosophy and black women for autonomous spaces in which to hold dialogues. Subsequently, I illustrate the difficulties which can be encountered in intercultural dialogues by referring to a debate between Innocent Asouzu and Heinz Kimmerle, and explore how an understanding of their difficulties can provide insights that might be beneficial to dialogues in which African women philosophers participate. Thereafter, I explore how the theory of intersectionality also applies to women in African philosophy, and address possible alliances and issues of marginalization, such as between intercultural philosophy and philosophies of (sexual) difference, as suggested by Kimmerle and Irigaray. Finally, I show how suggestions offered by female African philosophers such as Oyeronke Oyewumi, Sophie Oluwole, Awino Okech, and artist Zanele Muhoni, can offer different perspectives on the origins as well as on the ways out of marginalization. The diversity of approaches developed by the female African philosophers in this work is indicative of a pluralism among African philosophers. Just as there is a plurality among feminist and among African philosophers, there is also plurality among women in African philosophy. However, the work of the African women discussed in this chapter is from countries where English became the dominant language under colonization. There are important differences between these countries, but also between francophone, anglophone and lusophone African countries; the latter are not dealt with here.

## Autonomous spaces for dialogue

In July 2017 the Nyansapo Festival, an Afro-feminist festival, took place in Paris. This small occasion became an international news item, as it was allegedly going to be 'forbidden for whites'. Anne Hidalgo, the mayor of Paris, even tried to prevent the festival from taking place. In fact, the festival was open to all, except for some workshops which were exclusively for black women. Journalist Rokhaya Diallo (2017) draws a parallel with the French feminist movement, which was built on the idea of non-mixing, a strategy seen as necessary for oppressed groups seeking emancipation. That black women now wish to apply the same principle of non-mixing turns out to be so much more controversial, illustrates – according to Diallo – the attitude of the ruling white politicians.

In another blog written about this festival by a philosopher of Afro descent, as she calls herself, she mentions that her mindset during the festival was colored by an invitation from a fellow philosopher she received just beforehand. She refers to an invitation to a reading group on African philosophy, and questions why she is the only person of African descent who had been invited. She assumes that all the other invitees had already been involved with the project before, are able to do it for a living and wonders what would be her role in this reading group.

The fellow philosopher whom she refers to, who invited her, is me. Besides her assumptions about the gathering not being correct (she was invited from the onset like other participants, including others of African descent; and no, regretfully the other participants are also not able to do this for a living), for me, the blog revealed a felt need for activist women of African descent to have autonomous spaces for dialogue. In her blog, she refers to her affinity with black women in general and the hardships they experience as black women living in Paris. Maybe there is indeed something more, which would be hard for me to understand as a philosopher who is not of African descent, as she states. I felt challenged to think about this, and about what I and other philosophers working in the field of intercultural philosophy can learn from it, which is part of what I am exploring in this chapter.

Hountondji addresses a similar need for autonomous spaces of reflection for African philosophers and, in relation to that, criticizes ethnophilosophy. The roots of ethnophilosophy are in ethnographic studies and cultural anthropology, in which the investigators try to force a Western concept of philosophy on traditional African cultures (Hountondji, 2002). His critique is not so much aimed at collective thought or oral tradition not being philosophical, neither is it exclusively aimed at Westerners, but it is about the 'reductive reading of African civilizations to empty them of their creative tensions' (Hountondji, 2002, p. 103). However, these cultures transmitted a pluralism of beliefs and systems of belief that need to be taken into account. Furthermore, he indicates a need for an autonomous space for reflection and discussion in which questions that are relevant to African people are the guiding ones. He argues that this is in contrast to the current situation in which questions formulated by the West are dominant in philosophy as well as in science. He refers to this as 'theoretical extraversion', which finds its origin in economic extraversion. He describes extraversion as 'concentration on an audience that lives in its vast majority elsewhere' (Hountondji, 2002, p. 138). For Hountondji, the problem of extraversion is that it focuses on questions which have been formulated to serve an interest of the West and not those of people living in Africa (Hountondji, 2002, p. 138).

There are parallels between the need for African philosophers to have autonomous spaces for reflection to counter a tendency of extraversion, and the need of African and Afro-descent women to gather and share their experiences without the intervention of white women. Also, for women in African philosophy, the basis for their philosophical questions should be the experiences and questions that are relevant to them. However, Hountondji clearly focuses on the questions and does not object to answers to these philosophical questions being valid for others and studied outside of Africa. I would argue that at some point, this would even be very productive if the aim is to counter marginalization.

Osha (2008) states that the presence of sexism in African philosophy was inherited from its encounters with Western philosophy, and connects this with the creation of African philosophical practices as these practices have embraced the *logos* of the Western philosophical text. Osha points to similarities between the histories of the white feminist movement and the

African struggle against colonial domination. In both historical trajectories, body and mind were forcibly appropriated. The white female and the African subject both suffer from white male dominated systems of oppression. At the same time, the language to speak out against that oppression is framed by the oppressor and contains mechanisms which perpetuate marginalization and exclusion. Feminist theorists recognized the important connection between language, identity, authenticity and freedom. In Western philosophy, both feminist philosophers and male philosophers who think about difference, have deconstructed the dominant language and offered alternatives. Osha states that in African philosophical texts, the discursive foundations remain mostly unquestioned (Osha, 2008). He makes a plea for questioning the phallocentric regimes as well as advocating counter-phallocentric alternatives (Osha, 2008). Osha thus articulates the need for autonomous spaces in which one's own language can be developed. Furthermore, Osha's work also reminds us that there are similarities between the white feminist struggle and the African struggle against colonial domination, but that interventions thus far, coming from feminist and intercultural philosophy, have not yet contributed to solving the problem of marginalization of African women in philosophy.

## Possibilities and pitfalls of intercultural dialogue

Considering the domination of a phallocentric regime, I realize the irony of citing mostly male philosophers thus far, but I argue that we can learn from them about the possibilities and about the pitfalls of (intended) intercultural dialogues. Reflecting on this might help us understand the challenges faced in dialogues with marginalized philosophies.

In 2007–2008 a debate took place between two fellow philosophers, both working in the field of African philosophy: Heinz Kimmerle[1] and Innocent Asouzu. Heinz Kimmerle (1930–2016) had a chair in intercultural philosophy at the Erasmus University in Rotterdam. Innocent Asouzu is a professor of philosophy at the University of Calabar. The source of their debate dated back to 2004. In that year Asouzu published his book *The Method and Principles of Complementary Reflection in and Beyond African Philosophy*. In 2005 Kimmerle wrote a review of this book, and agreed with much of it. But his main criticism is that the book is not really embedded in the debate within African philosophy, as it hardly refers to other African philosophers. In his review Kimmerle tries to relate Asouzu's work to these other philosophers. In line with Asouzu's statement that regional philosophies are useful and necessary, Kimmerle considers Asouzu's approach an addition to other regional African philosophies, while at the same time acknowledging his renewing value to African philosophy in general.

Kimmerle sent his review to Asouzu with the intention of publishing both the review as well as Asouzu's response together. However, when he received a sixteen-page response from Asouzu which, according to Kimmerle, contained many misunderstandings and false assumptions, he renounced that intention. Besides, in 2006 a review of the book by Franz Gmainer-Pranzl had already appeared in the journal *Polylog*, with positive comments and some critical questions, in line with Kimmerle's ideas.

In 2007 Asouzu published two books.[2] In both books he criticizes Kimmerle and other Western and African philosophers who work in the field of intercultural philosophy as 'ethnophilosophers'. Asouzu distinguishes between unintended ethnophilosophy and ethno-philosophy *proper*, which is 'that variant of philosophical methodology which considers collecting, describing and informing over the general worldview of a people the target of philosophical investigation. It thereby underestimates the role which personal critical reflections plays in inquiry' (Asouzu, 2007, p. 37). Unintended ethnophilosophical commitment is not always evident. It is this last form Asouzu accuses Kimmerle of. Both forms share 'the common weakness of the danger of forgetting or missing the target of philosophical inquiry' (Asouzu, 2007, p. 44).

In a subsequent issue of *Polylog* (2008), Kimmerle responds to both Asouzu's books. The response is introduced Anke Graness. She states that:

> the exchange between Asouzu and Kimmerle is not only an important contribution to intercultural philosophising ... but in its pungency it's also symptomatic for intercultural dialogue and *Polylog* as the risk of misunderstanding and misinterpretation is big and the injuries caused by colonialism, inferiority accusations and exclusions, the dominant Western political, economic and cultural system, are far from being cured, happen each time again and are a burden (ibuaru) that intercultural philosophy will need to bear for a long time.
>
> (Graness, 2008 p. 99, translated from German)

Asouzu's book *Ibuaru* starts with Kimmerle's review of Asouzu's 2004 publication and the following nearly 300 pages are a reply to critics anchored around Kimmerle's 'Reaction' (Asouzu, 2007, pp. 24–316). Asouzu's assumptions are pungent. He states that Kimmerle's advocacy of African philosophy is 'marked by elements of disdain and parsimony, as is characteristic of most so-called Western thinkers in their relationship to matters concerning other cultures' (Asouzu, 2007, p. 34). He later refers to this as a benevolent type of mindset, with a deep sense of mission and mentions that 'this is that obdurate attitude that hardly changes and listens' (Asouzu, 2007, p. 35).

Asouzu refers to this mindset as unintended ethnocentric commitment, which he considers one of the greatest challenges facing *intercultural philosophy* (Asouzu, 2007, p. 35). Asouzu's assertions stand in sharp contrast to what Kimmerle perceives to be the task of intercultural philosophy, namely to equally value all philosophies of the world. Kimmerle argues that intercultural philosophy aims to gather forces and include all cultures to enable philosophical dialogue between different positions. He deems this necessary in order to counter the danger of fatal developments in world history caused by the exclusive dominance of any one culture. Kimmerle also discusses how the concept of intercultural philosophy has been colored by historical experiences, such as feelings of guilt for the colonial period, the world wars, the Shoah, and neo-imperialism, which he believes should all lead to modesty with regards to philosophical concepts (Kimmerle, 2008). Kimmerle's position seems to actually resonate with Asouzu's fear of philosophical methodology turning into a type of 'compensatory therapy aimed at addressing perceived unjust superimposition of alien thought categories as these relate to those nations and people that have been the unfortunate victims of colonialism and conquest' (Asouzu, 2007, p. 39). Asouzu also warns of those who feel they are victimized. Both colonizing nations and victims therefore feel a need to make some restitution or amends (Asouzu, 2007). However, that Kimmerle is aware of the danger of any philosophy dominating other philosophies does not necessarily imply that he acts out of guilt.

Kimmerle states that 'intercultural philosophical dialogues presuppose that the philosophies of all cultures are equal in value and in rank, and different in style as well as in content' (Kimmerle, 2011 p. 137). However, what he does not address is how this equality is achieved, given that it cannot automatically be obtained by entering a dialogical space. There are structural power inequalities that are historically and politically rooted, and which will not automatically disappear the moment one enters into dialogue, regardless of the good intentions of participants. One cannot deny power relations in a globalized context, particularly with the kind of dialogues which are intended to create a more level playing field within the discipline of philosophy. Suransky and Alma elaborate on the particular historic and political circumstances in which dialogues take place and the importance of acknowledging these within the dialogue. They argue that in order to use the transformative potential of dialogue, it is important to explicitly address the structural power inequalities and privileges enjoyed by some at the expense of others. The tensions created by inequality could and should be explored in the dialogue (Suransky and Alma, 2017). Just as stating that – morally speaking – a dialogue should be based on equality does not automatically eliminate power dynamics, stating that philosophical dialogues should not be influenced by emotional personal and historical experiences does not solve the issue. It might be more constructive to explicitly explore and address differences and inequalities, and reflect on the dialogical setting and prior experiences of different participants in such dialogues.

## Intersectionality and alliances

Audre Lorde (1984) addressed the neglect of black women in the feminist movement in her famous speech 'The Master's Tools Will Never Dismantle the Master's House'. As a black lesbian feminist in the 1960s and 1970s in the USA, she experienced similar systems of exclusion within different civil rights movements fighting for inclusion. Within the feminist movement, black and lesbian women were marginalized, within the gay and lesbian movement, black people were marginalized, and within the black liberation movement women were marginalized. She characterizes the absence of poor women, black and Third World women and lesbians in the discussion of feminist theory as academic arrogance and makes a plea for valuing difference as a crucial strength. She states that 'Difference must be not merely tolerated, but seen as a fund of necessary polarities between which our creativity can spark like a dialectic' (Lorde, 1984 p. 110). With this she indicates both the need to form alliances between different feminist groups, as well as the difficulties black feminists experience within feminist groups and black liberation movements.

'Intersectionality' investigates how different socially and culturally con-structed categories interact and how this causes complex levels of inequalities. Crenshaw explores how the experiences of colored American women are frequently the product of racism and sexism and how these experiences are neither represented in the discourse of antiracism, nor in feminism (Crenshaw, 1991). Liberation rights were fought for in the black liberation movement and in women's rights movements, without considering how racism and sexism intersect. Crenshaw (1991) shows in her research on battered women of color that 'where systems of race, gender and class domination converge, intervention strategies of women who do not share the same race or class background will be of limited help' (p. 1246).

Marginalization of African philosophy has been influenced by racism, and marginalization of women in philosophy by gender discrimination. The intersection of these two categories not being taken into account, might be an important reason why interventions against the marginalization of African philosophy or of women in philosophy have had little effect. Crenshaw shows how the focus within marginalized groups is often on the most privileged group members among the marginalized and how this exacerbates the position of members who are multiply burdened (Crenshaw, 2016). Within global academic philosophy, it is clear that there too the voices of the most privileged groups within the marginalized, namely being white and Western in feminism, or being a man in African philosophy, have been given the most prominence. African women philosophers have been subject to marginalization within African philosophy, within feminist philosophy and within the canon of philosophy altogether. The intersection of race and gender has contributed to this.

Crenshaw (2016) further indicates that we assume that claims of exclusion must be unidirectional. Women in African philosophy are framed as a category by using concepts of gender with the risk of neglecting the diversity among them. At the same time, by ignoring the intersection of race and gender and not recog-nizing African women as a group, which is subject to both marginalization based on gender and based on race, initiatives to counteract marginalization in either of these domains have not been beneficial.

Using affinity between different marginalized groups as point of departure, such as affinity between feminist philosophers and African philosophers, could lead to particular attention given to women in African philosophy. Santos illustrates how an alliance between different social movements can deepen the counter-hegemonic-potential of both, and states that the Mexican Zapatista movement's choice of a female leader is based on an affinity between the indigenous movement and the women's liberation movement (Santos, 2012).

In a colloquium series in Toronto (2015), Sandra Harding indicated a weak complementarity between post-colonial studies, that have been dominated by the South, and feminist studies, that have been dominated by the North. Both tend to be marked by their distinctiveness in their field and both are critical of how academia co-produces and co-constitutes the 'other'. Harding argues that both feminist and post-colonial studies offer counter-histories, position themselves against certain policies, are against their discrimination in modern sciences, and offer alternatives. Harding pleads for a strong complementarity, as these domains can strengthen each other (Harding, 2015).

Similarly, Irigaray and Kimmerle suggested an alliance between intercultural philosophy and the philosophies of sexual difference. They both created spaces to value differences and both offered alternatives to a Western male philosophical discourse.

Such an alliance could be of pivotal importance to understand the exclusion of women in African philosophy and move toward their inclusion based on consciously embracing difference. Kimmerle was indeed influenced by the ideas of philosophers of difference such as Derrida and Irigaray. The themes Kimmerle touched upon in his work were, in every regard, dimensions of the 'other', such as: marginalized women, manipulated nature, degraded animistic religion, and excluded strangers. Kimmerle suggested that there is an affinity between intercultural philosophy and the philosophies of difference as worked out by, for example, Martin Heidegger, Jacques Derrida and Luce Irigaray. He mentions that: 'The philosophies of difference and the ways they deal with the new "concept" of difference can be seen as a preparation of Intercultural philosophy' (Kimmerle, 2011, p. 137).

French philosopher of difference Luce Irigaray switches from a philosophy of difference, in particular of sexual difference, to an intercultural philosophical dialogue. This transition has been worked out in her book *Between East and West: From Singularity to Community* (Irigaray, 2002). Kimmerle critically considers her arguments and agrees with her conception of 'mutual respect between the sexes that remain insurmountably different as the nucleus of a new, more humane society' as a model to practice intercultural philosophy, and he suggests an alliance between intercultural philosophy and philosophy of sexual difference (Kimmerle, 2011). Irigaray does not privilege one gender over another, nor does she aim at a reversal of power, but rather she points to the possible coexistence of perspectives, of subjectivities, of worlds and of cultures. Her point of view relates to going beyond oppositional thinking, toward a constitution of horizontal relations between the sexes (Kimmerle, 2011). However, even though Irigaray pleads to move beyond opposites and hierarchical ordering, Kimmerle critically maintains that she places sexual difference at the top of the hierarchy of all differences. For Irigaray, this is the starting point for a re-founding of society. I agree with Kimmerle (2011) when he argues that differences of all kinds have their own status and can be arranged in different ways. Irigaray takes an important step in arguing for equal treatment of those who are different without the necessity of becoming the same. However, at least in the earlier mentioned publication, she retained a dichotomous way of thinking between man and woman, black and white. Irigaray still presupposes fixed gender categories. For a fruitful alliance between philosophies of difference and intercultural philosophy, we would need to allow for hybridity, a mixing of identities within persons and cultures, which actually happens in a dynamic world. If there is an encounter between genders and between philosophies of different cultures, their initial positions will most likely change in a dialogical process, without them becoming completely the same.

## Beyond categories: allowing space for hybridity

In her research on gender discourse, Oyeronke Oyewumi (1997) explores how 'gender' has been constructed. In *The Invention of Women: Making an African Sense of Western Gender Discourse*, Oyewumi argues that gender was not a category for social organization in traditional Yoruba society and that social organization was determined by relative age. As she puts it, 'what is missing in many Western-derived analyses is the realization that more important categories may be at work, categories informed by and constituted from the indigenous frame of reference' (Oyewumi, 1997, p. 77).

According to Oyewumi, gender categories were a new tradition that European colonialism institutionalized in Yoruba as well as in other cultures. Naturally, she does not mean that anatomical differences between men and women were not recognized, but rather that they were not seen as a determining factor for social organization. Oyewumi states that many of the gender distinctions in Western texts about the Yoruba have resulted from a false interpretation or automatic assumption that people referred to as leading politicians, priests, or even gods, were male, even though Yoruba names are mostly gender-neutral. As the European colonizers were in charge of institutionalized education in Nigeria and students were taught in English, the gender distinction was assimilated by the educational system and by Yoruba society itself. This resulted in women being excluded or marginalized in fields that they would formerly have had access to – political and economic life for instance.

Her extensive research only refers to Yoruba society, so we cannot draw conclusions about the place of women in other African societies before colonization. Opinions differ even about the Yoruba tradition. However, Oyewumi's work offers a major contribution to both African and feminist philosophy. It does so by demonstrating how gender has been constructed by Western privileging of the visual, body-oriented differences. This has led to a restrictive 'world-view', which she suggests replacing with 'world-sense'. It opens up the possibility of a world 'beyond gender', and enriches philosophical practice by expanding beyond the visual.

Sophie Oluwole also conducted research on Yoruba society. She, however, shows that gender categories did exist in pre-colonial times, but that this did not necessary imply an inferior position for women in Yoruba society. She gives various examples to show that women were present in political and military affairs. Proverbs about women's faults are sometimes referred to as indications of women's lower status, but neither men nor women were seen as perfect. Therefore, these proverbs do not necessarily mean that women had an inferior position. In Oluwole's opinion, the lesser representation of women in political affairs does not demonstrate that they had less power either, as Yoruba people did not see politics as a game of numbers. In most cases, the single female representative had a veto as she was the voice of all women and respected as such (Oluwole and Sofoluwe, 2014). Many indigenous African societies did not exclude women from roles in spiritual, economic and political matters as was done in most Western religious, economic, and political institutions. However,

> although there is abundant historical evidence that no specific public sphere was closed to women in Yoruba societies, men dominated the literary sphere and Classical Yoruba Oral tradition to such an extent that women's views were either not recorded or downplayed as it happened in Western literature ...
>
> (Oluwole and Sofoluwe, 2014, p. 8)

Here as well, the reproduction of knowledge plays an important role in the marginalization of women.

Agnes Atia Apusigah critiques Oyewumi's proposal. She sees a danger in adopting a static stance on the question of difference. A static stance closes off possibilities for dialogue and negotiation and for acknowledging any possibility of cultural crossover (Atiah Apusigah, 2008). Instead, Atiah Apusigah pleads for a complex, rather than simplified, framing of difference and brings in a relativist position, in which the difference is framed according to the context. According to Atiah Apusigah, 'It depends on whether our emphasis is on issues of the history of discourse, realities of African women or purely academic engagement' (Atiah Apusigah, 2008, p. 43).

Oyewumi argues that gender difference is a colonial construction in Yoruba culture. Her main contribution is to show that there are also other categories at work. Oluwole shows that gender difference was taken into account in social organization in traditional Yoruba culture, but not necessarily hierarchical. Atiah Apusigah shows that in a complex organization, there will be privileging of certain categories depending on what issue is at stake. However, it becomes clear from the work of Oyuwemi and Oluwole that knowledge reproduction and its organization, whether through traditional Yoruba culture or the institutionalized colonist education system, plays an important role in the marginalization of women in Yoruba culture.

Coetzee and Halsema (2018) demonstrate the fertility of cross-cultural dialogues for feminist philosophy by comparing the works of Oyewumi and Irigaray. They show where both philosophers overlap in their critique of a Western culture, but also where they differ. Oyewumi's arguments show that there are different epistemological foundations in the way the world as a whole is approached and between Yoruba and Western culture. By relating her work to the work of Irigaray, Halsema and Coetzee show that Irigaray remains within a Western world-view. The work of Oyewumi reveals how Western feminism has universalized the notion of gender (1997). Halsema and Coetzee argue that Oyewumi's work, in which sexual identity is 'constituted in multiple dynamic and shifting relations with others who are different', shows that there is no need to limit sexual identity to two clearly distinguishable categories (Coetzee and Halsema, 2018).

For the same reason, Kenyan feminist Awino Okech is critical of the notion of complementarity, which is often considered to be particular to African feminism, as it does not accept separatism from the other sex (Mekgwe, 2008). Okech argues that feminism defined in this way remains oppositional and shaped by imperial constructions of gender (Okech, 2013). She looks for a gender analysis beyond gender. An alliance with the queer movement could possibly offer valuable alternatives as it could dismantle the reproduction of a normative heterosexuality by the family, state and economy (Okech, 2013). With this conclusion, Okech offers an important indication that alternative alliances with feminists and African philosophers are possible.

Being queer and the possible alliances this offers is more than just a theory. There are real women behind the queer movement – just as there are real women behind the theory of intersectionality – who have experienced the hardship of being marginalized in different ways. That it is about more than theory is made painfully clear by South African photographer and visual artist Zanele Muholi, who made portraits of the brave women who fight the reality of a sexual identity beyond heteronormativity. One of the walls of the Stedelijk Museum, Amsterdam's modern art museum, where she had a solo exhibition in 2017, is dedicated to all the people who were raped or killed because of being queer in South Africa. In an interview in the *New Yorker* she states 'I'm one of us … I'm not observing from a distance' (Scott, 2015). It shows how the work of African women not only enriches the discipline of (intercultural) philosophy through the suggestion of a fluid notion of categories like gender and culture, but it also creates awareness that the theory would not have been there without their practices.

## Conclusion

This chapter shows that there is a variation in the perceived need for dialogues and the settings in which these could take place. There is a need for autonomous spaces for dialogue which relates to the life world of women in African philosophy and can contribute to developing new language. Additionally, there is a need for dialogue in which the 'inter' is present, allowing for philosophers from different places and genders to enrich each other's thinking. It has been illustrated that critical confrontations, power inequalities, and emotional experiences of, among others, colonial history should be part of a dialogical process. As scholars in the humanities, we must face these challenges as they are, in dialogue, where we can check and rethink assumptions and broaden our world to encompass different world-views.

Alliances between different groups of philosophers can lead to critical reflection on the dominant discourse, as well as to self-criticism of all participants in dialogue. Possible alliances between feminist and post-colonial studies, or between philosophy of sexual difference and intercultural philosophy, can help constitute change, and alliances with the queer movement, for instance, could help to deconstruct categories like culture or gender altogether. Affinity between these different disciplines is not only grounded in the fact that they differ from the dominant Western male discourse, but also because they have been forced to fit into categories which have been constructed from a Western male perspective and use a language which was constructed from this same perspective. 'Non-fitting' elements have been excluded or not valued as equal.

My involvement with this topic stems from the feeling of shared responsibility and a need to use all the knowledge available to face local and global challenges. I also wish for a world without one dominating center and a periphery, but which allows for a plurality of centers depending on the context.

First and foremost, it is women in African philosophy who know how to best counter their marginalization, and therefore their questions and answers should be central to the dialogue about marginalization of women in African philosophy. Therefore, we might need a different 'table setting', when philosophers from all backgrounds meet. In order to find out what this 'table setting' might be, one needs to ensure that African women can take their seat at the table. It is a pre-condition to realize that these tables might not be situated in places that usually dominate teaching and publishing in the discipline of philosophy. It would be logical to expect critical reflection by African women philosophers to arise where the need is felt the strongest. Therefore, this might be in non-Western universities or outside the academic world altogether, at platforms where there is space for different voices, for instance at an Afro-feminist festival, and through different means of expression, such as art. Intercultural and feminist philosophies can help to recognize a need for different table settings.

# Note

1 Since 1988, Kimmerle dedicated most of his research to African philosophy, he was cooperating intensively with African colleagues and received a honor doctorate of UNISA.
2 *Ibuanyidanda: New Complementary Ontology. Beyond World-immanentism, Ethnocentric Reduction and Imposition*; and *Ibuaru: The Heavy Burden of Philosophy beyond African Philosophy*, both by the same publishers (Lit Verlag).

# References

Asouzu, I. (2007). *Ibuaru: The Heavy Burden of Philosophy beyond African Philosophy.* Vienna/Berlin: Lit Verlag.
Atiah Apusigah, A. (2008). 'Is Gender Yet another Colonial Project?' *Quest*, 201(2), 23–43.
Coetzee, A. and Halsema, A. (2018). 'Sexual Difference and Decolonization: Oyěwùmí and Irigaray in Dialogue about Western Culture'. *Hypatia* doi:10.1111/hypa.12397.
Crenshaw, K. (2016). 'Demarginalising the Intersection of Race and Sex: A Black Feminist Critique of Anti-Discrimination Doctrine, Feminist Theory, and Racist Politics'. In H. Lutz, M. T. Herrera Vivar and L. Supik (eds), *Framing Intersectionality: Debates on a Multi-Faceted Concept in Gender Studies* (pp. 25–29). New York: Routledge.
Crenshaw, K. (1991). 'Mapping the Margins: Intersectionality, Identity Politics, and Violence against Women of Colour'. *Stanford Law Review*, 43, 1243–1246.
Diallo, R. (2017, 6 June). 'When an Afro-feminist Festival Defies White Supremacy'. *Al Jazeera, Opinion.* www.aljazeera.com/indepth/opinion/2017/06/afro-feminist-festival-defies-white-supremacy-170605175645563.html.
Eze, E. (1998). *African Philosophy: An Anthology.* Malden, MA: Blackwell.
Garfield, J. and van Norden, B. (2016, 11 May). 'If Philosophy Won't Diversify Let's Call It What It Really Is'. *New York Times.*
Graness, A. (2008). 'Einleitung zu H. Kimmerle: 'Die schwere Last der Komplementaritat''. *Polylog Zeitschrift für Interkulturelles Philosophieren*, 19, 100–111.
Graness, A. (2015). 'Is the Debate on "Global Justice" a Global One? Some Considerations in View of Modern Philosophy in Africa'. *Journal of Global Ethics*, 11(1), 133–136.
Harding, S. (2015, 17 October). 'Objectivity and Diversity: Tensions for Feminist Postcolonial Research'. You Tube. www.youtube.com/watch?v=w_qa87-54yQ.
Hountondji, P. (2002). *The Struggle for Meaning: Reflections on Philosophy, Culture and Democracy in Africa.* Athens, OH: Ohio University Press.
Irigaray, L. (2002). *Between East and West: From Singularity to Community.* New York: Columbia University Press.
Irigaray, L. (2008). *Sharing the World.* London/New York: Continuum.
Kimmerle, H. (2005). *Jacques Derrida: Interkulturell Gelesen.* Nordhausen: Traugott Bauz.
Kimmerle, H. (2008). 'Die Schwere Last Der Komplementaritat: Antwort Auf Innocent I. Asouzus Kritik an Der Interkulturellen Philosophie'. *Polylog Zeitschrift für Interkulturelles Philosophieren*, 19, 100–111.
Kimmerle, H. (2011). 'Respect for the Other and the Refounding of Society: Practical Aspects of Intercultural Philosophy'. In H. Oosterling and E. Plonawska Ziarek

(eds), *Intermedialities: Philosophy, Arts, Politics* (pp. 137–162). New York: Rowman & Littlefield.

Kimmerle, H. (2015). *Interculturele Filosofie: Een Studieboek*. Antwerp/Apeldoorn: Garant.

Kimmerle, H. and Schepen, R. (2014). *Filosofie Van Het Verstaan*. Antwerp/Apeldoorn: Garant.

Lorde, A. (1984). 'The Master's Tools Will Never Dismantle the Master's House'. In A. Lorde, *Sister Outsider: Essays and Speeches* (pp. 110–114). Berkeley, CA: Crossing Press.

Mekgwe, P. (2008). 'Theorizing African Feminism(s): The "Colonial" Question'. *Quest*, 20(1/2), 12–18.

Mosima, P. (2016). *Philosophical Sagacity and Intercultural Philosophy, Beyond Henry Odera Oruka*. Leiden: African Studies Centre.

Okech, A. (2013). 'In Sisterhood and Solidarity: Queering African Feminist Spaces'. In S. Ekine and H. Abbas (eds), *Queer African Reader* (pp. 11–26). Dakar/Nairobi/Oxford: Pambazuka Press.

Oluwole, S. and Sofoluwe, A. (2014). *African Myths and Legends of Gender*. Lagos: Ark Publishers.

Osha, S. (2008). 'Philosophy and Figures of the African Female'. *Quest*, 20(1/2), 164–191.

Oyewumi, O. (1997). *The Invention of Women: Making an African Sense of Western Gender Discourse*. Minneapolis/London: University of Minnesota Press.

Santos, B. (2012). 'Public Sphere and Epistomologies of the South'. *Africa Development*, 37(1).

Spivak, G. C. (1988). 'Can the Subaltern Speak?' In C. Nelson and L. Grossberg (eds), *Marxism and the Interpretation of Culture* (pp. 90–91). London: Macmillan.

Suransky, A. C. and Alma, H. (2017). 'An Agonistic Model of Dialogue'. *Journal of Constructivist Psychology*. ISSN: 1072–0537 print / 1521–0650 online. doi:10.1080/1 0720537.2017.1298487.

Scott, A. (2015). 'Zanele Muholi: A South African Photographer Brings Her Life Work to Brooklyn'. *The New Yorker*. 18 May. www.newyorker.com/magazine/2015/05/18/out-look.

# 6 Dealing with the trauma of a loss

Interrogating the feminine experience of coping with a spouse's death in African traditions

*Elvis Imafidon*

## Introduction

The Ugandan poet and scholar, Okot p'Bitek (1964), aptly captured the duty of an African philosopher when he said,

> The role of the student of traditional philosophy, it seems to me, is, as it were, to photograph as much of and in as great details as possible, the traditional way of life, and then to make comments; pointing out the connexions and relevance of the different parts. In this way, the belief of a people whether in one God or in a hierarchy of forces or in a number of spirits or in magic and witchcraft will emerge.
>
> (p. 34)

Doing African philosophy therefore could never really end with narrating or describing African traditions and belief systems. Rather, it primarily and essentially involves 'making comments', critical and analytical ones at that as, for instance, has been done with African communitarianism, and 'pointing out connexions and relevance of the different parts' as, for instance, an African environmental ethicist may do when she tells us about the relevance of African ontological beliefs for the moral status of the environment.

This chapter emerges from the same desire: to record and critically comment on a particular aspect of African traditions showing its connexion to a larger body of beliefs and ideologies. The aspect of African traditions that I focus on here are the experiences and challenges of the female folk in coping with, and healing, the pains caused by the death of a spouse. Dying as a human event is directly experienced by the dying subject. But death – the state of being dead – is directly experienced and dealt with by the living, particularly those closest to the one who has died. Such persons are often traumatized and need to be supported to cope and deal with the emotional and psychological challenges that often crop up due to the death of a loved one. Although many essays have been written on widowhood practices and mourning rites in African cultures, little has been said about a philosophical analysis of the nature, approaches and challenges of coping with the trauma faced by such women. What is often available in existing literature are legal, sociological, anthropological, economic and religious perspectives of widowhood and mourning rites. Philosophical perspectives on the intricacies of that traumatic experience are still quite rare.[1]

Furthermore, as is evident in the existentialist discourse on death,[2] philosophical thoughts on, and accounts of, death in the history of (Western) philosophy focus primarily on the futility of trying to make sense of the concept of death itself. Little attention is usually paid to the experiences of the living dealing with the loss of a loved one which, I think, constitutes a fundamental aspect of the philosophical discourse on death. I intend in this chapter to shift the horizon of discourse from the former to the latter, specifically from an African philosophical perspective.

I begin, in the first section, with an analysis of the trauma of death particularly as felt by a woman who has lost her husband in death. I show that the issue of coping with, and healing from, the trauma is essential for the well-being of the bereaved if she is to resume a measure of normal life after the loss and identify certain factor that may propel quick recovery, healing and effective coping. I then discuss, in the second section, the understanding of death in African traditions not as an event marking an end, but as an event signifying a passage to a different form of being and existence. The discussion of the African understanding of death is a necessary prerequisite to understanding the feminine experience of coping with a spouse's death. This is because the African conception of death implies the manner in which the woman who has lost her spouse is treated.

In the third section, I develop and defend two theses concerning the feminine experience of coping with a spouse's death in African traditions. First, there is an obvious sexist treatment, marginalization and gender bias against women whose spouses have died when compared with the treatment of men who have suffered the same traumatic experience. This is clearly seen in the requirements for mourning the death of a spouse that are imposed on women. Second, the social structures available in African traditions for coping with the traumatic loss of a spouse please the men folk more than the women folk. In fact, the structures do not only marginalize the woman but may traumatize her more and hinder the process of coping and recovery from the loss. In pursuance of these theses, I draw evidence from, and critically interrogate, rich cultural heritages in Africa such as those of Southern and Eastern Nigeria.

The fourth section unravels different levels of an epistemology of ignorance that may help to explain and understand the tension between individual and communal expectations with regard to coping with a spouse's death, the basis for the ideas and beliefs of mourning rites for women in African traditions, and the inherent paradox in the sexist treatment of women, perpetuated by women in conformity with societal expectations for mourning. I conclude from these analyses that a philosopher in Africa researching African thoughts and traditions is saddled with the crucial responsibility of critiquing cultures and traditions within the African place and space of discourse with the primary goal of liberating persons from indefensible ideologies.

## The spouse's death as traumatic experience

Death is generally a difficult experience to deal with, both in scholarship and in real life. Scholars have for long grappled with the nature of death with little or no success. Socrates once aptly expressed the futility of attempting to understand the concept of death in these words:

> To fear death, gentlemen, is no other than to think oneself wise when one is not, to think one knows what one does not know. No one knows whether death may not be the greatest of all blessings for a man, yet men fear it as if they knew that it is the greatest of evils. And surely it is the most blameworthy ignorance to believe that one knows what one does not know.
>
> (Socrates, 1997, p. 27)

Socrates' words remind us that we can never say with certainty what death is. But when death occurs, we are sure of the feeling it leaves behind for the living. It is often the feeling of meaninglessness and difficulty in comprehending the experience, particularly for those closely related to the deceased. Sartre (1969) therefore says that,

> Death is never that which gives life its meaning. It is on the contrary that which as a principle removes all meaning from life. If we must die, then, our life has no meaning because its problem receives no solution and because the very meaning of its problem remained undetermined.
>
> (p. 545)

The confusion that sets in and the difficulty of coping with experiencing a relative's death is strongly felt, for instance, when a couple lose a child, when a child loses a parent, when a teenager loses her best friend, and when a person loses his or her spouse. The loss of one's spouse in death can bring so much grief. The United States Military's *Cumberland Country Schools* (CCS) explain why this is so:

> The death of a spouse can be one of the most painful events a person ever experiences. The loss of your spouse can mean the loss of your partner, lover, best friend, confidant, and the parent of your children. In addition to dealing with the loss emotionally, a surviving spouse often faces major life changes that can be stressful. Coping with the loss of your spouse involves working through the emotional grief while adjusting to new circumstances.
>
> (n.p.)

When a spouse dies, grief certainly sets in. But how this grief plays out may vary from one person to another. For some, it may consist of shock, anger, fear, denial, sadness and frustration. Bolby-West identifies a number of phases common to grieving spouses.

1   A numbness phase that may last from a few hours to a week and may be interrupted by outbursts of extreme anger or distress. Coping with every-day tasks is difficult, due to incomprehension, denial and preoccupation with the loss.
2   A phase of yearning and searching for the lost figure which can last months or, often years. A period of intense inner struggle in which awareness of the reality of death conflicts with a strong impulse to recover the lost person and the lost family structure.
3   A phase of disorganization and despair; feelings of hopelessness in which the grieving person is aware of the discrepancy between his [sic] inner model of the world and the world which now exists.
4   A phase of greater or less degree of reorganization, development of new set of assumptions that includes finding a new personal identity.

(Bolby-West, 1983, p. 282)

A number of factors determine how well grieving spouses will do in phase four. These may include religious beliefs, supportive family members and friends, a supportive social structure and a change of environment. For instance, Rosemary Eccles explains what helped her to cope with and gradually adjust to the death of her husband:

My own faith in a great God, who has said, 'All things work together for the good of those who love him.' My dog, who needed daily walks, enabling me to think, pray, and cry privately as I trudged through the woods and fields. My friends, many of whom invited us for meals and especially one who rang every night for a chat, allowing me to share the little and big things of each day at great sacrifice of time to herself. My children, who all share my faith, and so together we could face the many problems ahead in quiet confidence and trust in God.

(Eccles, 1989, p. 1599; Wojtkowiak et al., 2010, pp. 363–373)

It is more difficult for a grieving spouse to cope with such a huge loss if a number of such factors are absent. It is very important that in such a time, the grieving spouse is around friends and family members, engages in many recreational activities rather than remaining indoors, and is free to express himself or herself in the most convenient way such as crying, talking about the events surrounding the spouse's death, or feeling like staying away from the place where the spouse died.

In many cases of a spouse's death, women can be more traumatized than men and find it more difficult to cope or move on. There are a number of reasons for this. In many societies, many women depend largely on their husbands for financial support. Some require full financial support while others may require partial support. When the husband of such a woman dies, it is not only traumatic but destabilizing. This is worsened when there are children to care for which requires a great deal of financial stability. In such cases, the trauma of the loss does not go away easily and may persist for a long time.

Another important reason why women may be more traumatized in the event of the loss of their spouse is because in many societies, particularly in African cultures, it may be difficult for the woman to remarry, particularly if she is advanced in years, say in her late forties or so. Men who are widowed even in their fifties may not find it as hard to remarry as women who are much younger. This has serious implications for the grieving widow that may cause her more trauma. She may have to face the weighty responsibility of parenting alone for a long time. And even when the bereaved woman is able to eventually remarry, difficult adjustments may be necessary. She may need to relocate with her children, if any, to the home of her new husband, adjust to new relatives and in-laws, and struggle to bring up her children within the new arrangement.

Again, in many parts of the world a bereaved woman is saddled with more mourning responsibilities and restrictions than a bereaved man. Of course this is our focus in this chapter and we shall be elaborating on this from African perspectives in due course. Notwithstanding the peculiarities of the feminine experience, a spouse's death is generally traumatic for both men and women, and the literature on the philosophy of death needs to pay more attention to an analysis of such trauma and how it could be better coped with.

## Understanding death in African traditions

Death is an event that occurs in every human society and understanding how such an event is conceived in an African space of dwelling consists of understanding how Africans conceive the reality and existence under which such events are subsumed. The literature now abounds with much consensus on the nature of African ontology/metaphysics. Polycarp Ikuenobe aptly describes the African view of reality as presented by many other writers on the subject when he says,

> In the traditional African view, reality or nature is a continuum and a harmonious composite of various elements and forces. Human beings are a harmonious part of this composite reality, which is fundamentally, a set of mobile life forces. Natural objects and reality are interlocking forces. Reality always seeks to maintain an equilibrium among the network of elements and life forces. ... Because reality or nature is a continuum, there is no conceptual or interactive gap between the human self, community, the dead, spiritual or metaphysical entities and the phenomenal

world; they are interrelated, they interact, and in some sense, one is an extension of the other.

(Ikuenobe, 2006, pp. 63–64)

The African people therefore hold the view that there are a number of beings or entities, physical and non-physical, that exist in the universe. In other words, the universe of beings consists of two realms of existence, the visible and invisible, intertwined and interlocked to form a whole, a unit and communal system. Within such a realm of existence, there exist categories of beings both physical and non-physical. Such include the divinities, ancestors, humans, animals, the physical environment and the Supreme Being. Events within such an ontology are therefore alleged to have implications for both the physical and non-physical aspects of reality. For instance, taboos, rituals, festivals and ceremonies do not only yield negative and positive results for the physically living, but also for the invisible segment of reality.

Death in an African culture therefore involves not just the physical loss of life of a person but the transition of that person into the non-physical realm of existence. This transition or passage seems to be more important in a typical African community than the actual death itself, as seen in the numerous rituals and rites of mourning, burial and passage. There are two main reasons for this. First, it is important for the community of the living to ensure that the dead is properly rested in the invisible realm of existence by, for instance, performing the necessary rites to initiate the dead into the ancestral cult. This first reason is essential for preventing the second reason: the dead, who is only physically dead, may become wrathful and harmful to the living if he or she is not properly translated into the invisible realm of existence. Hence, in the words of Lee and Vaughan (2008, p. 344),

the deceased must move from a state of impurity or contagion to a state of ritual purity and harmony with the spirit world. This transition can be guided by the living through close attention to the ritual preparation and internment of the body.

They add, interpreting Evan-Pritchard's earlier position[3] that 'the dead could only find their place as ancestors, rather than vengeful ghosts, if their loss had been properly registered, not only by the individuals closest to them, but by the social groups of which they are members' (Lee and Vaughan, 2008, p. 342).

The six-point summary of the African notion of death presented by Richard Moore is apt and instructive:

i   Death is not an arbitrary event. It comes only at its proper time, strikes young or old. The event is always significant and can show of a portion of truth. It can also be divined, explained, or even averted by those who know and follow the proper rituals for doing this.

ii   The dead, especially the recent dead, are still a part of the living. They both influence it and make demands upon it. They may be blamed, but they must always be served. Otherwise they will not be at rest

iii   The dead can be reborn amongst us. Such rebirth is often recognized in the naming of a child.

iv   Energy has primacy over matter. It precedes, controls, and survives all material forms. The energy or force of the dead man does not perish with him but passes into new manifestations. Death feeds life and makes renewal possible.

v   Nevertheless, the actual event of death causes a sense of shock, grief, and loss to all those concerned. Many funeral rituals, especially those of the 'second burial' type, are designed to express and purge that grief. As the ritual proceeds, so the loss is recognized and socially accepted. Finally, in the last stages of the celebration, cheerfulness keeps breaking in.

vi   While this sense of loss persists, it frequently finds expression in a sort of ambivalence as to whether the dead one is really gone or not. This ambivalence, often found in funeral songs, also helps to adjust the grief which death brings to the living, since it puts off the moment when the finality of personal death must be recognized.

(Moore, 1968, p. 17)

In addition to these apt descriptions of an African understanding of death, it is important to add that in traditional African communities there exists the notion of good and bad death.[4] Whether the death of a person is good or bad depends on certain circumstances surrounding the death. A good death results from a normal community-accepted life or a life well lived in the eyes of the community. Generally this would involve a morally clean life, getting married and having children and dying under normal circumstances such as after a brief illness or in one's sleep at a reasonably advanced age. Persons who die in such a condition are said to have died a good death and are given a befitting burial and all the accompanying rituals and rites to transport them to the non-physical realm of existence. A bad death, on the other hand, results from unusual circumstances such as death through suicide, unusual or unexplainable illness, accident and so on. A person who dies at a young age and without any child at the point of death may also be considered to have died a bad death. In such cases, many rituals are done to ensure such deaths do not bring calamity to the immediate family and the community at large. Bad deaths usually attract a quiet and, at times, shameful burial, depending on the circumstances, to serve as a deterrent for the living.[5]

However, whether it be a good or bad death, the living must perform some rituals and rites and honor certain taboos in order to ensure that the dead do not interact with the living in a vengeful manner or bring calamity to the living. As we shall discuss shortly, the expectations from the living during the experience of death may become more of a burden than a relief for a bereaved woman.

## Coping with the loss of a spouse in African traditions: the woman's experience

In many indigenous African communities, when a woman loses her spouse through death she is immediately confronted with a deeply entrenched structure of mourning and burial that she is expected to fit into. There are three interrelated reasons for her to readily and fully comply with the funerary expectations of her community: first, the moment her spouse dies, she has become impure and somewhat contaminated and requires cleansing, without which she may never be viable for remarriage; second, any failure on her part to fulfill the funerary expectations is immediately interpreted within her space of dwelling as utter disrespect for the late husband and his kin, and this may quickly raise suspicions as to her innocence in the death of her spouse; third, the rituals, rites and attitude expected of her during the period of mourning is regarded as essential for the peaceful transition of the departed to the non-physical realm of existence, which is essential to protect her from being pursued by or otherwise endangered by the malevolence of the dead.

The nature of the mourning and burial rites and rituals that a bereaved woman is expected to fulfill is similar in many African communities but there are also slight variations from one community to another. Hannah Edemikpong gives an apt description of what is often expected of bereaved women in Nigerian communities. She says,

> Some of the mourning rites include seclusion and general isolation, in which the widow is in confinement. All hairs of her body, including her pubic hairs, and the hair of her children are shaved with one razor. The widow is forbidden to go to the market or the farm and is prohibited from talking to anybody outside the kin family. She is also deprived of personal hygiene and can only wear a dirty cloth, known as a sackcloth, throughout the mourning period, which lasts from three to six months or sometimes a year. She must always sit on the floor and eat with unwashed hands and broken plates. If the women in her family see her secretly attempting to attend to her personal hygiene, she might be whipped, spat upon or reprimanded that she is attempting to beautify herself so as to attract men. They may even accuse her.
>
> (Edemikpong, 2005, p. 34)

Among the Igbo of Nigeria, for instance, much is expected from the bereaved woman. A. M. Okorie gives a vivid description of what is expected from a widow among the Igbo. He explains how the woman's process of mourning begins immediately after the death of the husband through verbal expressions consisting of loud and continuous weeping and wailing to express her pain and shock (Okorie, 1995, p. 79). To be sure, as Edemikpong explains above, not fulfilling this expectation well may result in blame and scorn being heaped on the woman. So the question is not whether or not the bereaved is immediately able to express her shock and pain vocally by weeping and wailing. She has no choice other than to do this in order to avoid the anger of the husband's relatives and others of the community. As Okorie points out,

> The widow's behavior when the husband was alive and her relationship with relatives of her husband determine the intensity of her mourning. The negligence of mourning rituals may rob her of her late husband's property, and love of the community. Sometimes this can be tyrannical on the widow, especially if she has not been relating well with her husband's sisters [the *Umuada*] The *Umuada* are the enforcement agency and decide how severe the mourning should be. The *umuada* surround the widow, commanding her to make sure she obeys the rules of mourning rites.
>
> (Okorie, 1995, p. 80; Tasie, 2013, pp. 155–162)

The mourning and wailing is immediately followed by the need for the bereaved woman to fulfill certain hideous and horrible requirements related to cleansing, last respects, seclusion and lengthy mourning. For instance,

> The days before the burial of the man are always horrible for the widow as she is made to stay in the same room with the corpse where she is required to be waving away flies from perching on the fast and progressively decomposing corpse. She is supposed to sit down and raise an early morning cry before anybody is awake and this continues till the day the husband will be buried. Her most painful ordeal occurs at night before her husband's burial They make sure she stays awake all night with bitter kola (*aku ilu*) in her mouth to remind her of the bitterness of the death of her husband. Furthermore, if the widow had disputed with the husband shortly before his death, the widow will be made to lie with the corpse for many hours and in addition pay heavily in cash as a fine.
>
> (Okorie, 1995, p. 80)

After the burial, she is expected to start the seclusion period. This, Okorie explains, 'is a period of deep mourning and it lasts for seven native weeks (*izu asa*), totaling twenty-eight days. During this period the widow never eats with or talks to anybody except her fellow widows. She should never greet or respond to any greeting, but if she does, she is believed to have passed ill-luck to the greeter or responder. She wears only rags, sits on a piece of wood, and sleeps on a mat or banana leaves ... she may not wash her face nor bath' (Okorie, 1995, p. 81). This is followed immediately by the following rituals:

> the widow is taken at night by the patrilineal daughters to the bad bush far from the residential zone of the community for bathing and cleansing. The bathing has to take place on the grave of the deceased husband, especially if it were to be in some part of Owerri. The cloth which she used during the seclusion period is burnt ritually or given to the older

attendant widow. She now puts on the real black cloth for the rest of the morning period which is supposed to last for a year as a sign of grief and love for the departed. The day after the cleansing, she exercises her restricted liberty as she is received back into the family and can now cook what others can eat and have the freedom to talk to people.

(Okorie, 1995, p. 81)

These experiences of the bereaved Igbo woman is true of what women experience in the southern part of Nigeria among the Binis and Esans, for instance, when they lose their spouse. Mamphela Ramphele succinctly summarizes what an African widow goes through in the following words:

The widow becomes the embodiment of loss and pain occasioned by the sting of death, and her body is turned into a focus of attention, as both subject and object of mourning rituals. The individual suffering of a widow is made social, and her body becomes a metaphor for suffering.

(Ramphele, 1996, p. 99)

But do men in these African communities go through the same hideous and dehumanizing treatment as women do? The evidence shows that they do not. The mourning period for men is shorter than it is for women. They are not strictly expected to seat near the corpse of the woman, shaving their hair, eat from broken plates, wear rags, put on black (or white) clothing for a year, and so on as women are. Among the Igbo, for instance,

a man is not expected to wail openly like a woman. His facial courage is supposed to be a first aid condolence, comfort and hope for the children who are psychologically broken down. After the burial of the wife, the widower is expected to mourn for at least six months or one year. In strict traditional obedience, the man may mourn for only twenty eight days. This is based on the idea that the absence of the woman makes her unimportant to the surviving husband except through her children and kin. Hence, it differs from that of a widow who undergoes intensive rituals at the hands of the *umuada*.

(Okorie, 1995, p. 82)

Okorie adds that,

At the end of the mourning, the man goes to the nearest river and dips his feet into the water, pulls the inner pair of pants he wears and throws it away. Although the reason for this ritual is not told, yet it could likely be a rite of purification and breakage of marital accord, since the Igbo philosophy accepts that the spirit of the dead hovers around, looking for normal life relationship. Again, the death of a spouse renders the living one impure and therefore he or she needs ritual purification. Nevertheless, after the ceremony at the end of the mourning, the man is expected to be free and may marry a new wife. Mourning, therefore, is understood as an expression of the widower's grief, love and respect for the dead. But for the widow, the process can be brutal and inhuman in practice.

(Okorie, 1995, pp. 82–83)

Among the Esan people of Southern Nigeria, the bereaved man is expected to have sexual relations with a girl two weeks after the burial of the wife. It is believed that this will help ward off the spirit of the wife so that he can move on with his life and probably remarry.

The sexism in the treatment of bereaved males as against the treatment of bereaved females is therefore obvious and undeniable. Women bear more of the horrible burdens of burial and mourning. While the man is encouraged to 'man up', recover and move on with his life, the death of a man is constantly and continuously rubbed on the woman's injury for a longer period of time. Under these conditions, can the woman recover easily from the trauma of losing a spouse? The chances are slim. She may become even more traumatized. The stress and communal expectations may hinder quick recovery from the incident and prevent her from easily moving on with her life and living a normal life. This is worsened if the couple had children and those children are still young. She may not be able to care for them properly while fulfilling all her obligations to her departed spouse. In fact schooling and normal life may become difficult for the children as their mother may not be available to cater for them. Some widows have thus made painful statements on how such widowhood practices further traumatize them. Here are some examples:

I am accused of being a witch who killed her husband.

(Terezinha, Zambezia Province, Mozambique, 1997)

We have no shelter; my children can no longer go to school.

(Ishrat, Bangladesh, 1995)

We are treated like animals just because we are widows.

(Angela, Nigeria, 1999)

I and my children were kicked out of the house and beaten by the brothers-in-law.

(Seodhi, Malawi, 1994)

My husband died of AIDS and slept with many women; I am now dying, but his family blames me for his death.

(Isabel, Kenya, 1996)[6]

Thus, the deeply entrenched structure of mourning and burial of the dead in African cultures further traumatizes the woman and hinders the process of coping and recovery from the loss. There is therefore an obvious tension between individual and communal expectations with regard to coping with a spouse's death. What may be responsible for this tension? What is the basis for the ideas and beliefs of mourning rites for women in African traditions, and why is there an inherent paradox in the sexist treatment of women, perpetuated by women in conformity with societal expectations for mourning? The section that follows explores a patriarchal epistemology of ignorance with its inherent harmful ideologies that is responsible for the problems faced by bereaved women in African cultures.

## A patriarchal epistemology of ignorance and the perpetuation of harmful ideologies

In *Race and Epistemologies of Ignorance*, Shannon Sullivan and Nancy Tuana gives a precise explanation of what an epistemology of ignorance consists of, an explanation that aptly captures what I have in mind when I talk about a patriarchal epistemology of ignorance. In their words,

> The epistemology of ignorance is an examination of the complex phenomena of ignorance, which has as its aim identifying different forms of ignorance, examining how they are produced and sustained, and what role they play in knowledge practices ... Ignorance often is thought of as a gap in knowledge, as an epistemic oversight that easily could be remedied once it has been noticed. It can seem to be an accidental by-product of the limited time and resources that human beings have to investigate and understand their world. While this type of ignorance does exist, it is not the only kind. Sometimes what we do not know is not a mere gap in knowledge, the accidental result of an epistemological oversight ... a lack of knowledge or an unlearning of something previously known often is actively produced for purposes of domination and exploitation.
>
> (Sullivan and Tuana, 2007, p. 1)

This of course captures the point Charles Wright Mills makes in his *The Racial Contract*, where the term 'epistemology of ignorance' may have first appeared. Mills had given a fine analysis of how the idea of white folks as superior and black folks as inferior was established through an epistemology of ignorance that was in no way accidental but one that was carefully doctored and actively produced over centuries for the purpose of the racial domination of blacks by whites.[7] The pioneers of the active production of a form of ignorance that describes black folks as inferior, pre-logical or non-human were not 'ignorant' of the fact that their views were not rationally defensible but saw this form of an established knowledge of ignorance as necessary if they were to successfully exploit the black 'race' within accepted moral standards of behavior.

Hence, although it may have been wrong, for instance, as at the time of the racial contract to take fellow humans as slaves, there was certainly nothing wrong in taking as slaves some black folks within the framework of an epistemology of ignorance that described them as not having the capacity to be humans. Otherwise, how could we resolve, for instance, the paradox of Kant's moral theory that among other things promotes respect for human dignity, and Kant's verbal support for slavery and racism? However, centuries later, when such an epistemology of ignorance had become deeply entrenched into the fabric of the Western society, it produced citizens who saw, and still see, the racial distinction as a given and infallible knowledge.

The same game, as I see it, is played out in the African woman's experience of coping with the loss of a spouse. It is enveloped by an actively produced and purposive patriarchal epistemology of ignorance. In African traditions there is deeply rooted patriarchal arrangement to sustain an egoistic superiority over women. The goal is to promote, by means of certain deeply entrenched ideologies of reality and existence, the idea that men are superior and women are inferior, that men are strong and women are weak. Thus while men, for instance, do not need to perform any rituals or rites when they loss their wives because a woman's spirit cannot harm them, the women need to perform all sort of hideous rituals in order to protect them from the strong spirits of their dead husband and his ancestors. Hence it is not uncommon to hear such reasons as the following as to why men hardly undergo what women face during burial and mourning:

> for the man, physical strength and biological difference between man and woman remove the psychological fear upon which the religious belief that the dead can harm a living relative hinges. Again, man in a typical rain forest and agrarian society like that of the Isiokpo, is naturally endowed with superior physical strength than the woman, to cope with the arduous task of fending for his family, and therefore needs not to undergo any rites at the demise of his wife to acquire this dexterity.
>
> (Tasie, 2013, pp. 160–161)

The ancestral patriarchy that theorized these ideas about existence and reality (particularly the theories about the status of the dead and their degree of interaction with the living, both men and women) are well aware, like the pioneers of the racial contract and just as Kant was, that such ideas are not always rationally defensible. They are aware that they have created an epistemology of ignorance, claiming to be ignorant about the actual facts of life just as the racial contractarians claimed they were ignorant that black folks were like any other human beings, and veiling the facts with harmful and indefensible ideologies. Such ideologies are then handed down from generation to generation until they attain the status of a given, some sort of revealed knowledge that cannot be altered, a framework or structure that beings within the community must fit, or at least strive hard to fit into. Matsobane Manala (2015) is thus right to say that,

> these rites were conceived and applied in accordance with the whims of and to the benefit of patriarchy. The stated positive assessment is definitely not meant to benefit the poor widows but to strengthen the hegemonic and imperial patriarchal system.

This active production and sustenance of ignorance in African traditions explains why those who have assimilated such ideas about being as infallible seem justified in enforcing them. This also explains why women who should display fellow feeling to a bereaved woman, and close relatives whom the bereaved woman may have hoped for as source of comfort, are often the ones who impose these horrible practices on the bereaved woman because such ideas have become part of their sub-consciousness. They do not question them; they simply implement them.

Thus although only a few men may have taken part in the formulation of the patriarchal epistemology of ignorance and its supporting ideologies, virtually all men within the African community benefit from it. And such an epistemology of ignorance may go unnoticed, unaddressed, and un-revised; but unless it is addressed and revised, the hostile environment that a bereaved woman must endure in coping with the death of her spouse will thrive as before, and the inhuman treatment will continue.

## Overcoming the epistemology of ignorance

Harmful ideas and knowledge claims about reality, constructed within an epistemology of ignorance to guarantee a particular kind of behavior, thrive more in human societies where the social structure is consciously designed to subdue reason with authority. Traditional or indigenous societies in Africa have, for good reasons, been presented in the existing literature as authoritarian in nature due to the manner in which they subdue individual autonomy, override the individual will and relegate the individual's free use of reason to the background. Kwasi Wiredu aptly describes what it means for an African community to be authoritarian, or to override reason with authority:

> What I mean by authoritarianism may be stated in a preliminary way as follows: Any human arrangement is authoritarian if it entails any person being made to do or suffer something against his will, or if it leads to any person being hindered in the development of his own will. This definition is likely to be felt to be too broad. It might be objected that no orderly society is possible without some sort of constituted authority which can override a refractory individual will. Anybody wishing to elaborate on this kind of objection has a rich tradition of both Western and non-Western philosophical thought to draw upon. Let me here cut the matter short by

making a concession. We might now say that what is authoritarian, is the *unjustified* overriding of an individual's will ... a society would be seen to be revoltingly authoritarian in as much as a person's will would usually be the result of the manipulations by others.

(Wiredu, 1980, p. 2)

In African traditions, many of the ideas about the condition of the dead that are harmful to the living, particularly to the widow as shown in this chapter, are harmful because of their authoritarian stance, which tends to unjustifiably override the individual's will. Even when such ideas defy all forms of rational evaluation, their perpetuators still hide under the veil of communal authority on the matter.

If this is the case, then to overcome such harmful ideas about being and reality, the tables must be turned. Reason, human autonomy and enlightened perspectives must be valued over authoritarian perspectives. The enthronement of reason over authority would ensure that ideas about reality, such as those about the dead, are not just superimposed on persons in the community of beings through an authoritarian structure therein, but are subjected to rigorous rational evaluation and validation. This is because enlightened and rational persons do not simply allow others to lead them or tell them what to do; rather, they are convinced by rational explanation of why they should do what they are required to do. Kant (1989 [1784]) is thus right to describe enlightenment in the following words:

Enlightenment is man's emergence from his self-imposed immaturity. Immaturity is the inability to use one's understanding without guidance from another. This immaturity is self-imposed when its cause lies not in lack of understanding, but in lack of resolve and courage to use it without guidance from another. *Sapere Aude*! [dare to know] 'Have courage to use your own understanding!' – that is the motto of enlightenment.

(p. 54)

Africans therefore need to willfully and consciously exert themselves to use their own reasoning in evaluating issues, rather than rely completely on social authority. In fact, Kant describes the inability of persons to rely on their own ability to reason as laziness and cowardice. In his words,

Laziness and cowardice are the reasons why so great a proportion of men, long after nature has released them from alien guidance (*natura-liter maiorennes*), nonetheless gladly remain in lifelong immaturity, and why it is so easy for others to establish themselves as their guardians. It is so easy to be immature. If I have a book to serve as my understanding, a pastor to serve as my conscience, a physician to determine my diet for me, and so on, I need not exert myself at all. I need not think, if only I can pay: others will readily undertake the irksome work for me.

(p. 54)

Therefore, to overcome harmful ideologies, Africans must avoid being lazy in the Kantian sense and consciously enthrone the reliance on reason in all human affairs. A few persons in different African communities have refused to believe in the harmful ideas about mourning and burial of the dead as described above, because they were not rationally convinced that such practices were necessary. Their refusal to accept such ideas and participate in the corresponding rituals and rites may have isolated them from communal life, but surely protected them from harm. The reliance on reason rather than authority emancipates and liberates humankind from the authoritarian, rigid, fixed and static social, economic and religious structures through the rational critique of power, which seeks the individual's freedom from rationally indefensible ideologies and mythologies. This is why the legacy of the Enlightenment has been the notion of critical reason, and it is intrinsically intertwined with the critique of foundationalism with the aim of producing a normative though fallibilistic perspective on reality.

To be sure, the enthronement of reason is not meant to discard or trivialize an authoritarian perspective. Rather it is to subject such perspectives to the court of reason in order to critique and validate them. Such validation will help to identify which ideas about reality are rationally meaningful and should be held on to and which are not. In the words of Georgia Warnke (1995),

> We need not simply succumb to the cultural values and prejudices with which we initially understand specific situations of action. Rather we can rely upon discourses of application that can justify our judgments of the appropriateness of applying specific normative principles to specific cases.
>
> (p. 138)

Thus, we do not just accept the necessity to do things because tradition says so. Rather, we do things because we are rationally convinced that we should. In this way, epistemologies of ignorance can be exposed and questioned, and their authoritarian attitude to reality can be subjected to critical reflection. This will result in fewer harmful ideas about reality.

## Conclusion

Our analysis has shown that the ancestors of African communities were great thinkers and theorists who, in the quest to protect a patriarchy, formulated ideas that were not always in the best interests of all in the society. They employed methods of authoritarianism and mystification to enforce and entrench such ideas into the fabric of the community and the minds of the people. Most such ideas have remained unchallenged for ages and continue to favor one segment of African society while causing harm to others, as we have clearly seen in the case of widowhood. Philosophers researching and writing on issues and ideas within the African space and place therefore have a lot to do. We are saddled with the crucial responsibility of critiquing African cultures and traditions with the primary goal of liberating persons from indefensible ideologies and fostering the reliance on reason and human autonomy.

## Notes

1 One major philosophical essay focusing on coping with the trauma of the death of a loved one in African traditions is Isaac E. Ukpokolo's (2012) essay, 'Memories in Photography and Rebirth: Toward a Psychosocial Therapy of the Metaphysics of Reincarnation among Traditional Esan People of Southern Nigeria'.
2 See for instance, Sartre's view of death in Sartre (1969), *Being and Nothingness*; and Heidegger's view of death in part 6 of Heidegger (1988), *Being and Time*.
3 Evans-Pritchard had earlier said about the Nuer that 'Death is a subject Nuer do not care to speak about', which is best meant to explain the extent of the Nuer fear that a deceased person may not have been properly buried (see Evans-Pritchard 1949, p. 62).
4 See Wiredu, 1992.
5 Cf. Lee and Vaughan, 2008, p. 345.
6 These experiences are quoted in Manala (2015, p. 4).
7 See Mills, 1997.

## References

Bolby-West, L. (1983). 'The Impact of Death on the Family System'. *Journal of Family Therapy*, 5, 279–294.

Cooper, J. M. (ed.) (1997). *Plato: The Complete Works*. Indianapolis, IN: Hackett.

Cumberland Country Schools (CCS). *Coping with the Death of a Spouse*. The United States Military. http://mil.ccs.k12.nc.us/files/2012/06/Loss-of-Spouse.pdf.

Eccles, R. (1989). 'Coming to Terms with the Death of a Loved One'. *British Medical Journal*, 299 (6715), 1598–1599.

Edemikpong, H. (2005). 'Widowhood Rites: Nigerian Women's Collective Fight against Dehumanizing Tradition'. *Off Our Backs*, 35 (3/4), 34–35.

Evans-Pritchard, E. E. (1949). 'Burial and Mortuary Rites of the Nuer'. *African Affairs*, 48, 56–63.

Heidegger, M. (1988). *Being and Time*. J. Macquarrie and E. Robinson (trans.). Oxford: Basil Blackwell.

Ikuenobe, P. (2006). *Philosophical Perspective on Communalism and Morality in African Traditions*. Lanham, MD: Lexington Books.

Kant, I. (1989 [1784]). 'An Answer to the Question: "What is Enlightenment?"' In Hans Reiss (ed.), *Kant: Political Writings* (pp. 54–60). Cambridge: Cambridge University Press.

Lee, R. and Vaughan, M. (2008). 'Death and Dying in the History of Africa since 1800'. *The Journal of African History*, 49 (3), 341–359.

Manala, M. (2015). 'African Traditional Widowhood Rites and Their Benefits and/or Detrimental Effects on Widows in a Context of African Christianity'. *HTS theological studies*, 71(3), 1–9.

Mills, C. W. (1997). *The Racial Contract*. Ithaca, NY: Cornell University Press.

Moore, G. (1968). 'The Imagery of Death in African Poetry'. *Africa: Journal of the International African Institute*, 38 (1), 57–70.

Okorie, A. M. (1995). 'African Widowhood Practices: The Igbo Mourning Experience'. *African Journal of Evangelical Theology*, 14 (2), 79–84.

p'Bitek, O. (1964). 'The Self in African imagery'. *Transition*, 15, 32–35.

Ramphele, M. (1996). 'Political Widowhood in South Africa: The Embodiment of Ambiguity'. *Daedalus: Social suffering*, 125(1), 99–117.

Sartre, J-P (1969). *Being and Nothingness*. London: Methuen.

Socrates. (1997). 'Apology'. In J. M. Cooper (ed.), *Plato: The Complete Works*. Indianapolis, IN: Hackett.

Sullivan, S. and Tuana, N. (eds) (2007). *Introduction to Race and Epistemologies of Ignorance*. Albany, NY: State University of New York Press.

Tasie, G. I. K. (2013). 'African Widowhood Rites: A Bane or Boon for the African Woman'. *International Journal of Humanities and Social Science*, 3 (1), 155–162.

Ukpokolo, I. E. (2012). 'Memories in Photography and Rebirth: Toward a Psychosocial Therapy of the Metaphysics of Reincarnation among Traditional Esan People of Southern Nigeria'. *Journal of Black Studies*, 43(3), 289–302.

Warnke, G. (1995). 'Communicative Rationality and Cultural Values'. In Stephen K. White (ed.), *The Cambridge Companion to Habermas* (pp. 123–144). Cambridge: Cambridge University Press.

Wiredu, K. (1980). *Philosophy and African Culture*. Cambridge: Cambridge University Press.

Wiredu, K. (1992). 'Death and Afterlife in African Culture'. In K. Wiredu and K. Gyekye (eds), *Person and Community: Ghanian Philosophical Studies*. Washington, DC: Council for Research in Values and Philosophy.

Wojtkowiak, J. and Rutjens, B. T. (2011). 'The Postself and Terror Management Theory: Reflecting on after Death Identity Buffers Existential Threat'. *Interdisciplinary Journal for the Psychology of Religion*, 21 (2), 137–144.

Wojtkowiak, J., Rutjens, B. T. and Venbrux, E. (2010). 'Meaning Making and Death in a Secular Society: A Dutch Survey Study'. *Archive for the Psychology of Religion*, 32 (3), 363–373.

# 7 Human rights discourse

## Friend or foe of African women's sexual freedoms?[1]

*Louise du Toit*

## Introduction

This chapter investigates whether international and human rights discourse, and international frameworks and legal developments, could and should be used as a lever to support African women's struggles for greater sexual freedom and autonomy. The first section of the chapter gives an overview of the current state of the global debate on the advantages and potential benefits, as well as the numerous obstacles and problems with human rights discourse, particularly when these are invoked in postcolonial contexts. This overview is focused on demonstrating that the central paradox of human rights traditions can be understood in terms of the tension within human rights claims between the immanent and the transcendent dimensions, or between the 'is' and the 'ought', or between fact and ideal. I argue that the paradoxical, and in many instances contradictory moments detectable in human rights struggles are neither contingent nor fully avoidable. Since the radical emancipatory potential of human rights lies precisely in their ability to critique what is, and to keep alive the promise of a better world, this tension should be kept alive. I furthermore show that violence (whether perpetrated by pro- or anti-human rights groups) is the closing down of this fruitful tension, an immanentization of rights, which kills its promise. By listening to different thinkers' various concerns about the use of human rights, I also start to show in this section *how* human rights claims can best be drawn upon in the struggle for African women's sexual freedoms. Seven important themes in this regard are crystallised in conclusion.

The second section of this chapter is devoted to considering South African women's ongoing struggle for sexual freedom. The real contribution of the chapter lies in this section, where I bring the 'lessons' learnt from criticisms of human rights claims in the international arena to bear on this specific issue in the South African postcolony. I first discuss, in broad strokes, the actual treatment of international human rights by the newly created South African Constitutional Court, and I lament the fact that the watershed verdict of the International Criminal Tribunal for the former Yugoslavia (ICTY) declaring war rape as a crime against humanity in 2001 has not found stronger resonance in our sexual offences legal reform process. I show further that the same paradox identified in the global debate on human rights, is at work in our local context, and I analyse this tension through the lens of monumental versus memorial moments of constitutional interpretation in South Africa. Taken to their logical extremes, both these moments tend to quash the promise embodied in the new Constitution, and thus they need to be kept in balance. However, in the case of women's sexual autonomy, instead of a fruitful or productive tension between the monumental and memorial moments of constitutional interpretation, we find that two violent, but opposing frameworks reinforce each other in order to resist women's claims. Thus I conclude that, while the current profile of human rights works against the creation of an indigenous feminist call for an end to sexual violence, the power of human rights *or something like them* remains an indispensable tool for African women's fight for sexual liberation.

## Paradox keeps human rights alive

### Douzinas and the 'fight for transcendence in immanence'

Human rights discourse remains paradoxical to the core. In Part 1 of his book, *Human Rights and Empire: The Political Philosophy of Cosmopolitanism*, Costas Douzinas (2007, p. 8) 'explores the paradoxical ways in which the ideal, transcendent position of natural law and human rights has been reversed turning them into tools of public power and individual desire'. When these rights, expressed as a corrective ideal, lose their transcendent character, they soon function ideologically. As Douzinas views it, currently the two main ideological uses of human rights discourse entail 'public power', mostly state and imperial power, and 'individual desire' by which he refers to the colonisation of rights talk by capitalist power where rights typically get reduced to, and perverted into the satisfaction of individual and private desires. With the current rapid rise of a new middle class in post-colonial Africa and South Africa, corruption, conspicuous consumption of the leading classes, and the growing gap between rich and poor, the latter form of perversion of the liberation and anti-colonial struggle, has become particularly salient in this context. In his earlier *The End of Human Rights*, Douzinas (2000) claimed starkly that 'human rights have only paradoxes to offer' and in the later book he goes even further, stating, '[t]he paradoxical, the aporetic, the contradictory are not peripheral distractions awaiting to be ironed out by the theorist. Paradox is the organising principle of human rights ...' (Douzinas, 2007, p. 8). We should thus not expect that human rights could be invoked in any cause or context without the danger of their perversion being present.

Indeed, from Douzinas' overview of the history of natural and human rights, it becomes exceedingly clear that the driving impulse behind such claims or assertions throughout history has been the attempt to critique and oppose the immanent and totalising power of state or empire, in particular in so far as these structures drew their authority from custom and tradition (Douzinas, 2007, p. 12). Such contestatory claims constituted appeals to various elements, including to nature, to God or to human reason or human nature as supposedly transcendent sources beyond the current power dispensation. Nature, God or Reason, believed to ground or found human rights, were seen as proclaiming 'higher', timeless, supra-cultural moral laws that could be successfully evoked in order to resist local custom and to explode totalitarian, closed systems of power. Proponents of such claims were thus, in effect, searching for some authoritative 'thing' or some 'place' external to the instituted and established order from where critique on the bounded, self-grounding and self-reinforcing whole could be leveraged. In practice, then, '[h]uman rights are part of a long and honorable tradition of dissent, resistance and rebellion against the oppression of power and the injustice of law' (Douzinas, 2007, p. 13). This tradition rested on assumptions of access to some form of higher moral authority.

Yet, paradoxically, as regularly as human rights have been invoked in the struggle for greater freedom or justice, they have also been appropriated to bolster absolute sovereignty in the immanent powers they set out to resist. Rights claims and their particular moral force have since their inception been 'usurped by those against whom they were supposed to be a defence', states Douzinas (2007, p. 13). Rights claims have thus been used in justifications of capitalist expansion, bourgeois interests, and increasingly, of invasive, neo-colonial wars. Some of the most glaring recent examples concern US justifications of their military attacks on Middle Eastern states in the name of women's rights. And so, for Douzinas (2007, p. 13), 'the radical potential of right [is] both revealed and concealed in human rights'. Umut Özsu (2008, p. 863), in his review of Douzinas' *Human Rights and Empire*, describes this structural ambivalence at the heart of human rights as the 'unique ability of rights discourse to shuffle back and forth between the vitality of modernity's promise and the violence of its practice.' The two most prominent problematic aspects of current human rights discourse that need addressing for Douzinas, are their implication in 'the projects of colonialism and imperialism [the ideological gloss of emerging empire] in which they have been affiliated' and the 'stultifying processes of commodification to which they continue to be subjected' (Özsu, 2008, p. 863).

How to do this? For Douzinas, the answer to this dilemma entails that 'the work of critique must be grounded in a commitment to safeguard the distance between the utopian promise and current profile of human rights', in other words, between transcendence and immanence (Özsu, 2008, p. 863). This means that intellectual and activist critique 'has to remain both mindful of and faithful to the need 'to discover and fight for transcendence in immanence'' (Özsu, 2008, p. 863). When struggles for greater freedom for oppressed peoples depend on keeping alive the transcendent claim (longing, protest, refusal) within the immanent context, then one can understand why Douzinas sees violence as constituting the opposite move of the 'closing down or forgetting of the gap' (2007, p. 287). Violence closes the gap with the assertion that the actual or the real in some preferred form actually corresponds with the ideal. It is clear that such a claim, this type of violence, may just as easily take the form of a rejection as of an appropriation of human rights discourse. It is not an exaggeration to say that these are the two most prevalent forms that armed violence currently assumes. For Douzinas, what these two globalised, opposing, forms of violence share is a resolute erasure of the transcendent nature of human rights claims. Whether they are pro- or anti-human rights, they curtail the idealistic dimension, and thus close down the utopian promise of human rights at their best. Put simplistically, the one side claims to represent and embody human rights, and the other combats human rights coached in its own particular version of such an incarnated, immanent form of human rights. By reducing and solidifying human rights in superficially opposed ways, both sides in actual fact collaborate to destroy what is most radical, most promising and most powerful about them. This is namely that they can open up radically new possibilities in stultified cultural environments such as the religious and patriarchal fundamentalisms often underlying both these dominant forms of globalised violence. Advocates of human rights should therefore work to keep open and emphasise the gap, the difference between positive law (immanence) and the ideals of justice (transcendence). In contrast to violence thus conceived, critique entails 'care for the distance, the cultivation of its memory and possibility' (Douzinas, 2007, p. 287).

### The need for a thin conception of human rights

With this emphasis on the need to care for the distance and to cultivate the memory and possibility (promise) of the gap between immanent and transcendent, Douzinas seems to place a special emphasis on an aspect of human rights discourse to which he referred earlier in his analysis of the necessary vagueness of human rights: 'the "human" in human rights is a floating signifier; "human rights" is a thin, underdetermined concept' (Douzinas, 2007, p. 8). A central aspect of their apparent vagueness is the fact that human rights claims are *moral claims* made by individuals or groups that may or may not be recognised by the particular legal system in, or against which they are made (Douzinas, 2007, p. 9). Human rights discourse thus has an undeniably moral dimension that aims to limit and shape political and legal power by stating in descriptive language what 'ought to be' the case. In contexts where human rights claims are most persistently made, they are least likely to be acknowledged; there is clearly something deeply paradoxical when a black woman in apartheid South Africa claims that she has 'a human right to moral equality and dignity'. Her claim amounts to a metaphorical (figurative, imaginative) one in which she claims that she possesses something because she does not possess it; she *simultaneously does and does not have* moral equality and dignity. As Douzinas (2007, p. 10) explains, 'right' in this sense clearly does not refer to any kind of 'positive or legally enforceable right [but rather] to a claim about what morality demands', in contrast with the positive law. As such, it amounts to an aspirational claim or a call for reform of the current legal and political system. Such a claim would only have power in a context where there is a chance of its being heard or received by some sympathetic audience, even if that audience is located elsewhere, outside of the narrow context. The same claim would have had (did have) resonance in South Africa in the 1980s, since there would have been (and was) resonance internationally, but no such resonance in the South Africa of the nineteenth century, for instance.

In addition, for human rights champion Michael Ignatieff, the emphasis in human rights should fall on the ethical and moral dimension, but then more specifically on the negative moral category of cruelty. In 2001, Ignatieff delivered the Tanner Lecture Series called 'Human Rights as Politics and Idolatry', in which he considered and responded to the best known criticisms of the international human rights framework. These included the allegations that

> human rights are vague and unenforceable; [...] they are more symbolic than substantive; they cannot be grounded in any ontological truth or philosophical principle; in their primordial individualism, they conflict with cultural integrity [...]; they are a guise in which superpower global domination drapes itself; they are a guise in which the globalization of capital drapes itself [...].
>
> (Brown, 2004, p. 451)

In response to these objections Ignatieff defends a *negative and minimalist* conception of human rights. He believes human rights may be grounded more securely in the notion of cruelty than in any supposedly shared notion of what constitutes the good for humans. Here he follows the intuition of his teacher, Judith Shklar, who claimed that it is easier to reach universal and transcultural consensus on what is bad about human suffering intentionally inflicted (cruelty as a crime against the deep-seated human capacity for compassion) than about what is the good life. Ignatieff's conception of human rights is thus negative, in the sense that he claims we should 'put cruelty first' and use human rights instruments merely to 'stop unmerited suffering and gross physical cruelty [... such as] torture, beatings, killings, rape, and assault' (Ignatieff, 2001, p. 173). It is minimalist in a sense that is closely connected with its negativity: for Ignatieff, human rights should not prescribe the good or the right, but rather fight against what we can all (universally, presumably) agree on to be unequivocally evil or wrong. In other words, the universality of human rights is

> compatible with a wide variety of ways of living [with many different cultures and world views] only if the universalism implied is self-consciously minimalist [... and] a decidedly "thin" theory of what is right, a definition of the minimum conditions for any kind of life at all.
>
> (Ignatieff, 2001, pp. 56–57)

One can see here an attempt to ground human rights in some transcendent, supra-personal and, at the same time, minimalist account of what human life requires to be worth living. Douzinas would probably criticise Ignatieff's strategy as merely another attempt to reduce and then fix the meaning of human rights, which goes against their grain, but what the two thinkers share is an insistence upon a 'thin' conception of right.

### *The political dimension of human rights*

Wendy Brown (2004) criticises another aspect of Ignatieff's argument, in that she sees his emphasis on the moral dimension of human rights (focused only on cruelty and suffering) as ultimately a refusal to acknowledge the *political dimension* in which, against which and from which human rights claims inevitably operate. Although Brown agrees that human rights claims necessarily couch themselves in moral (extra-legal or transcendent) language, she is also concerned that human rights activists (and, increasingly, bureaucrats), in the process of doing so, dangerously deny or ignore the inevitable political dimension of their work:

> What are the implications of human rights assuming center stage as an international justice project, or as *the* progressive international justice project? Human rights activism is a moral-political project and if it displaces, competes with, refuses, or rejects other political projects, including those aimed at producing justice, then it is [...] a particular form of political power carrying a particular image of justice, and it will behoove us to inspect, evaluate, and judge it as such.
>
> (Brown, 2004, p. 453)

Human rights claims, in their attempt to retain their universal thrust, are often couched in impossibly abstract ('thin') terms such as the entitlement of each individual to moral equality or in terms of their stand against the immorality of politically induced suffering (Brown, 2004, p. 453). If they remain on this level of abstraction, they are irrelevant for people's political struggles. Yet, the moment that activists try to promote these principles in any concrete context, that is, to say what it means in context for people to have moral equality, the force and efficacy (if any) of such principles is dependent on taking on some decidedly political dimension. Brown's example in this regard is the supposedly 'humanitarian' intervention in Iraq by the United States and Britain, where the local people simply 'traded one form of subjection for another'. The power to interpret what human rights could or should mean in those contexts was not worked out within the contexts themselves. Brown says that any 'moral' intervention seems unable to refrain from being at the same time a political intervention.

Posing as a type of 'merely moral' anti-politics, the *political* effect of 'liberal individualist' humanitarian interventions like these for Brown is that they do not empower individuals as political actors and autonomous agents, but rather '[cast] subjects as yearning to be free of politics, and, indeed, of all collective determinations of ends' (Brown, 2004, p. 456). Add to this Sylvia Tamale's (2008, p. 52) observation that 'first world' feminists often represent 'third world' women as helpless victims of their cultures, and as 'objects devoid of any agency' and one gets an even stronger sense of how human rights interventions from afar may both deny and stunt political, interpretative agency in their 'humanitarian' interventions. In this way, the human rights flag carried by the (sometimes war) ship of liberal individualism may, in fact, announce and promote the end of politics, struggle, and resistance, in a gesture of ultimate self-refutation. Douzinas (2007, pp. 6–7) formulates this paradoxical effect more strongly: 'the "victories for freedom and democracy" in Afghanistan and Iraq [...] have been drowned in a human rights disaster for the local people' (2007, pp. 6–7).

And so, like Douzinas, Brown also concludes that human rights are inherently much more paradoxical than Ignatieff acknowledges, especially in their political effects and concrete manifestations: '[a]s such, [rights] are not simply rules and defenses against power, but can themselves be tactics and vehicles of governance and domination [... they] can simultaneously shield subjects from certain abuses and become tactics in their disempowerment' (Brown, 2004, p. 459). She adds succinctly: 'there is no such thing as mere reduction of suffering or protection from abuse – the nature of the reduction or protection is itself productive of political subjects and political possibilities' (Brown, 2004, p. 460). One could add that suffering itself never constitutes a brute fact. It is instead always embedded in a context whose interpretation and meaning are politically contested. To see this, one should only consider the media spectacles of suffering created with the aim to justify certain wars and aspirations and to condemn others. Consider the dearth of images of suffering that do not serve the most powerful political agendas (Guantánamo Bay, victims of the US military invasions of Iraq and Afghanistan, Israel's brutal practices of occupation, supported by the USA) to understand to what extent our grasp of the global distribution of suffering is mediated politically, financially, ideologically, and otherwise.[2]

It might seem on the face of it as if Douzinas and Brown are pulling in opposite directions, with the former emphasizing the need to retain the transcendence of human rights (to heed the 'gap' between the real and the ideal) in order to avoid becoming ideologically subservient, and the latter emphasizing that human rights only ever become effective politically, and that to claim otherwise is likely to serve ideological purposes. Yet I would suggest, following thinkers like Debra Bergoffen, Judith Butler and Drucilla Cornell,[3] that by coming at the issue from different sides, Douzinas and Brown are highlighting the need to keep alive the paradox at the heart of human rights. Brown emphasizes the violence that is likely to follow if the immanent, political dimension of human rights is ignored; Douzinas draws attention to the violence that results from forgetfulness about the transcendent, moral dimension of human rights. Cornell explains this paradox by drawing a key distinction between the *concept* of justice and any particular *conception* of justice, arguing that 'the concept of justice [cannot] be fully realized in a conception of justice' (Cornell, 1995, p. 14). Yet, for any conception of justice to retain its force, it should draw energy and inspiration from the concept of justice. It is on the level of the conception of justice that both African (and other postcolonial) thinkers and feminists 'demand greater room for political contestation' (Cornell, 1995, p. 14). Such contestation is always in principle possible because, for Cornell (1995, p. 16) justice is a 'limit principle': '[j]ustice is not something to be achieved, it is [rather] something to be struggled for'. Similarly, Douzinas (2007, p. 13) states, 'Every exercise of right, every rearrangement of social hierarchy, opens in turn a new vista, which, if petrified, becomes itself an external limitation that must be again overcome.' Judith Butler (2001, p. 430) argues along the same lines, saying:

> What is permitted within the term universal is understood to be dependent on a consensus [and ...] presumes that what will and will not be included in the language of universal entitlement is not settled once and for all, that its future shape cannot be fully anticipated at this time.

It is clear that for these thinkers, the universal should be kept radically undecidable, 'transcendent', in Douzinas' terms. Butler also wants to protect the ideal or promise expressed in the universal aspiration of human rights, and she counter-intuitively approaches this task by insisting that we remember precisely the *particularity of its historical emergence*. She calls this a performative contradiction: by remembering the concrete, particular, specific, historical roots and contexts of the emergence and revision of any universalising concept, any particular expression of justice, one keeps alive its core meaning, namely the way in which it emerges in protest and in refusal to *what is*. This would ideally remind us of the possibility that it may, and in fact, must always be interpreted anew, that the critical-hermeneutical task of deciding what the political thrust of human rights should be in any given context, is never exhausted. This is also why Butler aligns the universal with the 'not yet', with 'that which remains unrealised', and its articulation with challenges to its existing formulations (Butler 2001, p. 431, as discussed in Bergoffen 2003, p. 125). Bergoffen (2003, p. 125) notes that Butler resists 'align[ing] the universal with an absolute unerring content', and does not ignore, but rather draws attention to 'the disjunction between the specificity of the content and the claim to universality', which is a necessary and ever-present disjunction, a tension that should at all costs be kept alive. Bergoffen detects a similarity between Butler's 'politics of hope and anxiety' and Derrida's (1997, p. 29) 'democracy of the perhaps' and sees them as linking 'the possibility of justice to a thinking that frees the thought of the future from its betrayal [...] by already determined concepts of universality' (Bergoffen 2003, p. 126). Bergoffen (2003, p. 125) formulates this concern very well:

Dethroned from their position as absolute Platonic realities, universals become embedded in material realities – sites where the tension between the specificity of those articulating the universal appeal and the absolute resolution articulated in the particulars of the appeal become politically productive.

The next section is devoted to bringing this international, philosophical debate on the nature, status and structure of human rights to the current South African context, and to asking how human rights discourse could or should function in women's struggles for sexual freedom. In particular, by keeping in mind the themes that have crystallised in this section, the question to be answered is *how* could or should human rights frameworks and claims be made productive in South Africa, in fighting for African women's sexual autonomy and freedoms? The themes to be kept firmly in mind include the following: (i) protecting human rights claims against their usurpation and monopolisation by state power; (ii) protecting human rights claims against their usurpation and monopolisation by imperial powers such as the USA and others; (iii) protecting human rights claims against being co-opted into a capitalist frame which reduces them to individual need satisfaction; (iv) keeping alive the transcendent claim or dimension of human rights; (v) neither negating nor avoiding the political dimension of human rights, which is closely linked to the need for local contestations over what specific human rights, such as bodily integrity, should mean in particular contexts; (vi) maintaining the 'human' in human rights as a thin concept and thus actively challenging ideological understandings of the human 'from below', e.g. where humanity or dignity is conflated with middle-class existence or male embodiment; (vii) similarly, preserving the proposed thinness of human rights conceptions and safeguarding the distance between the concept and the conception of justice by resisting interpretations of human rights claims that are overtly individualistic or abstract and that thereby threaten cultural integrity. A golden thread running through most of these themes is the need for South African women to work out for and amongst themselves what transcendent human rights principles such as bodily integrity could and should mean within local places, and then to find or create responsive audiences both inside and outside the country to help put pressure on governmental and other structures to rearrange power relations within the young state in order to improve the protection of women's and girls' sexual integrity.

## Sexual freedom in the postcolony

### *Women's sexual rights as human rights*

In the previous section could be seen how feminist theorists such as Bergoffen, Butler and Cornell cautiously adopt and adapt human rights discourses to be used in specific struggles, thereby emphasizing the need for such discourses to be activated. On the one hand they suggested that we cannot today do without the universalizing and transcendent moral claims emanating from these discourses, and on the other hand they showed that this can only happen if their concrete application remains eternally open to fresh and competing interpretations, i.e. in Douzinas' terminology, if they resist the violence of closure. They want the content, but also the structure and status of human rights discourse to remain open to political contestation. As soon as the universalizing thrust or aspiration gets bogged down by being equated with something like individual desire satisfaction, with public power, with imperialist interests or even with liberal individualist feminism, it becomes self-defeating. In the limited space available here, I want to briefly consider what this critical appropriation of human rights discourse may imply for (South) African women's struggle for sexual freedom.

Although it is possible to make a convincing argument that South African men's sexual freedoms are also not optimally realised, my focus here is on the sexual unfreedom of women and girls in the country. With an annual South African Police Service rape report rate of 66,000 and apparently still on the increase,[4] and with more than 40 per cent of the victims of rape being under the age of 18 (Jewkes et al., 2009), the impact of actual and threatened sexual violence severely violates women's sexual freedom as well as many other of their most basic freedoms guaranteed in our Bill of Rights, such as freedom from violence, the right to bodily integrity, freedom of movement, and so on. Moreover, I would argue that these cruelties are not generally framed as grievable under our current dispensation. Now and then a particularly cruel or sensational rape or rape-and-murder grabs the media headlines: think of baby Tshepang from Upington, Anene Booysen from Bredasdorp, and Ina Bonnett, victim of the 'Monster of Modimolle'. Yet, if one considers the actual numbers of victims involved – approximately 180 reported cases per day – then it is clear that the phenomenon does not receive the high-level political and public response that it deserves. South African society seems to be largely reconciled with, and thus complicit in, sexual violence as firmly woven into the daily fabric of our lives. One could thus reasonably expect that international and human rights frameworks can and should be more strongly enforced or applied within the South African legal and governing systems, regarding this issue. But in light of the concerns around human and international legal frameworks explored above, how could this be done?

When these questions are raised, it should be noted that there has been an intensification and expansion of international attention to sexual violence, especially after the February 2001 verdict in the Kunarac case of the ICTY (see Bergoffen, 2003). In this instance, three men were sentenced for war rape, condemned by the Tribunal as a war crime as well as a crime against humanity. It was the first time in history that war rape had been condemned and sentenced internationally as such a severe crime. Bergoffen's extensive analyses of this watershed verdict show that its power was derived from political pressure mounted by lobby groups on the issue of war rape around the world in the wake of the UN Fourth World Conference on Women in Beijing in 1995; the retention of the transformative, transcendent and aspirational thrust carried by the vocabulary of 'crimes against humanity' and, importantly, the openness of the Tribunal to allowing its understanding of the 'human' in human rights to be informed and finally changed by women's testimonies about war rape, i.e. 'from below'. Bergoffen (2012) demonstrates the latter by showing how a certain interpretation of women's sex-specific vulnerabilities to rape was incorporated into the Tribunal's definition of the 'human' in human rights at the cost of the traditional, invulnerable and heroic idealised male body.

In my view these developments in international and human rights law should have more profoundly affected our domestic frameworks in South Africa for dealing with sexual violence than they finally did. It is a pity that they did not feature more strongly during the reform process, which culminated in the new Sexual Offences Act of 2007. Although there are differences between rape as an explicit strategy of war and ethnic cleansing as it was employed in the former Yugoslavian conflict, on the one hand, and the high levels of 'everyday' rape that happen in South Africa as a post-conflict society, on the other, there are also, scholars realise, important overlaps and insights that are transferable between pre-, post- and armed conflict contexts. It could arguably be demonstrated that South Africans have a long history of self-exceptionalism, in which the alleged uniqueness of South African circumstances (and later after liberation of South African autonomy *vis-à-vis* the West) have been used as rationalizations for resisting international pressure. To be fair, such resistance is tied up with legitimate struggles for self-determination against ongoing pressures exerted by imperialist, neo-colonial and other globalizing powers and interests. Yet, a blanket rejection of international pressure in the name of autonomy and self-determination and in the name of custom and tradition constitutes a kind of violence and closure – the kind of violence most typically challenged by the universal and moral thrust of human rights. It kills the promise of a better life just as surely as does an invasive war waged under the banner of humanitarianism.

### Human rights in South Africa

How should South Africans then respond to international human rights and humanitarian frameworks and activities? Renowned South African legal philosopher Lourens du Plessis draws attention to the mixed reactions of the then newly created Constitutional Court of South Africa to international and human rights frameworks. On the one hand, in the very first case handled by that Court, the *Makwanyane* case in which the constitutionality of the death penalty was contested, the Constitutional Court triumphantly declared the death penalty to be unconstitutional.[5] They did this, not only in the name of the South African Constitution, but explicitly also in the name of human rights standards worldwide (Du Plessis, 2000, p. 387). Du Plessis adds that two justices, Mokgoro and Madala JJ, went further than this and 'solemnised a marriage of Western and African human rights values' with reference to Ubuntu (Du Plessis, 2000, p. 387). Interestingly, among this and other 'remarkable judgements' of the Constitutional Court which 'have given short shrift to the remnants of long-cherished biases' on the basis of the newly celebrated human rights culture in the country, Du Plessis (2000, p. 388) lists rights and freedoms regarding gender and parental roles and prominently also gay and lesbian rights. There was thus, at least initially, great enthusiasm for the application of human rights standards to the opening up of sexual freedoms for all South Africans.

Following the work of Johan Snyman (1998) in this regard, Du Plessis distinguishes between a monumental and a memorial approach to the Constitution. The confident thrashing in the name of human rights of 'long-cherished biases', held by the majority of South African citizens he calls a monumental moment of constitutional interpretation. He contrasts with this the memorial moment in constitutional interpretation where the emphasis is more on mourning (of past victims) than on triumph or celebration – echoing the ideas of Shklar and Ignatieff discussed earlier. For Du Plessis, the memorial moment limits triumphant constitutionalism by allowing for a multiplicity of perspectives, for voices coming from concrete, local contexts, and for political contestation. In particular, Du Plessis is concerned that the voices of actual and potential victims of constitutional decisions should be more clearly aired and prioritized. This would mean, for example in the case of the death penalty decision, that victims of violent crime should have ideally been given a chance to testify about the impact of criminal violence on their lives, thereby giving a voice to the majority of South Africans who seem to favor the return of the death penalty. At the same time, South Africans should have been reminded of the unsavoury political role that the death penalty had played in apartheid South Africa. These emphases imply a much more modest constitutionalism and, for Du Plessis, they give better effect than monumental constitutionalism to an 'open community of constitutional interpreters'. One aspect of this latter notion is that the Constitution does not 'belong' in any sense to the Constitutional Court, but that its promise along with its interpretation instead belongs to all South Africans.

One could thus plausibly link Du Plessis' notion of monumental constitutionalism to the transcendent, universal aspiration of human rights, and thereby with their radical and disruptive potential and promise, which should clearly be protected. On the other hand his understanding of memorial constitutionalism insists on the difficulty of deciding what a specific human rights claim should mean in any particular, concrete context; in other words, he acknowledges the difficulty of simultaneously keeping alive the promise of human rights and contextualizing them, making them politically effective. Like Butler, Bergoffen and others discussed above, Du Plessis (2000, p. 385) makes a clear case for striking a constant, if dynamic, balance between the memorial and monumental moments of constitutional interpretation:

the promise(s) which a constitution holds can only emerge from contradictory modes of dealing with that constitution as memory. In other words, *the manner in which we deal with the Constitution as memory predetermines the fulfilment of the Constitution as pledge.* The Constitution as memory is a *monument* and a *memorial* at the same time. In purpose and style these constitutional modes of existence are largely contradictory, but they need not necessarily exclude or eliminate each other.

Like Wendy Brown, Du Plessis is clearly uncomfortable with the persistent tendency to treat human rights as a purely moral category and thereby to depoliticize them. He dislikes the way in which the Constitutional Court adopts an a-political, 'merely moral' human rights stance on certain issues, thereby denying that they in fact interfere politically, or that their actions have political effects and consequences in the sense of actually redistributing power. This was for him particularly striking in the *Azapo* case where the Constitutional Court resisted clear principles of international law in order to make what it considered to be strategic political moves by granting amnesty to apartheid perpetrators (Du Plessis, 2007). This is doubly ironic since the Court then went on to defend its stance as motivated by morality alone, and to thereby be elevated above politics and political pressures, operating somehow from a pure moral realm beyond political considerations (Du Plessis, 2007, pp. 53ff). In doing so, the Constitutional Court insisted on the transcendent moment of human rights, but without acknowledging the complexity of interpreting their meaning in context, i.e. their necessary immanence. We have seen time and again how global imperialist powers make a similar claim to neutrality and objectivity when they most glaringly serve their own power interests. Taken to extremes, memorialism and monumentalism may actually constitute the two opposing types of violence that Douzinas warns against: both tend toward the closure or fixation of the promise and disruption of human rights claims in an attempt to exert control over others. Whether the claim is one of the triumphant 'realisation' of human rights ignoring local protests and concerns, or whether it is an opposition to human rights in the name of local 'political necessities' that 'require' certain 'sacrifices' to be made, neither of these strategies respects the promise (and thus necessary transcendence) of any human rights claim worth its salt.

### Human rights and sexual violence

In conclusion, let us focus more narrowly on the everyday nature of sexual violence committed against women and girls in this country, and the promise contained in human rights discourse to put an end to it. I agree with Helen Moffett's (2006) analysis, which shows that the debate and political contestations around sexual violence in South Africa get bogged down by a racialization of the issue which occludes the fact that sexual violence is overwhelmingly intra-racial and intra-communal, and an issue of sexual rather than racial power.

Of course, nothing in our country is untouched by race dimensions and it would be naive to assume this is untrue for sexual identity and sexual violence. The history of the sexual dimension of colonial power in South Africa still needs to be researched extensively (see Thomas, 2007 and Gqola, 2015). But what I see as happening is that the issue of sexual violence is/gets racialized *so that* it can then be pronounced taboo and thereby removed from public debate. Read in feminist terms, what we get is a dominant public strategy which declares male honor to carry more weight than female bodily integrity and sexual freedom, in a context where racial stereotypes of course also impact on these different valuations (see for an important discussion of these issues, Hassim, 2014). The wider frame in which I understand the passivity, the silence and the complicity around sexual violence in our country is the clash in our context between the two global frames referred to earlier, both of which exert the violence of closure. On the one hand there is the too Western-monopolized and US-dominated human rights framework which threatens indigenous traditions because it treats human rights as immanent, and on the other, there are the ossified systems of control that are acknowledged as authentically and traditionally 'African' which resist those same immanentized human rights claims, often with no clear normative frame to put in their place. And of course, most typically, the clash between these two misogynist traditions chooses as its battleground women's sexual bodies. Viewed from women's perspective, these two interpretative frames that seem to oppose one another are, in fact, deeply complicit in maintaining women's sexual unfreedom. Drawing on Douzinas, one could say this is because both are strongly invested in existing power distributions (one global, one local) and therefore repress the radical potential of transcendent human rights claims such as African women's right to sexual integrity in postcolonial contexts.

If the struggle for women's sexual freedom and in particular their freedom from sexual violence in the South African postcolony is to be successful (without which the democracy is postponed and the liberation has not yet happened), it is very important that we understand the nature of the beast which dominates the public discourse, as set out earlier. It is imperative that we understand the deeply paradoxical nature of human rights. It is important that women realize that neither of these two opposing agendas serve their interests and I suggest that it is crucial that women unite across race, class, ethnicity and religion in solidarity around issues of sexual violence and oppression, in order to ensure that racial, class, religious and other agendas do not hijack the debate. The next step would be to insist on a link between, on the one hand, the promise and power contained in human rights discourse, which historically played a decisive role in our political transition in this country, and on the other, the power and authority of women to express what sexual freedom and the basic right to bodily integrity as promised in the Constitution *mean in our local contexts*, cultures and neighborhoods. I thus propose that it is necessary to resist and refuse the tendency of the dominant discourses to force the sexual violence debate into a stalemate by pressing the issue into the service of national (or race or class) interests.

Women (and their male allies) should insist on again and again returning this debate back to the question of what the basic human right to bodily integrity should and could mean when the proclamation of that right is allowed to critique and explode local and international interpretative frames equally that want to limit and contain its promise. The power of human rights should be mobilized in order to combat the often invisible cruelties committed against women in the everyday in the way that Ignatieff proposes, but then not by naively claiming to be 'merely moral', or to be minimalist and purely negative in approach. It is a truism that, if you want to end the banal invasions of women's bodies, the violent appropriation of their humanity through the subjugation of their sexuality, it will require a radical redistribution of power (see MacKinnon, 2005). It will be political and it cannot but be political, and we should not shy away from this. Not only will women and men in the process insist on and highlight the public-political nature of the pervasive 'private, sexual' violence made possible by the current nature of the state and government structures, but they will also assume real political power for women (see Nedelsky, 2011). At the same time, feminists would challenge Western-monopolized human rights frameworks by reactivating forgotten indigenous traditions of women's sexual freedoms and autonomy (cf. Oyewumi, 1997), and would challenge local authorities to state in so many words that African traditions oppose women's right to bodily integrity and autonomy, and to substantiate those claims. Also, claims to tradition will hereby be removed from the murky realms of the untouchable and the timeless, and brought into the living gathering of people, the *lekgotla*, where they belong, for scrutiny and rein-terpretation, for inquiring rigorously about whether they (still) serve the flour-ishing of human life and Ubuntu principles, or not (see the essay by Oelofsen in this anthology). Neither the promise of human rights nor the meanings of African traditions should be handed on a tray to powerful groups who have no real interest in women's lives and consider the sacrifice of women's sexuality to 'higher causes' as justifiable (see Chimakonam's essay in this anthology).

Finally, I want to draw attention to the close affinity between the proper transcendence of human rights claims and the transgressive imagination. Stories in all cultures have served the purpose of critiquing the violent closure of meanings and worked to open up avenues for thinking and acting differ-ently. In a dynamic African past which some contemporary commentators want to close down and freeze in time according to their own power-invested interpretations, stories have played the same role. In a recent anthology Jean Lombard (2014) from Cape Town collected a variety of stories dealing with the legendary big Water Snake of the Groot Gariep – the largest and longest river in our country, winding its way through an arid landscape. What strikes the reader about this series of stories, a small selection out of a large multi-cultural tapestry of southern African stories about the Water Snake, is how the snake represents the male sexual organ, the Phallus, on the one hand, but how closely aligned the Water Snake is to women's sexuality and women's procreative powers, on the other. The Water Snake is the perfect example of what the ancient Greeks called the *pharmakon*: the medicine which could also be a poison, the deeply ambivalent phenomenon. The snake lives in the deepest hollows of the river – in a land where water is the most precious resource and the source of all life. The river itself presents as mythical, supernatural – a large body of water winding its way through a semi-desert. The Water Snake is closely associated with the river itself, and highlights both its life-saving and life-threatening aspects. The Water Snake carries a bright stone on its forehead, which it takes off and hides in the reeds when it feeds. This stone is marvellous and enticing and brings riches to the one who can get hold of it. Yet, the same stone can act as a trap by which the snake can catch a person for prey. In some stories, the snake swallows all the water of a river or fountain so that the humans starve.

Also sexually speaking, the Water Snake is deeply ambivalent, representing both the pleasure and the dangers of sex itself. It is mostly regarded as straightforwardly threatening to men and boys – it eats them. But the snake has a more complex relation with women and girls. When girls reach puberty, in some cultures it is customary that the young girl ('die maagmeisie' in the Afrikaans language, translating roughly to 'virgin girl') gets introduced ceremonially to the Water Snake – an initiation and an acquaintance that is understood to empower her, especially in her womanly role of life-bearing (see Deacon in Lombard, 2014). In addition, in almost all of the stories recorded, ranging from Sotho to Xhosa to Griekwa cultures, the Water Snake seeks to marry a girl, to find a wife. It is said that once a woman has had intercourse with the snake, she will lose sexual interest in men. According to one storyteller, the woman 'gets wise under the water' and no man can give a woman the kind of pleasure that the snake can (Strauss in Lombard, 2014, p. 39): '*Ek en jy kan tog nie met haar gedoen kry wat die slang met haar gedoen het nie. Die slang gee haar 'n anner soort lekkerte*' (translated by author: 'You and I surely cannot manage to do with her what the snake has done with her. The snake gives her a different kind of pleasure.').

I read this as the kind of legend that plays an important corrective or balancing role in a male-dominated society. In a world where male sexuality is constructed as dominant, stories of the Water Snake place emphasis on female sexuality – not only on its procreative and life-giving and life-sustaining aspects, but also, very importantly, on the female capacity and desire for pleasure. The exaggerated, impossible pleasure that the Water Snake is capable of bestowing on his wife (or anyone's wife!) acts as a reminder of women's capacity and need for sexual pleasure, and thus for transcendence. The Snake, in its mythical proportions, embodies something transcendent, something which by its very nature pushes against the boundaries of the immanent, the given, the closed, the tradition and the custom, and in her close association with the Snake, the 'maagmeisie' also transcends the immanent. The Water Snake makes the impossible possible and stretches the imagination. It inspires awe, and serves as a reminder of how human sexuality is embedded in nature and how both its constructive and destructive powers ultimately transcend our limited powers of comprehension and control.

In line with the thinking of Ugandan legal philosopher Sylvia Tamale (2008), I also think it is strategically important to revisit African cultural traditions in an effort to deliberately work against 'the totalising effect of obscuring the potential that culture may hold as an emancipatory tool', especially for women's sexual powers, freedoms and autonomy (Tamale, 2008, p. 49). Tamale wants to pursue a 'constructive approach to African sexual rights', an approach that works through rather than against or around African culture, and I agree with this strategy. It is important that African feminists highlight both the positive, emancipatory, as well as the negative and restrictive aspects of contemporary African cultures. From such a perspective we shall also be better placed as African scholars to highlight both positive and negative aspects of contemporary Western cultures, where, as far as women's sexual freedoms are concerned, there are also many systemic problems. We should consistently fight the stereotypes which portray, for example, Europe as completely woman-friendly when compared with 'patriarchal, oppressive' Africa. These pictures are purely and simply false.

Echoing the two South African Constitutional Court judges referred to earlier, Tamale (2008, p. 60) urges us to 'find those values that resonate from indigenous cultures that will speak to the rights repertoire, as feminists know it' and build our case that way. Through her investigation into the contemporary Baganda cultural practice of Ssenga (sexual initiation of a girl by the paternal aunt), Tamale discovers not an outdated, static and oppressive practice as African cultures are usually portrayed, but instead a practice that has adapted to changing realities such as HIV and AIDS, and which now serves to help young Baganda women 'negotiate agency, autonomy and self-knowledge about their sexuality', as well as their sexual autonomy and economic independence. As in the Water Snake stories of South Africa, we find in Ssenga an emphasis on women's sexual pleasure. According to Tamale (2008, p. 62), these young African women are empowered through a contemporary version of sexual initiation, into using 'the erotic as an empowering resource to claim justice'. In the midst of the real and the immanent, empowering new possibilities are opened up through a redescription, a reimagination of the world. What young girl raised in the contemporary West can lay claim to this kind of sexual empowerment through cultural initiation?

To return to the question which is the title of this article, on the one hand, the current profile of human rights, narrowly associated with Judaeo-Christian legal traditions and, increasingly, with liberal individualism and the gradual capitalist destruction of the political sphere, probably constitutes more of a foe than a friend to African women's sexual freedom aspirations. On the other hand, they may still prove to be (even if in a somewhat transformed guise or form) an indispensable ally. Something *like* them (in their imaginative power to inspire and empower by picturing things otherwise than they are; recall, 'it was and it was not the case') may very well be necessary to leverage critique against ossified, closed systems that resist calls for change and that insist on only one correct (resolutely patriarchal) reading of the African past, against systems that kill stories and the possibility to imagine things wildly differently. Just as African tradition is open to interpretation and contestation, human rights should be, too. We should not conceive of human rights as dogmatic absolutes or irreplaceables. We should rather focus on the kind of stories that human rights at their best allow us to tell. They allow us to consider a world in which women's sexuality is celebrated and revered, women's sexual pleasure cultivated, and where there are real sanctions placed on anyone violating them. They allow us to say in our current, deeply oppressive context: 'We simultaneously have and do not have an equal moral right to sexual integrity and autonomy', but not to blow this message into the wind. Instead, they also help to create an audience who could 'catch' that story, echo it, and help to give birth to the world evoked by it.

Should we dare to once again let loose the spirit of the Water Snake on the South African landscape? Allow the poison of the snake to do its healing, its protective as well as its destructive work (destroying unjust systems of political power)? Can the Water Snake of a truly transcendent but at the same time materially embedded (in the boegoe and the clay of the Groot Gariep) human rights discourse assist us to embrace the risks of an uncertain future of sexual freedom for all? Can we call again on the Water Snake to revitalise an indigenous tradition of sexual freedom and celebration, and to 'discover and fight for transcendence within immanence', as Douzinas suggests?

## Notes

1 This essay was first published in the journal *Acta Academica* 46(4) (2014), pp. 49–70, © UV/UFS ISSN 0587–2405, www.ufs.ac.za/ActaAcademica, and is reprinted here with permission from the author and publishers.
2 In this regard, consider Judith Butler's (2003, 2009) notion of 'grievable lives' and the work of Dubravka Žarkov, *The Body of War: Media, Ethnicity, and Gender in the Break-up of Yugoslavia* (Žarkov, 2007).
3 The discussion over the next two paragraphs is closely modelled on, and draws freely from an article I have published elsewhere (see Du Toit, 2013).
4 http://rapecrisis.org.za/rape-in-south-africa/.
5 *S v Makwanyane* 1995 6 BCLR 665 (CC).

## References

Bergoffen, Debra. (2003). 'February 22, 2001: Toward a Politics of the Vulnerable Body', *Hypatia* 18 (1), 116–134.
Bergoffen, Debra. (2012). *Contesting the Politics of Genocidal Rape: Affirming the Dignity of the Vulnerable Body.* New York and London: Routledge.
Brown, Wendy. (2004). 'The Most We Can Hope For … Human Rights and the Politics of Fatalism', *The South Atlantic Quarterly* 103 (2/3), 451–463.
Butler, Judith. (2001). 'The End of Sexual Difference?' In *Feminist Consequences: Theory for the New Century*, edited by Elisabeth Bronfen and Misha Kavka, pp. 414–434. New York: Columbia University Press.
Butler, Judith. (2003). 'Violence, Mourning, Politics', *Studies in Gender and Sexuality* 1 (4), 9–37.

Butler, Judith. (2009). *Frames of War: When Is Life Grievable?* London and New York: Verso.

Cornell, Drucilla. (1995). *The Imaginary Domain: Abortion, Pornography and Sexual Harassment.* New York: Routledge.

Derrida, Jacques. (1997). *Politics of Friendship.* Trans. George Collins. New York: Verso.

Douzinas, Costas. (2000). *The End of Human Rights.* Oxford and Portland, OR: Hart.

Douzinas, Costas. (2007). *Human Rights and Empire: The Political Philosophy of Cosmopolitanism.* Oxford and New York: Routledge-Cavendish.

Du Plessis, Lourens. (2000). 'The South African Constitution as Memory and Promise', *Stellenbosch Law Review* no. 3, 385–394.

Du Plessis, Lourens. (2007). '*Azapo*: Monument, memorial or … mistake?' In *Law, Memory and the Legacy of Apartheid: Ten Years after Azapo versus President of South Africa*, pp. 51–64. Pretoria: Pretoria University Law Press.

Du Toit, Louise. (2013). 'In the Name of What? Defusing the Rights-Culture Debate by Revisiting the Universals of Both Rights and Culture', *Politikon: South African Journal of Political Studies*, Febuary, 15–34.

Gqola, Pumla Dineo. (2015). *Rape: A South African Nightmare.* Auckland Park: MF Books Johannesburg.

Hassim, Shireen. (2014). 'Violent Modernity: Gender, race and bodies in contemporary South African politics'. *Politikon: South African Journal of Political Studies*, 41 (2) 167–182.

Ignatieff, Michael. (2001). *Human Rights as Politics and Idolatry.* Princeton, NJ: Princeton University Press.

Jewkes, Rachel, Naeemah, Abraham and Shanaaz, Matthew. (2009). 'Preventing Rape and Violence in South Africa: Call for Leadership in a New Agenda for Action'. *Report, Gender and Health Research Unit, Medical Research Council.* www.mrc.ac.z a/gender/prev_rapedd041209.pdf.

Lombard, Jean. (2014). *Die Ding in die Riete: Verhale Byeengebring deur Jean Lombard.* Kaapstad: Tafelberg.

MacKinnon, Catharine A. (2005). *Women's Lives, Men's Laws.* Cambridge, MA: Belknap Press of Harvard University Press.

Moffett, Helen. (2006). 'These Women, They Force Us to Rape Them: Rape as Narrative of Social Control in Post-apartheid South Africa', *Journal of Southern African Studies* 32(1), 129–144.

Nedelsky, Jennifer. (2011). *Law's Relations: A Relational Theory of Self, Autonomy, and Law.* Oxford: Oxford University Press.

Oyewumi, Oyeronke. (1997). *The Invention of Women: Making an African Sense of Western Gender Discourses.* Minneapolis, MN: University of Minnesota Press.

Özsu, Umut. (2008). 'Book Review: Costas Douzinas, *Human Rights and Empire: The Political Philosophy of Cosmopolitanism.* Abingdon: Routledge-Cavendish, 2007', *European Journal of International Law* 19, 862–864.

Snyman, Johan J. (1998). 'Interpretation and the Politics of Memory', *Acta Juridica* 312, 317–321.

Tamale, Sylvia. (2008). 'The Right to Culture and the Culture of Rights: A Critical Perspective on Women's Sexual Rights in Africa', *Feminist Legal Studies* 16, 47–69.

Thomas, Greg. (2007). *The Sexual Demon of Colonial Power: Pan-African Embodiment and Erotic Schemes of Empire.* Bloomington, IN: Indiana University Press.

Žarkov, Dubravka. (2007). *The Body of War: Media, Ethnicity and Gender in the Break-up of Yugoslavia.* Durham, NC: Duke University Press.

# 8 African philosophy's injustice against women

*Bernard Matolino*

## Introduction

In this chapter I seek to analyze the state of African philosophy as a tool of oppression, exclusion and discrimination against women. While women are said to have enjoyed a privileged position in traditional African societies (Amadiume, 1987; Oyewumi, 1997), that privilege does not appear to extend to philosophy. Both in the traditional articulation of African philosophy and in the modernized, professionalized practice of this art in universities, women have been kept at the margins, while the discrimination has not been a straightforward loud and public barring of women from the academy. The most likely reason for this occurrence is that philosophy has been a preserve for males that has been handed down to male heirs. Yet another occurrence which I seek to analyze has been that the fight to assert the existence of African philosophy was essentially a fight between males. White males having doubted and castigated the African as having no philosophical standing, it was African males who stood up to register the existence of African philosophy and counter their white counterparts' racist attitudes. I seek to argue that since Western philosophy was dominated by males, African philosophy has, in an uncanny way, followed this pattern by permitting or even encouraging men to dominate. This has essentially defeated the whole purpose and project of the growth and development of African philosophy as a counter-hegemonic enterprise. Thus African philosophy can no longer claim to be a philosophy that promotes the humanity of the African and the African's intellectual standing as a philosopher. It only does so with the proviso that such an African is primarily male and the female can only be affirmed derivatively. This shared, dubious domination of philosophy by males, I argue, is a continuation of the hierarchization of humanity on grounds of race and sex. Tragically, the female African finds herself at the very bottom of the hierarchy of the oppressed and excluded. For African philosophy to be the fully emancipatory tool that it was initially conceived as, it must become more alert to its potential participants and how they are being left behind. African philosophy must self-correct by promoting the inclusion of female voices and interpretations of the world.

This will not only enrich its discursive standing but will return it to its originally inclusive mores.

## The dominance of males in philosophy

If we look at the history of Western philosophy, it is without a doubt a history of how the enterprise has been mainly dominated by males; needless to say white males. The dominance of males was enabled by the distinctions they created which favored their standing in relation to philosophy. As Fiona Jenkins and Katrina Hutchison (2013) point out, there is

> a well-developed feminist argument that western philosophy was formed around an overlapping series of conceptual oppositions – reason/emotion, mind/body, culture/nature – coding a hierarchical understanding of the relationship of masculine and feminine that can be discerned throughout the 2,500 year history of the subject.
>
> (p. 2)

I suggest that not only were these conceptual oppositions false but they were ostensibly advanced from the specific world view of white males. This specific world view is limited and cannot be taken as representative of all of humanity's experiences. The distinctions which were built into the essence and development of Western philosophy, by its males, were neither universal nor easily provable. Rather, they amounted to a self-promoting view that Western males had about themselves regarding the rest of humanity. These dichotomies, while giving the white male an upper hand, were clearly incapable of capturing the entire reality of human experience. Woefully, even in the context in which they arose, they failed to give credence to the views of the other half of humanity, namely females.

This claim is amply supported by Jean Grimshaw and Miranda Fricker, whose analysis points to the nature of Western philosophy as having been presented as masculine by virtue of being predicated on reason that is both universal and objective. The subject of philosophical analysis, they state, was taken to be free of limitations such as class, gender, race or a social and historical standing. Rather, the subject was viewed as universal, and at times as having no body, and was assumed to be 'capable of God's eye view'. They state that in contemporary times, any discussion of the location of philosophers has been dismissed

> as a form of sociology of knowledge which has no relevance to questions about the truth or adequacy of philosophical theories themselves. But from a feminist perspective, questions about the social location of knowers, or those who claim to know, are not extrinsic to philosophy. Rather, they should be at its very heart, since the gendering of philosophy, and its frequent exclusion of women, are based on the denial of this location, on

the assumption of a 'universality' which is in fact a concealed partiality. The 'human' subject in philosophy has often turned out to be a male subject.

(Grimshaw and Fricker, 2003, p. 554)

However, in the professional development of philosophy, this narrow view became the dictum by which philosophy was to be defined. The view that only specific people were capable of doing philosophy meant that those who did not belong to the designated group such as women and non-whites were doomed as incapable of the project of philosophizing. The scandal, as Jenkins and Hutchison point out (2013, pp. 4–6) is that while philosophy claims to be the core of humanity, it speaks for that humanity from a narrow, male, white standpoint. Such a narrow construal of philosophy is not only impoverished by its very denial of the rest of humanity to participate in the task of philosophizing, but as Jenkins and Hutchison point out, is mind boggling. This is particularly so when we consider the etymology of philosophy.

If wisdom – Sofia – has historically been represented as a woman, how does philosophy's claim to represent a kind of cultural and human wisdom fare in view of the still narrow representation of humanity in the ranks of its practitioners, and the class, race, and gender composition of its elite? How indeed, does this impact its claim to represent, criticize, or interpret the theoretical dimensions of the social sciences? Should we care to ensure that women come to practice philosophy in numbers comparable to men, for reasons that go beyond equity goals (though they include them), to invoke the good of the discipline itself?

(Jenkins and Hutchison, 2013, p. 5)

Jenkins and Hutchison then go on to bemoan the absence of people of color in the practice of philosophy and argue that the exclusion of people of color, just like the exclusion of women, impoverishes philosophy itself so that it cannot be considered to be representative of humanity. But if we return to the theme of the exclusion of women, there are two aspects to that exclusion. The first, as I have already pointed out, is to be found in the very origins of philosophy in the West. This is found in the dichotomization of characteristics into those that are seen as male and philosophical and those that are seen as female (or representative of other races) and non-philosophical (Haslanger, 2008, p. 213). Thus the manner in which philosophy originates is specifically seen as a male concern and one that is either best understood or best executed by men. The second aspect of the exclusion of women has to do with how the modern academic, professionalized practice of philosophy in university departments is either deliberately, or by tradition, made to be a male domain. Stories of women's exclusion are premised on the very belief that philosophy is 'hard' and is not meant for women (Haslanger, 2008, p. 211). Worse, as Haslanger chronicles her experience, even when she excelled and passed with high first grades in graduate school, she was made the butt of jokes about her gender when she was encouraged to have herself tested to determine if she was not a male after all. While Haslanger admits that there has been progress and times have changed with respect to the position of women in the academic pursuit of philosophy, she holds that 'there are trends that have continued throughout my time in the profession, because I see evidence of them today' (2008, p. 210). Such evidence, she argues, is found in both outright discrimination and unconscious bias.

While it is easy to condemn or criticize outright bias as engendered by base discrimination against women, such a critique would be a far easier target and may actually contribute to hiding the real problem with the conceptualization of philosophy. A more subtle method of discrimination that is encapsulated in the origins of philosophy as masculine is well apprehended by Haslanger when she writes:

> As feminist philosophers have been arguing for decades, the familiar dichotomies with which Anglophone philosophy defines itself map neatly onto gender dichotomies – rational/emotional, objective/subjective, mind/body; ideals of philosophy – penetrating, seminal, and rigorous; and what we do – attack, target and demolish an opponent, all of which frame philosophy as masculine and in opposition to the feminine. These ideals and dichotomies are not only gendered but also are relevant in considering challenges philosophers of color face; like women, non-whites are often perceived through schemas that represent them as less rational and more identified with nature and the body than whites. Even if one consciously rejects these assumptions, they may continue to work at the schematic level.
>
> (2008, p. 213)

What is evident from Jenkins and Hutchison, Grimshaw and Fricker, and Haslanger, is that modern Anglophone philosophy is based on dichotomies created right from its beginning. These dichotomies essentially pit white males against the rest of humanity. But these dichotomies, as Haslanger so ably points out, accord those characteristics considered to be hallmarks of being male to be consistent with the ideals of philosophy. That which is rational, objective, and of the mind frames philosophy as masculine while that which is emotional, subjective, and of the body, is not philosophical but feminine and non-white. With these distinctions, philosophy then is a male domain. Its attribute of being a male domain is seen in the very manner in which philosophy is done. It retains those characteristics that are seen as properly masculine as Haslanger argues; the qualities of penetrating, seminal and rigorous (argumentation) are a reserve for the philosopher white male. To attack, target and demolish an opponent is stuff of which male legends both real and fictional are made of. Hence, I suggest, philosophy is modeled on a gladiatorial system with all the trappings of warrior heroes. The rest of humanity can either be just spectators of the heroic gladiators or be left behind in their emotional, subjective and embodied experiences which are anathema to philosophy.

It is this nature of philosophy, or at least the view that Anglophone philosophy must essentially retain these characteristics, that leads to the overt and sometimes subtle discrimination against women and other races. It is as if there is a sort of an honor code that exists among philosophers themselves as to how philosophy is done and who qualifies to get into that project of philosophizing. Just like some clubs or organizations are seen as serving the gentry or limited to a select few, philosophy by its so-called hallmarks becomes an exclusive club of gentlemen who understand how to duel with each other in smart ways yet at the same time treat females with courtesy and non-whites with patronizing objectification. In the eyes of these gentlemen, they are the only ones who are supposed to understand the rules of combat, how an attack is launched, and in the event of coming under attack – how it is repulsed, and if subdued how to change one's position without betraying a fundamental misunderstanding of the rules of the game.

While other members of the human race may be allowed a peek into this game, they are not expected by the players to fully understand what the game is all about. Indeed it is like a professional footballer having a discussion with a zealous supporter on the last game the player featured in. The player can only be condescending or dismissive of the zealous supporter's view – it is after all merely a view from the stands. And there is a good reason why the supporter is in the stands: she is said to lack both the talent and temerity to be in the thick of things, so to speak. Philosophy is indeed a game, a game of brilliant minds, involving sparring, watching your opponent closely and punching as hard as possible whenever you can. It is also a game that is understood by a select few. And that select few knows how to choreograph its way around major themes, points, and sub-points within a philosophical debate. They are also quick to notice an impenetrable wall of argument and know when to retreat either to think the matter further or to abandon the fight. Any philosopher knows how to recognize a superior mind, and even if they disagree with that mind they can easily come to concede that such a mind is beautiful but probably misguided.

Besides the core business of philosophizing or reading texts philosophically, every philosophy student is also taught some non-philosophical values attendant to philosophy. I remember, when I had just started my Ph.D., how it was impressed upon me never ever to betray any emotional attachment to my position by showing offence when my position came under sustained attack by senior and highly experienced professors. Going through the motions of the first conference presentation, taking questions, withstanding the attacks and downright ridicule had to be handled 'philosophically'. And as a male, I had to handle that as a man. I have very indignant memories of my first ever international conference. For some very stupid reason I had not cared to notice who the keynote speaker was going to be. I prepared a paper criticizing some aspect of the keynote speaker's thoughts. Worse, I included the keynote speaker's name in my title. My session was filled to the brim with people eager to hear my 'critique'. When I arrived at the conference and realized that the keynote speaker was the subject of my 'critique' fear seized me. I confided to a colleague of my precarious situation. He chided but strengthened me. I read the paper to a capacity audience with the guru in attendance. I am convinced the paper was silly and the critique hopeless. One of the guru's former students denounced my project as unphilosophical, worthless, a waste of everyone's time. He encouraged me to abandon any attempt at philosophizing henceforth. The attacker was a full professor of repute. His attack was withering and merciless. I conceded and attempted to restate my position in a cold manner. At tea the attacker thought my demeanor praiseworthy and retracted his position that I should abandon philosophy. He expressed regret that he had left the continent instead of hanging around to train youngsters like myself. The attacker and I are now on most cordial of terms. I continue to view him with admiration and whenever I meet him, which is too infrequent, I enjoy both his stories as well as his presentations, and of course his unrelenting attacks on poor unsuspecting presenters. As for the guru, he refused to express an opinion on my views, but he lectured me a bit afterwards on other issues. I have gone on to develop a few points both for and against the guru in my work. In case you were wondering, this episode did not involve white Anglophones but black African males. But that is philosophy! All philosophers have to know how to attack, when to attack and most importantly who to attack. It is a rigorous, cold-blooded game of pure rationality, at least we think so.

But this sort of thing is something that is expected of males, or only appears to be acceptable when done by males. Philosophy itself originates and operates within the confines of real societies where discrimination against girls and women has a very strong presence and history. Girls are supposed to be tame and well behaved, mothering and nurturing, socialization states. It is an abnormality, as Haslanger points out, when a woman is seen slugging it out with the men. Hence the jokey suggestion to get herself examined to check whether she is not a man after all.

The simple point is that the gladiatorial nature of philosophy is seen as temperamentally more suited to men. Moreover, not any man can participate in it; those who do must be special men. And when they enter the theatre of gladiators they have to go through the rituals of merciless humiliation. If they can live up to it they get inducted into the rarefied field of philosophy where only one thing counts: brute rationality. They are then tasked with raising the next generation of philosophers, and as properly inducted members they must choose carefully who, in the next generation, will carry the torch of brute rationality.

But philosophy is about the human condition. This or that human being is the proper subject of philosophy, the proper beneficiary of philosophical endeavor. When this or that human being seeks to participate in philosophical discourse but does so from a perspective that is not insistent on brute rationality, they are treated as being unphilosophical. It is worse still if they turn out to be women or persons of color. Yet a simple, self-evident truth is that we all have ideas about our condition and existence as human beings. While we do not have all to become philosophers, there will always be philosophers or potential philosophers in all human groups. The philosophers who might emerge from their particular group are those who reflect on the basics they have learnt or observed from their group. They might have questions about some aspect of existence or may seek to find answers to questions that already exist. The determinant of these possibilities is always the location of the people and their lived experience. It can never be a uniform appeal to the rigors of rationality. This does not mean that the rigors of rationality count for nothing. What it simply means is that such rigors may appeal to a particular group for a variety of reasons that may not be present in another group.

However, what must be admitted is that the ultimate aim of philosophy is to grasp or interpret reality in ways that guarantee making sense of that reality. Life is about what we perceive and what we see. But what we perceive and see is not always easily accessible to all of us by way of simple and direct impressions. What is available to us may only be the half of it or may be presented in confusing and contradictory ways. Our own frame of reference and/or background gives us the ability to move on to the philosophical level of attempting to understand what reality is, from a philosophical view.

If this understanding of philosophy is correct, then an admission must be made that there is not just one single way of doing philosophy. While rigorous pursuit of cold rationality is one way, there are other possible avenues of philosophizing which are perfectly legitimate ways of attempting to grasp reality through philosophical lenses. While it is agreed that philosophy is essentially about reason, what is not universally agreed on is the very nature of reason itself. If philosophical reason was to be seen as of the male, Anglophone sort, it would fail to correlate with other people's experiences. It would be as if the experiences of other people did not matter unless aligned to the male Anglophone experience. But here is the problem: the male Anglophone experience, while a legitimate way of both experiencing reality and approaching it philosophically, is but just one form of experience. There are myriad other experiences and philosophical realities which must be allowed to work their own philosophical commitments. This ultimately includes how female Anglophones and non-whites both see reality, including the reality of their relations with white male Anglophones. It also includes how each set of players chooses to interpret their own reality as a lived experience in tandem with other people and other agencies that shape their lives. Refusing to acknowledge the need for the articulation of such philosophical experiences is nothing short of tyranny.

The discrimination that women share with non-white males in philosophy is one suggested by Haslanger above. It is believed that the only group that is capable of rationality in the sort of way that philosophy is done in the

Western world are white males. Indeed, Lucien Lévy-Bruhl (1995, originally published in 1910) offers a lengthy but false discourse on how primitives think. The falsity of his discourse does not so much lie in the description of primitive mentality but in the underlying belief that the Western mind is one that is of a superior form and that any positive trajectory of thought must aim at arriving at Western logic. The problem is presenting Western logic as if it were the most pure form of thinking that necessarily defines thinking-proper. As Kwasi Wiredu (1995) notes, this comparison is hopeless. Wiredu argues that each epoch has a specific philosophical outlook. Traditional societies compare well while non-traditional societies do not compare well to traditional societies. Lévy-Bruhl's thinking that the Western modern mind is one that is most sophisticated betrays his own misunderstanding of what a possible fruitful comparison will have to do. Such a fruitful comparison, according to Wiredu, must be between traditional Western societies and traditional African societies. The result of such a comparison will show that both societies share a fundamental spiritistic outlook on life. What then is called the primitive mind is not typical of only a certain people or race but is generally shared by traditional societies everywhere. However, as Wiredu argues, the desire to maintain the traditional and spiritistic references in Africa is driven by various agendas, such as those of nationalists who seek to find an authentic African political outlook, by African-Americans in search of their roots, or Westerners looking for an exotic diversion.

But the tag that women are different from men is well maintained in philosophy's founding texts and figures. Jenkins and Hutchison (2013, p. 2) point to Kant and Schopenhauer, who defend the view that women are intellectually inferior to men. The point is that the stereotype of women and other races that cannot philosophize in the same manner as white males is well established; both are charged with being overly emotional and incapable of seeing reason.

## African philosophy as a site of counter-hegemony

As already argued, the development of Western philosophy as a specialized field of reflecting on reality and how humans apprehend it was not presented as limited to the specific context from which it originated. On the contrary, its founders and practitioners spoke and wrote of that specific reality as if it was the sole reality that was supposed to be true of all humanity everywhere. Those human beings who failed to live up to these expectations were either seen as perfect targets for the 'civilization' project or were condemned to a sub-human status. These complementary views proceeded to work together to create the snooty position that the West had about its standing and accompanying mission to conquer the so-called 'uncivilized' nations.

With the colonial mission well underway, and the oppression of the black person institutionalized, the philosophical status of the African continent was equally condemned. Black political leaders and activists took it upon themselves to debunk the inferiorization of the black person and subsequently agitate for their freedom. It was this process that saw the birth of African philosophy. The political struggle was not merely restricted to the political freedoms and political claims of black people; it was also fittingly extended to apply to the pride and standing of African people vis-à-vis cultural achievement. Such cultural achievement would have been a derivative of the philosophical standing of the people. Little wonder, then, that the pioneering stalwarts of Africa's struggles for political freedom also dabbled in political philosophy. Not only did they aim at articulating a philosophical orientation that would be both local and an informant of the political trajectory that newly independent states were to take, they also sought to affirm the reflective capacity of the black person.

Whether by historical coincidence or design, the nationalist/ideological orientation in philosophy, as identified by Henry Odera Oruka (1998), was made of men. For Oruka what was important in his male oriented view was that a new class of gladiators, one can say, had emerged in the African context. This class had fought the political fight and was now at the forefront of the philosophical fight. However, it is quite curious that Oruka sees the political trend, as one promoted by men alone. This claim completely ignores the contribution of women in the Mau Mau in Kenya, and in the struggle for independence in Algeria, and the Aba women's riot in Nigeria, for example. That Oruka fails to identify the philosophical underpinnings of such gallant efforts testifies to the deliberate creation of a male-dominated narrative, conceptually and practically.

Another group of thinkers identified by Oruka as professional philosophers also emerged, and it was exclusively composed of men. The three names credited with spearheading this group are Peter O. Bodunrin, Kwasi Wiredu and Paulin Hountondji. This was another class of gladiators that was interested in advancing the idea that there indeed was a brand of African philosophy that could live up to the rigors and demands of Western philosophy. Indeed, the rigor is evident in the harsh chastisement of the elevation of traditional philosophy to the status of African philosophy, and in the condemnation of backward Western views on the capacity, or lack thereof, of the black person to philosophize.

It could possibly be a matter of chance that the black man, not the black woman, emerges at the forefront of philosophizing on the African continent. But it would be naive to seriously believe that the dominance of males in African philosophy is an accident. What is much more likely is that philosophy in Africa pretty much followed the same structural form of emphasizing what are considered to be male characteristics at the expense of non-male attributes. Now, Ogotemmeli occupies a permanent place in traditional African philosophy, but whatever one's attitude or thoughts about him, his conversation with, or lecture to, Marcel Griaule makes for compulsory reading. For a start, the sage philosopher Ogotemmeli demonstrates that it is false to think that Africans were incapable of speculation of a philosophical kind. But according to Griaule, very early on in his book *Conversations with Ogotemmeli*, at the very beginning of the encounter between these two men the following is what apparently first troubled Ogotemmeli:

> The longest task of the first day was the choice of a place for the conversations. The space in front of the dwelling-house, even if the aged Ogotemmeli remained indoors, and even if the white man bent his head towards him and spoke in low tones as if in the confessional, was, according to Ogotemmeli, open to the objection that interviews there might excite the eternal curiosity of the women. The minute courtyard on the other side of the building, on the other hand, which was exposed to all the winds from the north, might be watched by children hidden in the ruined granary. There remained the courtyard itself with its wretched dung-heap, its hollow stone, and its dilapidated wall with a gap in the middle of it just high enough for curious eyes to look through.
>
> Ogotemmeli still hesitated; he had much to say about the inconvenience of the courtyard for the purpose of conversations between men of mature years. The European for his part did not open his mouth except to agree; he even stressed the indiscreet nature of walls and the stupidity of men, and naturally, the unconscionable curiosity of women and their insatiable thirst for novelties.
>
> (Griaule, 1970, pp. 12–13)

What we should read into the above quote is not merely the process of choosing a place. On the contrary, what is at play is how philosophy is deliberately made to be a male endeavor and how it is actively to be hidden from women, children and probably some 'stupid' men. It is quite clear that the two interlocutors view themselves as mature men, men of wisdom, who are under some obligation to keep philosophical exchanges between themselves as representatives of the European and African view. The eternal curiosity that is accorded women is not seen as something good but as only aroused when the women intrude into conversations they should not be participating in. Only a little later the women's curiosity is described in very harsh terms as 'unconscionable'. There is agreement between these two mature men that women should be kept out of philosophy as they bring something so bad that it warrants describing as unconscionable to the project of loving wisdom.

If Ogotemmeli represents a part of the development of the history of philosophy in Africa, or if his is a part that should be known by all engaged in African philosophy, then his views on the barring of women from philosophy must be exposed. While there are views that women were accorded a special and protected status in African societies, as far as Ogotemmeli was concerned that status did not extend to cover philosophical issues.

If African philosophy can be said to run counter to the hegemony of Western philosophy and is a vista through which we could transcend the limited male Anglophone manner of seeing and understanding philosophy, then it has also to provide ways in which women's status and views on philosophy may be handled. The origins of African philosophy lay in the attempt to show the African as naturally suited to philosophy as the European. The importance of such a demonstration lay in the fact that the project of philosophizing and the ability to philosophize was seen as evidence of the humanity or civilized status of a people. The idea of philosophizing shows the ability of a people to engage with the world around them in ways that are distinctly human. They are evidence of a self-reflecting engagement. It is in the articulation of that self-reflective engagement that the human being transcends her biological matter to become a fully rational animal. But two things are at play here; the first is the process of becoming self-reflective. It is crucial that we note that self-reflection means exactly that: self-reflection. If it is done in engagement with the outside world what is at play is the individual's own understanding of her own self and her external world and how she ultimately makes sense of it. The second aspect is that the rational engagement that the individual uses to make sense of the world is specific to the forces and factors that shape her own rationality. The development of African philosophy, particularly in its modes as the nationalist/ideological trend and the professional trend, sought to advance these very aspects of human reality.

African philosophy is conceived as a place where the prerogative of the subject to speak on her or his own behalf and account is legitimized. The legitimacy to claim philosophical ability lies in the shared essence and nature of being human. We cannot help but be entities that wonder. And it is in wonder that philosophy begins. Wondering is an essential and integral part of this species. What is contingent is the stuff that we could wonder about and how we eventually wonder about that stuff. But wonder we will. For example, all philosophers of all traditions and of all peoples have wondered on the purpose of life and the possibility of an afterlife. What matters is that these are questions that have occurred to philosophers and they are questions they have earnestly sought to provide answers to. What does not matter is that there are different conclusions reached in answer to these questions.

What African philosophy does is to show that the notion and process of wondering about one's surroundings and one's own place in those surroundings is an inescapable part of our constitution. We cannot ignore that aspect of ourselves because it is constitutive of what contributes to the making of our nature. What has only to be distinguished, as shown by Wiredu, is the idea of wondering in a traditional set-up and wondering in a modern set-up. In other words traditional philosophy is not to be equated with modern philosophy, and cross-cultural comparisons between modern versions of philosophy and traditional versions will only yield an unjustified claim to superiority of the modern version.

African philosophy, as a site of counter-hegemony in relation to Western philosophy, achieves two things; first, from the articulations of traditional philosophy to its modern version, we see how philosophy is not a closed project but one that is given to constant change and revision. Philosophical issues in

Africa, just as in the West, can be categorized according to the epochs from which they originate. We could talk of traditional philosophy and modern philosophy. Modern philosophy could have its antecedents in traditional philosophy and that traditional philosophy can be subdivided into facets such as pre-colonial, colonial, and post-colonial traditional philosophy. This would be similar to the stages that are given to Western philosophy such as ancient, medieval, modern, and contemporary philosophy. From this we can see how philosophy is time-specific and how even within the same geographical area it can go through radical changes. Second, philosophizing is a natural and essential human trait. What cannot be disputed is that all humans philosophize. However, what is likely to be debated is the exact nature of philosophizing in each context and how that procedure is deemed to live up to the requisite task of philosophizing. A simple definition of philosophy which is to be found in its etymology is 'love of wisdom'. Wisdom is a poly-term and notion that cannot be confined or reduced to a particular orientation. As there are many accounts and experiences of the world, so also are there many accounts of interpretation.

## African philosophy's injustice against women

While I do not seek to suggest that there is a straight comparison between the plight of women in philosophy in the West and those in sub-Saharan Africa, I wish to argue that there are some shared similarities in the professional outlook of philosophy that actively discriminate against women. While it is true that women's struggles may be said to share some characteristics, particularly in philosophy, it is equally true that there are differences in those struggles. However, the similarity that I wish to pursue here has to do with how philosophy has been constructed as a male domain right from its conception, both on the African continent and in the Western world, and how that attitude has been subtly perpetuated in the academies of both spheres. The charge I seek to prove is not necessarily one of straightforward sexist bigotry, but a rather subtle exclusion of women by way of the very conception of philosophy as an activity that is exclusively male.

The failure of African philosophy to be an effective counter-hegemonic style of philosophizing relative to the domineering Western enterprise lies at the roots of what the pioneering figures in modern African philosophy sought to achieve (Wiredu 2009, pp. 1–36; Hountondji, 1996, pp. 55–70). These pioneers either received a significant part of their training or obtained their doctorates from their former metropole. They followed a strict curriculum which naturally emphasized the philosophical greats of the colonial masters and their associates. What was being transferred to our first generation of professional philosophers was the 'proper' way of doing philosophy, namely the Western, male-dominated mode of philosophizing. Thus the professionalization of philosophy on the African continent was largely externally generated. The trained philosophers were sensitized to the combative method of philosophizing which emphasized rigor, reason (seen as clarity of thought), and the twin beauties of attacking and defending. There is so much to be said in favor of this approach. The good that can be said about it is that there is nothing wrong with being rigorous, emphasizing reason, and having the ability to attack one's opponents and defend one's position.

However, these attributes, as argued above, are the hallmarks of the distinction that traditional Western philosophy has kept alive to actively discourage women from doing philosophy. These attributes are not only seen as something that properly constitutes the activity of doing philosophy but as the mark of sensible men who qualify to be philosophers. As Kant and Schopenhauer maintain, the distinction between men and women is to be found in that men retain mental attributes while women are bodily creatures. The same distinction is also extended to apply to non-whites, particularly Africans.

The founding professional philosophers on the African continent worked very hard to disprove the charge that Africans were overly bodily. At the same time they had to disprove the authenticity of other competing strands of African philosophy. The outcome of the combination of these two goals was that African philosophy had to be made to appear as technical as the philosophy of the metropole. In becoming ever more technical or as closely technical as the philosophy of the metropoles, African philosophy unwittingly started excluding the possibility of incorporating other voices within its context that could contribute to the development of a truly counter-hegemonic form of philosophy. The emphasis was, for example, on how the integrity of 'philosophy' was going to be maintained even with the prefix 'African'. But what the maintenance of that integrity really amounted to was the retention of the stereotypical attributes associated with Western philosophers.

An example of how alternative ways of philosophizing on the continent were resisted suffices to capture the point I seek to make. When Léopold Sédar Senghor (1964) tailored his philosophy along the lines of Aimé Césaire's notion of *négritude*, with clear and unapologetic emphasis on the negro's difference from the white person (including the philosophical), he was condemned for reducing philosophy to some levels that were hardly recognizable as philosophy. His emphasis on emotion as a mode of knowing was condemned as denying the negro the right to claiming that he could know in the same rigorous manner as the white person. While these rejections of Senghor's position could be valid or well stated, what they fail to notice is that philosophical discourse cannot be limited to the Western white male understanding of it. Philosophical thought can begin in any manner and form and it can be started by anyone, including those suspected of being overly emotional such as women and black people.

Thus what has developed now into a fully-fledged modern African philosophy bears all the hallmarks of Western philosophy. Although philosophy is admittedly not regulated in the same way as professions such as law and medicine, those who retain the title of philosopher are men and women formally employed at universities and colleges. They not only have the authority to run their departments, but they constitute what is recognized as a legitimate body of producers of specific and expert knowledge through peer evaluation. It is therefore very hard, if not impossible, for anyone outside university structures, or for anyone who does not subject herself to this peer-review system, to claim the title, let alone be accepted as a philosopher.

In Africa, women who wish to follow the path of philosophizing have to deal with the structurally sanctioned male codification of philosophy, and have to overcome this codified system which operates at every level of being a philosopher. Louise du Toit describes the picture I have painted of the reasons for the absence of women in African philosophy as a developmental explanation. However, she does not take this to be the full picture. On the contrary, she argues that women have deliberately chosen not to take up philosophy. In relation to the possibility of women entering philosophy in the future, and the reasons why the first generation of women chose not to take up philosophy she writes:

> But of course, even if more African women enter the discipline at a later stage, it leaves open the possibility that the first generations consciously or sub-consciously resisted entering it, found it unhelpful or unsatisfactory, possibly even oppressive. Without being able to go into too much detail here, I must mention one further distinction, namely between the philosophical ideal of open, flexible and equal exchanges of ideas and the closed, inflexible and highly unequal ways in which the discipline is very often institutionalized. Flawed institutionalization might in other words be to blame more than 'the discipline as such', but then it might be precisely what makes philosophy philosophical that has been seen as unpalatable or an obstacle. I will pursue this line of thought below. For the sake of my argument, I ask the reader to entertain with me the possibility that African women thinkers currently not only reject Philosophy as a discipline, but that they prefer literary writing as a form of intellectual self-expression.
>
> (du Toit, 2008, p. 416)

She then goes on to argue that the fictional writings of women, in which they present issues from their perspectives, is a direct challenge to the masculine presentation of the world. Though philosophy, she maintains, presents itself as if it were speaking about universals applicable to all, it actually only speaks from the perspectives of men. She states that this situation is not only unique to African women challenging African philosophers but can be seen in the West, especially with Plato's feminizing of poetry. That process, according to du Toit, shows

> the extent to which Plato was in an ironic sense right when he feminized poetry – he was being honest about the masculine nature of his philosophical enterprise, and contradicting his own universalizing aspirations.

> Masculine fears and interests can only pose as universal for so long as the feminine is framed as an inferior, deviant or lacking version of the masculine-universal.
>
> (2008, p. 426)

I find it hard to accept du Toit's main thesis. While she agrees that part of the problem is the historical presentation of philosophy as a masculine endeavor which does not allow women in, she then proposes that the absence of women in African philosophy is an expression of a preference for other modes of intellectual activity such as writing fiction. On top of that she claims that the ideal of philosophy as open is different from the actual practice of institutionalized philosophy which is closed and masculine. The reason why I find du Toit's conclusion hard to accept is that it surely would be strange for people to protest against something by avoiding confrontation with the very object of the injustice that is caused by that thing. While it is perfectly legitimate to, in some instances, boycott a product or some other article of trade, as a result of dissatisfaction with some aspect associated with it, the same cannot be said of the struggles by women vis-à-vis the masculinity of philosophy. It is odd that women can be said to choose fiction writing over showing their capabilities in philosophizing. While fiction writing may be a legitimate form of expressing women's experiences, it is hardly the most effective way of starting the process of reforming philosophy. If it is a conscious decision made by women as du Toit claims, then it remains to be seen how effective they think their strategy is in forcing philosophy to reckon with its sexist outlook.

If this were a serious choice that women are said to really have made it can only mean that it is a choice by default. It is not really a choice but something they eventually choose to do because of the great hostility to women that is naturally associated with philosophy. I suggest that what du Toit describes as a choice is actually a far cry from what real choices are made of. It is not as if women are given a fair chance to pursue philosophy with the dignity and respect accorded white males who choose to pursue it. The choice that du Toit says women make is not even a choice since it is a commonly accepted principle that fiction writing is less rigorous than philosophy, far less strenuous. It is unusual to make a choice that confirms one's suspected inferiority.

A more promising strategy would be one where women force philosophy to reckon with its false assumption that there is something about philosophy that makes it inherently and uniquely ill-suited for 'real' women to do. African philosophy has a particular obligation to aggressively promote the presence of women in its ranks, as its basic foundation is one of protest against the monolithic interpretation of philosophy from the Western white male's view.

## Conclusion

The failure of African philosophy in relation to women is in the way that it has presented itself as an alternative to a cynical and domineering system while at the same time retaining the same structures of exclusion inherent in the very system it seeks to replace. African philosophy, by seeking to challenge the dominance of the view of white males, had a lot of promise in contributing to the development of multiple approaches to philosophical engagements. However, in its attempt to show itself as capable of analytical rigor it has been forced into a corner of exclusivity. That exclusivity has no merit, as it is simply an option of philosophizing from a male perspective. If African philosophy is to regain its initial promise of inclusivity, it must do more to get rid of its structural trappings in a male oriented framework of philosophizing. This should not be taken as suggesting that African philosophy should abandon reason, but it must be seen as a call for African philosophy to genuinely acknowledge the plural nature of reason.

# Reference

Amadiume, I. (1987). *Male Daughters, Female Husbands: Gender and Sex in an African Society.* London: Zed Books.

du Toit, L. (2008). Old wives' tales and philosophical delusions: on the problem of women and African philosophy. *South African Journal of Philosophy*, 27 (4), 413–428.

Griaule, M. (1970). *Conversations with Ogotemmeli: An Introduction to Dogon Religious Ideas.* London: Oxford University Press.

Grimshaw, J. and Fricker, M. (2003). Philosophy and feminism. In N. Bunnin and E. P. Tsui-James (eds), *The Blackwell Companion to Philosophy* (pp. 552–566). Hoboken, NJ: John Wiley & Sons.

Haslanger, S. (2008). Changing the ideology and culture of philosophy: not by reason (alone). *Hypatia*, 23 (2), 210–223.

Hountondji, P. J. (1996). *African Philosophy: Myth and Reality.* Bloomington, IN: Indiana University Press.

Jenkins, F. and Hutchison, K. (2013) Introduction: Searching for Sofia: Gender and philosophy in the 21st century. In K. Hutchison and F. Jenkins (eds), *Women in Philosophy: What Needs to Change?* (pp. 1–21). New York: Oxford University Press.

Lévy-Bruhl, L. (1995). How natives think. In A. G. Mosley (ed.), *African Philosophy: Selected Readings* (pp. 40–61). Englewood Cliffs, NJ: Prentice-Hall.

Oruka, H. O. (1998). Sage philosophy. In P. H. Coetzee and A. P. J. Roux (eds), *Philosophy from Africa: A Text with Readings* (pp. 98–108). Johannesburg: International Thomson Publishing.

Oyewumi, O. (1997). *The Invention of Women: Making an African Sense of Western Gender Discourses.* Minneapolis, MN: University of Minnesota Press.

Senghor, L. S. (1964). *On African Socialism.* New York: Praeger.

Wiredu, K. (1995). How not to compare African thought with Western thought. In A. G. Mosley (ed.), *African Philosophy: Selected Readings* (pp. 159–171). Englewood Cliffs, NJ: Prentice-Hall.

Wiredu, K. (2009). *Philosophy and African Culture.* New York: Cambridge University Press.

# 9 Conceptual decolonization in African philosophy

## Views on women

*Oladele Abiodun Balogun*

### Introduction: the meaning of African philosophy

To define African philosophy is as problematic as defining philosophy as an academic discipline. The reason is because of the varied conceptions of the discipline, arising mainly from the different philosophical orientations on the debate surrounding the existence or non-existence of African philosophy. It is not the purpose of this chapter to undertake an elaborate discussion on the meanings and history of African philosophy. My attempt at discussing the idea of African philosophy is only to state succinctly its meaning. In this regard, two important definitions of African philosophy shall be given. First, African philosophy can be seen as a rational and systematic inquiry into the fundamental problems confronting the African world, with a view to understanding and providing plausible solutions to them. As a corollary and second, African philosophy can be defined as an analytical, critical and reconstructive evaluation of both African traditional cultural experience and modern cultural heritage in pursuit of useful living for the Africans. Its nature consists of clarifying concepts, puzzles and problems that are embedded in issues of life and rooted in African belief systems. African philosophers expose and explain various beliefs, values and ideas before they begin to analyze and interpret them in their philosophical investigations. In an attempt to do this, they subject all issues and objects of their investigations to systematic reflection. Consequent upon this is critical evaluation, which reflects the argumentative nature of the discipline. By its very nature, African philosophy thrives on mutual criticism in a culture of rational dialogue. African philosophy is an intellectual engagement with reconstruction of values, beliefs and social norms supposedly held to be obsolete and absolute. It, in addition, compares various world-views for the purpose of obtaining cross-cultural understanding and perspectives. Indeed, it is a cognitive discipline that examines African experiences, that calls into question all the different aspects of African life – religion, politics, social life, morality, economy, technology and other fundamental issues by offering new interpretations and syntheses of African experiences.

What I have said above in some way corroborates what others have said. A host of African philosophers like Peter Bodunrin (1984), Kwasi Wiredu

(1991), Bruce Janz (2009), Jonathan Chimakonam (2015), have all offered opinions as to the nature and goal of African philosophy as a discipline. For lack of space, I will not detail their submissions here. One point of convergence for all is with regard to the nature of African philosophy as a reflective enterprise with reason as its tool. This shows that philosophy is the same everywhere irrespective of which tradition is mentioned.

Thus African philosophy offers the context for my discussion in this chapter, which concerns two hotly debated issues, namely women and decolonization. In this postcolonial era, is there a need to decolonize the colonial legacies? What has the colonial culture done to the African idea of womanhood? And taking into account the postcolonial realities, is there a need to decolonize the concept of women? These questions shall direct the course of my inquiry in this chapter.

First, I present a preliminary discussion on the themes of colonization and decolonization. Second, I single out the concept of women and attempt to decolonize it within the bourgeoning field of African philosophy. Third, I use the Yoruba cultural framework as my context to show just how Western or colonial influence could distort our conceptual accumulations in African philosophy and to make the case for the veracity and necessity of conceptual decolonization as a strategy. In the next section I will discuss the concept of colonization vis-à-vis conceptual decolonization as articulated by Wiredu.

## Colonization vs. decoloniation

The concept of decolonization presupposes colonization. Whenever one thinks of colonization, especially colonization in Africa, what comes to mind includes the external political domination of natives, or, the partition of Africa and the eventual physical conquest of the continent. While it includes these, colonization and its effects entail more than the political repression and domination of the African continent by the European nations. Besides the geographical mapping and partitioning of the continent, political colonization also translates to the colonization of African thought and the entirety of African ways of life. Much as political colonization has been officially declared over across the world (though not without its newly clothed form of imperialism and neo-colonialism), mental colonialism remains very much alive, decades after the end of political colonization in Africa. Mental colonialism involves the unavoidable influence and involvement of alien modes of thinking in the thought process, attitude and approach to life of indigenous Africans. The three principal avenues of mental colonization which one can readily identify here are language, religion and politics.

The mental colonization of the Africans by the erstwhile colonizers through the above avenues has led to an uncritical assimilation of the conceptual schemes embedded in foreign languages and culture in contemporary ways of life and modes of thought among Africans. 'The African today', Wiredu (1995, p. 22) rightly notes, 'as a rule, lives in a cultural flux characterized by a confused interplay between an indigenous cultural heritage and a foreign cultural legacy of colonial origin'. The most fundamental and subtle consequence of this cultural condition is 'the historical superimposition of foreign categories of thought upon African thought systems' (Wiredu, 1995, p. 19). This superimposition, besides the pernicious effects it has had on contemporary African society, has generated distortions of African world-views. Given this situation, Olusegun Oladipo (1996, p. 19) in consonance with Wiredu says that the need for conceptual decolonization in African philosophy has become very urgent.

Indeed, one of the major preoccupations of contemporary African philosophers should be the task of conceptual decolonization. Conceptual decolonization, Oladipo (2006, p. 143) observes, 'is not out of any obeisance to the god of authenticity, but a desirable step in making African philosophy an aspect of African social and cultural experience'. Such a task is unavoidable in Africa today because many of the problems of self-understanding and other pre-dicaments experienced on the continent are closely connected with the uncritical superimposition of alien categories of thought on African conceptual understanding. The pernicious effects of this on the distortion of African world-views, values and cultural understanding are not too difficult to imagine.

Wiredu is one of the originators of the idea of conceptual decolonization in African philosophy (Oladipo, 2006, p. 144). His idea can be regarded as a key aspect of what the Kenyan writer Ngugi Wa Thiong'o has called the decolonization of the mind (Oladipo, 2006, p. 144). To Ngugi, African minds have been colonized as a result of their interaction with the West. Their minds have been trained and conditioned to see things and analyze events using the Western canon, and as a result they have been unwittingly carrying out their business of analysis with 'conceptual ontologies' embedded in the foreign languages of colonization (Afolayan, 2006, p. 46).

Furthermore, Ngugi argues that Africans were colonized linguistically by the West, in such a way that the language of the West has been used politically as an instrument of cultural alienation, thus any attempt by the Africans to force themselves from this cultural alienation should not be carried out within the ambit of the European languages (Afolayan, 2006, p. 46). In other words, to Ngugi, the European languages played a formidable part in separating Africans from their languages and the denial of their collective self, more especially in binding them as a continent to a cultural and cognitive structure of dependence which neo-colonization and imperialism perpetuate (Afolayan, 2006, p. 46).

The thrust of Ngugi's argument is that the uncritical adoption of European languages in undertaking the task of philosophy in Africa will be disastrous for African conceptual schemes and cultural understandings, and he concludes that decolonization of mind can only be successful and meaningful if European languages are overthrown in our attempt to shift the center away from the West. This is further corroborated by Wiredu's assertion that: 'The English language, as Ngugi sees it, cannot lay any claim to a cultural or political innocence; every part of the grammatical and semantic structure is shot through with the imperialistic ethos' (Wiredu, 1995, p. 90).

While it is true that Ngugi's argument is open to criticism, I think he has successfully established a case for the decolonization of African concepts in an attempt to differentiate African belief systems from those of the West, otherwise, the Western culture would totally subsume and swallow African culture, all in the name of universalism or globalization.

Wiredu's idea of conceptual decolonization can be regarded as an offshoot, or better still, an extension of Ngugi's decolonization of the mind. The reason for Wiredu's advocacy of conceptual decolonization is not far-fetched. Such a task is unavoidable in Africa today because many of the problems of self-understanding and other predicaments experienced on the continent have to do with the uncritical superimposition of alien categories of thought on African conceptual understanding. The pernicious, distorting effects of this on African world-views, values and cultural understanding are not too difficult to imagine (Wiredu, 1995, p. 33).

Conceptual decolonization entails two inter-related issues. First, it negatively involves the avoidance or reversal 'through a critical conceptual self awareness of the uncritical assimilation in African philosophical traditions which have exercised considerable influence on African life and thought' (Wiredu, 1995, p. 33). Wiredu argues that cultural flux in Africa which has brought about a confused interplay between an indigenous cultural heritage and a foreign cultural legacy of colonial origin has produced a lot of distortions of African world-view. As if this is not enough, this cultural flux which is characterized by confused interplay of both indigenous and foreign cultures has led to superimposition of foreign categories upon African thought systems (Wiredu, 1995, p. 33). To lend credence to the argument of Wiredu, it is discovered that in some recent books on African philosophy even those written by Africans, a lot of these distortions and superimpositions of alien accretions in interpretations of African conceptual schemes are glaring. Therefore, it is the submission of Wiredu that the task of conceptual decolonization must be urgently carried out in order to produce modern African philosophy that is relevant and truly represents African belief systems.

Second, it positively means judiciously exploring the resources of our own indigenous conceptual schemes in our philosophical meditations on even the most technical problems of contemporary philosophy (Wiredu, 1995, p. 33). The second side of conceptual decolonization, according to Wiredu, encourages the Africans to look inward and to make use of the indigenous resources available to them in undertaking philosophical meditations, so as to bring about the correct images and interpretations of African conceptual schemes (Oladipo, 2002, p. 42). Olusegun Oladipo summarizes the two sides of conceptual decolonization when he avers:

> The two sides of the meaning of conceptual decolonization given by Wiredu are complementary. They involve the comparable utilization of

different languages in philosophical thinking, with a view to guarding against the uncritical assimilation of conceptual schemes embedded in foreign languages and cultures and at the same time, promoting an adequate understanding of the intellectual foundations of African culture.

(Oladipo, 2002, p. 13)

In an attempt to pursue his agenda of domestication and decolonization of foreign ideas, Wiredu argues that a modern African philosopher must be ready to subject all inherited foreign categories of conceptualizations to systematic and critical reflection, in other words, the African must direct her thought in all modes of conceptualization emanating from the colonial past that cannot stand the task of due reflection (Wiredu, 1995, p. 95). Such concepts which must be decolonized according to Wiredu include: Reality, Being, Death, Afterlife, Mind, Soul, Spirit, and host of others (knowledge inclusive) (Bewaji, 2006, p. 7).

Conceptual decolonization has the benefit of promoting cross-cultural understanding in African philosophical studies. It is helpful in the search for African identities, as it promotes the understanding of the intellectual foundations of African culture. In view of the importance of conceptual decolonization, African philosophers are enjoined to take it seriously in their philosophical endeavors with the hope of overall progress in modern day Africa.

## Colonialism and women's image in contemporary Africa

One of the effects of colonialism on contemporary African society is the widespread of distorted view of womenfolk which has led to discrimination against women. This can be traced to the colonial impact. According to Sophie Oluwole, at the beginning of colonial rule in Nigeria, pregnancies and/or marriage marked the end of an educated woman's career (Oluwole, 1995, p. 18). In other words, the colonial philosophy encouraged the subjugation of women, denial of equal rights with their male counterparts, oppression of women and unjust treatment as second fiddles in the society. Our argument in this chapter is that with the introduction of colonialism, the original African view of women has been distorted and bastardized due to the foundation of the oppressive philosophy of the West. An exploration of the metaphysical and epistemological origin of the oppression of women in the West would be of utmost importance to buttress our claim. Metaphysics, as practiced in the West, started as an objective study of nature but with an inherent disguised form of evaluation which entails an implicit classificatory element (Oluwole, 1995, p. 18) of either superior or subsidiary/inferior. This kind of analysis can be seen in the writings of the Ionian philosophers like Thales, Anaximander and Anaximenes. For example, on the one hand, Thales observed that although there were changes everywhere, that things changed from one form to another. Nevertheless, there was continuity in the midst of the changes. There was always something which did not change but remained permanent and persisted through the change which to him could be regarded as the fundamental stuff underlying everything. He opines that water is the original element from which all things are made. Water is the underlying unit in all things (Omoregbe, 1990, p. 72). On the other hand, Anaximander held that the original element, the primary stuff from which all things are made is a neutral element which is infinite, eternal and indeterminate; while to Anaximenes, it is air (Omoregbe, 1990, p. 73). This kind of philosophy is also reflected in the epistemology of the West, which regards truth as superior to opinion and knowledge as higher than belief. The philosophy of Plato and his successors like Aristotle also displayed the discriminatory element. For example, when Aristotle was justifying slavery, one of his premises was that the male can be regarded as superior, being always stronger than the subsidiary female. This kind of philosophy is the beginning of the oppression and the unjust treatment of women which is now predominant in contemporary African society. To exacerbate the crisis of oppression, Judeo-Christian thought, as exemplified by the Bible, treats women as inferior to men. They are not supposed to lead like men, they are to always keep quiet in the church and be submissive to their husbands at home. This point is well captured by Oluwole when she argues

> Judeo-Christian thought and Hellenism both share similar conception of the woman. Man is the primary stuff from which a woman was originally made. The woman caused the downfall of man and by implication, that of his descendants. Sinful Eve put an everlasting blemish on Saint Adam.
> (Oluwole, 1995, p. 20)

With the philosophical undertone of the colonial masters as exemplified above, and their administrative activities, women were relegated to the background. They were rendered invisible by the exclusively male colonial domination. Women were deliberately neglected by the colonial masters, especially the British. Many women were stripped of their titles. Thus, they were neglected and excluded from the political sphere. In the words of Nina Mba, during the colonial period, women were considered unsuitable for the rigors of public life, hence they were not allowed to vote, to contest elections, to sit in parliaments, or to be employed in the civil service. The British administrators created an atmosphere in which there were no women at any level and therefore, they did not expect or wish to find women involved in government in southern Nigeria (Mba, 1982, p. 39). In the area of the economy, colonialism promoted the rule of men over women, which was contrary to the initial division of labor between men and women during the pre-colonial era. It offered men greater incentives for going into large scale distributive and retail trades and eventually they superseded women. In agriculture, even where women were farmers, the men were encouraged to take over because as weaker vessels, the women were considered not to be as energetic or strong as their male counterparts. This caused women to be regarded as economically weak and feeble and accordingly subservient to their male counterparts. The imposition of the British legal system on Africa further deteriorated and distorted women's value. A number of changes which were introduced by the new legal system affected women negatively. Colonial values, which were anti-women in most cases, replaced the indigenous value placed on women. As against the indigenous legal system which allowed women some property rights, the imposed British system not only took away these rights from women but made them the property of their husbands.

In the area of religion, most of the religions practiced in Nigeria such as Christianity and Islam, relegate women to the background. Apart from the fact that these religions make men automatic rulers over women, women are also seen as things of dirt and also symbolize the unclean which should not be allowed near holy things. In the mosque, women are totally separated from the men and they cannot be allowed to occupy and pray on the same row with men because they are considered as inferior. Most of them are kept at home and the introduction of *pudah* system worsened the situation in that even when they are allowed to go out, their faces must be covered because they are regarded as the property of men. In Christianity, women are still struggling to overcome St Paul's injunction on women to keep silent in the church, and even today the right to ordination still eludes most women.

The problems and crises of women's oppression are also manifested in gender inequality, role differentiation and denial of educational, political and employment opportunities as masterminded by the colonial master. Lirieka Meintjes-Vander Wal (quoted in Grimshaw, 1986, p. 26) asserts that:

> Gender inequality is common to all women ... and is expressed in the home, the work place and in the public domain. Women tend to be poorer than men, often own less property than men, and are more likely to be unemployed. Those who are employed often receive fewer benefits, subsidies and recognition on the basis of gender and marital status.

She explains further that the work performed by women is not even recognized as an occupational activity and that women's opportunities to enjoy their rights and freedom are often hindered by societal and religious norms that discriminate against women. Feminists (both male and female) whatever their disposition, believe that women have been at the receiving end of unequal treatment and unnecessary discrimination in all spheres of life: socio-economic, political and religious.

Ayesha. M. Imam (1997, p. 3) has this to say concerning gender inequality:

> Despite constitutional provisions of equality before the law, women citizens are often constructed as dependants on husband in tax laws, as not competent to travel autonomously in provision for acquisition of visas and passports; as financial risks in requiring approval for loans and scholarship from husbands, and so on. Male citizens often have the

ability to pass on citizenship to children. They can often also decide both for themselves and for their wives whether or not they will have passports, travel, get loans or work – all of which are underwritten by state provisions imbued with particular gendered ideologies about masculine [sic] and control. The relationship of men and women citizens to the state are clearly not the same, and, are in both cases gendered relationships.

Similarly, Norman Vincent Peale (1971, p. 235) submits that:

If the good lord chooses to divide the human race into distinctive sexes, I do not see why anyone should try to blur the distinction. It seems to me that a man should possess and occasionally display the basic character-istics of the male animal ... a drive to be dominant in all areas, including marriage.

This kind of orientation portrayed by Peale explains why some men think it is their natural right to oppress the women as we have it in Nigeria. Also in the work of Buchi Emecheta, *The Slave Girl*, Ojiebeta the heroine learns that every woman, whether slave or free, belongs to some male. At birth, she is owned by her father and when she is sold, she belongs to a new master who has paid something for her and would control her.

Educationally, inequality also exists. Only a few women wrote anything prior to the dawn of the modern era in Nigeria, for three reasons. First, they rarely received the education that would enable them to write, as it was generally believed then that a woman's education ends in her kitchen. This explains why many women were not sent to school, especially in northern Nigeria. Second, not until recently were they admitted to public roles as administrators, bureaucrats, lawyers, notaries or university professors, where they might gain knowledge of the kinds of issues that occupy the minds of the literate public. Third, the culture imposed silence upon women, considering not speaking out as a form of chastity (Barnes, 1984, p. 328, quoted in Grimshaw, 1986).

## Decolonizing the concept of women: the Yoruba example

In decolonizing the concept of 'women' in modern Yoruba thought, it must be realized that before the Yoruba came in contact with the West, there was no women's oppression. The idea of women's liberation was alien. Our argument is that there was no gender crisis in Yoruba thought. It is prominent today as a result of Western experience. In other words, it is part of the pernicious effect of colonialism on African soil. This is because the Yoruba value system was characterized by a dual gender structure which emphasized, between the sexes, distinct but balanced and complementary functions. Colonialism con-tributed to the oppression of the Yoruba woman. Women had significant power and influence in Yoruba society before the advent of colonial rule. It was colonialism that undermined the legitimacy of women's political power by introducing philosophies which have oppressive undertones, and by so doing provided a philosophical basis for the oppression of women. It must be emphasized that in pre-colonial Yoruba thought, as in its society, both men and women were instruments of social, political and economic change. To substantiate the above, an exploration into the position and role of women in traditional Yoruba thought suffices.

The Yoruba pantheon consists of male and female deities. As Chinweizu puts it, 'in the Yoruba Pantheon, whereas Ogun is male and the god of war, Oshun is female and the goddess of river' (Chinweizu, 1993, p. 3). Within this pantheon, male and female cults existed, and both men and women could serve as priests and priestesses. Among the Ijebu for instance, 'Agemo' is a male cult with sixteen principal priests; while 'Olomitutu', who is a river goddess, has female fertility cult with priestesses (Adeoti, n.d., p. 49). In many other cults, however, membership is neither segregated by sex, nor are roles assigned on that basis. In fact, in some male cults, women are allowed membership and assigned important roles equaling those of men. One of such is the Egungun cult among the Ijebu Igbo people. Despite being male dominated, the Egungun cult permits priestesses in its activities.

Esaogbin Esufunke was the Orisagbemi of Agbowa and the Itale Oke-Sopin was a priestess of the Egungun cult in Ijebu Igbo. She had her own masquerade and knew all that went on in the group, including those behind the mask. Iya Agan, a woman, held a position (similar to the Egungun priest) popularly known as Oje. Iya Agan was free to go with any kind of Egungun and could enter into their shrines and grooves. Besides Iya Agan, who occupied a key position, other women sat on the supreme council of the Egungun cult. They included Iyalode and Iyamode. who were vested with the power to deal with several matters affecting the cults (Adeoti, n.d., pp. 62–63).

From the above, one can see that there was gender dualism among the Yoruba. Gender dualism in the context of this discourse means a well ordered society where power and responsibilities were shared between men and women and acknowledged as such, both in the home and the wider social milieu. Such sharing, it should be noted, did not preclude specialization. Specialization, however, was not based on sex (Chinweizu, 1993, p. 8).

Gender dualism was also reflected in the social organization of Yoruba society. This society was patrilineal: all members of the extended family lived in the same compound known as Agbole. The man was the head of the family and had authority over his household. The wives were expected to respect and honor him. Such respect did not necessarily imply male dominance. The men paid adequate attention to their wives, providing for them in times of illness and so on.

At home, the responsibilities were shared among the husband, wife and children. The husband was mainly responsible for providing food, shelter and other such needs of the family, sometimes with the assistance of the wife. The wives, however, were mostly concerned with the family affairs of home management and care of the children. The children supported their parents whenever the need arose.

Decisions at home were not taken by the husband alone. He was never seen as all wise, omniscient or a dictator. Wives took active part in decision making and, at times, children were not exempted. This is supported by the following Yoruba proverbs: *Eni kan ki gbon tan* meaning 'no one is omniscient or all wise'; *Omode gbon Agba gbon nia fi dale Ife* meaning 'children are wise, elders too are wise'; *Bo'kunrin ri ejo, Bo'birin pa, Ani kejo sa ti ku* meaning 'A snake seen by a male and killed by a female will not generate any problem, what matters is the death of the snake.' All these proverbs express the basis of Yoruba culture and emphasize the equal place of men and women in gender relations. Whether a problem at home is tackled by a husband or his wife, what matters to the Yoruba is whether the problem has been solved.

In the economic sphere, there was no gender conflict among the Yoruba because even in occupations where men dominated, there were typical divisions of functions among male and female and any keen woman could enter, excel and shine therein. As Chinweizu rightly puts it:

> Zoned to men are plantation farming, hunting, fishing and long distance trading. These are the activities which take place in the unsafe areas beyond the town walls. Within the safety of the town walls, women engage in food processing and local trading. In the technical crafts, which also are conducted in town, some are in the male sphere: iron smelting, smithing (iron, gold, copper, etc), tanning, carving, divination, drumming, etc. Others are in the female sphere, spinning, dyeing, pottery, bead making, etc.
>
> (Chinweizu, 1993, p. 4)

In Ijebu Igbo, women undertook those activities that were zoned to their male counterparts. For instance, some of the Ijebu women were specialists in plantation farming just as they were diviners. There appears thus to have been some harmony in the performance of functions between the two sexes in the economic sphere. As a matter of fact, the activities zoned to men were never regarded as superior nor were those of the women seen as inferior. Hence, the Yoruba would say *Agbajo owo la nfi soya*, meaning 'Total involvement for higher heights.'

In the political sphere, gender dualism was manifest in the valuation of contributions to the administration of the society. While it did seem that men dominated the scene, women's contribution was significant. For instance, Erelu and Iya Abiye were titled members of Osugbo secret cult which is one of the legislative arms of the town. The functions of these women were so important in the administration of the town that it has assumed a proverbial dimension:

*Da' gi ge, da' gi ge*
*Aake kan ko lee da gi ge*
*Da' gi la, da' gi la*
*Eele kan o le dagila*
*B'o s'erelu*
*Osugbo o lee da awo se*

Cutting alone, cutting alone
The axe cannot cut alone
Splitting alone, splitting alone
The wedge cannot split alone
Without Erelu (the women's representative)
Osugbo (the secret society) cannot operate alone.

(Oluwole, 1993, p. 13)

The above saying confirms that both sexes were recognized in political administration. In fact, if the Erelu was absent from Osugbo, no decision would be reached.

Furthermore, in every town of the Yoruba, there was an Iyalode or its equivalent charged with running the affairs of women in particular, and the society in general. Thus Mba (1982, p. 5) asserts 'Among the Ijebus, the Iyalode participated at all levels of policy making, including that of the Osugbo secret cults and the council of Iwarofa Chiefs.' Moreover, oral tradition tells us that exceptional women became the Oba (king) and regents in exceptional times and circumstances in Yorubaland (Mba, 1982, pp. 5–6). At such times, men who were under them were cooperative. This shows that in Yoruba society, no one was regarded as inferior or played second fiddle.

Another essential feature of Yoruba thought is the stress on epistemological relativity. To the Yoruba, nothing is absolute and nobody is omniscient. Unlike Western epistemological absolutism, the Yoruba did not treat some things as subsidiaries and some as absolute. As a result, the characterization of the subsidiaries as inferior and the absolute as superior did not arise. According to Oluwole:

> When the Yoruba thinker talks of Olodumare, Orunmila, and Esu, he [sic] creates the principle of explanation that transcends human limitation, but they never reach the level of absolute. Hence, the principle of epistemological relativity applies to these beings who the Yoruba man create in his own image rather than the reversed model. In Hebraic thought, Olodumare is therefore, neither omniscient nor absolutely benevolent. He asks questions and concedes learning from lesser being, just as Orunmila, the god of wisdom does.
>
> (Oluwole, 1993, pp. 7–8)

The stress on epistemological relativity is reflected in the fact that Orunmila, who is regarded as the god of knowledge, does not know everything. He still learns from Amosun, his son. Hence, the oracular saying:

*Eni mo yi ko to hun*
*A dia fun Orumila*
*Ti yio ko ifa lowo Amosun*
*Omo re.*

He who knows this may not know that
This is the oracular injunction to Orunmila
Who had to learn from Amosun
His own son.

Other proverbs, such as the under listed, confirm epistemological relativity in Yoruba thought.

a   *Ogbon oduni were e mii*
b   'Wisdom this year is fuller next year.'
c   *Ogbon ologbon ki je ki a pe agba ni were*
d   'The sage learns from others' wisdom, therefore it is anathema to call him a dunce.'
e   *Af'ogbon ologbon sogbon ko te boro*
f   'He who shares from others' wisdom will not be disgraced.'
g   *Bi olugbon ti gbon ni Aresa na gbon*
h   lsquo;As Olugbon [a king] is wise, so also is Aresa [a king of another town].'
i   *Ologbon aye kan ko te ra re nifa*
j   *Omiran kan ko fira re joye*
k   *Obe to mu kii ge eku ara re*
l   'No wise man consults himself as an oracle
m   No knowledgeable person makes himself a chief
n   A sharp knife does not carve its own handle.'

All these proverbs are indicators of the absence of absolutism among the Yoruba. No matter the level and certainty of one's knowledge, one still needed to learn from others. The Yoruba believed that one gender is not superior to the other when it comes to epistemological issues. Emphasis was on collective deliberation and resolution of issues. Hence, the saying, '*A npe gbo ni, A ki pe go*' (collective deliberation leads to knowledge and not foolishness).

## Conclusion

In conclusion, the above exercise in conceptual decolonization of the concept of women in contemporary African thought, using the Yoruba as an example, has shown us that it is high time we revived and encouraged the awareness of the complementarity of male and female roles as contained in the gender dualism of the traditional Yoruba. In addition, the exercise also serves as a catalyst to rehabilitate traditional African attitudes to women and gender in order to guide our daily lives. In other words, as Chinweizu (1993) puts it, when it comes to views on women in contemporary Africa, we must be Afrocentric rather than Eurocentric or Arabocentric.

## References

Adeoti, S. O. (n.d.). 'The Role of Women in Ijebu Igbo Religious Beliefs and Cultic Practices'. *M.A. thesis* submitted to the Department of Religious Studies, Faculty of Arts, University of Ibadan.

Afolayan, A. (2006). 'The Language Question in African Philosophy'. In *Core Issues in African Philosophy*, edited by Olusegun Oladipo (pp. 41–58). Ibadan: Hope Publications.

Imam, A. M. and Mama, A. (eds) (1997). *Engendering African Social Science: An Introductory Essay*. Dakar, Senegal: CODESRIA.

Bewaji, J. A. I. (2006). 'Olodumare: God in Yoruba Belief and the Theistic Problem of Evil'. *African Studies Quarterly*, 6 (1).

Bodunrin, P. (1984). 'The Question of African Philosophy'. In *African Philosophy: An Introduction*, edited by Richard A. Wright. 3rd edn (pp. 1–23). Lanham, MD: University Press of America.

Chimakonam, J. O. (2015). 'Dating and Periodization Questions in African Philosophy'. In *Atuolu Omalu: Some Unanswered Questions in Contemporary African Philosophy*, edited by Jonathan O. Chimakonam (pp. 9–34). Lanham, MD: University Press of America.

Chinweizu, I. (1993). 'Gender and Monotheism: The Assault by Monotheism on African Gender Diarchy'. Paper presented at the International Conference on African Philosophy and Feminism, Lagos, 3 December.

Grimshaw, J. (1986). *Feminist Philosophers: Women's Perspectives on Philosophical Traditions*. London: Wheatsheaf.

Janz, B. B. (2009). *Philosophy in an African Place*. Lanham, MD: Lexington Books.

Mba, N. E. (1982). *Nigerian Women Mobilized: Women's Political Activity in Southern Nigeria, 1900–1965*. Berkeley, CA: University of California Press.

Oladipo, O. (1996). *Philosophy and the African Experience: The Contributions of Kwasi Wiredu*. Ibadan: Hope Publications.

Oladipo, O. (2006). 'Issues in Definition of African Philosophy'. In *Core Issues in African Philosophy*, edited by Olusegun Oladipo (pp. 9–20). Ibadan: Hope Publications.

Oladipo, O. (ed.) (2002). *The Third Way in African Philosophy: Essays in Honour of Kwasi Wiredu*. Ibadan: Hope Publications.

Oluwole, S. B. (1993). 'African Thought: The Search for Intellectual Identity'. Paper presented at the International Conference on African Philosophy and Feminism, Lagos, 7–8 December.

Oluwole, S. (1995). 'Madonna and the Whore in Traditional Thought'. *Journal of Philosophy and Development*, 1 & 2, (1). Ago-Iwoye, Nigeria: Ogun State University.

Omoregbe, J. (1990). *Knowing Philosophy: A General Introduction*. Lagos: Joja Educational Research and Publishers Limited.

Peale, N. V. (1971). *The Adventure of Being a Wife*. Englewood Cliffs, NJ: Prentice Hall.

Wiredu, K. (1991). 'On Defining African Philosophy'. In *African Philosophy: The Essential Readings*, edited by Tsenay Serequeberhan. New York: Paragon House.

Wiredu, K. (1995). *Conceptual Decolonization: 4 Essays Introduced by Olusegun Oladipo*. Ibadan: Hope Publications.

# 10 Women in the his-story of philosophy and the imperative for a 'her-storical' perspective in contemporary African philosophy

*Mesembe I. Edet*

## Introduction

One of the central issues that confronts contemporary African philosophy is the problem of the historiography of African philosophy. Whereas the history of Western philosophy is clear on the evolution of thoughts within it, African philosophy is not yet clear on the structure of its history. Granted that the works of Barry Hallen (2002), D. S. Masolo (1994), B. Abanuka (2001), M. Osuagwu (1999) and others have attempted to articulate this history, it is evident, as Chimakonam (2014, 2015) demonstrated, that there have been distortions concerning the periodization and a general incomprehensiveness with regard to content.

Obi Oguejiofor in considering the possibilities of such a history, perceives enormous problems with the project, which have to do with 'the dearth of research on the different traditions, the systematization of different philosophic thoughts, and a clear and consistent periodization' (Oguejiofor, 2002, p. 130). His views appeared in 2002 in a collection of essays edited by Olusegun Oladipo, *The Third Way in African Philosophy*, in honour of Kwasi Wiredu. In my view these perceived 'problems' have been overtaken by developments in contemporary African Philosophy.

Contemporary African philosophy is bubbling with rigorous formal philosophical activity; there is intensive research in the different traditions, there is systematization of different philosophic thoughts; it is being developed in branches and compartments, and philosophical systems and schools have also emerged. Perhaps the main problem is the absence of a comprehensive presentation of the history, in which both the male and female epistemic viewpoints are accommodated. However, major doubt remains if such a project is worthwhile or can even be carried out any time soon.

But despite the scepticism or circumspection about the possibility of a comprehensive narrative history of African philosophy, it has not discouraged some scholars from focusing attention both on the possibility and the necessity of the project, and indeed making efforts accordingly. Evidently, the writing of such a history which will accommodate both masculine and feminine perspectives is long delayed, and has become an imperative because it is the historical approach that has been very significant in the elevation of the status of Western philosophy as the universal philosophy which other regional philosophies are encouraged to ape. Western philosophical narrative is able to evoke the statistics of time (or date) and space (or places), as well as characters, events, ideas, problems, topics, questions, doctrines, contexts and methodologies. African philosophy is no exception to these claims of a history.

But in aping Western philosophy we must pay critical attention to its historiography and the way in which this has developed, arguably, in ways which perpetuate the stereotyping of philosophy as masculine and excludes women in the construction of historical knowledge. Women have engaged in philosophy throughout the field's history and there were women philosophers since ancient times, but very strangely, almost no woman philosophers have entered the Western philosophical canon. They have been systemically left out. The Western narrative turns out to be a masculine story. Whether one is reading Russell, Copleston, Stumpf or Jones, what is clear is that the history of Western philosophy is masculine in character, overwhelmingly dominated by male characters, and women are virtually invisible.

This situation raises the 'feminine problem in philosophy' or what may be called 'the problem of women and philosophy' generally. Until the emergence of feminism as a theory and as a movement, Western philosophy did not seem to consider this problem as fundamental, because there seemed to be tacit agreement by men, pro Aristotle, that women do not have the rigor for philosophy. For so long Western philosophy omitted the energy, creativity and potential of half of humanity, and many coming into the philosophical field have not been able to see how much influence women have had in the field. My aim in this chapter is to show how this error of Western philosophy is repeating itself in the nascent narrative of African philosophy. The focus therefore will be to explore ways whereby the exclusion or under-representation of women in African philosophy can be addressed.

## The history of philosophy as his-storical

There is general agreement that history is an organized and critical study of such past activities of human beings as have produced sufficient effects on the subsequent course of events or on other human beings in the course of events. Though history is not just a study of past events, nor is it an uncritical cataloguing of significant past events, still it is a study of all past events. History is or ought to be analytical and critical as the historian seeks to understand significant past events and interpret them in the light of her or his own knowledge of the present.

The word 'history' is derived from the Greek word 'historia' meaning 'knowledge obtained by enquiry into the past' (Erim, 2004, p. 6). There have been diverse reactions to history and historians throughout the ages and various forms of prejudices are held against the discipline. A major problem which confronts the discipline has to do with historiography, that is, dealing with the methods of writing history and its purpose.

Available evidence shows that Western philosophy which aspires to universality and to be the paradigm or norm for other regional or cultural philosophies is essentially masculine in character. Louise du Toit observes that, 'within this masculine symbolic order, women were rendered either functional/instrumental and for-men, or invisible and inaudible' (du Toit, 2008, p. 414). What is indicated here is that women are presented as incapable of creating worthwhile critical and scientific knowledge, and men are put at the centre and made to establish and constitute the canons of knowledge, whilst women's perspective is under-valued.

Going further, Adeshina Afolayan describes the history of Western philosophy as 'the history of the individual philosophers whose thoughts constitute its framework, which is a tradition of texts' (Afolayan, 2006, p. 22). While there were women philosophers since the earliest times and some were accepted as philosophers during their lives, almost no woman philosophers have entered the Western canon. Some of the notable female philosophers include Aspasia of Miletus (c. 470–400 BC), Nicarete of Megara (fl. c. 300 BC) and Catherine of Alexandria (282–305 BC) in the ancient period of Western philosophical history; Hypatia (fifth century AD), Aedesia of Alexandria (fifth century AD) and Catherine of Seneca (1347–1380) in the medieval period; Margaret Cavendish (1623–1673) and Laura Bassi (1711–1778) in the modern period; and the likes of Hannah Arendt (1906–1975), Simone de Beauvoir (1908–1986), Sandra Harding, Susan Wolf, Jessica Wilson and Ayn Rand in the contemporary period, and many more, but these have remained obscure or marginal in the Western canon.

This exclusion is not accidental. Rather it is conscious and deliberate and reflects the fact that Western historiography bears a burden of male bias in the construction of historical knowledge. Thus I maintain that the Western historical narrative in philosophy lacks scientific integrity and the essential authenticity in view of its exclusion of the woman's perspective. This able-bodied maleness of the Western philosophical historical narrative is replicated in the invisibility of women in historical texts of Oriental philosophy, which similarly ignores women's lives, experiences, contributions, voices, perceptions, representations and struggles, showing still an uphill battle for the recognition of women philosophers in Oriental philosophy and confirmation perhaps that the project of history writing is gender-blind and privileges male representations.

This gender-blind *his-storic* deterministic conception of history, particularly history of philosophy necessitates the development of *her-story*. Her-story is history written from a woman's perspective, emphasizing the role of women and taking serious cognizance of the creative work that women have done in the development of knowledge. Robin Morgan, in a book of her selected writings, states that the debut of the word 'herstory' was in the byline of her article 'Goodbye To All That', in early 1970, in the first issue of the 'underground' New Left newspaper *Rat* after it was taken over by women to clean it of sexism. According to her, she identified with the W.I.T.C.H. movement, decoding the acronym as 'Women Inspired to Commit Herstory' (Morgan, 2014).

Her-story is a neologism coined as a pun on the word 'history' as part of a critique of conventional historiography which is traditionally written as his-story, that is, from the masculine point of view. Even if the term is comic, it needs to be taken very seriously as it is a term pregnant with implications and consequences for academia, especially philosophy, the field where concepts are fundamental, indeed concepts are everything.

I am throwing up this concept in philosophy, especially African philosophy, to emphasize that women's lives, experiences, deeds, contributions, voices, perceptions, expectations, representations, struggles and participation in human affairs have been for long neglected or undervalued in standard histories and that serious cognizance must be taken of the creative works that women have produced in the development of knowledge, and how these have affected the philosophic temper. Otherwise, history thus becomes, as Erim O. Erim very rightly remarks 'the biography of great men' or 'the narrative by a man who wasn't there' (Erim, 2004, p. 4), lacking essential intellectual authenticity or scientific integrity. Her-story in African philosophy will enrich philosophy, especially African philosophy, and cure the disservice to philosophy which the Western philosophical narrative has done to the field, and thereby prevent Western history of philosophy's venture of apparent *her-storycide* with its masculinist canon; a gesture of purposeful killing (neglect) of the women's perspective of history.

## The history of contemporary African philosophy project

The project of writing the history of African philosophy is ongoing and there are several identifiable efforts in that direction. Oguejiofor reports about Theophile Obenga's article of 1986 in which he outlined a possible period-ization of that history which includes the Pharaonic period (2780–330 BC), the Patristic period (first to fourth century AD), the Moslem period (c. 800–seventeenth century), and the contemporary Negro-African period (eighteenth century–present day) (127). M. Bilolo adopted a similar four-epoch approach and identified the periods of pre-Alexandrian African philosophy (Egypt–Nubia–Libya); Alexandrian African philosophy (Graeco-Roman period) and the Coptic-Islamic African philosophy (seventeenth–nineteenth century AD).

Oguejiofor also tells us of the work of Claude Sumner who worked on 'Ethiopian Philosophy, tracing its history from the *Physiologue* to the later rationalist period of Zaera Yaekoba', and of Osuagwu who did 'separate works of varying volumes on Egyptian, medieval and contemporary periods of African philosophy' (Oguejiofor, 2002, p. 127). It would seem that these scholars, in embarking on this project of the historiography of African philosophy were mainly focusing on the question of its periodization. This was also the focus of the International Conference on African Philosophy which held in 1995 at the Saint Peter and Paul, Ibadan, Nigeria. Oguejiofor writes that the conference dwelt on the theme of 'The problems of history and historiography of African philosophy'. The papers presented at the conference covered all the different periods into which a history of African philosophy may be divided, including the Ethiopian.

It is remarkable that these works which focus mainly on the possible periodization of African philosophy, with different understandings and interpretations of philosophy, both informal and formal, completely ignore and exclude the thoughts and voices of women, as the characters selected as representative of the various periods under discourse are men. On the question of the possible periodization of African philosophy, it is no surprise at all that different views on the historical origins and periodization of African philosophy abound among scholars of African philosophy.

With scholars such as Lacinay Keita (1984), Henry Olela (1984) and Innocent Onyewuenyi (1993), from the mere titles of their reflections and works one easily concludes that they attribute much antiquity to African philosophy. Momoh (2000) and Omoregbe (1985) likewise in their contributions to the periodization debate endorse clearly the idea of its great antiquity. But in their understanding and interpretation of 'ancient African philosophy' they completely ignore and fail to draw attention to the role of women. They neglect to acknowledge the significant function of women in traditional Africa as 'repositories of the past and guarantors of the future', as Leopold Senghor describes their work and importance (see UNESCO, 2014, p. 45).

The masculinist chauvinist tendency of these scholars is reflected and affirmed when we consider Omoregbe's submission that, 'all civilizations, all people, have their own philosophers, their own Socrates, their own Plato, their own Descartes, their own Hegel, etc. In this Africa cannot be an exception' (Omeregbe, 1985, p. 6). We see here that philosophy is attributed to men, showing still Omoregbe's uphill battle in recognition of women philosophers in African antiquity.

I do not at all begrudge these scholars for establishing their own canon of understanding and interpreting philosophy in this question of periodization of African philosophy. But my concern is with the historiography of contemporary African philosophy, by which I mean the formal philosophical activity which is a product of critical reflection carried out in the light of pure reason and with some training has constituted an organized corpus of knowledge on specific African experiences and on universal issues by African authors, indigenous and expatriate.

Very recently, some scholars have adopted a thematic approach in effort to articulate a history of contemporary African philosophy. Barry Hallen's *A Short History of African Philosophy* (2002) falls in this category. He discusses major ideas, figures, and schools of thought in philosophy in the African context. While drawing out critical issues in its formation, Hallen focuses on recent scholarship and relevant debates that have made African philosophy essential to understanding the rich and complex heritage of the continent.

Hallen builds on connections with Western philosophical traditions to explore African contributions to cultural universalism, cultural relativisim, phenomenology, hermeneutics and Marxism. Among the figures he discusses are Ptah-hotep (Egypt, 2,400 BC), Zar'a Ya'aqob (Abyssina, seventh century),

Anton Wilhelm Amo (Ghana, eighteenth century), and more recently W. E. Abraham, John Mbiti, Paulin Hountondji, V. Y. Mudimbe, Kwame Anthony Appiah, Kwasi Wiredu, Lucius Outlaw, Lewis Gordon, Godwin Sogolo and Wole Soyinka. There is only a single reference to and a passing discussion of a female viewpoint, this being that of the Nigerian sociologist Oyeronke Oyewunmi, who produced a work entitled *The Invention of Women: Making an African sense of Western Gender Discourses* (1997). And even though two works of the famous philosopher Sophie Oluwole are listed on the bibliography, her views are not specifically discussed.

Kwasi Wiredu also follows this gender-blind approach in his *Blackwell Companion to African Philosophy*. The anthology, which has a part that deals with the history of African philosophy, narrated in seventeen articles, all of which are authored by men, is evidence that emerging efforts in writing the history of African philosophy still tend to follow this unjust line of her-storycide. An anthology of forty-seven articles, covering seven parts including history of African philosophy, politics, ethics and aesthetics, the philosophy of religion, logic, epistemology, metaphysics and methodological issues, only features a solitary female in Nkiru Nzegwu, who contributed two essays. One of Nzegwu's contributions, entitled 'Feminism and Africa: Impact and Limits of the Metaphysics of Gender', is placed in part VII of the work, devoted to 'special topics' and is the last article in the anthology (see Wiredu, 2004).

Emmanuel Chukwudi Eze's *African Philosophy: An Anthology* (1998) seems to fare a shade better. Here, out of a total of fifty-one articles, women authored only those five essays specifically raising the question about 'philosophy and gender'. bell hooks authored two chapters and co-authored one, which means that in total, only five women authors were involved, as opposed to about forty-three male authors, some of whom also contributed more than one chapter (see Eze, 1998). The point I labor to make so far is that it is evident that contemporary African philosophy as a loose set of canonical texts and authors is currently clearly and overwhelmingly dominated by men and its historiography tends toward her-storycide. But of course, no one can justly deny that women have indeed contributed immense value to African philosophy.

Barry Hallen holds the view that 'the first truly comprehensive and detailed history of African philosophy was written by Kenyan philosopher D. A. Masolo' (Hallen, 2002, p. 108). This is in reference to Masolo's work entitled *African Philosophy in Search of Identity* (1994). In this work Masolo traces the history of the major themes, debates and participants in African philosophy since the 1940s. His purview includes francophone and anglophone philosophers in both the analytic and phenomenological traditions.

With regard to the 'comprehensiveness' and 'detail' of the work, I am circumspect in accepting that Masolo's 1994 effort was 'truly comprehensive' as Hallen opines, but the innovative brilliance of the work is that it is a critical narrative which does more than merely chronicle the themes, debates and characters. Masolo analyses and provides critical assessments of the various philosophers and the traditions they represent. He does this, ultimately, from the standpoint of his own philosophical position, but again he also ignores the woman's perspective and women's contributions to the development of contemporary African philosophy (see Masolo, 1994). Thus the work turns out again as his-story.

Chimakonam's entry on 'History of African Philosophy' in the *Internet Encyclopedia of Philosophy* is to my mind the most comprehensive, detailed and updated narrative on the subject, for the panoramic view it provides on the history of systematic African philosophy from the early 1920s to about 2014. Chimakonam's narrative, covering six thematic areas, represents a radically new approach to the historiography of African philosophy. He discusses the criteria of African philosophy, and its various schools, which cover ethno-philosophy, the nationalist/ideological school, philosophic sagacity, the hermeneutic school, the literary school, the professional school and the conversational school.

Chimakonam's narrative interestingly also highlights the 'movements' in African philosophy and identifies excavationism, Afro-constructionism and deconstructionism, critical reconstructionism and Afro-eclecticism and conversationalism. His engagement with the periodization question is indeed novel, and seems technically more accurate than what others have done as he identifies the Early, Middle, Later and Contemporary periods (see Chimakonam, 2014).

But it is also evident from Chimakonam's narrative that he has caught the his-story bug because he evinces an uphill battle in recognition of women philosophers. In his thirty-three-page narrative, Jennifer Lisa Vest and Sophie Oluwole are the only females mentioned. He characterizes Vest as belonging to the conversationalist movement of the New Era of African philosophy and Sophie Oluwole as belonging to the Afro-constructionist movement. In a listing of about eighty-nine items of 'references and further reading', Sophie Oluwole's *Philosophy and Oral Tradition* (2009) and Vest's 'Perverse and Necessary Dialogues in African Philosophy' (1999) are the only works authored by women. Much as Chimakonam's effort is impressively informative and offers a much anticipated new direction for the historiography of African philosophy, its inadequate recognition of the contributions of women leaves a gaping lacuna which only her-story can fill.

## The importance of the her-storical perspective in African philosophy

From the foregoing discussion, the point made is that just as women were excluded, neglected, marginalized or undermined in Western philosophy and Oriental philosophy, perhaps until recent times, the same challenge also confronts women in contemporary African philosophy. This is 'the problem of women and African philosophy', which du Toit (2008) describes as 'the absence of strong women's and feminist voices within the discipline of African Philosophy' (p. 413).

This issue of African philosophy and women raises many questions that demand further research from both males and females: what are the basic questions that engage contemporary African philosophy and how have women and feminists responded to these questions? Why are their voices, views and thoughts undermined? Why has it been difficult for their views and experiences to enter the African philosophical historical canon? Is it truly a conscious and a systemic marginalization? How has African philosophy marginalized women in its questions? What are the consequences or implications of this marginalization for Africa, Africans, African philosophy and philosophy generally, now and in the future? What can African philosophy learn from women and vice versa? Why are there so few women in African philosophy? Why are there points of tension? Are women truly averse to philosophy? Is there something about philosophy which makes the field seem unwelcome to women? Is there, as du Toit submits, a rejection of the philosophical genre of intellectual expression by African women intellectuals in preference to some other genre? If this is the case, what may feminist and other philosophers learn from this act of rejection? Very important and urgent is the question, why has African philosophy remained essentially his-storical? How can African philosophy establish and sustain her-storical perspectives in her narratives? (Come to think of it, why are disciplines referred to by the feminine pronoun while the voices of women in most disciplines continue to be repressed? I think this may be explained as the continuing expression of male subjugation of and dominance over women and the extension of that disposition to dominate entities and institutions and determine their direction in like manner, as if they were women.)

Contemporary African philosophy still seems not to have come to terms with the need to mobilize the energy, creativity and potential of women's intellect and rationality for philosophical engagement in order to enrich its contents. The consequence is that it is impoverished and under-nourished, just as philosophy is anywhere the presence of women's voice is undermined or marginalized.

If African philosophy is to be built on a holistic epistemological edifice, and if her historiography is to be intellectually authentic, it is imperative then that the narrative must draw from the experiences of both males and females. We cannot claim to have true, complete knowledge in African philosophy when its substance is drawn exclusively or lopsidedly from the experience and ideas of men. It is pertinent to take into consideration women's experiences, women's lives, voices, struggles, expectations and perceptions of African reality. The Nigerian Chimamanda Adichie (TedTalk, July 2009) has warned about 'the danger of a single story'.

Sophie Oluwole has worked so long and so hard to make clear what is specifically African in African philosophy. From a great number of publications, mention must be made of her book *Witchcraft, Reincarnation and the God-Head: Issues in African Philosophy* (1991), which offers a direction for the development of questions and discourses for metaphysics in contemporary

African philosophy. Oluwole in her book *Philosophy and Oral Tradition* (1999) also draws attention to the problem concerning what difference it makes to think in terms of orality rather than writing in the transmission of philosophy generally, and African philosophy especially. This question is fundamental for African philosophy's historiography. In this age of 'global expansion of thought' and homogenizing modes of knowledge, her work which compares Socrates and Orunmila is an amazing piece of comparative philosophy and a ground-breaking contribution not just to African philosophy, but also to inter-cultural philosophizing (see Oluwole, 2014).

The issues addressed in this work are some of those that surround that pernicious debate about the existence of African philosophy. Was there an indigenous African critical tradition of philosophy before the European incursion into the continent? If so, is it comparable to the well-known tradition of Western philosophy? Oluwole suggests that if fully understood, a combination of the African and Western traditions of philosophy will provide a sound basis for the development of non-culturally biased, world intellectual culture that promotes sustainable development.

What is the justice of any African philosophy narrative that takes into account sage philosophy and the works of the Kenyan Henry Odera Oruka, but ignores or disregards the work of Anke Graness? It is important to note that Graness is currently working as project leader of a FWF-funded research project on the 'History of Philosophy in Africa' at the University of Vienna, and her co-edited anthology on Oruka, *Sagacious Reasoning: H. Odera Oruka in Memoriam* (Graness and Kresse, 1997) is impossible to ignore in the whole corpus of African philosophy literature for the holistic understanding of sage philosophy and sagacious reasoning in African philosophy which the work provides.

African philosophy can further be enriched in content and not impoverished if it acknowledges and promotes the work and insights of the likes of the Kenyan Wangari Maathai. Though a biologist by training, Maathai has written and done so much on the theme of 'empowerment', developing several perspectives in her approach, namely empowerment's relationship to self-esteem, teamwork, and political action, its ambivalent relationship to formal education, and very significantly, the role of cultural traditions in providing alternatives to colonial-era cultural impositions and the current exploitative effects of neo-liberal capitalism (see Presbey, 2013).

Furthermore, how can African philosophical historiography underestimate the great works of Nkiru Uwechia Nzegwu, and her voice which resonates on the subject matters of feminism, womanhood and gender discourses in African philosophy. Nzegwu's book *Family Matters: Feminist Concepts in African Philosophy of Culture* (2006) is a genuinely ground-breaking text which holds great potential for the study of Africa and our historical understanding of the social and political dynamics which are at play in the construction of West African gendered social organization and the evolution of 'modern' families. The book challenges scholars to take much more seriously questions about the foundations of their disciplines. African philosophical historiography undervalues Nzegwu to its own peril. There are many more.

The point made is that African philosophy must recognize the need to create knowledge systems which emerge from the diverse and complex contexts in which both men and women live and work and sustain their being, and design methodologies of historiography which guarantee an innovative and transformative narrative that ensures epistemic justice.

Her-storicity is a new approach to African philosophical historiography which I recommend. Her-storicity considers his-story as an attempt at her-storycide, which I maintain is the killing (neglect) of women's perspective on history. Thus it is a form of rhetoric which provides arguments which validate the experiences of women in philosophy against a mainstream masculine narrative. It is a movement for justice that aims to create a discernible balance and equity between the voices of women which are truly marginal and the voices of men who constitute the African philosophical historical canon. Her-storicity is an epistemology which seeks to erect the African philosophical epistemological edifice on a foundation that guarantees intellectual authenticity in the effort to balance male and female epistemological claims and how these have affected the philosophical temper. It is a politics which compels a re-evaluation of received approaches and attitudes to historiography, and the development of research methodologies which address questions about the experiences, and ideas of men and women and engages their realities holistically without marginalizations.

Her-storicity is not reverse his-storicity. This programme of her-storicity purveys the methodological preconditions for the development of a new approach to narrating the contemporary African philosophical experience, one which will lead to the emergence of *Afro-herstoriscism*. Afro-herstoricism seeks to advance women's views and style of philosophizing, but will be inclusive of the male view.

## Conclusion

The points this chapter labors to make are straight and simple. First, the documented reflections of women in contemporary African philosophy, of individuals such as Sophie Oluwole, Anke Graness, Wangari Maathai, Nkiru Nzegwu, Ebunoluwa Oduwole, Betty Wambui, Gail Presbey and Louise du Toit, are impossible to deny or to ignore; the heritage they (and other female thinkers on the African condition too numerous to do justice to here) have bequeathed to African philosophy and the world deserves the recognition denied it for so long, and current African philosophical historiography must remediate this epistemic injustice.

Furthermore, I maintain that concepts are crucial in philosophical discourse and this work has thrown up fresh concepts, and keywords such as 'his-story', 'her-story', 'her-storycide', 'her-storicity' and 'Afro-herstoricism'. These concepts are pregnant with implications, consequences and creative possibilities for African philosophy and her place in the philosophical world. These concepts encapsulate the idea that women's lives, experiences, deeds, contributions, voices, perceptions, representations, struggles, problems, expectations and participation in human affairs have been too long neglected or undervalued in standard historical narratives, and that serious cognizance must be taken of the creative works that women have produced in the development of knowledge and how these have affected the philosophic temper. Contemporary African philosophy cannot run away from honoring its 'debts and duties' to women in African philosophy.

## References

Abanuka, B. (2001). *A History of African Philosophy.* Enugu: Snaap Press.

Adichie, Chimamanda. (2009). *The Danger of a Single Story.* http://ted.com. Retrieved, September, 2016.

Afolayan, A. (2006). 'Some Methodological Issues in the History of African Philosophy'. In O. Oladipo (ed.), *Core Issues in African Philosophy* (pp. 21–40). Ibadan: Hope Publications.

Chimakonam, J. O. (2014). 'African Philosophy, History of'. In James Fieser and Bradley Dowden (eds), *Internet Encyclopedia of Philosophy.* Retrieved 20 August 2016. www.iep.utm.edu/afric-hi.

Chimakonam, J. O. (2015). 'Dating and Periodization Questions in African Philosophy'. In J. O. Chimakonam (ed.), *Atuolu Omalu: Some Unanswered Questions in Contemporary African Philosophy* (pp. 9–34). Lanham, MD: University Press of America.

Du Toit, L. (2008) 'Old Wives' Tales and Philosophical Delusions: On *The Problem of Women and African Philosophy*'. *South African Journal of Philosophy* 27 (4), 413–427.

Erim, E. O. (2004). 'African Historiography: Trends, Praxis and Democracy in Nigeria'. *25th Inaugural Lecture,* University of Calabar, Nigeria, 11 November.

Eze, E. C. (1998) *African Philosophy: An Anthology.* Malden, MA: Blackwell.

Graness, A. and Kresse, K. (eds) (1997). *Sagacious Reasoning: H. Odera Oruka in Memoriam.* Frankfurt: Peter Lang.

Hallen, B. (2002). *A Short History of African Philosophy.* Bloomington, IN: Indiana University Press.

Keita, L. (1984). 'The African Philosophical Tradition' In R. A. Wright (ed), *African Philosophy: An Introduction* (pp. 57–76). Lanham, MD: University Press of America.

Masolo, D. A. (1994). *African Philosophy in Search of Identity.* Bloomington, IN: Indiana University Press.

Momoh, C. S. (2000). *Nature, Issue and Substance of African Philosophy* (pp. 1–22). Auchi: African Philosophy Projects Publications.

Morgan, R. (2014). *The Word of a Woman: Feminist Dispatches.* ISBN: ISBN: 9781497678071.

Nzegwu, N. (2004). 'Feminism and Africa: Impact and Limits of the Metaphysics of Gender'. In K. Wiredu, *Companion to African Philosophy* (pp. 263–275). Malden, MA: Blackwell.

Nzegwu, N. (2006). *Family Matters. Feminist Concepts in African Philosophy of Culture.* Albany, NY: State University of New York Press.

Oguejiofor, J. O. (2002). 'Kwasi Wiredu and the Possibility of a History of African Philosophy'. In O. Olusegun (ed.), *The Third Way in African Philosophy: Essays in Honour of Kwasi Wiredu* (pp. 17–34). Ibadan: Hope Publications.

Olela, H. (1984). 'The African Foundations of Greek Philosophy' In R. A. Wright (ed.), *African Philosophy: An Introduction* (pp. 77–92). Lanham, MD: University Press of America.

Oluwole, S. (1991). *Witchcraft, Reincarnation and the God-Head: Issues in African Philosophy.* Ikeja: Excel Publications.

Oluwole, S. (1999). *Philosophy and Oral Tradition.* Lagos: Ark Publications.

Oluwole, S. (2014). *Socrates and Orunmila: Two Patron Saints of Classical Philosophy.* Lagos: Ark Publications.

Omoregbe, J. (1985). 'African Philosophy: Yesterday and Today'. In P. O. Bodunrin (ed.), *Philosophy in Africa: Trends and Perspectives* (pp. 1–13). Ille-Ife: University of Ife Press.

Onyewuenyi, I. C. (1993). *The African Origin of Greek Philosophy: An Exercise in Afrocentrism.* Nsukka: University of Nigeria Press.

Osuagwu, M. I. (1999). *A Contemporary History of African Philosophy.* Enugu: Snaap Press.

Oyewumi, O. (1999). *The Invention of Women: Making an African Sense of Western Gender Discourses.* Minneapolis, MN: University of Mineasota Press.

Presbey, G. M. (2013). 'Women's Empowerment: The Insights of Wangari Maathai'. *Journal of Global Ethics* 9 (3), 277–292.

UNESCO (2014). *Philosophy Manual: A South–South Perspective.* Paris: UNESCO. ISBN: 978-92-3-101006-4.

Vest, J. L. (2009). 'Perverse and Necessary Dialogues in African Philosophy'. *Thought and Practice: a Journal of the Philosophical Association of Kenya.* New series, 1 (2): 1–23.

Wiredu, K. (2004) *Companion to African Philosophy.* Malden, MA: Blackwell.

# 11 Buffeted

## Developing an afro feminist response to environmental questions

*Betty Wambui*

## Introduction

In this chapter, I make the case that serious questions raised by the increasingly tragic impact of human interactions within our ecology, are in part answered by an exploration of indigenous and post/decolonial knowledges that find solutions to what is in contemporary times generally recognized as an unfolding environmental crisis. Using feminist scholars such as Wangari Maathai, Pala Achola, Vandana Shiva, Maria Mies, Ariel Salleh, Mary Mellor and others to explore the place of women in the debates that buffet environmentalism, I present a post/decolonial feminist take on the problem. Like these scholars, I make the argument that there is a real need to study and even recover the relationship of certain special populations (such as women) with our environment if we are to begin to understand and address the issues raised by our environmental crisis. This is especially important on the African continent where women's voices continue to require amplification as well as locational empathy and ingress. My position assumes that this exploration will unveil the ways in which modern and contemporary socio-political and economic practices have contributed to modes and forms of exploitation and destruction that have risked our eco and bio-diverse systems, yet also move us beyond this to a recognition of the possibilities that feminist knowledges, relations and imagination, especially afro ones, offer.

Following on the heels of feminists, environmentalists and indigenous peoples who have made the case that we are elements of the environment who have a particular relationship with it, and who face cataclysmic futures if we continue with business as usual, Maria Mies and Vandana Shiva (2014) in the Introduction to *EcoFeminism* ask us to consider their claim that 'If the final outcome of the present world system is a general threat to life on planet earth, then, it is crucial to resuscitate and nurture the impulse and determination to survive inherent in all things' (p. 3). It is to this urge not only to survive but also to flourish that eco theorists and eco activists especially on the African continent direct their energies. Each warning of impending disaster, each rise of the thermometer, each extermination of another species, retreat of forests, contamination of soil, seed, water, and other material bodies are seen as a call to urgently respond to this emergency that women and activists of all genders feel particularly deeply.

## Parsing the problem

The African continent, much like the rest of the world, has been subject to consumerist extraction practices that have continuing negative environmental consequences. This impact is especially clear across the global south where as Wangari Maathai and the Greenbelt remind us, trees are being cut down more rapidly than they can be replaced. Where, as Vandana Shiva and others have pointed out, indigenous/native covering is being depleted and, or quickly replaced with exotic and engineered species of plant and, increasingly, animal species.[1] This is often to the detriment of local ecosystems. We see this kind of loss not just in South America's Amazon, where we are told we lose the equivalent of a football field of plant life and the accompanying animal life every day, but also in the tropical forests of Africa.[2] Additional environmental problems such as those of the toxic contamination of streams, rivers, lakes and hidden watersheds – fresh and salt, have expanded beyond the global north into the global south, as has the destruction of swamps which for many years were seen not as living but as dead or useless ecological spaces from a global capitalist imperialist perspective.[3] These problems have worsened with industrial expansion in the global south for a complex of reasons, pre- dominantly colonialism and industrialization, the latter of which has been accompanied by loose regulations that have allowed the pouring of toxic effluence into clean water sources which, as environmental activists constantly remind us, are dangerous to life on earth.

These problems confront the South, indeed the world, at a time when ideological shifts that complicate responses have begun to take shape globally. Let us briefly discuss the history of one of these. Historically, the collusion of westernization and modernity resulted in the construction and deployment of ideologies that promoted ideas of objectivity and universality that distinctly excluded particular populations that were raced, sexed, gendered, classed, disabled and in various ways 'othered'. These ideologies targeted indigenous populations and their ecologies in ways that were deep and long lasting, pitting local populations against each other and putting in motion global environ- mental tragedies whose minimal gains continue to be weighted in favor of damaging effects. This latter fact may explain why at this stage, as many agree, not all are impacted similarly.[4] Differential equations such as these are not new in human history, nor is the difficulty of dislodging weighted pressure from subordinated life and lives. They are connected to past processes of extraction that have characterized global imperialism. The distribution of gains is also akin to other historical patterns where the dominant accumulates the most. Unique to our time however, as contemporary analysis and experi- ence now tell us, is that we are, or will; all eventually be subject to the impact of our unfolding environmental crisis. Aware or not, we all face the end of our futures if we do not exercise our agencies in directions that begin to reverse our current environmental status, although some are temporarily buffeted by capital and propaganda that allows them to question the reality of our common environmental crisis and delay action. I will not enter into this discussion, as it has been addressed by Salleh (2009), Maathai (2006), Mies (2014), Mies and Shiva (2014), Shiva (2008, 1997) and many other feminists and post/ decolonial writers. I will however say that attempts at redressing the harm caused by power in collusion with these ideologies has resulted in the last few decades in resistance and responses that have begun, in the face of imperialism, domination and globalization, to appreciate various and alternative epistemologies, both as sites of power and authenticity, both localized and particularized.[5]

This kind of alternative thinking has been able to make a powerful case against the historical impact of imperial and patriarchal exploitation as well as its continuing brunt. In resulting contemporary arguments, we are reminded by eco theorists and eco activists that we are linked by our gene pools and also by our sharing of our little blue planet and its resources. Part of the argument made has been that the impact of our poor stewardship has been, as I have described above, increasing harm to all life on our planet, a tragedy that we cannot allow to continue unfolding.

In summary, the environmental issue is a universal problem that calls for urgent action. It has for example seen increasing sea level rises, droughts, forest fires, heatwaves, tornadoes, earthquakes, melting ice caps, as well as increased cancers and asthmatic attacks. It is part of the explanation for increased human conflict over life resources that has increased wars in the past century, as well as new migration patterns that have produced new populations of refugees that are challenging and reshaping our socio-political relations. Because of a great increase in unregulated and unsupervised human animal and non-human animal contact, it also threatens us all with crossover diseases such as SARs (Severe Acute Respiratory syndrome)[6] and ultimately with extinction. These concerns all face us in the midst of the challenge of previously unexperienced concentrations of human beings in new and/or expanded organizational spaces, whether city or state. While this is our material reality, it is also the case that the past hundred years are ones in which we – women and indigenous peoples – have also began to emerge from the shadow of the simplistic yet seriously harmful erasure, reduction, diminishment and uniformity that imperial globalization constructs as universality and order. This emergence has enabled the epistemic revival of particular identities and perspectives that had previously been negated, accompanied by a desire not only to develop these further; especially in the face of our time and needs, but also to protect hard won sites of historic and cultural distinction that offer us different ways of thinking about, seeing and being in the world. All this leads us to an interesting juncture, where we face a universal problem that requires concerted action at the very moment that we desire, for good reason, to protect unique identities and autonomous, even sovereign, action.[7]

It is a juncture at which there is need to redistribute power in ways that enable marginalized groups and communities to contribute, maybe; even in direct action and in resistance to groups and individuals that have enjoyed power, privileges and advantages that have come at the cost of our common futures. It is to the easing of this impasse that I see afro feminism contributing.

## Our histories

Studies of patriarchal imperialism and western male-centered modernity remind us how central domination, dispossession and docilization are to control and subordination. The experience of afro women is especially interesting. Paying homage to localization as a site of epistemic lucidity, let me start by directing our attention to the example of the Kikuyu of Central Kenya.

Using scholars such as Tabitha Kanango (2005, 1987), Godfrey Muriuki (1994/2006), Wangari Maathai (2008, 1985/2004), L. S. B. Leakey (1952) and others to track the movement of this community into modernity reveals the special experience of sexed and classed subjects. Given our interest in this chapter, we focus mainly on the rough equivalent of the category modernity labels 'women'.[8] Surviving and reconstituted oral, material and literary archives present women in what we commonly refer to as traditional societies, and which Pala Achola (2010) calls 'original ones'[9] as having secure access to living resources and this as allowing, even encouraging, particular relationships with the environment. To illustrate, sources suggest that prior to colonial capture, land tenure rules among the Agikuyu ensured that most people were able to acquire or utilize land in ways that ensured that their living needs were met while sustaining the health of the ecology. Muriuki in 'A History of the Kikuyu 1500–1900' makes the claim that:

> Being primarily an agricultural people, the Kikuyu have been deeply attached to their land, which has been regarded by them as having more than an economic value. Largely because of the mode of migration and the topography there developed neither tribal nor individual ownership of land … . Land was owned by the *mbari* and its administration was entrusted to a *muramati* (guardian or custodian) who was the nominal head of the *mbari*. *Mbari* ownership of land was further reinforced by people's religious beliefs, especially reverence for ancestors which fostered a deep attachment to ancestral lands. The *mbari* land tenure was a safe guard against exploitation by any one member of the clan, however strong or influential he might have been. Moreover, in a society in which communal solidarity was essential for survival, the welfare of the less fortunate members was ensured by the rest of the community. Anyone without land, for example, became a *muhoi* (tenant-at-will) on someone else's land, with the assurance that save for misconduct his tenancy would be secure. Indeed the *ahoi* (tenants-at-will) were always welcome mainly

near the frontiers, where manpower was in great demand for performing various task.

(pp. 34–35)

Mechanisms ensuring community access are especially visible when one investigates the status of women among the Agikuyu, and similarly elsewhere as other scholars demonstrate.[10] Significantly, across much of the continent, women were most often the primary food producers. So, while land was culturally presented as belonging to and inherited by men in manners similar to those observed in the patriarchal north as the masculinist language in Muriuki's paragraph implies, property and ownership did not operate similarly for a variety of reasons. Significantly, as the quote emphasizes, ownership was always seen as transient and custodial in ways that were disrupted by colonialism and modernity. It is, however, spurious understandings of access and ownership that unfortunately were carried into post-independence states. That said, and focusing on access among the Agikuyu, it was expected that one of the things one ensured for one's daughters, one's sisters and one's wives was access to land for tilling and cultivation. Such access was not only a measure of family and clan status but also a material indication of care. Significantly, it was an important consideration at marriage negotiations. There are many stories told of how upon marriage a man would stake out a piece of *githaka*, i.e. wilderness, plough and harrow it; then gift it to his new wife as measure of their new relationship. If the land that the man claimed had been handed to his safe-keeping by his father or clan, the exchange was often signified by the planting of a tree. Men often planted trees on and around their homestead to signify the beginning of a new relationship or to celebrate something as significant as the birth of a child or another equally meaningful event.

Clearly, a thoughtful agro-forestry structured around what today we might read as heterosexuality was practiced around the exchange of land and its goods. Importantly, marriage contracts ensured that women who were primarily responsible for food and crop production would have land on which they practiced agronomy. This compares to men's roles in the period, which directed them to animal husbandry and agroforestry. Thus, we are told that while it was the man's job to plough, it was the woman's to plant and harvest crops. This work required women to have a working understanding not only of soil science, which they used to determine the utility of various tracts of land for different crops as well as of the kind of crop rotation that ensured the health of land, crops and human beings.[11] Legally, unless in exceptional circumstances, a man could not harvest or authorize the harvest of crop on what in the marriage contract was referred to as his wife's farm. A wife on her part could not cut down trees. Beyond these checks, there was also an understanding that beyond the cultured spaces were forces that replenish our environment – including plant and animal life – in ways that human and other domesticated lives should not interfere with. This stands in stark contrast to the kind of ideology characteristic of western modernity especially consequent to large scale industrialization in the seventeenth and eighteenth centuries which, as Carolyn Merchant (2006) and Ariel Salleh (2009) argue, seeks dominion and the subordination of all that is othered. It is instructive too to note that the Agikuyu, like many African communities on the continent and in diaspora, did not develop the kinds of binaries that scholars like Karen Warren (1994; Warren and Erkal 1997), Merchant, and Salleh[12] describe as common in the modern west. These are criteria which served to construct opposing categories like the natural and rational worlds, ones that harbor deep divisions between particular categories such as men and women, nature and society, civilized and barbarian, and so on. These are used to justify the domination of all that is othered and to produce that flattening that results from the deployment of anthromorphic lens that has brought us to the impasse we encounter in our ecological crisis. Instead, across the board, this community held a perspective that kept open a sense of interaction and interdependence between all lives. Indeed, similar to many other African groups, the Agikuyu generally understood that the task or role of each member was not to attempt to subdue and extensively redirect the ecosystem, but rather to promote cohabitation and coexistence of all including human beings as members of the living whole. While it is easy to think of this understanding only as reflexive intuition or even as instinctual, I want to make the case that it is part of an elaborate system at whose heart was indigenous afro feminist thinking and practice, one that found and continues to find meaning in relationships, and an awareness of the value of nurturing these.[13]

Before moving into a discussion of women's experiences in the colonial era, let me emphasize here the ways in which women's voices – vocal and material – were promoted in traditional societies such as that of the Agikuyu. First, let me invite you to see the requirement for access to land and procedures for securing this, as material articulation of both speech and right; insofar as these recognized and protected women in manners that allowed them to exercise agency, develop skills, expertise, and a compendium of knowledge that they; for example, transmitted inter and intra generationally. Significantly, mechanisms surrounding access to land allowed not only certain prerogatives around for example soil and crops, but also informed procedures for social and legal appeal to local and regional courts if these rights were denied or infringed; treating or at least attempting to treat all subjects – sexed, classed, abled or even those ethnicized, fairly.[14] In addition to this, and in spite of critiques drawn from analyses of sexed divisions of labor, note also the opportunities provided to develop epistemic standing around distinct divisions of labors of life, ranging from the practical to the theoretical around such topics as agriculture, forestry, health, medicine, craft, trade, the arts, and so on.

Significant in thinking about knowledges and their transmission in many African communities, are traditional or original educational systems.[15] Elaborate and formidable, these have been divided into at least two forms. First were the formal systems around which training schools connected to initiation systems such as age, circumcision, menstruation, marriage, conception, birthing, care, and so on were built. These training schools were ones in which skills emerging from centuries of accumulated knowledge in fields such as biology, herbology, mathematics and others were taught. It is also around these that crafts ranging from military to ironmaking, pottery to sisal weaving, and so on were shared. Some of these kinds of training required apprenticeships that were carefully structured and developed. Second, were the informal systems associated with practical experiences of living such as farming, herding, hunting and so forth, depending on the community in focus. Orality, as in storytelling, songs, dances, proverbs and more, were used often in this area to transmit elements of knowledge that were coded in and linked to water, soil, particular understandings of beauty and health, our food systems and the general ecosystem. Much of this transmission began and relied on complex parenting[16] for diffusion, especially sexed parenting. We must of course keep in mind the sophisticated ways that parenting was interpreted and practiced in many African communities to understand this. That is, we must keep in mind an intricacy that hosted, for example, biological and social parents. It was a system that allowed for some of this knowledge to survive colonial violence both on the continent and in diaspora. Altogether, what one finds in an exploration of these educational systems is a complex that is closely wrapped around what we might call womanist ways of being, which see relations and interconnections as central to life and the science of living.

### Colonial invasion – imperial power

While careful not; on one hand to essentialize or idealize, or on the other to victimize or under-rate traditional communities; it is nonetheless clear that the colonial period, not just in much of Africa but much of the global south, is characterized by a weakening, a hobbling – in some cases the damaging or destruction – of original and often effective socio-political mechanisms that provided opportunity for the training and development of skills, expertise and knowledges that served a range of needs including those signified by and operational around women and the environment. This effect was in part executed through the destruction of long standing, deep, extensive, local archives – human and non-human, some of which are briefly discussed above. There was, additionally, the attenuation of instructional resources, whether primary and informal ones, that historically were transferred by use of intimate training around families or the more formal secondary processes developed by and around specialists, clans and villages as mentioned above. The outcome of this was the destruction of internships and apprenticeships as well as the undermining of experimentation, and epistemic and material exchanges across villages and ethnic groups that has persisted into contemporary times across Africa.

Analyzing the various facets of this, Shiva (2005) and Mellor (1997), very much like Salleh (2009), invite us to expand our understanding of our environmental and political economies in a manner that I find useful. I see their work as helpful both in exposing the operation of colonialism – neo- and paleo-, while also encouraging us to exercise our radical imagination against the shackles imperial power deploys to limit vision. Salleh asks us to think of economies as either narrow or wide, that is, as attentive either primarily to the global flow of capital (narrow) or more interestingly to human relations in sustainable communities (wide). Mellor calls these latter 'provisioning economies'. Shiva makes the case that there are at least three kinds of economy, which she labels capitalist, sustenance and nature. All these analytic frames help make sense of colonial intrusion in many parts of the global south in ways that enable both a critique of their operation and the productive inclusion of sustainability to discussions of women and the environment. As Shiva argues on her part, what she calls sustenance economies were with colonialism replaced by capitalist ones which colonial imperial power promoted with varying degrees of success. Characteristic of these imposed systems was the introduction of money economies, the development of new patterns of consumption, the insertion of new modes of production for the satisfaction of the imperial center, the reorganization of new political systems with reassigned boundaries, and the Importation of legal systems that took precedence over original ones even as they (these imposed systems) had limited depth and connection to subordinated communities given the historical context of invasion. The radical nature of domination in the global south revealed by this understanding is vividly seen in settler colonies like Kenya where land was seized, labor exploited, indigenous knowledge systems systematically attacked, relations and identities especially, sex/gender, unsettled. In Kenya as in much of British colonial Africa, divide-and-rule tactics internally and externally wrecked communities and created lasting suspicion between neighboring communities, and internal dysfunction, in ways that continue to be felt. Like the ecofeminists above argue, I am convinced that processes and practices like these had serious and lasting impact on the environment – indeed on our ecosystems.

Of special relevance to this chapter are the ways that colonial laws targeted, criminalized and morally condemned indigenous practices that were particularly useful for women and, by association, the environment. Unable to accept the matrifocal and sometimes matrilineal nature of many Africana communities, imperial power often penetrated them by luring men with the enticement of patriarchal power. Often encountering the alterity that indigenous communities presented after training and immersion in the rigid binaries of the modern and enlightenment periods, many colonialists could not imagine alternatives beyond the linear, competitive, atomic ones constructed by modernity without fear of this 'other' they had fabricated to justify their domination. Knowing[17] that the colonial project of domination required allies on the inside, men were seen as easier recruits and courted thus. In complicated and incomplete ways, local men gained status and power that they had not exercised in original societies, even as imported Victorian and/or modernist ideas and interpretations of nature infected by racism, sexism, misogyny, homophobia or xenophobia were presented as objective and desirable under the guise of the biological, religious and socio-political, and used to justify new hierarchies and stratifications of societies in resulting configurations. This had tragic consequences in the ecosystem.

For example, though not accepted as equal to white men, Africana men in communities like the Kikuyu were issued license over women, children and nature in ways that were foreign to the group. It was power that extended into the political realm. For instance, though the Agikuyu, prior to colonial invasion were broad participatory democracies in which female social political power was exercised, chiefs, mainly male, were now instituted. Amongst them too, primarily using the tool of compromised religion, men were naturalized as heads of homes, societies, indeed of all nature as processes of emptying non-masculine life of value and dignity were engaged and engineered. New mores were developed around sexuality that utilized social shaming and certain interpretations of religion not only to control non-human nature but also to regulate women's bodies and the exercise of their agency while providing unusual sexual license to men. This stood in contrast to many traditional societies, including this one, where there was a dignity to the exercise of sexuality and a system in place that allowed both for sexual experimentation and the transmission of knowledges about sex and sexuality.[18] As one follows the development of this issue, one very clearly sees the impact of the exportation and imposition of Victorian mores into normative and legal standards across many colonized communities, especially in British colonies. In these areas, as indigenous structures were attacked and collapsed, women's agency progressively came under greater attack and control. Accompanying this was the introduction of concepts such as promiscuity, sometimes their redefinitions, as well as the deconstruction of traditional families and social institutions, for example that of polygamy and its partner structures which in certain instances were built around certain understandings of the environment. Jane L. Parpart (1986) reminds us that, echoing the status of western women, the status of African women was eroded as they were transformed into domestics, directed to and limited to private domains if they were 'good' women, especially subject for example to adultery ordinances and the emergent formations of masculine power if they challenged their new status.[19] These 'good' women of course existed alongside 'bad' women, often those who dared to go into emerging urban centers unaccompanied by men and who then sometimes entered the sex trade – sometimes driven there by new colonial laws but always protected by systems that needed the sexual services of these women to keep the newly constructed African men working in the urban centers.[20] While a binary was constructed around rural and urban, good and bad women, there was also on the other hand, a different development in the collapse of medicine persons and witch doctors into one; and attacks on women's bodies as for example harboring witchcraft even as under the guise of keeping social order,[21] nature and knowledge were reorganized.

Observing these and other processes, it for instance becomes clear that where in original societies there were mechanisms to ensure that women's voices were heard and protected, colonial systems criminalized both women's bodies and voices, destroying spaces such as that called the *baraza*[22] in many Kenyan communities. *Barazas* in their many forms across the region signified local hearings amongst neighbors and community members where all, and especially women, could appeal for justice knowing that their case would be heard by peers who often understood the contested issue in context. These traditional 'jurors' were often individuals whom litigants trusted, and who cared about both the plaintiffs and defendants as well as the larger enterprise that was their community. The losses incurred by the demolition of such processes are especially obvious when one looks at the economic and environmental impact of colonialism. It is work well explored by scholars such as Iris Berger (1999), Claire Robinson (1997), Christine Mathenge (2013), Lydia Potts (1990) and Ault and Sandberg (2006/2001), as well as others, especially around land and labor, both of which are closely linked to our environment. Let us discuss this further.

One of the impacts of colonial occupation, certainly in British Africa; and indeed across much of the global south, was land alienation. This especially impacted communities like the Kikuyu who were agricultural in visible, immediate ways. The effect on women who were primarily food producers and who had a history of access to and authority to cultivate land, was especially traumatic. As the settler economy gained traction, Kikuyu women found both that they no longer had access to the various tracts of land they had prior to colonial conquest, and also as discussed above, that mechanisms of redress were often blocked to them. The first limited women's access to the varieties of soils they needed to grow indigenous crops on which regional healthy diets depended, and resulted in agricultural pressure on soils that accelerated soil exhaustion, deforestation and soil erosion as women tried to ensure the survival of their communities on the small and nutritionally poor parcels of land they obtained away from this new economy. Robinson discusses some of the difficulties associated with the reinvention women had to contend with in her book *Trouble Showed the Way: Trade in the Nairobi Area, 1890–1990*,[23] as does Maathai in the documentary *Taking Root: The Vision of Wangari Maathai* (Merton and Dater 2008).

Significantly, the second points to the manner in which this process worked in conjunction with other acts of disempowerment. For example, as land was appropriated from local communities, the social status of women was also weakened, as were the social institutions to which they could appeal to for recompense. In addition and to emphasize my claims above, this happened as local hearings and courts were delegitimized and populations destabilized as men were forced into wage labor away from their rural homes and into new emerging urban centers, where they became participants in new money economies that relied not only on de-animation but also on environmental exploitation. Women whose labor was often demanded by settler elites and the emerging state and economic structures in the form, for example, of plantation labor, and as sources of state taxation,[24] were often left in broken, dysfunctional rural spaces where, much like in urban spaces, the ecology was drained of vigor and vitality.

Very importantly, colonial agents systematically and deliberately weakened assembled populations. By discouraging the reconstitution of communities by, for example, resettling members in disparate areas so as to make it difficult to recover common histories, which might inspire memory of common identities that might in their turn encourage revolt, colonial agents were able for a period, to some extent, to control local populations. Original groups were broken up, dispersed and resettled as a tactic to avoid uprisings. In such turbulent circumstances, women had to compensate for the absence of men and sometimes the complicity of men with imperial and patriarchal power, while often reconstituting families and communities in transition as groups were intentionally broken up and resettled in new habitats. The consequential impact of this disruption was far reaching, especially in relation to indigenous knowledges and ecologies. Attempting to compensate for loss of access to natural resources and their partners in sustainable living, all in the face of a delegitimization of social systems, knowledges, and authority, women, in this case Kikuyu women, worked smaller and smaller tracts of land to meet expanded needs and obligations; often no longer confident of their own expertise or that of inherited archives which, given the disruption of resettlement, premature deaths and forced westernization, were often incomplete and unstable. The resulting turmoil was felt not only in human society but also across the ecosystem as soil nutrients were depleted, soil sequestration banks broken, excessive hunting carried out, trees cut down, waters redirected and contaminated, and so forth. This period is significant also because as access was taken from communities, pressure to use land for cash crops in imitation of colonial settlers moved groups and individuals to replace various traditional agri- and agro-cycles, many of which prioritized deep eco-relations and nurture. This negative turn led to a weakening of the environment and, in many parts of the continent, a reduction of indigenous cover. The impact of this imbalanced human print had the kind of far reaching consequences, especially in places like the Central Province of Kenya, that inspired Wangari Maathai's work[25] on the environment.

## Struggle and resistance

Importantly, studies of indigenous peoples reveal that the experience of dislodgment, dislocation and disruption is not unique to the Agikuyu.[26] In ways that are eerily similar, Wilma Mankiller and Michael Wallis (1993) in documenting the experience of the Cherokee, an indigenous group in the United States, provide another example of a group victim to the impingement of imperial power. Similar to the experience of the Agikuyu, we see in the Cherokee evidence of the ways that lack of constitutional protection from subjugation exposes indigenous people to displacement, removals and attacks that are sometimes fatal to people, cultures, their knowledge systems and ecosystems. This is a pattern that seems characteristic of the workings of imperial power. Admirably, given forces directed against them, indigenous women stand up and out against what by most measures seem overwhelming odds. They frequently successfully resist complicity in global, fossil fuel-intensive, capital-rich consumerist cultures and markets. It is therefore to these women then, that we must look as we think about the serious challenge posed by environmental degradation and climate across the world in our lives and communities generally, but most especially in Africa. In considering the success of indigenous women, it is clear to me as it is to scholars such as Wallis, that in part, their resistance has relied on the cycle of knowledge production, transfer and distribution that for example Potts (1990) discusses in her seminal exploration of global labor mentioned above.[27] Considering women's responses to colonialism, Potts (1990) points out that in intentional ways, African women historically effectively controlled reproduction as a way of counteracting colonial masters and the colonial system's demand for exploited indigenous labor. The actions of such indigenous women in Africa, then were, and continue now, to be important on several levels. First, their past success demonstrates the reliability of indigenous knowledge practices. That is, it tells us that African women had a working understanding of human biology and chemistry that allowed them to utilize the flora and fauna around them within indigenous paradigms to great effect. Second is the revelation that they had what seems a sophisticated awareness of the nature and impact of the imposed sociopolitical relations into which they were forcibly thrust. It is these which they rejected in serious intentional ways. It is also this resistance that Potts argues is signified by their control and redirection of reproduction to avoid their instrumentalization for the creation of reservoirs of labor for imposed capital markets that deliberately or coincidentally worked to destroy original production and distribution systems of material and epistemic goods.

To counteract such feminist resistance colonial governments, as discussed earlier, challenged and worked to delegitimize a wide range of local epistemic practices and sources including such pillars as local midwives, who were an important part of womanist lore and knowledge. This is a tactic used successfully not just in the global south but also in the global north.[28] On many occasions, as has been well documented elsewhere, with modernization local midwives were stigmatized and replaced by western-trained nurses and midwives who were themselves trained to operate within narrow, rigid, patriarchal birthing systems that are male centered, male identified and male dominated.[29] It is from the brink of extermination (of communities and of knowledge systems) that these kinds of practices signify, especially for Africana peoples, that indigenous feminists have held back against apparently insurmountable odds. It is from the tools and strategies that have allowed this resilience and directed this survival that I am convinced we must learn, if our ecosystems are to flourish.

## Into contemporary times

Ault and Sandberg (2006/2001) discussing indigenous knowledge systems, argue that their destruction impacts not only food and health practices but extends further into social and political structures in ways similar to the ones I discuss above. For example, they argue that the erasure and sometimes eventual absence of indigenous knowledge systems leaves women and children with no legal recourse in contemporary society as indigenous legal protections are often subordinated into emergent contemporary ones, or destroyed completely.[30] In the course of this socio-legal transformation, as they and others have pointed out, women are often the last to be absorbed and trained in the function of new systems. They are also the ones most seriously harmed by the impact of such changes on society and the environment. Additionally, family and community loyalty restrain their utilization of emergent systems. Reluctance to report perpetrators of social and environmental harm even as patterns of abuse, assault and violence (domestic, environmental and otherwise) increases with new and expanding vulnerability as individual communities are thoughtlessly and violently penetrated by global processes, and demands on time and allegiance increase on members for the survival of their families and communities in now weaker ecosystems; women, children and the elderly are harmed in many ways by these processes. This assault I argue, distracts women from the work of collecting and preserving knowledge, of nurturing the earth and building community/ies.

The vulnerability that results from this turbulence is most visible in the impact of modernization on land relations – as one looks at retention, acquisition and exchange – on indigenous persons generally but most especially on women. Patterns indicate that as indigenous communities and their lands are encroached upon, members are forced out of traditionally held land and onto land that may have been treated with agri-chemicals such as methylbromide, sulpher dioxide, DDT, dieldrin, chlorinated pesticides, and so on; or forced to take jobs or to farm in ways that expose them to pesticides. One can see this pattern in the Kenyan Central Province and Highlands as one follows the introduction of cash crops such as tea, coffee, maize, wheat, and of course, the flour industry. Being forced into capital systems without capital – actual or metaphorical – be this social, economic or material, within weakened social systems has a particular impact on women, their health and the environment.[31] This observation becomes even clearer when one investigates the flour industry; tomatoes; French beans; tobacco; shoes and clothing factories, and digital assembly industries that are often highly populated by women and children and which are especially vulnerable to World Trade Organization (WTO) agreements and intellectual rights (PRG) regimes. Of interest to our discussion is the fact that when marginalized groups often led by and heavily populated by women for reasons such as those discussed above, are successful in withstanding attempts at grabbing and/or contaminating their land, plants and animals, they are often left open and susceptible to increasing attempts to claim the products of generations of knowledge collection and application. And so in our time, we see treatments and processes that are quickly moved from the global south, patented and expeditiously regulated in the global north. Painfully, we see that as communities, and often women, attempt to ensure that the seeds, plants, animals and microbes that they have protected against encroachment are not patented and modified – as hybrid, genetically modified organisms (GMOs) and so on – without their consent by transnational companies such as Calgene and Monsanto, their states and other instruments of penetration and acquisition, such as academic institutions and researchers, agricultural boards and forestry boards, are sometimes enabled to complete the destructive work of imperial power.

## Buffeted

Part of what I hope is clear from my discussion here is that the impact of all these pressures on the Africana world is a western modernity that has engineered a loss of connection with our ecosystem and indeed our environments. This is damage I insist, that is exacerbated by a loss of our indigenous knowledges that were often located with women and transferred by women. Recent work not only among the Agikuyu but also amongst other communities elsewhere provides us with good evidence for this conclusion. For example, research on the Kpelle women of Liberia who over time have protected over a hundred varieties of rice. There is also the example of the Kamba in Machakos, Kenya. Amongst them, forty five indigenous naturalized wild plants for medicinal and health care have been found. Or, practices amongst some communities in the Sudan where women's role as the protector of sorghum heads is significant given that this cereal is an important staple. This role has been threatened by war. A comparable role is that of Agikuyu women, they, in orginal communities were administrators of granaries. Another example  in Kenya is tied to the harvesting lore of the Luo that honors the idea of *chira*[32] which demands that we connect sexuality and harvest.

When these connections are violently disrupted and replaced within and without by paradigms that locate living relations and processes in the market, and this kind of knowledge is obtained and transferred in part or solely through western education or what is sometimes called formal schooling, product advertisement and/or the internet, something valuable is lost. This latter point I hope is also clear, as is its grave impact on our environment.

## Indigenous feminist thinking – alternatives

An afro feminist lens allow us to excavate and make visible indigenous systems as resilient training and archival systems of knowledge that honor sustainable living and create apprenticeships that respect the ecosystem – dealing wholesomely with all members and aspects of life, allowing balance and support not only for survival but for even better, for flourishing. Very importantly, an afro feminist lens relies on an understanding of the human agent as a steward who relies on human relations within healthy ecosystems. This perspective is not unique to the Agikuyu; it is present among other Africana communities. The building of communities and the care such relations demands is a skill that Africana women have had to sharpen in response to historic challenges. It is this that afro feminism brings as a contribution to mitigating our environmental crisis – this tool, this strategy unpacked, is an awareness that we must each bring our memories and histories, our stories and expertise, and contribute to treating the environment as a member of our family, reliant on our relations and in the same way in need of nurture.

This perspective relies on the kinds of intersectional readings, writings and activism that scholars such as Kimberley Crenshaw (1991) and Patricia Hill Collins (1998) advocate for; one that is nuanced by afro readings of sex and gender in Africa presented by scholars such as Amadiume (1987) and Oyěwumi (1997), as discussed earlier; one that engages in the kinds of culturally safe research Tuhiwai Smith (2012/1999) urges, focusing on layers of indigenous feminist knowledge that opens spaces for women's voices and experiences to be heard, as they break the silences imposed on them by colonialism, modernity and neo-colonialism, complicating research, findings and epistemes. In the reality of our world where the past is gone and urban centers grow rapidly, we must factor these latter and their flux into our considerations of the environment. They are integrally connected to discussions of the ecology, and they, like women, demand a breaking of dualisms such as urban/rural, controlled/wild, artificial/natural, human/nature. This is the kind of work that Salleh and Merchant call on us to do. It is work that Africana women are particularly ready for, as our excursion into the histories above shows. Moreover, it seems to me that given that it is afro women who most recently in living memory have had to constitute and reconstitute communities, they are particularly good at recovery and reinvention, which is what our crisis calls for. They have always, similar to what Barbara Demmings argued for, had to engage in two-handed activism (one hand inviting reconciliation, the other resistance) well aware that there is no such thing as pure activism or pure theory.[33] They have had to be pragmatic in their vision and practice, always with the objective of deep moral and social change. Afro women, I am saying, are positioned by their material circumstances and equipped by history to move us into our futures. In such a case, the contribution of African indigeneity to environmental debates becomes not just that of offering a last frontier in terms of natural resources (which capitalist imperialists see as another chance for exploitation) or for the nostalgic preservation of the traditional (which is all the romantics offer), but rather new ways for communities under attack to exist in our stressed ecosystems, maybe with an urban–rural symbiosis that offers new possibilities for future cities and community living. Adopting the work of Mies, Salleh, Merchant and others, this kind of afro womanist perspective recognizes the dangers of unfettered anthropocentrism and the careless consumption that undergirds fossil fuel capitalism. It is work that contributes to deconstructing the binaries of self and other, human and nature, remembering how such simplistic divisions have allowed both women and nature to be subjects of patriarchal domination and exploitation. Unique to my work in this direction is, first, a recognition of the ways in which women generally but in this case in afro cultures circumvent patriarchal domination to develop reciprocal, nurturing relationships with nature and the environment. Second, the making visible of communal knowledges, practices of sharing these, and the sacredness of our interdependence that calls for restraint and sustainable practices in our relationships with nature. This is a response to capitalist consumerism that draws on our memories of sustainable cultural practices and a recognition of our moment. It is from here that we should engage with the major debates of our time in Africa on women and the environment, such as those on deforestation and forestation, GMOs,[34] and others. It is from here that we must vocalize alterity.

## Notes

1  For example, fish as the tragic story of Lake Victoria in East Africa shows. Read for example: Robert M. Pringle, 'The Origins of the Nile Perch in Lake Victoria', *BioScience 55(9)*, 780–787. Retrieved 15 September 2017.

2  Continentally for example, in the Congo, nationally in my case, in Kenya, in the Aberdares, Mount Kenya, Mau Forest, Ngong Forest, Karuri Forest, and so on. See: www.un.org/apps/news/story.asp?NewsID=43417#.WKiYC28rLIU – UN News Centre. 'Cost of Deforestation in Kenya Exceeds Gains from Forestry and Logging, UN Joint Study Finds', 5 November 2012. Retrieved 18 February 2017. http://wwf.panda.org/about_our_earth/deforestation/deforestation_fronts/deforesta tion_in_the_congo_basin/#eastafrica – Africa Deforestation – Congo Basin, East Africa. Find also on this site, the *Annual Living Forest Report* that talks to my claim above, retrieved 18 February 2017; Republic of Kenya, *Report of the Commission of Inquiry into the Illegal/Irregular Allocation of Public Lands*. Nairobi: Public Printer, 2004; Amnesty International, Nowhere To Go: Forced Evictions in Mau Forest. London: Amnesty International, 2007; Wilson Mathu, *Forest Law Enforcement and Governance in Kenya*. Nairobi: Kenya Forest Service, 2007; Sheila Masinde and Lisa Karanja, 'The Plunder of Kenya's Forests. Resettling the Settlers and Holding the Loggers Accountable', in *Global Corruption Report: Climate Change*. Gareth Sweeney, Rebecca Dobson, Krina Despota, Diter Zinnbaue, eds, for Transparency International. London: Earthscan, 2011; Multiple reports including: Kenya, Ministry of Environment and Natural Resources, *National Forests Programme of Kenya*. Nairobi, Kenya: MENR, 2016. www.environment. go.ke/wp-content/uploads/2016/07/Kenya-NFP-draft-doc-2016-07-12-small-v2-1.pdf. Retrieved 18 February 2017.

3  I write this as the occupied South in the global north continues to resist occupation and extermination. I write as water protectors in the North Dakota are fighting to keep clean the waters of the Missouri River and the lands of the Standing Rock, Sioux Tribe, in the face of physical attacks against them and their allies. As capital pushes to build the North Dakota Pipeline that aims to transport tar sand oil from Canada to Illinois through a route that would be a disaster for these indigenous Americans, the First Peoples of this Continent, the route promises and already has in some instances destroyed indigenous peoples' knowledges and cultural archives as sacred sites and burial grounds have been ruined. I edit this paper in the wake of some of the most powerful hurricanes to sweep through the Atlantic into the

United States and parts of the Atlantic. Catastrophic flooding in portions of South Asia including India have also been experienced, as have a series of serious earthquakes in Mexico whose impact was muted by the various tragedies that were unfolding simultaneously: mudslides in Sierra Leone, flooding in the Marshall Islands, Puerto Rico, Barbuda and more. All this is in addition to wildfires across Washington and California, low harvests in parts of Europe and droughts in parts of East Africa. Each of these political and weather events hits communities, especially indigenous ones, especially hard.

More particularly in reference to swamps, now often called wetlands, visit the educational section of the *National Geographic* online: www.nationalgeographic. org/encyclopedia/swamp/. Retrieved 18 February 2017. http://africa.wetlands.org/ Homepage/tabid/2907/language/en-GB/Default.aspx – A site which tracks wetlands across Africa. www.kenyawetlandsforum.org/index.php?option=com_content&vie w=article&id=43&Itemid=30 – Retrieved 18 February 2017. This site hosts a summary of the work of the Kenya Wetlands Forum which in response to the Ramsar Convention and in collaboration with partners African and international advocates for the reclamation and protection of swamps, marshes and other wetlands in Kenya. On the Ramsar Convention itself, please visit www.ramsar.org/ – Retrieved 18 February 2017.

4 See Naomi Klein's 'Opinion' column in the *Guardian*, 20 November 2015, that addresses the challenges indigenous persons face to even be heard on the international stage during the United Nation's climate change talks – COP 21: https://www. theguardian.com/commentisfree/2015/nov/20/paris-climate-talks-protesters-hollande-violence. Follow discussions at COP22: https://www.theguardian.com/environment/ 2016/nov/18/poor-nations-pledge-deep-emissions-cuts-at-marrakech-climate-change-summit, or even: https://www.thenation.com/article/what-does-blacklivesmatter-have-do-climate-change/, as well as many other conversations that address this issue.
5 See for example, Lorraine Code, *Ecological Thinking: The Politics of Epistemic Location*. Oxford: Oxford University Press, 2006; Alison Jaggar. *Feminist Politics and Human Nature*. Lanham, MD: Rowman and Littlefield, 1983.
6 As well as swine flu, ebola, hantavirus(from mice and deer), taxoplasma gondii (hosted by house cats in their feces), avian influenza (birds), lyme disease (deer), rabies (from dogs and bats) and many more.
7 I use the language of 'autonomy' and 'sovereignty' guardedly yet intentionally. Aware that these are terms that are shrouded in debate yet also conscious that this decade of the twenty-first century has seen multiple arguments over what seem to be increasing demands by nation-states or at least groups (sometimes referred to as nationalist) within these to determine their futures separately from what has sometimes been called the global order. From Brexit in the United Kingdom to the 2017 national election in the United States, these voices can be heard in Holland, France, Germany and elsewhere. Different issues drive similar calls in different countries on the African continent where for complicated reasons members may feel unfairly treated within the international order, most particularly the International Court of Justice at the Hague. Additionally, within various nation states, groups and communities have become skeptical not only of large scale international initiatives but also of centralized federal direction and so there are increasing calls to act locally.
8 I use this term well recognizing that it is contested. For part of this debate, do read: Oyèrónké Oyěwùmí. *The Invention of Women: Making an African Sense of Western Gender Discourses*. Minneapolis: University of Minnesota Press, 1997; Ifi Amadiume. *Male Daughters, Female Husbands: Gender and Sex in an African Society*. London: Zed Books, 1987.
9 See Pala Achola's article, 11 June 2010 at www.womensmediacenter.com/feature/ entry/the-ground-we-stand-on. Here she justifies her use of this language.

10 https://afrikaneye.wordpress.com/2007/03/08/the-effect-of-colonlialism-on-african-women/. This anonymous article by 'Afrikan Eye' offers us good overview of many of the issues I will discuss and most especially as these connect to colonialism and women. As with all articles found on the web and elsewhere, it is important that one reads it carefully and critically.

11 For example, of yam and arrowroot, maize and beans, sweet potato and greens. The planting and rotation of these, all of which we are coming to admit are especially good for our health.

12 Each making a powerful case. See: Carolyn Merchant. 'The Scientific Revolution and *The Death of Nature*'. *Isis* 97(3) (September 2006), 513–533; Karen J. Warren (ed.), *Ecological Feminist Philosophies*. Bloomington: Indiana University Press, 1996. Ariel Salleh makes hers in 'From Feminism to Ecology', *Social Alternatives* 4(3), 8–12 (1984). www.socialalternatives.com, which can be found at www.arielsalleh.info/theory/eco-feminism/socialalts-art.pdf or Ariel Salleh, 'Essentialism – and Ecofeminism', *Arena* no. 94, 167–173 (1991), which can be found at http://arielsalleh.info/theory/eco-feminism/arena-essent/arena-essent-article.pdf. Salleh makes available these two important articles on the open web.

13 In spite of the controversy surrounding his work, which is written as he admits from a Christian perspective by a Christian, one ought not to enter this discussion without remarking on the work of John Mbiti. My object here though is to note the expanse of the living connections that he invites us to observe in many African perspectives. See: John S. Mbiti, *African Religions and Philosophy*. African Writers Series. East Africa: Heinemann, 1990; Ibid., *Introduction to African Religion*. African Writers Series. East Africa: Heinemann, 1991.

14 Read for example L.S. B. Leakey's discussion of rules around land acquisition between the Agikuyu and Ndorobo in *Mau Mau and the Kikuyu*. London: Methuen, 1954; as well as Godfrey Muriuki's *History of the Kikuyu 1500–1900*. Nairobi: Oxford University Press, 2006.

15 Read for example Nkiru Nzwegu's article 'Osunality' (or African Eroticism)' in Sylvia Tamale (ed.), *African Sexualities: A Reader*. Nairobi: Pambazuka Press, 2011.

16 For an interesting consideration of parenting in Africa but certainly elsewhere, see: Obioma Nnaemeka (ed.), *The Politics of (M)othering: Womanhood, Identity and Resistance in African Literature*. New York: Routledge, 1997; Bessie Muhonja and Wanda Thomas Bernard (eds), *Mothers and Sons: Centering Mother Knowledge*. Ontario: Demeter Press, 2016. Here, in articles contained in both anthologies, as one finds more frequently today, parenting is complicated and transformed both into epistemic lens and analytic tool.

17 Here in calling up the idea of 'knowing', an intentionality assigned to processes, institutions, agents.

18 Refer for example to: Wairimu Ngaruiya Njambi, 'Telling My Story', in *Gendered Bodies: Feminist Perspectives*, edited by Judith Lorber and Lisa Jean Moore. New York: Oxford University Press, 2011.

19 See not only: Jane L. Parpart and Kathleen A. Staudt (eds), *Women and the State in Africa*. Boulder CO: Lynne Rienner, 1989; Sharon Stichter and Jane L. Parpart (eds), *Women, Employment and the Family in the International Division of Labor*. Philadelphia PA: Temple University Press, 1990; but also John Iliffe, *Honor in African History*. New York: Cambridge University Press, 2005.

20 For example, see studies of areas such as Pangani in Nairobi and the work of scholars such as Luise White on prostitution in Kenya: Luise White, *The Comforts of Home: Prostitution in Colonial Nairobi*. Chicago, IL: University of Chicago Press, 1990.

21 See for instance one reading of this in Silvia Federici, 'Witch-Hunting, Globalization, and Feminist Solidarity in Africa Today', *Journal of International Women's*

*Studies 10(1)*, 21–35 (2008), which is available open web at: http://vc.bridgew.edu/
jiws/vol10/iss1/3.

22 Swahili for conferences, formal public meeting places, courts, assemblies.

23 Claire Robertson, *Trouble Showed the Way*. Here Robertson leads us into this
discussion by use of the competition against the bean and in favor for example of
maize (corn).

24 See for example *Northey Labour Circular* no. 1, 23 October 1919. http://digilib.syr.
edu/kenya/supp/1217/index.pdf.

25 Hear her voice not only in her book mentioned above – *Unbowed* (2008), but also
in various interviews and of course in the documentary of her life mentioned earliler,
*Taking Root* (2008).

26 Refer for example to: Wilma Mankiller and Michael Wallis. *Mankiller: A Chief
and Her People: An Autobiography by the Principal Chief of the Cherokee Nation*.
New York: St. Martins Press, 1993. This important work carefully discusses
Cherokee experience.

27 Lydia Potts, *The World Labor Market. A History of Migration*. London: Zed
Books, 1990.

28 Read for example: Christine Overall, 'Childbirth', in *Ethics and Human Reproduction:
A Feminist Analysis*. Winchester, MA: Allen and Unwin, 1987.

29 Allan G. Johnson, 'Patriarchy', in *Race, Class and Gender in the United States*,
edited by Paula Rothenberg and Kelly S. Mayhew. New York: Worth, 2014; A
particularly good analysis of reproduction is Christine Overall, *Ethics and Human
Reproduction: A Feminist Analysis*, Winchester, MA: Allen and Unwin, 1987.

30 Amber Ault and Eve Sandberg (2001), 'Our Policies, Their Consequences: Zambian
Women's Lives under Structural Adjustment', In I. Grewal and C. Kaplan, *An
Introduction to Women Studies: Gender in a Transnational World*. New York:
McGraw-Hill, 2006.

31 Think of body wellness and reproduction.

32 No harvest without the first wife (polygamous arrangements traditionally
common), authorizing it. Such authority comes with a reminder of the connection
of the need to nurture fertility in all its forms as the ritual calls for sexual relations
with that first wife who then authorizes harvest.

33 I owe this way of thinking about Barbara Demmings to Ynestra Kings, an eco-
feminist whom I heard discussing this kind of two-handed activism during the
2016 Left Forum in the panel titled 'Revolution and NonViolence'. From Demming,
Fanon and today's global movements.

34 This position seems to call for caution in regard to Genetically Modified Organisms
(GMOS). Their resistance to large quantities of pesticides and unknown impact on
human bodies is of concern. As is their impact on land and waterway contamination
as well as on the possibility of harmful animal–human–plant encounters.

# References

Achola, P. (2010). 'The Ground We Stand On'. 11 June. www.womensmediacenter.co
m/feature/entry/the-ground-we-stand-on.

'Africa Wetlands'. (n.d). http://africa.wetlands.org/Homepage/tabid/2907/language/en-
GB/Default.aspx. Retrieved 18 February 2017.

Amadiume, I. (1987). *Male Daughters, Female Husbands: Gender and Sex in an African
Society*. London: Zed Books.

Amnesty International. (2007). *Nowhere To Go: Forced Evictions in Mau Forest*.
London: Amnesty International.

Anonymous. (2007). 'The Effect of Colonialism on African Women'. Message posted to *African Eye*. https://afrikaneye.wordpress.com/2007/03/08/the-effect-of-colonlialism-on-african-women/.

Aulette, J. R. and Wittner, J. (2012). *Gendered Worlds*. New York: Oxford University Press.

Ault, A. and Sandberg, E. (2006). 'Our Policies, Their Consequences: Zambian Women's Lives under Structural Adjustment'. In I. Grewal and C. Kaplan (eds), *An Introduction to Women Studies: Gender in a Transnational World*. New York: McGraw-Hill.

Berger, I. and Robertson, C. (eds) (1986). *Women and Class in Africa*. New York: Homes and Meier.

Berger, I. and White, E. F. (1999). *Women in Sub-Saharan Africa: Restoring Women to History*. Bloomington, IN: Indiana University Press.

Code, L. (2006). *Ecological Thinking. The Politics of Epistemic Location*. Oxford: Oxford University Press.

Collins, P. H. (1998). 'It's All in the Family: Intersections of Gender, Race, and Nation'. *Hypatia* 13 (3), 62–82.

Crenshaw, K. (1991). 'Mapping the Margins: Intersectionality, Identity Politics and violence against Women of Color'. *Stanford Law Review* 43 (6), 1241–1299. Available open source at http://socialdifference.columbia.edu/files/socialdiff/projects/Article_Mapping_the_Margins_by_Kimberley_Crenshaw.pdf.

Federici, S. (2008). 'Witch-Hunting, Globalization, and Feminist Solidarity in Africa Today'. *Journal of International Women's Studies* 10 (1), 21–35. Available open web at: http://vc.bridgew.edu/jiws/vol10/iss1/3.

Iliffe, J. (2005). *Honor in African History*. New York: Cambridge University Press.

Jagger, A. (1983). *Feminist Politics and Human Nature*. Lanham, MD: Rowman and Littlefield.

Johnson, A. G. (2014). 'Patriarchy'. In Paula Rothenberg and Kelly S. Mayhew (eds), *Race, Class and Gender in the United States*. 9th edn. New York: Worth.

Kananogo, T. (1987). *Squatters and the Roots of the Mau Mau, 1905–1963*. Nairobi: East African Publishers.

Kanogo, T. (2005). *African Womanhood in Colonial Kenya, 1900–50*. Athens, OH: Ohio University Press.

Kenya. Ministry of Environment and Natural Resources. (2016). *National Forests Programme of Kenya*. Nairobi: MENR. www.environment.go.ke/wp-content/uploads/2016/07/Kenya-NFP-draft-doc-2016-07-12-small-v2-1.pdf. Retrieved 18 February 2017.

Kenya Wetlands Forum. (n.d). www.kenyawetlandsforum.org/index.php?option=com_content&view=article&id=43&Itemid=30. Retrieved 18 February 2017.

Kings, Y. K. (2016). 'Revolution and NonViolence: From Demming, Fanon and Today's Global Movements'. In *Left Forum*. New York: John Jay School of Criminal Justice.

Klein, Naomi. (2014, 12 December). 'Why #Blacklivesmatter Should Transform the Climate Debate'. *The Nation*. https://www.thenation.com/article/what-does-blacklivesmatter-have-do-climate-change/.

Klein, N. (2015). 'COP 21 UN Climate Change Conference, Paris: What's Really at Stake at the Paris Climate Conference Now Marches Are Banned'. *Guardian*. 20 November. www.theguardian.com/commentisfree/2015/nov/20/paris-climate-talks-protesters-hollande-violence.

Leakey, L. S. B. (1954). *Mau Mau and the Kikuyu*. 2nd edn. London: Methuen.

Maathai, W. (2006). *The Greenbelt Movement: Sharing the Approach and the Experience.* 4th edn. New York: Lantern Books.

Maathai, W. (2008). *Unbowed: A Memoir.* New York: Knopf Doubleday.

Mankiller, W. and Wallis, M. (1993). *Mankiller, a Chief and Her People: An Auto-biography by the Principal Chief of the Cherokee Nation.* New York: St. Martins Press.

Masinde, S. and Karanja, L. (2011). 'The Plunder of Kenya's Forests: Resettling the Settlers and Holding the Loggers Accountable'. In Gareth Sweeney, Rebecca Dobson, Krina Despota and Dieter Zinnbauer (eds) for Transparency International, *Global Corruption Report: Climate Change.* London: Earthscan.

Mathenge, C. (2013). 'The Evolving Legal Framework and Governance in Redressing Land Inequalities'. In Kenya Scholars and Studies Association (KESSA)2013. Available open source at: www.kessa.org/yahoo_site_admin/assets/docs/4_Mathenge _KESSA_Proceedings_2013.362144818.pdf.

Mathu, W. (2007). *Forest Law Enforcement and Governance in Kenya.* Nairobi: Kenya Forest Service.

Mbiti, J. S. (1990). *African Religions and Philosophy.* 2nd edn. African Writers series. East Africa: Heinemann.

Mbiti, J. S. (1991). *Introduction to African Religion.* 2nd edn. African Writers series. East Africa: Heinemann.

Mellor, M. (1997). *Feminism and Ecology: An Introduction.* New York: NYU Press.

Merchant, C. (2006). 'The Scientific Revolution and the Death of Nature'. *Isis* 97(3), 513–533.

Merton, L. and Dater, A. (Directors) (2008). *Taking Root: The Vision of Wangari Maathai.* Motion Picture. Independent Lens. DVD available from New Day Films.

Mies, M. (2014). *Patriarchy and Accumulation on a World Scale: Women in the International Division of Labour.* London: Zed Books.

Mies, M. and Shiva, V. (2014). *Ecofeminism (Critique. Influence. Change).* London: Zed Books.

Muhonja, B. and Bernard, W. T. (eds) (2016). *Mothers and Sons: Centering Mother Knowledge.* Ontario: Demeter Press.

Muriuki, G. (1994/2006). *A History of the Kikuyu 1500–1900.* 5th edn. Nairobi: Oxford University Press.

*National Geographic Online* (n.d.). www.nationalgeographic.org/encyclopedia/swamp/. Retrieved 18 February 2017.

Neslen, A. (2016, 18 November). 'COP22: UN Climate Change Conference, Marrakech – Poor Nations Pledge Deep Emissions Cut st Marrakech Climate Change Summit'. *Guardian.* https://www.theguardian.com/environment/2016/nov/18/poor-nations-pledge-deep-emissions-cuts-at-marrakech-climate-change-summit.

Nnaemaka, O. (ed.) (1997). *The Politics of (M)othering: Womanhood, Identity and Resistance in African Literature.* New York: Routledge.

Nzegwu, N. (2011). 'Osunality (or African Eroticism)'. In Sylvia Tamale (ed.), *African Sexualities: A Reader.* Nairobi: Pambazuka Press.

Overall, C. (1987). 'Childbirth'. In *Ethics and Human Reproduction: A Feminist Analysis.* Winchester, MA: Allen & Unwin.

Oyěwùmí, O. (1997). *The Invention of Women: Making an African Sense of Western Gender Discourses.* Minneapolis, MN: University of Minnesota Press.

Parpart, J. L. (1986). 'Woman and the State in Africa'. *Working Paper* 117, May. Halifax, Canada: Department of History, Dalhousie University.

Parpart, J. L. and Staudt, K. A. (eds) (1989). *Women and the State in Africa*. Boulder, CO: Lynne Rienner.

Potts, L. (1990). *The World Labor Market: A History of Migration*. London: Zed Books.

Pringle, R. M. (2005). 'The Origins of the Nile Perch in Lake Victoria'. *BioScience* 55(9), 780–787. doi:10.1641/0006-3568(2005)055[0780:TOOTNP]2.0.CO;2. Retrieved 15 September 2017.

Ramsar Convention. www.ramsar.org/. Retrieved 18 February 2017.

Republic of Kenya. (2004). *Report of the Commission of Inquiry into the Illegal/Irregular Allocation of Public Lands*. Nairobi: Public Printer.

Robinson, C. (1997). *Trouble Showed the Way: Trade in the Nairobi Area, 1890–1990*. Bloomington, IN: Indiana University Press.

Salleh, A. (1984). 'From Feminism to Ecology.' *Social Alternatives* 4 (3), 8–12. Available open source at Social Alternatives, www.socialalternatives.com. www.arielsalleh.info/t heory/eco-feminism/socialalts-art.pdf.

Salleh, A. (1991). 'Essentialism – and ecofeminism'. *Arena* 94, 167–173. Available open source: http://arielsalleh.info/theory/eco-feminism/arena-essent/arena-essent-article.pdf.

Salleh, A. (2009). *Eco-Sufficiency and Global Justice: Women Write Political Ecology*. London: Pluto Press.

Shiva, V. (1997). *Biopiracy: The Plunder of Nature and Knowledge*. Boston, MA: South End Press.

Shiva, V. (2005). *Earth Democracy: Justice, Sustainability and Peace*. Boston, MA: South End Press.

Shiva, V. (2008). *Soil Not Oil: Environmental Justice in a Time of Climate Crisis*. Boston, MA: South End Press.

Skinner, L. (2012). *Recycle or Reimagine: Tracking the Direction of the U.S. Environmental Movement*. New York: Rosa Luxemburg Foundation.

Smith, L. T. (2012/1999). *Decolonizing Methodologies: Research and Indigenous Peoples*. 2nd edn. London: Zed Books. Available open source: https://nycstandswithstan dingrock.files.wordpress.com/2016/10/linda-tuhiwai-smith-decolonizing-methodologi es-research-and-indigenous-peoples.pdf.

Stichter, S. and Parpart, J. L. (eds) (1990). *Women, Employment and the Family in the International Division of Labor*. Philadelphia, PA: Temple University Press.

UN News Centre. (2012). 'Cost of Deforestation in Kenya Exceeds Gains from Forestry and Logging, UN Joint Study Finds'. 5 November www.un.org/apps/news/ story.asp?NewsID=43417#.WKiYC28rLIU. Retrieved 18 February 2017.

Wairimu, N. N. (2011). 'Telling my Story'. In Judith Lorber and Lisa Jean Moore (eds), *Gendered Bodies: Feminist Perspectives*. New York: Oxford University Press.

Warren, K. J. (1994). *Ecological Feminism*. London: Routledge.

Warren, K. J. (ed.) (1996). *Ecological Feminist Philosophies*. Bloomington, IN: Indiana University Press.

Warren, K. and Erkal, N. (eds) (1997). *Ecofeminism: Women, Culture, Nature*. Bloomington, IN: Indiana University Press.

White, L. (1990). *The Comforts of Home: Prostitution in Colonial Nairobi*. Chicago, IL: University of Chicago Press.

WWF Global. (n.d.). 'Africa Deforestation. Congo Basin, East Africa'. http://wwf.panda. org/about_our_earth/deforestation/deforestation_fronts/deforestation_in_the_congo_b asin/#eastafrica. Retrieved 18 February 2017.

# 12 Ecofeminism in Africa
## The contribution of Wangari Maathai

*Anke Graness*

## Introduction

The exclusion of women philosophers and feminist theory from the history of philosophy has been widely criticised, and a number of ground-breaking research projects and publications have furthered the reconstruction of women's contributions to philosophy during the last few decades.[1] Considering these debates, it is puzzling to see that overviews and compilations of African philosophy rarely include women philosophers or African feminist theory.[2] Their contributions are still generally neglected in African philosophical discourse,[3] and not only in philosophy, for example the wide-ranging *Oxford Encyclopedia of African Thought* (2010) does not – to my sincere astonishment – include any female thinker of African descent, not even Nobel Prize laureate Wangari Maathai.[4]

It is time to advance and intensify discussion of the theories and concepts developed by African women and to include their contributions in relevant discussions and publications. African female thinkers and African feminist theory offer interesting insights into several theoretical areas and questions, as well as topics with political significance. One of those topics is the intersection of feminist theory and environmental protection. The most outstanding example here is the theoretical and practical work of the remarkable Kenyan scientist, feminist, and ecological and political activist Wangari Maathai (1940–2011), winner of the Nobel Peace Prize in 2004.

In this chapter I will reflect on her contribution from a philosophical perspective and focus particularly on the system of ethical values which Maathai developed in her practical work for environmental protection and poverty reduction in the rural areas of Kenya. The chapter is divided into four sections. The first section explores keystones in Maathai's theory; the second introduces the concept of ecofeminism and one of its main theoreticians, the Indian scholar and ecological activist Vandana Shiva; the third elaborates on similarities and differences between Maathai's and Shiva's approaches; and the fourth section draws conclusions concerning the need for further discussions of Maathai's ideas.

## Wangari Maathai and the spiritual crisis of our world

A member of the Kikuyu community, Wangari Maathai was born in 1940 in Nyeri, a rural area of Kenya. Unlike most Kenyan women of her time, Maathai had an extensive formal education. She obtained a degree in biological sciences (1964) and an M.Sc. (1966) in the USA, and pursued doctoral studies in Germany and at the University of Nairobi before obtaining a Ph.D. in veterinary anatomy (1971) from the University of Nairobi, thereby becoming the first woman in East and Central Africa to earn a doctoral degree. She became chair of the Department of Veterinary Anatomy in 1976 and an associate professor at the University of Nairobi in 1977. In both cases, she was the first woman in the region to attain those positions.

In addition to her work at the University of Nairobi, Maathai became involved in a number of civic organisations in the early 1970s. She was a member of the Nairobi branch of the Kenya Red Cross Society and became its director in 1973. She was a member of the Kenya Association of University Women, and the National Council of Women of Kenya (NCWK). Through her work for these various voluntary associations, it became evident to Maathai that most of Kenya's problems were rooted in environmental degradation. Based on this finding, in 1976 Maathai introduced the idea of community-based tree planting, an idea which she continued to develop into a grassroots organisation, the Green Belt Movement (GBM). The GBM was founded in 1977 under the auspices of the NCWK. The GBM takes a holistic approach to development by focusing on environmental conservation, poverty reduction, community development, and capacity building. While the main target of the Green Belt Movement is to combat desertification, deforestation, water crises, and rural hunger, the movement also makes an important contribution to the empowerment of women in Kenya. It organises women in rural Kenya to plant trees to combat deforestation, restore their main source for firewood and generate income, while preserving their lands and resources. Moreover, it offers education and professional training for women. Maathai explained the focus on women in her Nobel laureate speech in 2004 as follows:

> Throughout Africa, women are the primary caretakers, holding significant responsibility for tilling the land and feeding their families. As a result, they are often the first to become aware of environmental damage as resources become scarce and incapable of sustaining their families.
>
> (Maathai, 2004)

Since the start of the movement in 1977, over 51 million trees have been planted in Kenya.[5] Over 30,000 women have been trained in forestry, food processing, bee-keeping, and other trades that help them earn income. And entire communities in Kenya have been motivated and organised to prevent further environmental destruction and restore that which has been damaged. For her work with the Green Belt Movement, Maathai was awarded the Nobel Peace Prize in 2004, becoming the first African woman to win that prize.

Maathai's activism was motivated by practical issues and problems. As she emphasizes repeatedly,[6] the Green Belt Movement originated from her involvement with the rural population of Kenya. In discussions with them it became apparent to her that there was a lack of resources, especially of basic goods like clean water, adequate food and firewood, and secure income. Soon Maathai realised that all these problems were rooted in a damaged rural environment, and that women were especially affected by such environmental problems as deforestation, soil erosion, and desertification. Thus, improving the condition of the environment entailed improving the condition of women, and even more fundamentally, preserving and healing the earth entailed preserving and healing humankind. Or as she expresses it:

> Through experience and observation, I have come to realize that the physical destruction of the earth extends to humanity, too. If we live in an environment that's wounded – where the water is polluted, the air is filled with soot and fumes, the food is contaminated with heavy metals and plastic residues, or the soil is practically dust – it hurts us, chipping away at our health and creating injuries at a physical, psychological, and spiritual level. In degrading the environment, therefore, we degrade ourselves and all humankind.
>
> The reverse is also true. In the process of helping the earth to heal, we help ourselves.
>
> (Maathai, 2010, p. 17)

Healing the world and healing ourselves are two inseparable tasks; conversely, 'to destroy what is essential to life is to destroy life itself' (Maathai, 2010, p. 18).

Planting trees seemed to be a concrete and accessible response to environmental as well as social and economic challenges. The benefits of trees are multiple: they help stem soil erosion and improve the health of the soil, making it possible to grow nourishing food. They provide firewood, fodder for livestock, and shade. They regulate rainfall and provide a habitat for small animals and birds (Maathai, 2010, p. 32). Beyond those benefits, through their involvement in the GBM, women gained a degree of power over their lives, especially their social and economic position and their status in the family. As a matter of fact, tree planting not only contributed to the improvement of living conditions of Kenyan rural women, but also laid the ground for many women to participate actively in social and political processes. Here too, Maathai was a role model or 'trailblazer regarding her early entry into electoral politics' (Presbey, 2013, p. 282). Despite all obstacles, including verbal and even physical attacks on her, she ran for election to parliament in 1982 and subsequent years, finally winning a seat in 2002. In 2003 she was appointed Assistant Minister for Environment and Natural Resources. Thus, her own commitment contributed to the escalation of women's participation in

Kenyan electoral politics over the last thirty years and an increase in democratic reforms in Kenya.

However, the GBM was not driven only by passion and the vision to improve the lives of Kenyan rural women, but also by certain core values. Maathai describes these as follows:

1   Love for the environment, a love which can be demonstrated in one's lifestyle and in activities like planting trees or protecting animals.
2   Gratitude and respect for Earth's resources. According to Maathai, this entails the three R's of Reduce, Reuse and Recycle.
3   Self-empowerment and self-betterment.
4   The spirit of service and volunteerism.

(Maathai, 2010, pp. 14–15)

For Maathai, such values are 'part of the human nature' (Maathai 2010, p. 16). Thus, she seems to stand for a fundamentally positive or altruistic conception of human beings, which takes them to be protective of and caring toward creation, not destructive and exploitative. According to her, human beings are guided by 'the god within us, the Source' (2010, p. 183), a voice that tells us the difference between right and wrong, alerts us when injustice is committed, and urges us to act against it.

Maathai considers the present-day ecological crisis to be at once a physical crisis and a crisis of values and ethical norms. She identifies a number of symptoms of moral decline which indicate that the voice within us which she describes seems to be silent today. Besides overconsumption and an insatiable craving for more that she believes are the main causes of environmental destruction, she also observes a deterioration of the commitment to serve the common good and work for the betterment of the community. She states, 'The farther people moved away from traditional life and became "modern", the less willing they were to serve. Everything had to be paid for, and those who couldn't pay were pushed out' (Maathai, 2010, p. 33). Maathai calls such an attitude a 'modern deficit in values' (ibid.). She argues that the prevailing value system, a selfish, monetized attitude to life, in particular a belief that every natural phenomenon is a commodity, must be changed before the present-day ecological crisis can be overcome. Maathai strongly doubts that scientists and economists who attempt to address ecological challenges like air pollution by commodifying, for example, carbon dioxide output, can provide a sustainable, or even practical answer to such challenges, because what they try to monetize is indeed priceless. In her opinion, spiritual or ethical values are more fundamental than science and data to finding sustainable solutions to ecological problems. She maintains that finding such solutions requires, in addition to the values of the GBM, honesty, transparency and, of course, a genuine will to work for change. The willingness to work for true change is above all what is lacking in today's international politics; most of the climate treaties negotiated at several world climate summits have yet to be ratified.

Consequently, the challenge of ecological crisis requires not only practical scientific and technical solutions, but also a new level of consciousness and substantial changes to the prevailing value system. Maathai suggests adopting the four values of the GBM to create sustainable change in our relationships to the environment and between ourselves. Of the items on that list of values – love for the environment, respect for the Earth, self-empowerment, and community service – the last two are crucial to her thought (see e.g. Maathai, 2010, chs 7, 8 and 9). Self-empowerment, or self-betterment, as Maathai calls it (2010, p. 135), is a fundamental value in her conceptual system.[7] She argues that the passive attitude of many Kenyans[8] contributes to numerous problems which the country faces today. By failing to take responsibility as members of the community, blaming others (the state, the government, colonialism) and remaining passive, Kenyans are hindering genuine change in their country. It is vital to abandon such passivity and adopt the conviction 'that one can improve one's life and circumstances – and the earth itself' (ibid.). Maathai describes a practice of GBM seminars that help participants take a step toward active participation: listening to participants to see how many of their problems are of their own making. 'By acknowledging our own destructiveness', Maathai argues, 'we have an opportunity to remedy it' (2010, p. 145). Homemade problems can usually be solved without waiting for someone else to take action. And thus, 'Through accepting their own responsibility, they can empower themselves ...' (2010, p. 135). Where passivity and inertia are elements of a very destructive disempowerment of individuals and communities, awareness of our own responsibility contributes to a new consciousness of our own opportunities to change prevailing conditions. Maathai's method of empowerment flows from acknowledgment of our own destructiveness and our responsibility for it. Disempowerment underlies Africa's gravest problems, argues Maathai. To remedy this, she calls on Africa's leaders to create conditions in which people may build confidence, recognise their inherent dignity, and develop a sense of self-worth (Maathai 2009, p. 274). However, Maathai warns, passivity and inertia can be used by authorities for their own ends. Ultimately, self-empowerment, self-reliance, and acknowledgment of one's own power to change (Maathai 2010, pp. 15, 130) are core values not only with respect to economic and social improvements but in the political sphere as well. Maathai states:

> Entire communities also come to understand that while it is necessary to hold their governments accountable, it is equally important that in their own relationships with each other, they exemplify the leadership values they wish to see in their own leaders, namely justice, integrity and trust.
> (Maathai, 2004)

Now, one could think at this point that such a strong focus on self-empowerment and individual responsibility is a sign of support for radical liberal ideas. Libertarianism not only considers individual liberty to be the most important political goal, but also holds that the role of the state in society ought to be severely limited. A radical interpretation of the liberal idea of self-ownership holds that human beings have absolutely no obligation to support one another.[9] Such an interpretation requires individuals be left on their own and holds them solely responsible for their personal success or failure. But this is not what Maathai has in mind when she focuses on self-empowerment and self-knowledge. Contrary to such radical formulations of liberalism, Maathai connects the responsibility of individuals for the improvement of their life with valuing selfless service and the use of volunteer labour for the benefit of the community – which clearly indicates a high appreciation for harmonious communal life and solidarity, instead of selfish individualism. In Maathai's view, self-empowerment is not meant solely to improve one's personal situation; it must contribute to a greater, common good which is, according to Maathai's understanding, the preservation of the Earth as a healthy ecological system.

Ecofeminism focuses on the preservation of the Earth, the improvement of women's lives, and the particular responsibility of women to use their knowledge for the regeneration of Earth's resources. To my knowledge, Maathai did not identify herself and her work as a part of this movement; however, there are a number of obvious similarities with ecofeminism in her approach and goals. Moreover, Maathai was quite aware of the work of such representatives of ecofeminism as Vandana Shiva. For this reason, I will introduce the concept of ecofeminism in the following section, using Vandana Shiva's theories as an example.

## Ecofeminism: environmental protection and the empowerment of women

The dominant tradition of European thought has strictly separated subject and object, nature and culture, emotion and reason, and female and male human beings. In this dualistic view, men were considered to be the creators of culture and civilisation, equipped with reason and a will to rule, whereas women were equated with nature, their physiology being seen as closer to nature, not least because of their capacity to give birth, and characterised as emotional, unreasonable, and ripe for conquest. The objective of culture/men was to subsume and transcend nature/women. Thus, the subordination of both nature and women is the explicit aim of such a paternalistic world-view. Incidentally, the equation of women with nature can be found not only in the works of such European male scholars as Kant, Schopenhauer, and Nietzsche, but also in the works of feminist thinkers like Simone de Beauvoir, who claims for example that 'the female, to a greater extent than the male, is the prey of the species' (de Beauvoir, 1953, p. 60).

The indispensable correlation between women and nature and the integral connection between the domination of women and of nature are the central tenets of ecofeminism. Ecofeminism differs from other feminist theories which still maintain a hierarchical and anthropocentric world-view. Or as Maria

Mies and Vandana Shiva argue, 'urban, middle-class women find it difficult to perceive commonality both between their own liberation and the liberation of nature, and between themselves and "different" women in the world' (Mies and Shiva, 1993, p. 5). This disconnection is due to the fundamentally dualistic nature of the 'Western' world-view, which divides reality into hierarchically arranged opposing parts; humans are seen as separate from nature, technology is seen as superior to indigenous knowledge, men as superior to women, and humans as superior to and separate from animals. In contrast to most 'Western' feminist theories, ecofeminism explicitly rejects any anthropocentrism and links the liberation of women with the liberation and preservation of nature.

Although ecofeminism has a conceptual framework with common features, it is not a homogeneous movement; it has taken many forms and comprises different positions. However, all representatives of ecofeminism condemn the patriarchal value system's separation of nature and culture as harmful and point out that women have been the primary victims of this split. They criticize modern (patriarchal) science and claim that a holistic knowledge of and approach to the world is necessary for sustainable environmental protection. Such knowledge seems to be preserved in many regions of the world by women, who often have a particularly close relationship to nature due to their roles in supplying food to their families, addressing medical issues, etc.

The Indian scholar and activist Vandana Shiva is a well-known representative of ecofeminism who plays a major role in the global ecofeminist movement. Shiva was born in 1952 in Dehradun, India. She studied physics at Panjab University, where she received a B.Sc. in 1972 and an M.Sc. in 1974. At the University of Guelph (Ontario, Canada) she completed an M.A. in the philosophy of science in 1977, and in 1978 she received a Ph.D. in philosophy at the University of Western Ontario with a focus on the philosophy of physics. She has a broad-based theoretical and practical commitment to environmental protection and poverty reduction. She has written extensively on indigenous knowledge, biodiversity, biotechnology and genetic engineering, intellectual property rights, and what she calls 'seed freedom' in her critique of patents for living organisms. She founded and has supported several NGOs in India and worldwide. For example, she is one of the leaders and board members of the International Forum on Globalisation and was involved in the Chipko movement, which resisted industrial forestry and logging in rural India.

Shiva considers the oppression of women and the oppression of nature to be deeply connected. In her article 'Women's Indigenous Knowledge and Biodiversity Conservation' (Shiva, 1993), she observes similar mechanisms being used to suppress gender diversity and biodiversity. She writes:

> Gender and diversity are linked in many ways. The construction of women as the 'second sex' is linked to the same inability to cope with difference as the development paradigm that leads to the displacement and extinction of diversity in the biological world.
>
> (Shiva, 1993, p. 165)

Shiva argues that the world-view that causes environmental degradation and injustice is the same world-view that causes a culture of male domination, exploitation, and inequality for women. At the root of these phenomena is a patriarchal, capitalist world-view – Shiva considers both to be closely connected[10] – which takes male humans as the measure of all value and regards them as standing apart from and above nature. In this view, nature is considered primarily an economic resource. The patriarchal, capitalist world-view also takes the male outlook to be the only valid guiding and ruling orientation. Thus, according to Mies and Shiva, the same masculinist mentality which destroys nature denies women the right to their own bodies and their own sexuality:

> We see the devastation of the earth and her beings by the corporate warriors, and the threat of nuclear annihilation by the military warriors, as feminist concerns. It is the same masculinist mentality which would deny us our right to our own bodies and our own sexuality, and which depends on multiple systems of dominance and state power to have its way.
>
> (Mies and Shiva, 1993, p. 14)

In Shiva's opinion, the patriarchal-capitalist world-view is incapable of treating women and males as equals despite their differences and unable to appreciate nature's diversity as a value in itself, for the 'patriarchal model of progress ... pushes inexorably towards monocultures, uniformity, and homogeneity' (Shiva, 1993, p. 164). The patriarchal model of progress is solely defined in terms of economic growth and the highest profit, and it presupposes uniformity as an effective instrument of high productivity. This particular concept of development has caused the present-day ecological crisis, for it considers nature primarily an exploitable resource for commodity production, not as an entity in its own right. Shiva argues that 'a denial of the rights of nature[11] as well as societies that revere nature was necessary in order to facilitate uncontrolled exploitation and profits' (Shiva, 1997, p. 106). In addition, in the patriarchal-capitalist world-view, only commodity production counts as production; therefore, most of women's heavy workload (including self-provisioning work as well as housework and child-rearing) is considered non-productive work.

To increase profitability, the patriarchal-capitalist economy resorts to tactics that have severe effects on biodiversity. One example is monoculture. Monoculture ensures high agricultural productivity of the production of specific cash crops. In turn, monoculture reduces the number of different crops cultivated and severely damages the environment, causing such problems as the degradation of soil fertility, and soil erosion. Moreover, monoculture requires heavy use of pesticides and fertilisers. In consequence, biodiversity is reduced both by reducing the number of different crops cultivated and by destroying other organisms (insects, animals, and plants) through the heavy use of chemicals or the elimination of the respective food source of the organism.

But monoculture has direct effects on humans too, argues Shiva. It is one of the main causes of malnutrition and severe nutritional deficiencies. Shiva claims that the problem of hunger and malnutrition is 'rooted in an obsolete and destructive food and agriculture system that is blind to the need for diversity, quality and … for a balanced diet' (Shiva, 2014). According to her, it is the reductionist mechanistic paradigm, which she also calls 'monoculture of the mind', that promotes monocultures. And she emphasizes that as a result of this monoculture model, the human diet has been reduced from nearly 8,500 species providing a diversity of nutrients to just eight crops, largely producing carbohydrates.

Particularly in her critique of so-called golden rice, a breed of rice that has been genetically engineered to biosynthesize beta-carotene in an effort to address the vitamin A deficiency suffered by 250 million people in developing countries, Shiva argues that the women of Bengal grow and eat 100 types of greens which can do the same. She claims that subsistence farming, which is based on a variety of crops, not only preserves biodiversity but is at the same time a solution to malnutrition (see Shiva, 2014) – a view which is strongly contested by a number of scientists.[12]

But biodiversity is not only fundamental to the fight against malnutrition; it is at the same time fundamental to the sustainability of self-provisioning farms, whereas monoculture creates dependencies. In a monoculture system, farmers can no longer provide themselves with the variety of plants needed for a balanced diet, but have instead to buy food they formerly produced for themselves. Thus, they are transformed from producer to mere consumer of food. Monoculture based on patented seed also forces farmers to purchase seeds instead of producing them, and in addition, to purchase the fertilizers and other items which cash crops require to survive.

Thus, monoculture has serious effects on communities, in particular on the lives of rural women. Monoculture displaces women in rural areas, for example in India, from their self-provisioning (but unprofitable) farms by integrating the land into huge farms for monoculture products and, through the use of patented seeds, by undermining their role as custodians of seeds. In consequence, women are transformed from experts in subsistence farming into unskilled laborers. The custodianship of seeds is in many traditional communities, according to Shiva, a role usually played by women that is closely connected with cultural elements such as festivals and rituals to celebrate the renewal of life. As a consequence, removing women from the custodianship of seeds displaces them from decision-making in their families and communities (Shiva 1993, p. 169). Thus, Shiva argues, the loss of biodiversity has serious consequences for nature and for the living conditions of women in many areas of the world, and she concludes:

> The marginalization of women and the destruction of biodiversity go hand in hand. Loss of diversity is the price paid in the patriarchal model of progress which pushes inexorably towards monocultures, uniformity, and homogeneity.
>
> (Shiva, 1993, p. 164)

Shiva describes women's work and knowledge as being characterised by diversity, contrary to the patriarchal-capitalist world-view and model of progress.[13] She claims that women have a special connection to the environment through their daily interactions with it, a unique connection generally ignored up to the present day. For example, women in subsistence economies produce in partnership with nature and are experts in their own right about the holistic ecology of nature's processes. Furthermore, their role as seed custodians makes them custodians of biodiversity. Shiva writes, 'Women have been seed custodians since time immemorial, and their knowledge and skills should be the basis of all crop-improvement strategies' (Shiva, 1993, p. 168), for in her opinion, women have a holistic view of the world and would develop new agricultural strategies that show respect for nature.

Among indigenous peoples, the conservation of seeds is often closely related to a concept of 'sacredness of seeds' (Shiva, 1993, pp. 169ff), which takes the seed as a symbol for the mystery of life.[14] Yet the sacredness of seeds is based on a world-view which runs counter to the patriarchal-capitalist world-view that values profit only and views seeds as a commodity. Thus, acknowledging the expertise of women in subsistence economies requires a fundamental change from a patriarchal-capitalist world-view to a view which perceives the interconnectedness of nature and human beings and is conscious of the connection between women's lives, work, and knowledge and the preservation of nature.

To sum up, Vandana Shiva considers the oppression of women and the destruction of nature to be inherently connected. She argues that the patriarchal-capitalist world-view and mode of production and their mechanisms of exploitation are at the root of the present-day ecological crisis. As an alternative to the prevailing world view, which is at the same time responsible for the oppression of women, Shiva suggests a new world-view which draws on the knowledge of women as well as on indigenous concepts. According to Shiva, both have a holistic view of our world, appreciate diversity, are closely connected to nature, and, thus, may enable us to avoid ecological destruction.

## Maathai and Shiva: similarities and differences

Obviously, Shiva's and Maathai's theories share some important features, including their commitment to environmental protection, which is closely linked with their desire to reduce poverty; their passion for tree protection and planting; their focus on the knowledge and experiences of women and on traditional environmental knowledge as it is expressed in such things as sacred groves and taboos; and their political activism on the national and international levels. It is also interesting that both originally started their careers as natural scientists.

However, there are also significant differences between Maathai's and Shiva's thought. In her theoretical work and her activism in the GBM, Maathai takes a different approach to that of Shiva, whose work is known to Maathai (see Maathai, 2010, p. 97). I consider two differences to be crucial. First, while Shiva's argument is explicitly anticapitalistic, Maathai – although she is fully aware of systemic injustice and the structural reasons for poverty and many ecological problems (see e.g. Maathai, 2009, pp. 48ff) – focuses on the spiritual and ethical dimensions of these problems. She views such values as self-empowerment, self-knowledge, and respect for the Earth, and such practical concerns as good governance and leadership essential to the success of the struggle to heal the earth's wounds, and our own. For her, the fundamental change necessary to 'replenish the earth' is a renewal of values and a shift in consciousness.

Although her theory focuses on values, she is well aware of the need to engage in practical political involvement. She realizes that environmental degradation flows from a lack of good governance, and that planting trees can be a significant political act:

> Although initially the Green Belt Movement's tree planting activities did not address issues of democracy and peace, it soon became clear that responsible governance of the environment was impossible without democratic space. Therefore, the tree became a symbol for the democratic struggle in Kenya. Citizens were mobilised to challenge widespread abuses of power, corruption and environmental mismanagement. In Nairobi's Uhuru Park, at Freedom Corner, and in many parts of the country, trees of peace were planted to demand the release of prisoners of conscience and a peaceful transition to democracy.
>
> (Maathai, 2004)

Since the commitment for the preservation of the environment and the democratization of the society are intertwined, issues of political participation, good governance, and responsible leadership are the second focus of her work. Maathai has clear ideas of what constitutes good governance.[15] In her opinion, good governance is based on three pillars or legs, like the traditional African stool. The first leg is democratic space, where rights are respected; the second leg is sustainable and accountable management of natural resources; and the third leg is a culture of peace, comprising such values as fairness, respect, compassion, forgiveness, recompense, and justice (Maathai, 2010, pp. 56–57).

Arguably, the main point of her work is that good governance, democratization, and commitment to environmental protection essentially require a renewal of social values. Without such an ethical renewal, people will be unable to change their attitudes to natural resources, modes of production, and, ultimately, humanity's way of living with one another as citizens of a particular country and inhabitants of the Earth. The wholesale rejection of social systems and production methods, such as Shiva's approach demands, is alien to Maathai's intentions. While Shiva's approach seems to suggest a kind of conversion to a certain world-view, Maathai's approach is open to a plurality of opinions – as long as they respect certain core values.

Second, her approach encompasses nature and *all* oppressed people, including men. Maathai underlines that the collaborative efforts of both men and women are needed to solve ecological problems and to lessen poverty. She pronounces several times in her writings the need for men *and* women to commit themselves to the spiritual and ecological regeneration of the Earth. What she wants is a genuine partnership 'where gender equity is respected and men and women share responsibilities fairly' (Maathai, 2009, p. 278). Such an approach follows a line of argumentation which is supported by quite a number of African feminists, including Chikwenye Ogunyemi (1985), Molara Ogundipe-Leslie (1994), and Mary Kolawole (2004). All of them stress the need for collaboration between men and women for the improvement of the society and warn of the pitfalls of 'Western' feminism's one-sided concentration on women's perspectives alone.[16]

Nevertheless, Maathai's work and the work of the GBM encourage women in particular to come together and make changes in their communities and country in order to advance the society. Maathai gives two reasons for such a gender-specific approach: First, rural women suffer the most from environmental destruction because of their responsibility for securing the necessities of life for their families. Deforestation and erosion deprive them of access to resources like firewood, clean water, and fresh food and make it extremely difficult for them to fulfil their responsibility. Thus, activities like tree planting are particularly useful for improving the livelihood of rural women.[17] Unlike women, a majority of African men spend much time working in urban centres, often forced by the dire need to earn money to sustain their families (Maathai, 2010, pp. 275ff). Consequently men are less directly affected by environmental changes. Second, as a result of their intensive agricultural work, rural women are equipped with a deeply grounded knowledge of ecology and agriculture as well as practical experience, which makes them successful in such activities as tree planting.

Both of the reasons for addressing women first (their economic needs and special knowledge) result from certain historical, economic, and political developments. Colonialism has had a particularly strong influence on the present-day status and role of African women. As Maathai argues in her chapter 'The African Family' (Maathai, 2009, pp. 275ff.), the colonial system uprooted the African man from his family and forced him to seek employment far from home. Consequently, women were forced to work in the fields and to sustain their families single-handedly. Thus, Maathai avoids an essentialist or homogenising view; in contrast, Shiva disregards history when she sees women as guardians per se of biodiversity, and considers female knowledge or a woman-focused system to be the proper means to achieve environmental protection.[18] When Shiva distinguishes between female and male knowledge, and even talks about a 'masculinist mentality', she perpetuates the dualistic world-view she criticizes by employing exactly the same binary patterns (men–women; homogeneity–diversity, mechanistic versus organic thinking). Such an approach does not only erase differences of power and experiences among women, but still seems deeply rooted in a heteronormative matrix. Issues like social and class differences between women; the assignment of privilege according to skin color, religion or culture; women's involvement in the machinery of exploitation and oppression, and so on, can hardly be addressed using such an approach. Maathai avoids such generalizations and explains that the situation of women in Kenya today and their relationship with nature results from historical processes and power relations (see particularly her analysis in *The Challenge for Africa*).

Maathai offers a truly holistic approach to ecological protection and poverty reduction by including all different forms of knowledge: women's knowledge and men's, scientific knowledge and traditional knowledge, modern values and traditional values. In contrast to Shiva, who considers only the positive aspects of subsistence farming (for example, the protection of biodiversity), Maathai also has an eye for the negative aspects of certain forms of subsistence farming, which – like certain forms of industrialized agriculture – also cause soil erosion and water loss (see Maathai, 2009, pp. 11ff). Thus, Maathai avoids generalizations about different forms of knowledge and refrains from favoring one knowledge system over another. Rather, she suggests a critique of different forms of knowledge, modern and traditional, from many regions of the world, with respect to their contributions to environmental protection and the harmonious coexistence of all forms of life on Earth.

In sum, Maathai's careful examination of complex structures and relationships saves her from one of the crucial pitfalls of ecofeminism, namely an essentialist conceptualization of women's relationship with nature, and makes her approach a valuable contribution to the ecofeminist movement. Maathai successfully overcomes the prevailing dualistic view and analyses the complex historical, economic, and political causes of ecological and social problems. Such careful analysis is the basis of satisfactory solutions to profound problems, which is probably part of the secret of the Green Belt Movement's success.

## Wangari Maathai and philosophy

Wangari Maathai was first and foremost an ecological activist, a feminist, and a natural scientist. So, why consider her practical and theoretical work as philosophical issues here?

There are several reasons. Not the least is the fact that the relationships between human beings and the world, between nature and culture, between freedom and the responsibilities of the individual, have been central philosophical issues for centuries. Maathai's work concerns all of these topics, and the clearly defined answers she presents to these questions are worthy of deeper exploration.

In conclusion, I want to come back to her focus on the renewal of values as the precondition for sustainable ecological protection and poverty reduction. As we have seen, Maathai regards a fundamental change of consciousness the key to a spiritual and ecological regeneration: movement toward a love of the environment demonstrated in one's lifestyle and actions, a respect for Earth's resources, self-empowerment and self-improvement, and a spirit of selfless service and disinterested volunteerism driven by non-monetary values. Throughout her work, Maathai recommends focusing on ethics and values to instil such character traits as gratitude for the earth's gifts, respect for the earth and our fellow humans, and the responsibility to work for the common good. Ultimately the solutions she identifies for the main challenges faced by Africans (and others) do not begin with economic and political change – which is the basic assumption of the development strategies, NGOs, and national and international political solutions that have thus far failed to provide sustainable solutions. In contrast, Maathai argues that the challenges humanity faces are 'moral, spiritual, cultural, and even psychological in nature' (Maathai, 2009, p. 4). Or as she puts it at the end of her book *Replenishing the Earth*: 'the questions of how or whether we will heal Earth's wounds are spiritual ones ...' (Maathai, 2010, p. 193).

Significantly, a crucial philosophical question arises here, namely the issue of the relationship between values and social structures, and ultimately between theory and practice. Does a change of attitudes and consciousness lead to social change? Or is social change the precondition for new ethical values, and in the end, a different practice? The question of which comes first is an old one, which culminated in the nineteenth-century Marxian notion that social existence determines the consciousness of men and women. Marx's controversial thesis has been widely debated in philosophy and other social sciences for the last 150 years.

In contrast to such a Marxian or materialist stance, Maathai argues that a renewal of our values is the precondition for 'healing the world and ourselves'. However, her claim raises several questions that have to be addressed. First, why did we lose certain values, like solidarity and selfless service, as she asserts? What is the reason for the 'modern deficit in values' and a monetised approach to the world? Is such an attitude not a direct response to the requirements of the capitalist system, and, thus, structurally determined? Although her approach is problematic in some ways, Shiva's understanding that the capitalist system is based on a certain set of values and a certain world-view offers a valuable insight into the close link between a social system, its mode of production, and a certain value system. Thus, Maathai's focus on values as the precondition for a social and ecological renewal provokes further philosophical investigation into the nature of the relationship between value systems and social systems, and the ways a value system can be changed. Maathai's almost Socratic approach of talking to the people, asking them to name their most fundamental daily problems, and finding out which problems are homemade and can be solved by the people themselves, might play an important role in such investigations.

And finally, I would like to address the important intercultural dimension of her work. Particularly with regard to the list of values proposed by

Maathai, we have not only to ask if the list is complete and whether it provides an adequate answer to today's challenges, but also to question whether such values will be interculturally acceptable.

Maathai's approach is already guided by an intercultural and comparative view, not least because of her own work on an international level and membership in international organisations. For example, with regard to the tree, the focus of her activism, Maathai describes the appreciation of the tree in different cultures, religions, and regions of the world. Trees are valuable not only as an economic resource or as part of the ecosystem; their value comes not only from the fact that they clean and retain water, regulate the climate, enrich the soil, emit oxygen, entrap carbon, conserve flora and fauna, and supply humans with food, medicine, firewood, and building material. Trees are also sites of healing, consolation, meditation, and communion with other human beings, spirits, and gods. They are inspiring entities and create inspiring places. In many cultures they are or were in former times the locus of judgment and governance. In a brief survey, Maathai reminds us about the function of trees in different religions and cultures, from the Jewish mystical tradition of the Kabbalah to the Hindu Upanishads to Christianity; from the ancient Egyptian culture to the Mayan civilisation in Central America to Norse mythology; she discusses the importance of the oak tree for the ancient Germans and the importance and function of trees in different cultures in Africa. She suggests that a system of taboos and sacred groves – as found in many cultures and religions – could reinforce the respect for nature. Maathai shows that, in almost all cultures of the world, the power and value of trees and forests far exceeds mere economics to encompass a deep spiritual dimension. Her reflections draw on different concepts and norms, including the Christian tradition in which she was raised and educated, her own Kikuyu heritage, other African traditional cosmologies and value systems, the Kabbalah, the Japanese *mottainai*[19] principle, and Latin American liberation theology. Here deeper philosophical analysis is still needed. This applies, for example to the *mottainai* principle, which Maathai mentions several times but unfortunately doesn't elaborate on. On this point in particular one would wish for further investigation by experts in Japanese philosophy. The same applies to her brief mention of the spiritual value of trees in different cultures and religions.

For Maathai, the most admirable result of the various attempts to save the environment is the ongoing dialogue that has emerged between scholars and practitioners of different religions: 'a coming together of a global consensus among religious and spiritual traditions that Earth matters' (Maathai, 2010, p. 180). Intercultural philosophy is one of the ways to continue these dialogues. And Wangari Maathai's work should play a central work here.

## Acknowledgement

This work was supported by the Austrian Science Fund (FWF) V 348 Richter Programme.

## Notes

1 See among others: Ménage, 1984; Waithe, 1987–95; Deutscher, 1997; Rullmann et al. 1994–95.
2 For example, see Eze 1997; Hallen 2002; Makumba 2007; Ochieng'-Odhiambo 2010.
3 And not in Africa alone. The neglect of women's thought and theory in academia is still a widespread problem throughout the disciplines and world regions.
4 Maathai is mentioned only in the last sentence of the entry on 'Environmentalism' (vol. I, 339). Among the few female thinkers honored with their own article are Afro-American feminists and writers like Angela Davis, Zora Neale Hurston, Toni Morrison and Alice Walker, and African women of European descent like Nadine Gordimer and Ruth First. Even though all these women rightly found their place in the encyclopaedia, it is nevertheless amazing that the editors did not include one single black African female scholar, artist or activist.
5 See www.greenbeltmovement.org/.
6 Maathai authored four books: *The Green Belt Movement* (2003); *Unbowed: A Memoir* (2007); *The Challenge for Africa* (2009); and *Replenishing the Earth: Spiritual Values for Healing Ourselves and the World* (2010).
7 For deeper exploration of her concept of empowerment see Gail Presbey's excellent article (2013).
8 While Maathai's writings refer mainly to her compatriots in Kenya, we easily can extend her argument to many other nations across the world, including the industrialised ones.
9 See for example Robert Nozick, who argues that helping is a moral option (virtue), but not mandatory. It is mandatory merely that we do not harm each other (negative duty) (Nozick 1974).
10 Here Shiva, as well as further representatives of ecofeminism, argue along the same lines as a number of other feminist and postcolonial thinkers, for example the Afro-American scholar bell hooks. Hooks explains in her book *The Will to Change: Men, Masculinity, and Love*: 'I often use the phrase "imperialist white-supremacist capitalist patriarchy" to describe the interlocking political systems that are the foundation of our nation's politics' (p. 17). Thus, even though patriarchy is older than capitalism, scholars like Shiva or hooks assume a specific link between the two political systems mainly due to the exploitive character of both.
11 'Rights of nature' are defined by the Global Alliance for the Rights of Nature, where Shiva serves as an Executive Committee member, as follows: 'Rights of Nature is the recognition and honoring that Nature has rights. It is the recognition that our ecosystems – including trees, oceans, animals, mountains – have rights just as human beings have rights. Rights of Nature is about balancing what is good for human beings against what is good for other species, what is good for the planet as a world. It is the holistic recognition that all life, all ecosystems on our planet are deeply intertwined.' http://therightsofnature.org/what-is-rights-of-nature/, accessed 9 September 2016.
12 See for example Justus Wesseler and David Zilberman (2014) and Patrick Moore (2013).
13 Elsewhere she even speaks of a 'feminine principle' which is based on inclusiveness and its recovery in men, women, and nature, a recovery of 'creative forms of being and perceiving' (Shiva 1989, p. 53).
14 The book *Sacred Seed* (2014), a collection of essays compiled and edited by Vandana Shiva and Bartholomew, the ecumenical patriarch of Constantinople, draws on the knowledge of mystics, shamans, monastics, and priests to illustrate the profound sacredness of the seed in ancient and modern traditions.

15 Several chapters of Maathai's book *The Challenge for Africa* (2009) are dedicated to those issues, most prominently 'Pillars of Good Governance: The Three-Legged Stool', pp. 48–62, and 'Leadership', pp. 111–128.

16 The concept of 'gender mainstreaming' – used as a strategy for making women's as well as men's concerns and experiences an integral part of policies and programmes in all spheres of the society – is comparatively young (the earliest laws institutionalizing it in the European Union were passed in 1997 and 1999) in relation to African feminists' critique of 'Western' feminism (particularly the representatives of so called second-wave feminism, e.g. Simone de Beauvoir), which concentrated for decades on issues of the emancipation and equality of women.

17 This is certainly the case in Kenya and other African countries. However, the question has to be raised of whether this argument is true on an international scale.

18 To claim that diversity 'is the principle of women's work and knowledge' (Mies and Shiva 1993, p. 164) is itself an essentialist concept of womanhood. Essentialism means here a perspective which assumes that certain individual or social features are (biologically) fixed, immutable and inevitable.

19 The Japanese word *mottainai* refers to the waste of something useful, like food or time. Buddhists apply the word to the waste or misuse of something sacred. The term encompasses respect, gratitude, and conservation of resources.

## References

de Beauvoir, S. (1953). *The Second Sex*. Translated by H. M. Parshley. New York: Knopf.

Deutscher, P. (1997). *Yielding Gender: Feminism, Deconstruction and the History of Philosophy*. London and New York: Routledge.

Eze, E. C. (1997). *Postcolonial African Philosophy: A Critical Reader*. Cambridge, MA: Blackwell.

Hallen, B. (2002). *A Short History of African Philosophy*. Bloomington, IN: Indiana University Press.

hooks, b. (2004). *The Will to Change: Men, Masculinity, and Love*. New York: Atria Books.

Irele, F. A. and Jyifo, B. (eds) (2010). *The Oxford Encyclopedia of African Thought*. New York: Oxford University Press.

Kolawole, M. (2004). 'Reconceptualizing African Gender Theory: Feminism, Womanism and the Arere Metaphor'. In *Rethinking Sexualities in Africa*, edited by Signe Arnfred, pp. 251–266. Uppsala: Nordic Africa Institute.

Maathai, W. (2003). *The Green Belt Movement: Sharing the Approach and the Experience*. New York: Lantern Books.

Maathai, W. (2004). Nobel Lecture, Oslo, 10 December 2004. www.nobelprize.org/no bel_prizes/peace/laureates/2004/maathai-lecture-text.html, accessed 31 August 2016.

Maathai, W. (2007). *Unbowed: A Memoir*. New York: Anchor Books.

Maathai, W. (2009). *The Challenge for Africa*. New York: Anchor/Random House.

Maathai, W. (2010). *Replenishing the Earth: Spiritual Values for Healing Ourselves and the World*. New York: Doubleday.

Makumba, M. M. (2007). *An Introduction to African Philosophy: Past and Present*. Nairobi: Paulines Publications Africa.

Ménage, G. (1984). *The History of Women Philosophers*. Translated by Beatrice Hope Zedler. Lanham, MD: University Press of America.

Mies, M. and Shiva, V. (eds), (1993). *Ecofeminism*. London and New Jersey: Zed Books.

Moore, P. (2013). 'By Opposing Golden Rice, Greenpeace Defies Its Own Values – and Harms Children'. *Toronto Globe and Mail*, 8 October.

Nozick, R. (1974). *Anarchy, State, and Utopia*. New York: Basic Books.

Ochieng'-Odhiambo, F. (2010). *Trends and Issues in African Philosophy*. New York: Peter Lang.

Ogundipe-Leslie, M. (1994). 'Stiwanism: Feminism in an African Context'. In *Re-Creating Ourselves: African Women and Critical Transformations* (pp. 207–241). Trenton, NJ: Africa World Press.

Ogunyemi, C. O. (1985). 'Womanism: The Dynamics of the Contemporary Black Female Novel in English'. *Signs* 11 (1), 63–80.

Presbey, G. (2013). 'Women's Empowerment: The Insights of Wangari Maathai'. *Journal of Global Ethics* 9 (3), 277–292.

Rullmann, M., Gründgen, G. and Mrotzek, M. (eds) (1994–95). *Philosophinnen*. 2 vols. Zürich/Dortmund: Edition Ebersbach im eFeF.

Shiva, V. (1989). *Staying Alive: Women, Ecology and Development*. London: Zed Books.

Shiva, V. (1993). 'Women's Indigenous Knowledge and Biodiversity Conservation'. In *Ecofeminism*, edited by M. Mies and V. Shiva (pp. 164–173). London and New Jersey: Zed Books.

Shiva, V. (ed.) (1994). *Close to Home: Women Reconnect Ecology, Health and Development Worldwide*. Philadelphia, PA: New Society Publishers.

Shiva, V. (1997). *Biopiracy: The Plunder of Nature and Knowledge*. Cambridge, MA: South End Press.

Shiva, V. (2014). 'Golden Rice: Myth, not Miracle'. *GM Watch*, 12 January. http://gm watch.org/index.php/news/archive/2014/15250-golden-rice-myth-not-miracle. Accessed 13 September 2014.

Shiva, V. and Bartholomew, Ecumenical Patriarch of Constantinople (eds) (2014). *Sacred Seed*. Point Reyes, CA: The Golden Sufi Center Publishing.

Waithe, M. E. (ed.) (1987–95). *A History of Women Philosophers*. 4 vols. Dordrecht: Kluwer.

Wesseler, J., Zilberman, D. (2014). 'The Economic Power of the Golden Rice Opposition'. *Environment and Development Economics* 19 (6), 724–742. doi:10.1017/S1355770X1300065X.

# 13 Women in the kitchen of philosophy

## Re-asking the questions of African philosophy

*Egbai Uti Ojah*

## Introduction

African philosophy is a relatively young tradition. Some historians of African philosophy have dated its emergence as a systematic discipline to the twentieth century (Chimakonam, 2014). Thus for nearly a century of its existence as a discipline, the questions of African philosophy have largely overlooked the female perspective; it is therefore about time to re-ask the questions that drive inquiries in African philosophy. By re-asking the questions, I do not mean the abandonment of old questions; I mean the integration of other relevant perspectives like that of women. As men dominate the African philosophical place, most of them have taken it for granted that women either cannot philosophize or do not have the right to philosophize. Thus the question 'who has the right to philosophize in a given place?' will drive my inquiries in this work.

For much of the twentieth century, African philosophers asked metaphilosophical questions bordering on the discipline's existence or otherwise. Some of the prominent voices in this regard include: Henri Maurier (1984), Richard Wright (1984), Peter Bodunrin (1984), C. S. Momoh (1985), and others. Recently, some like Pantaleon Iroegbu (1995), Innocent Asouzu (2004), Jennifer Lisa Vest (2009) and Bruce Janz (2009), have begun asking or at least advocating for phenomenological questions concerning new ideas in the discipline. While some inquire about method, others ask about system building and some others ask about the 'African predicament' and other specific themes (Andreski, 1970; Oguejiofor, 2001; Awoonor, 2006). But even with these new dynamics, women and the roles they can play in the development of the discipline are relegated to the background.

No doubt, there are now some African women who produce feminist literature in support of the female perspective in scholarship as well as intellectual freedom specifically in African studies. A few good examples are Ogundipe-Leslie (1994), Oduyoye (1995), Ogwu (1996), Nzegwu (1996), Oyewumi (1997) and Oheneba-Sakyi (1999); but even these efforts have not in a concerted way established a strong philosophical basis for the justification of female epistemic perspective, especially in African philosophy. What these well-meaning women do can easily be criticized by their chauvinistic contemporaries as agitations of a few misguided diaspora women who have been corrupted by the cultures of what the Igbo would call *nwa-bekee* or the outsider European.

My concern in this work is to produce a philosophical necessity and justification for the viability of the female voice in the African philosophical place. I will argue that African women can philosophize or think for themselves and even for the society, for the singular reason of being humans and possessing the faculty of reason. If there is such a thing as the right to philosophize, it should be the natural entitlement of all humans unregulated by the positive law. Nobody has and should have the power to determine who is to exercise his or her ability to think and hold informed opinions on issues of concern. Even the rule of law, that is the bastion of modern organization and functionality of a society, is grossly limited and cannot regulate the human activity of reflection.

To this end, I am of the view that the marginalization of women in Western philosophy has had severe consequences for civilization. For example, it is hard to believe that had women as much influence in international politics and diplomacy as men did in the twentieth century, the first and second World Wars would have occurred. Even if the first may have occurred, few could argue that the second would have taken place. The reason is not far-fetched. One can argue with a measure of confidence that the agony of the loss of lives of fathers, sons and husbands in the First World War would have been enough to spur women to avert the Second World War, if there had been an influential number of women in international politics and diplomacy. Needless to emphasize here that women suffered greater anguish from the losses caused by those two great wars.

Again, when we leaf through the pages of recent human history, we are bound to observe the cracking family structures. And of course, the collapse of the family structure inevitably spreads repercussions in the society. We must ask: on what do we blame most of the family crisis in our societies today? Evidently, since the mid-twentieth century, women have been on the rampage fighting for their rights, using all manner of strategies including what might be called family guerrilla warfare. As insignificant or private as the society might think of this, it is mounting untold stress on different family units which in turn impact the society heavily. Today in almost every society, all manner of gender issues or gender inspired issues perturb us all. Specifically, one can list issues such as unequal wages for equal work, employment in specific fields and professions as some are still considered the domain of men, issues concerning inheritance as some cultures still pass on inheritance along the male line; in some cultures a man may smoke cigarette but a woman should not, a man may drive but a woman should not, and the list goes on. Within the family units, some of these problems tend to become violent in nature, others become deadly. Now, it may be argued that the cultural, social and political conventions implicated in the gender imbalance that creates these frictions, especially at the level of family units, are one way or the other inspired by long conspiracy of silence by the philosophers of Western civilization. In postcolonial times, we see different African societies copying the West by entrenching and enforcing cultural, social and political patterns of male domination. I will argue that African philosophers (males and females working together) can and should prevent such pattern from taking root in the African place by liberalizing the episteme of African intellectual space so that African women can participate in the enterprise of African philosophy and express their reflections. The reason I focus primarily on women's freedom to think and express their thoughts is because it is the first point of liberation. It is difficult to accomplish the task of ending women's subordination, if actors do not first liberate women intellectually and free them from the mental chains of our social, cultural and political history. The denial of the natural right to think and express oneself is tantamount to full scale dehumanization. And this is what women in Africa suffer amidst the silence of the African philosopher. Again, I talk of the African philosopher as a genderless construal.

In the first part of this chapter, I will investigate the right to philosophize: who has it? And who does not have it? I will try to connect a culture of subjugation to the current perception of women philosophers in Africa. I will speculate on what should be the proper place of women philosophers in Africa. In the second part, I will question the questions of African philosophy. I will recommend that it is the burden of African philosophy to correct the anomaly of its lopsided questions by re-asking its questions in ways that will accommodate not only the concerns of women but most importantly, the voice of women.

## Who has the right to philosophize in the African place?

First, it is important that I clarify the analogy of 'kitchen of philosophy'. The kitchen is the part of a home where meals are prepared. In the African world-view, it is bad manner to talk while preparing meals. It is the female gender that is associated with this anonymous place and the thankless task of preparing meals for the family and most especially for the men. It is taken for granted in many an African culture that one of the basic duties of the woman is to prepare meals for her husband. In native African architecture, the location of the kitchen is usually at the back of the compound where visitors and outsiders do not get to. The kitchen has a couple of symbolic meanings: (a) it is a place that sustains life. Women are vehicles of life in the sense that they are the ones that men send on the errand of bringing human life into the world, so it is their duty to sustain it by constant nourishment; (b) the kitchen is a place for the weak and ambitionless gender. Men are comfortable with women controlling the place from which their nourishment comes because they are thought of as weaklings who lack ambition like men. In which case they constitute less threat; (c) when women are posted to the kitchen which is located at the back of the house, almost hidden from sight, it signifies relegation to the background where they are not to be heard; (d) the big structure of the house that stands in front of the small kitchen located behind it symbolizes the power of the man and vulnerability of the female gender. The female gender represented by the small kitchen is expected to be perpetually thankful to the man who provides, protects and thinks for her; (e) it is the right of the man to occupy the main house and the duty of the woman to remain in the small kitchen behind quiet, silent and anonymous; (f) the kitchen above all else is not a place to employ the brain and the speech act, both instruments of philosophy; it is rather a place to engage the limbs.

From the above, the analogy of 'kitchen of philosophy' is evoked to depict the type of mindset that can determine what the place of women in African philosophy might be. In African philosophy, women are expected to be anonymous. Anonymity is their virtue. They are expected to be in the background, silent and grateful to men whose 'right' it is to think for both genders. This implies that women are not really subjects capable of thinking for themselves or the world for that matter. In this guise, African philosophy can very easily reduce them to objects. As objects of thought, African male philosophers are at liberty to choose when and how to think about them. They may even choose to regard them aesthetically, in which case there might not be any need to consider the objects reflectively. They could become objects of admiration and at most, of sexual fantasy. Indeed, how many African male philosophers see beyond sexual objects when they look at women? This rhetoric question constitutes serious food for thought but I will not investigate it further here.

What I will do however, is to show that all of this epistemic marginalization demonstrates the gripping power of the stereotype that presents women as means to serve men's ends rather than ends in themselves, especially in African cultures. As means they are mere objects. Philosophy on the other hand is an activity of human subjects. Men therefore represent the definition of humanness in which the female gender is an appendage of some sort, not complete enough to practice reflection and yet not so incomplete as to be denied the tag of humanity. The female gender is a human, but not quite in the sense of the male gender, hence, she is not worthy of holding an informed opinion. Since philosophy is a mental activity, which leads one to hold and express informed opinions, and since many African sages think that the female gender is not intellectually equipped by nature to achieve this feat, they relegate her to the background and banish her to the kitchen. In the kitchen of philosophy, there is no reflecting, speculating, pontificating, extrapolating, conversing, arguing; all you have is silence/agreement, and this is where women should belong. The above categorizations have been adopted by modern African philosophy from the traditional ethno-philosophical orientation propagated by nameless African philosophers of the pre-systematic era (Chimakonam, 2014). Innocent Asouzu has also described these precolonial African sages as anonymous African philosophers (2004). In recent time, Nigeria's president Muhammadu Buhari has been quoted as saying that his wife, the First Lady, belongs in his kitchen and the other room (*Vanguard News*, 2016). If the president of Africa's most populous nation holds this view in the twenty-first century and gets away with it, then that gives us an idea, with respect to cultural, social and political complicities, of women's subordination in postcolonial Africa. Granted that there may be many Nigerians, and by extension African men, who do not share this type of despicable opinion with Mr Buhari, but the worrisome question is: what is the level of cultural, social and political sensitivity concerning women' subordination in Nigeria and Africa at large? Obviously, it is still abysmally low; otherwise, such a comment would have been enough to cost Buhari his job. Even in a country like Nigeria where women outnumber men, Buhari's job was never threatened, let alone his marriage. The fact that he got away with this scandal without a scratch speaks of the high level of intellectual marginalization women have suffered in Africa. Buhari's declaration that his wife belonged to the kitchen and to the bedroom also spoke volumes for his perception of women as house maids and sex objects who are not made to use their brains. If not for anything else, the idea of the kitchen of philosophy should be able to arouse our consciousness and persuade us to revisit the question of right to philosophize once again, and that will be my focus.

Who has the right to philosophize in the African place? This question in the context of this work is not about race but about gender. Even at that, the question might not make so much sense at the surface level, but deep down, it underlies the basic ethos that influences the philosophical attitude in sub-Saharan Africa. In parts of postcolonial Africa it is almost a cultural crime to be a woman in philosophy. To be specific, philosophy does a couple of things to the mind. The first is to set it on the path of argumentation. A philosophical mind is not supposed to accept a position without questioning. The second is to set it on the path of informed individual opinion. Philosophy trains the mind and equips an individual with the ability to hold one's own opinions and take responsibility for them. The third is to set it free from any conceptual impositions. No student of philosophy can be regarded as properly trained if she still venerates authority. I will revisit the question of who has the right to philosophize in the next section.

Now, all of the three things highlighted above which philosophy education impacts are antithetical to the traditional African mores that African women are expected to live by. For example, an African woman is supposed to be virtuous, and one may add that the first principle of virtue is anonymity. To argue for or against positions, to hold one's own informed opinion, and not to venerate the authority of men are *virtueless* means of conduct. But the problem, it seems, is not really about the moral quality of such conduct that is regarded as *virtueless*; after all, those are the exact same patterns of conduct that African men live by; it is the fact that men are the ones who make these rules and set them to apply to only women. One way this works is that men are the ones that shape the cultural, social and political life of a sexist society. Where they have not enacted laws, they form and mould opinions about who is a virtuous woman and who is not, usually, in accordance with their masculine predilections.

So, somehow, and in a very sincere way, the question that should be at issue is; who determines who has the right to philosophize in the African place? As soon as we summon the courage to ask this latter question, we open the door to thoughts that will question some of the uncritical assumptions that underlie the African life-world, which in turn undergird our mode of philosophizing in Africa.

I will not go into some of these uncritical assumptions that fuel the arguments against women's intellectual ability. Some feminist scholars have addressed these assumptions almost comprehensively (See: Horney, 1967; Lynne, 1983; Midgley and Hughes, 1983; Nzegwu, 2006; Alcoff and Kittay, 2007; Shaw and Lee, 2012; Chuku, 2013). What, however, will occupy my attention is the fact that men are the ones that make laws, conventions and norms which the society adopts. Men are still the ones that rule the society and determine its destiny. So, they really are the ones who determine who has the right to philosophize. But is it supposed to be so? Obviously not! Philosophy promotes freedom wherever it is practised. It seeks to liberalize reason in all places in the world. It cannot at the same time stifle freedom and imprison reason in the African place.

From the foregoing, it is clear that for African philosophy to thrive, it needs to reinvent itself. Some have argued that it needs to downplay its commitment to metaphilosophical debates and focus more attention on phenomenological issues (Janz, 2009; Vest, 2009; Chimakonam, 2015). Others have also argued against African philosophy's over-commitment to the question of its existence (Janz, 2015) carried over from the middle and later periods of its history. What it should be focused on in this contemporary period are themes that reposition its fortunes. African philosophy must now identify important themes that have been excluded or ignored in its discourses so far or that correspond to the experiences of Africans in today's world. Examples of such themes that African philosophy should investigate, to name a few, are climate change, the environment, and of course the question and perspective of women in post-colonial Africa's social and intellectual spheres. African philosophy must reinvent itself to address some of these relevant issues that have been sidelined for much too long. To do this effectively, African philosophers must take steps to re-ask the questions of African philosophy in order to accommodate these perspectives and themes.

## Re-asking the questions of African philosophy

Instead of asking, for example, about the existence or non-existence of African philosophy, whether it is on the same footing or can compete with Western philosophy, whether it can be compared with Western philosophy, we can ask: what can African philosophy do for Africa? How can African philosophy solve the everyday problems in Africa? How can it negotiate the challenges facing women in particular? How can it dethrone the culture of subservience and inspire a new culture of questioning?

However, it is not just questioning that is needed; it is a specific line of questioning. African philosophy has been asking questions, but a load of them have been essentialist and a pointless reaction to Western demagoguery. This is why we talk of a re-asking of the questions of African philosophy. Perhaps Bruce Janz captures it properly when he states:

> The question of African philosophy needs to be re-asked, not from an essentialist but from a phenomenological and hermeneutical point of view. Instead of carving territory, there should be a way to rethink this nascent field through its own theoretical structures, rather than through a metaphysical attitude inherited from elsewhere. If this can be done, then the conversations that African philosophy has with other philosophical pursuits, other disciplines, and other sets of commitments, can yield a positive result.
>
> (2009)

In the above, Janz counsels African philosophers to redirect their critical energy toward the center in order to investigate the internal structures of the discipline. This is one veritable way of developing the discipline. By focusing on the theme of women in this work, I heed this call.

In the preceding section I argued that just about anybody irrespective of gender has a right to philosophize. If biologists and physiologists have proven that men are physically stronger than women, they are yet to prove that the same is the case with recourse to the human brain. And incidentally, you do not require muscles to do philosophy. What is required is the brain – the seat of the faculty of reason – and women possess this brain as men do.

It is clear that what has kept women marginalized in philosophy generally and African philosophy in particular is a chauvinistic strategy to subjugate the opposite sex. What is happening to women in philosophy is not different from what is happening to them in sport, politics, the corporate business world, religion, etc., and this is fuelled by cultures that are inclined, whether consciously or unconsciously, to the privileging of men over women. A good number of scholars have bemoaned cultural complicities in subjugating and silencing the female voice (See: Achike, 1977; Afonja, 1990; Amadiume, 1997; Ewelukwa, 2002). My charge in this work is to question this fundamental problem with a specific focus on the field of African philosophy.

To do this, I would like to begin by re-asking the main questions in African philosophy today to accommodate women. Instead of asking, as some like Uzukwu (1982), Anyanwu (1984) and Onunwa (2011) do, what is the good life for 'man' in this place?, we may ask what is the good life for 'humans', men and women alike? This type of question makes a space for the female gender, but besides balancing gender concerns, it also could make room for the female voice. For example, in entertaining this question, we are committed to separating, in a gender-sensitive way, our analysis of what the good life might mean for men and for women. We might discover, as ideas are poured out by male and female thinkers alike, that some of the things men want out of life in general might vary from some of the things women want out of life. Is this not worth studying? Of course, it is, and what does it tell us? It tells us that we may have been leaving out some important layers in our epistemological enterprise when we gloss over the feminine perspective or bury such a perspective within the masculine viewpoint. The idea of a masculine human ideal as in contrast to that of the feminine human ideal might seem odd, especially as it tends to bifurcate humanity, but has nature not bifurcated humanity all along? Are we to deny that the physiologies of men and women are different? We know this for a fact and cannot deny it. But difference in gender is not the same as inequality of gender; only chauvinists argue for the latter. What I argue for is that differences in gender might translate to differences in ideals. Thus one can creditably ask, do men have some ideals that are somewhat different from those of women? Put in another way, are these ideals in some ways different from the feminine human ideals? My intention is to highlight this concern and not to investigate it here for lack of space.

Also, instead of asking what is the criterion for knowledge in the African place (conceived through a masculine lens)? We may ask, what are the criteria for knowledge in the African place? And are there different categories of perception for men and for women? If there are, what constitutes their basic epistemic structures? Recently, philosophers like Nkiru Nzegwu (2003), Lorraine Code (2007) and Elizabeth Potter (2007) have discussed issues surrounding feminist epistemology in greater detail, and as a result, revisiting the subject here will amount to an unhelpful digression. My intention is to highlight the issue here and not to discuss it in detail.

Further, instead of asking how Africans perceive reality, as some have done (Iroegbu, 1995; Asouzu, 2004, 2007; Ogbonnaya, 2014), which is discussed from masculine viewpoints, we may ask, what forms of perceptions of reality exist in the African place? The latter question might be able to open new vistas for thought and enable us conduct a more accommodating philosophical investigation. Also, instead of asking who has the right to philosophize in the African place which produces masculine pontifications, we may ask: what does it mean to philosophize in the African place? And instead of asking how do we philosophize in the African place, we may ask: how ought we to philosophize in the African place? The latter question brings on board the normative dimension of epistemology in African philosophy. J. O. Chimakonam has recently investigated this issue in his work 'The Knowledge Question in African Philosophy: A Case for Cogno-Normative (Complementary) Epistemology'.

In the work, Chimakonam among other things seeks to investigate the connection between knowledge and morality, which crystallized into his theory of cogno-normative epistemology or complementary epistemology (2015). This theory states that knowledge can be subjected to value analysis. What this entails is that our knowledge should have moral content, especially in a post-colonial Africa afflicted by all kinds of problems. As he put it: 'That which must be knowledge for the modern Africa struggling to shake off the evils of poverty, backwardness, racism, conflicts and effects of colonialism must have positive moral content' (2015). In other words, we must be able to distinguish between good and bad and not just accurate and inaccurate in the question of knowledge.

Following from the above, it is not good to suggest that someone does not have the right to reflect and hold an own informed opinion on matters simply because she is a woman. There is a moral problem involved in denying women the right to philosophize. It is similar to saying that they are not humans. And this is condemnable. Every human being that possesses the faculty of reason is capable of philosophizing. Philosophizing is not a right which by law could be awarded to some and denied others. When, as a dominating gender, men attempt through cultural means to write off the female gender from the act of philosophizing, we must call attention to the bad logic that undergirds their claims. Nzegwu clearly exposes this bad logic, especially as it permeates academia, in her work 'The Politics of Gender in African Studies in the North'. For her, to suggest that one lacks intellectual rigor/ability simply because of her gender is spurious (2001). It is all a baseless assumption to infer from the biologically correct premise that men are physically different from women to the psychologically incorrect conclusion that they must be mentally superior to women. There is no science in this world that has and can prove that the brain of the female is inferior to the brain of the male. Even the difference in morphology, some have clearly argued, does not translate to a superior–inferior dichotomy (Midgley and Hughes, 1983).

Thus the question of who has the right to philosophize, whether across gender or race, is a mischief that should not arise. Human beings, the ones evolutionists call *homo sapiens*, possess the faculty of reason which can be deployed to philosophical activity. This faculty is never vitiated by race or gender, but it can be improved upon through specialized training. However, training or no training, no human can claim the right to philosophize on the basis of racial or gendered categories. We must therefore reject the cultural, religious and all forms of traditional strategies that tend to exclude women from philosophical activities. These, as Nzegwu suggests may amount to what she calls gender imperialism (2002). This is a scenario where males dominate and impose their epistemic structures on females, particularly in academia.

It is important at this point to clarify the epistemological, ontological and ethical implications of any convention that denies women the right to philosophize. We must understand that the human society is run and directed by humans. Laws which guide human conduct in the society are products of arguments and deliberations during town hall meetings. The exclusion of the female gender in these meetings and gatherings is a denial of their ability to philosophize. In all of this, there are two philosophical activities that stand out, namely reflection and expression. If women are posted to the kitchen of philosophy or in another rendition relegated to the background or banished from town hall meetings where their voices are not heard and where their opinions are not sought or where their presence is not required, which is the norm in many an African society today, their perspective and contributions are eliminated. This is a form of epistemic injustice which Miranda Fricker talks about (2007). She conceives epistemic injustice as 'a wrong done to someone specifically in their capacity as a knower' (2007). We cannot afford to go on like this in Africa with regard to the place of women. The exclusion of any gender in the decision making processes of any society or community of humans amounts to the ontological denial of their humanity and that is unjust by any framework. We are simply saying that women are not fully human as men are. This is morally despicable and out of date for a twenty-first-century world. African philosophy and philosophers have a moral duty to address this age's long-term wrongdoing to the female gender. Thus any question in African philosophy which does not accommodate the perspective of the female gender commits epistemic injustice.

## Conclusion

In this chapter I have been able to do a couple of things, namely: I provided explanations of the analogy of women in the kitchen of philosophy. I drew inspiration from the traditional African world-view that locates the place of the female gender in the kitchen, thus denying her the right to reflect, ask questions, and hold informed own opinions on matters that concern her and her immediate environment. The analogy of a kitchen thus harps on the idea of anonymity as a virtue for the female gender. I went on to establish that this type of treatment of women in traditional pre-colonial Africa has been carried over to the postcolonial time and now amounts to female subjugation/marginalization orchestrated by the male gender. I argued that it is a despicable strategy which should be quashed in twenty-first-century Africa. I addressed the issue of who has the right to philosophize and concluded that human beings, irrespective of gender or race, can philosophize and that the question of right does not even arise. My proposal was a project of re-asking of the African philosophy questions by which African philosophy can reinvent itself anew and weave its questions in ways that cover the phenomenological sphere of inquiry and most importantly, accommodate the relevant and pressing issues of our time which includes women. On the whole, my argument in this chapter has focused on establishing the fact that there is no way to overcome women's subordination without including and battling intellectual marginalization, and this is where African philosophy has a major role to play.

## References

Achike, O. (1977). 'Problems of Creation and Dissolution of Customary Marriages in Nigeria'. In Roberts, S. (ed.), *Law and the Family in Africa* (pp. 145–158). The Hague: Mouton.
Afonja, S. (1990). 'Changing Patterns of Gender Stratification in West Africa'. In Tinker, I. (ed.), *Persistent Equalities: Women and World Development* (pp. 198–209). New York: Oxford University Press.

Alcoff, M. and Kittay, F. E. (eds) (2007). *The Blackwell Guide to Feminist Philosophy.* Malden, MA: Blackwell Publishing.

Amadiume, I. (1997). *Reinventing Africa: Matriarchy, Religion and Culture.* London: Zed Books.

Andreski, S. (1970). *The African Predicament: A Study in the Pathology of Modernisation.* New York: Atherton Press.

Anyanwu, K. C. (1984). 'The Meaning of Ultimate Reality in Igbo Cultural Experience'. *Ultimate Reality and Meaning,* 7, 84–101.

Asouzu, I. I. (2004). *The Method and Principles of Complementary Reflection in and beyond African Philosophy.* Calabar: University of Calabar Press.

Asouzu, I. I. (2007). *Ibuaṛu: The Heavy Burden of Philosophy beyond African Philosophy.* Zurich: Litverlag.

Awoonor, K. (2006). *The African Predicament: Collected Essays.* Accra: Sub-Saharan Publishers.

Bodunrin, P. (1984). 'The Question of African Philosophy'. In Wright, R. A. (ed.), *African Philosophy: An Introduction.* 3rd edn (pp. 1–23). Lanham, MD: University Press of America.

Chimakonam, J. (2014). 'African Philosophy, History of'. In Frasier, J. and Dowden, B. (eds), *The Internet Encyclopedia of Philosophy.* ISSN 2161–0002. www.iep.utm.edu/afric-hi/.

Chimakonam, J. (2015). 'The Knowledge Question in African Philosophy: A Case for Cogno- Normative (Complementary) Epistemology'. In Chimakonam, J. (ed.), *Atuolu Omalu: Some Unanswered Questions in Contemporary African Philosophy* (pp. 67–81). Lanham, MD: University Press of America.

Chuku, G. (2013). *The Igbo Intellectual Tradition: Creative Conflict in African and African Diasporic Thought* (pp. 267–293). New York: Palgrave Macmillan.

Code, L. (2007). 'Feminist Epistemologies and Women's Lives'. In Alcoff, M. and Kittay, F. E. (eds), *The Blackwell Guide to Feminist Philosophy* (pp. 211–234). Malden, MA: Blackwell Publishing.

Ewelukwa, U. U. (2002). 'Post-colonialism, Gender, Customary Injustice: Widows in African Societies'. *Human Rights Quarterly,* 24, 424–486.

Fricker, M. (2007). *Epistemic Injustice: Power and the Ethics of Knowing.* Oxford: Oxford University Press.

Horney, K. (1967). *Feminine Psychology.* New York: Norton.

Iroegbu, P. (1995). *Metaphysics: The Kpim of Philosophy.* Owerri: International Universities Press.

Janz, B. B. (2009). *Philosophy in an African Place.* Lanham, MD: Lexington Books.

Janz, B. B. (2015). 'African Philosophy: Some Basic Questions'. In Chimakonam, J. (ed.), *Atuolu Omalu: Some Unanswered Questions in Contemporary African Philosophy* (pp. 67–81). Lanham, MD: University Press of America.

Lynne, S. (1983). *Intruders on the Rights of Men: Women's Unpublished Heritage.* London: Pandora Press.

Maurier, H. (1984). 'Do We Have an African Philosophy?' In Wright, R. A. (ed.), *African Philosophy: An Introduction.* 3rd edn (pp. 25–40). Lanham, MD: University Press of America.

Midgley, M. and Hughes, J. (1983). *Women's Choices: Philosophical Problems Facing Feminism.* London: Weidenfeld and Nicolson.

Momoh, C. S. (1985). 'African Philosophy: Does It Exist?' *Diogene,* 33(130), 73–104.

Nzegwu, N. (1996). 'Philosopher's Intellectual Responsibility to African Females'. *APA Newsletter,* 90 (1), 130–135.

Nzegwu, N. (2001). 'The Politics of Gender in African Studies in the North'. In Veney, C. and Zeleza, T. P. (eds), *Women in African Scholarly Publishing* (pp. 111–168). Trenton, NJ: Africa World Press.

Nzegwu, N. (2003). 'The Epistemological Challenge of Motherhood to Patriliny'. *JENDA: A Journal of Culture and African Women Studies*, 5. www.jendajournal.co m/issue5/nzegwu.html.

Nzegwu, N. (2002). 'O Africa: Gender Imperialism in Academia'. In Oyeronke, O. (ed.), *African Women and Feminism: Reflecting on the Politics of Sisterhood* (pp. 99–157). Trenton, NJ: Africa World Press.

Nzegwu, N. (2006). *Family Matters: Feminist Concepts in African Philosophy of Culture.* New York: State University of New York Press.

Oduyoye, M. A. (1995). *Daughters of Anowa: African Women and Patriarchy.* Maryknoll, NY: Orbis Books.

Ogbonnaya, L. U. (2014). 'The Question of Being in African Philosophy'. *Filosofia Theoretica: Journal of African Philosophy, Culture and Religions*, 3(1), 108–126.

Oguejiofor, J. (2001). *Philosophy and the African Predicament.* Ibadan: Hope Publications.

Ogundipe-Leslie, O. (1994). *Re-creating Ourselves: African Women and Critical Transformations.* Trenton, NJ: Africa World Press.

Ogwu, J. (1996). 'Perspectives of the Critical Impediments to Women in the Decision-making Process'. In Osinulu, C. and Mba, N. (eds), *Nigerian Women in Politics* (pp. 35–42). Lagos: Malthouse Press.

Oheneba-Sakyi, Y. (1999). *Female Autonomy, Family Decision Making, and Demographic Behavior in Africa.* Lewiston, PA: Edwin Mellen Press.

Onunwa, U. (2011). 'Humanistic Basis for African Traditional Religious Theology and Ethics: A Challenge to the Church in Nigeria'. *Filosofia Theoretica: Journal of African Philosophy, Culture and Religions*, 1 (1), 39–61.

Oyewumi, O. (1997). *Invention of Women: Making an African Sense of Western Discourses on Gender.* Minneapolis, MN: University of Minnesota Press.

Oyewumi, O. (2002). 'Conceptualizing Gender: The Eurocentric Foundations of Feminist Concepts and the Challenge of African Epistemologies'. *Jenda: A Journal of Culture and African Women Studies*, 2 (1).

Potter, E. (2007). 'Feminist Epistemology and *Philos Sci*'. In Alcoff, M. and Kittay, F. E. (eds), *The Blackwell Guide to Feminist Philosophy* (pp. 235–254). Malden, MA: Blackwell Publishing.

Shaw, S. and Lee, J. (eds) (2012). *Women's Voices, Feminist Visions: Classic and Contemporary Readings.* 5th edn. New York: McGraw Hill.

Uzukwu, B. (1982). 'Igbo World and Ultimate Reality and Meaning'. *Ultimate Reality and Meaning*, 5, 188–209.

*Vanguard News.* (2016). 'My Wife Belongs to My Kitchen: Buhari Responds to Aisha's Interview'. *Vanguard Newspaper*, 14 October. www.vanguardngr.com/2016/1 0/wife-belongs-kitchen-buhari/.

Vest, J. L. (2009). 'Perverse and Necessary Dialogues in African Philosophy'. *Thought and Practice: A Journal of the Philosophical Association of Kenya*, New series, 1 (2), 1–23.

Wright, R. A. (1984). 'Investigating African Philosophy'. In Wright, R. A. (ed.), *African Philosophy: An Introduction.* 3rd edn (pp. 41–55). Lanham, MD: University Press of America.

# 14 Are women marginalized in African philosophy?

*Uduma Oji Uduma*

## Introduction

This chapter is inspired by the roundtable discussion at the International Colloquium on 'Marginalization in African Philosophy: Women and the Environment' hosted by the University of Calabar, Nigeria in collaboration with the University of Johannesburg, South Africa in partnership with the Conversational School of Philosophy. The Colloquium, which held from September 21, 2016 to September 23, 2016 focused on women and the environment, noting specifically that the entrenched traditional world-views which privilege men over women and humans over the environment make it difficult for the modern day challenges posed by the neglect of these issues to become obvious. On the issue of marginalization of women in African philosophy, it is urged that the United Nations General Assembly in 1996 adopted the Beijing Declaration and Platform for Action (BPfA) as a programme of action against gender inequality, yet 20 years after, the assessment of the BPfA implementation does not show much progress in the sub-Saharan Africa. Worried about how women's subordination affects the economy and socio-political development in the society vis-à-vis the economic, social, political and educational roles which women can play for the growth of a state, the pertinent questions that arise here were articulated as follows: to what extent do world-views inspire women's subordination in sub-Saharan Africa? To what extent do governments, academia and corporate bodies condone this? What roles has philosophical education played to ameliorate or escalate this problem? What are the questions of African philosophy and how do they accommodate women? How has African philosophy marginalized women in its questions? To what extent can African philosophy help in solving this problem?

From these underpinnings and questions, I was asked to discuss the question: 'Are women marginalized in African philosophy or is African philosophy marginalized by women?' It was, and still remains, my position that there is no epistemic justification for asserting any of the two disjuncts; as such, both in the weak and strong senses of the disjunction, the truth-value correlation of the disjuncts in the disjunctive question is false. It is pertinent to underscore here that this roundtable question stems from the grossly erroneous Western-inspired feminist drumming that today's status of African women as second class citizens is rooted in, hence reflective of, traditional African societies' perception and treatment of women as inherently inferior and thus not only peripherized but indeed subjugated. Regrettably, most Africans and non-Africans alike bandy this sentiment. Nevertheless, it is unarguable that the number of women engaged on scholarship in African philosophy is abysmal, yet there is no evidential support for the omission of women philosophers from the historical surveys of African philosophy. There is also no evidential support of a conscious process of making African philosophy a male-dominated profession or an attempt to keep male control of the production of ideas in African philosophy. The question of women's marginalization in African philosophy is thus a dumb one. The temptation, therefore, may be to infer the corollary that the paucity of women engaged in philosophy is a result of African philosophy being marginalized by women. And here too there is neither evidential nor epistemic justification that it is the African philosophy genre that is peculiarly, or in isolation, marginalized by women. From questions raised in the roundtable discussion, I began to be fascinatingly awash with how much Western feminist scholarship has, with blinkered and distorting finesse, misguided African feminist philosophy. This inspires the need to restructure the curricula of the philosophy programme of universities in Africa to see how much of African perspectives and experiences will speak to us about the place of women in African philosophy. But before addressing the question of women's marginalization in African philosophy it is important to look at the question of women's marginalization generally.

## Marginalization of women in philosophy

It is notoriously bandied that academic philosophy as practiced today excludes, marginalizes, and trivializes women philosophers and the contributions that they make to the discipline (Hutchinson and Jenkins, 2013). Tracy Bowell captures this succinctly when she avers

> For women, philosophy is the least welcoming of the humanities disciplines. Women's underrepresentation as scholars, as students and as subjects of enquiry is unsurpassed by any other of those disciplines. It has a gender profile more similar to (though sometimes worse than) disciplines in the STEM (Science, Technology, Engineering and Maths) areas. A gender gap exists at almost all levels, with men outnumbering women from undergraduate students to professors.
>
> (Bowell, 2015, pp. 4–5)

Rini (2013, pp. 127–142) discussing in depth, reels out statistical evidence; according to her, only one woman was appointed to a permanent (but part-time) position in a New Zealand philosophy department between 2005 and

2013, while 20 men have been appointed. In Australia, women hold 28 percent of continuing positions in philosophy departments, in the USA, the percentage has remained at around 21 percent for the past decade, while in the UK, it stands at around 25.4 percent (Hutchinson and Jenkins, 2013, appendix 1). While noting that statistical evidence is often tainted and fraught with fallacies, yet it does not eviscerate the epistemic validity of the claim of paucity of women in philosophy. It is also pertinent to underscore that the situation in universities in Africa is not quite different from the statistical picture that Rini bandies. In my undergraduate days, we had only one female philosophy teacher and the same could be said to be the case throughout my postgraduate days. Amongst us, the first ten Ph.D.'s in the Department of Philosophy at the University of Lagos, only one woman could be counted. As a teacher of philosophy, the experience is no different. In our department at Ebonyi State University, Abakaliki, the department for over 17 years has had only one female teacher in its employment. During my sabbatical visit to the University of Cape Coast Ghana between July 2009 and July 2010, there was no female philosophy faculty member; even now in 2017, nearly 8 years since, there is still no female philosophy faculty member in that university. The situation is no different at Nnamdi Azikiwe University, Awka in Nigeria; the Philosophy Department is 20 years old, it was established in 1997, and there is no female philosophy teacher. At the University of Nigeria, Nsukka, one of the oldest philosophy departments in Nigeria, established over 45 years ago, it took it over 40 years to engage their first female philosopher academic staff, a graduate assistant for that matter.

It is also notable that in Nigeria today there are just four female professors of Philosophy, namely: Sophie Oluwole (first female professor of Philosophy in Nigeria), Dorothy Olu Jacobs (Ucheaga), Ebun Oduwole and Ashiata Bolatito Lanre-Abbas.

In her seminal article on the situation of women scholars and students in philosophy, Haslanger writes of her 'rage' about how she and others have been treated and how many women and others who are marginalized in philosophical discourses and in the professional, academic practice of philosophy, continue the struggle to be recognized and respected as philosophers (2008, p. 210). As she and others note, many simply give up that struggle; some scholars are lost to more welcoming intellectual homes – to disciplines that are more outward looking – while others are lost to the academy altogether.

In fact, it is claimed by many feminist historians of philosophy that 'the philosophical canon taught at European and American universities does not include women philosophers'.[1] According to Zdenka Kalnická (2010, pp. 143–144), 'Witt (2000) claims that in a 1967 *Encyclopedia of Philosophy* containing information about 900 philosophers, no women were present, and the same was said by Waithe about *The Encyclopedia of Philosophy* from 1981'.

E. O'Neill (1998), however, argues that an omission of women philosophers from historical surveys was not always the case. According to her, in the seventeenth century, women were often included in history of philosophy books, for example in *The History of Philosophy* by Thomas Stanley, popular and widely read by his contemporaries. O'Neill further submits 'that the situation began to change during the eighteenth and nineteenth centuries; and by the twentieth century, women philosophers were erased from the history of philosophy entirely'. She indicates several causes of this phenomenon, such as the process of making philosophy a profession and purification of philosophical discourse, the omission of those conceptions which did not 'win' in the course of time, and, especially, the attempt to keep male control of the production of ideas (O'Neill, 1998, pp. 17–34).

However, assuming but not conceded that there is male bias in the historical survey of philosophers, the evidence for a claim of gender equality in the discipline of philosophy is so thin that, no matter how we orchestrate allegations of bias in the historical survey, this alone cannot satisfactorily explain the paucity of women in the enterprise of philosophy. Neven Sesardic and Rafael De Clercq elaborate on this when they aver that:

> a number of philosophers attribute the underrepresentation of women in philosophy largely to bias against women or some kind of wrongful discrimination. They cite six sources of evidence to support their contention … In each case, we find that proponents of the discrimination hypothesis … have tended to present evidence selectively. Occasionally they have even presented as evidence what appears to be something more dubious – for example, studies supporting the discrimination hypothesis based on data that have been reported 'lost' under suspicious circumstances. It is not the aim … to settle the question of the causes of female underrepresentation in philosophy. Rather, we argue that, contrary to what many philosophers claim, the overall information available does not support the discrimination hypothesis.
>
> (Sesardic and De Clercq, 2014)

The point for Sesardic and De Clercq above is that gender disparity is not sufficient to ground discrimination. They thus cite EEOC v. Bloomberg L. P., 07 Civ. 8383(LAP), NYLJ 1202618858451, at *1 (SDNY, Decided September 2013) where the U.S. District Court for the Southern District of New York dismissed a complaint about sex discrimination by saying: '"*J'accuse!*" is not enough in court. Evidence is required', and concludes by saying 'We should expect nothing less in philosophy' (Sesardic and De Clercq, 2014).

Notwithstanding, however, even in centuries eulogized by feminist historians of philosophy for their gender sensitivity, the number of women philosophers was very few. The question: why are there few women philosophers? Thus remains a very germane and pungent one.

The view expressed by Hegel in his *Philosophy of Right* to this vexed question is that:

Women can, of course, be educated, but their minds are not adapted to the higher sciences, philosophy, or certain of the arts. Women may have happy inspirations, taste, elegance, but they have not the ideal. The difference between man and woman is the same as between animal and plant. The animal corresponds more closely to the character of the man, the plant to that of the woman. In woman there is a more peaceful unfolding of nature, a process, whose principle is the less clearly determined unity of feeling. If woman were to control the government, the state would be in danger, for they do not act according to the dictates of universality, but are influenced by accidental inclinations and opinions. The education of woman goes on one only knows how, in the atmosphere of picture thinking, as it were, more through life than through the acquisition of knowledge. Man attains his position only through stress of thought and much specialized effort.

(Hegel, 2001 [1820], pp. 144–145, par. 166, note)

For Hegel, in the above quotation, women come to knowledge through the imaginary, while men come to knowledge through work; this naturally disposes women to simply be unsuited to philosophy. Linda Martín Alcoff (2013) apparently shares Hegel's persuasion. According to her, female would-be philosophers are deterred by the academy's combative, 'rough-and-tumble' style of debate. The emerging suggestion here, as Louise Antony couches it, is that 'there's something about philosophy and something about women that makes the one alien to the other' (2012, p. 227). Kant, before Hegel, insists that women were generally incapable of abstract thought; that women's faculties of understanding were merely 'beautiful', not 'sublime' like men's. For this reason, the idea of a woman philosopher was absurd. The odd woman who tried to do philosophy despite her handicap, Kant opines, would be unsexed by the attempt: 'she might as well grow a beard' (Kant, 1994, pp. 102–112).

This view, however, for obvious reasons, no longer enjoys currency in today's gender-sensitive society. Instead, feminist philosophers and philosophers of psychology have drawn on the importantly distinct idea that women approach things differently, and that philosophy is the victim for not fitting well with women's ways of thinking, not that women are either naturally or intrinsically handicapped to do philosophy. The postulate here is that the features of philosophy that make it alien to women are features that were detrimental to the practice of philosophy itself, so that it is the discipline that needs changing, not the women.

Those who canvass this position begin by positing that 'differences in intuition' is a major factor in the demographic gender imbalance found in academic philosophy. Wesley Buckwalter and Stephen Stich (2014) address this issue and claim to have found evidence of gender differences in people's responses to common philosophical thought-experiments. These differences which they speculate account for the paucity of women in philosophy are explained thus:

if women have different intuitions about standard thought-experiments than men do, and if men dominate philosophy, then women studying philosophy may come to the conclusion – or be told explicitly – that they just don't 'get' philosophy – that philosophy is not the subject for them.

In essence, for Buckwalter and Stich, women may be victims of a 'selection effect' within philosophy. The point here is that if agreement with the philosophical consensus is taken to be a *sine qua non* of philosophical ability, individuals with non-orthodox intuitions will be filtered out. If that consensus is forged within a community that is almost all-male, then it will be men's intuitions that will constitute the philosophical mainstream. If women, then, have systematically different intuitions from men's, then their intuitions will be less likely than men's to agree with mainstream opinion, and thus more likely to be filtered out. Women, in short, will be disproportionately selected against.

What is clear in Buckwalter and Stich is that they do not, like Kant, see gender disparity as symptomatic of inadequacy or weakness in women; or as Katy Waldman (2013) would couch it 'smear women as too fragile'. For them the demonstrable gender gap in philosophy is rather suggestive of unintentional sexism in the methodology and pedagogy of academic philosophy. They, Louise Antony (2012, p. 228) would say, are not making the retrograde claim that women do not belong in philosophy; their contention is rather that philosophy, to its discredit, does not welcome women. Indeed, Carol Gilligan (1982), in her book, *In a Different Voice*, had earlier portrayed philosophy as it is practiced as 'gendered', embodying or reflecting a distinctively male perspective that fails to listen to – even to notice – the 'different voice' in which women speak. According to her, mainstream ethical theory improperly enshrined what was in fact a male style of moral reasoning as the best and highest form while neglecting an equally valuable mode of ethical thinking that was characteristic of women. Male theorists could not hear what women had to say about morality because women spoke 'in a different voice'. Also, Janice Moulton (1993, pp. 149–164) argues that philosophy's 'adversarial method' was off-putting to women and antithetical to feminist values. More than that, however, Moulton challenged the utility of the method, arguing that it fostered intransigence and discouraged sympathetic consideration of opposing views, undercutting the goal of discovering the truth.

Camille Paglia, in explaining the dearth of women in philosophy, also emphasized what prima facie would pass for unintentional sexism in the methodology and pedagogy of academic philosophy when she says:

I feel women in general are less comfortable than men in inhabiting a highly austere, cold, analytical space, such as the one which philosophy involves. Women as a whole – and there are obvious exceptions – are more drawn to practical, personal matters. It is not that they inherently lack a talent or aptitude for philosophy or higher mathematics, but rather that they are more unwilling than men to devote their lives to a frigid space from which the natural and the human have been eliminated.

(Paglia, 2005)

Admittedly, Paglia in pointing out that women have peculiarities that inspire their underrepresentation in philosophy does not thereby consider women as fragile, less capable or intellectually diminished. Rather, there may be something to this, so she goes further and deeper to explicate:

Today's lack of major female philosophers is not due to lack of talent but to the collapse of philosophy. Philosophy as traditionally practised may be a dead genre. This is the age of the internet in which we are constantly flooded by information in fragments. Each person at the computer is embarked on a quest for and fabrication of his or her identity. The web mimics human neurology, and it is fundamentally altering young people's brains. The web, for good or ill, is instantaneous. Philosophy belongs to a vanished age of much slower and rhetorically formal inquiry. Today's philosophers are now antiquarians.

(Ibid.)

Paglia, as Katy Waldman aptly captures it, is saying that philosophy in general fails to evolve as quickly as the other humanities; its sexism is thus just a symptom of being mired in the past. But Waldman disagrees with Paglia; in fact she describes her postulation as 'the most tenuous possibility yet' in discussing philosophy's problem with women and worried that she is needlessly dragging gender into what seems like an individual preference for pragmatism over abstract-mindedness. She thus concludes by remarking that

if women perceive philosophy as a 'frigid space', it's probably because they are outnumbered and alienated, not because they consider theoretical musings somehow less 'human'. Likewise, the male philosophers propositioning their graduate students appear perfectly comfortable wallowing in the mud of everyday life. If only they had some respect for their medieval counterparts, who chose to personify philosophy as a fair, virtuous woman.

(Waldman, 2013)

Will Wilkinson (2005), however, debunks Paglia's postulation about the present day otiose practice of philosophy. He rather argues that philosophy as traditionally practiced is at its 'high water mark today'. According to him, 'more books of philosophy were published in the last ten years than in any other ten-year period of history. There are, without a doubt, more people well-trained in rigorous methods of philosophical inquiry than ever before'.

I do not only agree with Wilkinson that philosophy in recent years cannot be stigmatized as a dead genre – indeed, it has rather been fecundated. I am also convinced that it is ignorance (or at best mischief) of the history and value of philosophy that can warrant such a dismissal of philosophy as a moribund discipline. It is, therefore, both pertinent and instructive to underscore the fact that the suasion that philosophy has collapsed is vacuous because it is rather sadly a vestige of the traditional image of philosophers as the occupants of ivory towers, indulging in the philosophical equivalent of counting the number of angels that can fit on a pinhead. Philosophy in this context is construed as a concern that investigates issues which are divorced from any relevance to the so-called common man.

Thus Paglia, instead of indicating a new image of philosophy that represents a decline is only carrying over or relapsing to ancient misgivings about philosophy, particularly when it is contrasted with what we now call science. It is remarkable here that for a long time science was known as part of philosophy, later being spoken of as natural philosophy and eventually experimental philosophy. With the disengagement of the specialized sciences and the contributions of modern science, people started to ask questions of philosophy and wonder if it was good for anything given the apparent success of science. Even some philosophers began to insist that the experimental method was the only way to answer questions about the world and that philosophy could no longer be thought of as anything but idle speculation. Fortunately, however, some philosophers have always cautioned that the arrival of another way to approach questions was both a good thing and no reason to throw away the other methods that may, after all, still work better on some questions.

It is this, in a nuanced sense that indexed the strident and persuasive challenge for philosophy to show its practical usefulness in an age of science. In an age where everybody values usefulness and effectiveness, failure to rise to this challenge is prone to be regarded as a most serious defect, As Einstein has noticed: 'People like chopping wood, because it shows immediate results' (culled from https://twitter.com/EinsteinBOT). For good or for bad, philosophy is stigmatized as not having any utility of that kind. It is, therefore, widely perceived as a completely otiose activity in the world of universal nitty-gritty (know-how).

Russell in discussing the main sources of negative attitudes to philosophy elaborates the, already highlighted, influence of science, the pull toward *scientism* and *technocratic consciousness* (Russell, n.d., 'The Value of Philosophy'). He also discusses the influence of practical affairs (in fact of *pragmatistic, philistine consciousness*). According to Russell, *scientism* and *technocratic consciousness* recognizes only definite, applicable knowledge derived from scientific questions, while *philistine consciousness* values only practical action as an immediate response to everyday trivial (= little) questions. For Russell, s*cientism* does not bear the indefinite, uncertain character of philosophic study and *pragmatisticism* does not tolerate philosophic procrastination and the ineffectiveness of thinking. Both are insensitive to the beneficial effects of the uncertainty philosophers cultivate as their typical state of mind.

Russell is, however, convinced that both attitudes espouse a superficial view of philosophy based on some misconceptions. These misconceptions pertain to: (a) the ends of human life, and (b) the goods of philosophy.

The first group of misconceptions identifies ultimate human goals with acquisition, power or pleasure, whereas the other inappropriately measures philosophical goods upon the yardstick of positive, tangible and useful results of other human endeavors. These misconceptions are only prejudices of those people who are fascinated by material goods and the effectiveness of technology (Russell calls them 'instinctive men'). Who are they? And why are they 'wrongly called practical men'? They are *modern philistines* who view philosophical questioning as an idle game played by lazy, intellectual slackers who avoid real problems of everyday life. These philistines present themselves as advocates of practical needs and concerns. But the philistine notion of useful thinking is obviously formed upon the model of instrumental thinking ('what is the utility of this?') and does not take into account practical concerns regarding our personal existence, identity and the sense of life. And precisely these concerns make up the realm of the traditional 'practical philosophy' which deals with the problem of 'good life' and 'just community'. In view of this, the notion of 'useful' practicality in the sense of immediate and everyday 'utility' is very *narrow*. This is the reason Russell indicates that in fact it is wrongly called *practical* (it should be perhaps named *pragmatistic*).

The above discourse shows how defective Paglia's appreciation of philosophy is. And Wilkinson (2005), in demonstrating that philosophy, contrary to Paglia's vituperations, does *not* belong to a vanished age of much slower and rhetorically formal inquiry and that today's philosophers are *not* now antiquarians, writes

> And as travelers to this little piece of the information superhighway may be aware, philosophical conversations and debates can be conducted *over the internet*, and they are. It's probably a good bet that there were more words written last year in online discussions of philosophy than were written about philosophy in *any other year of human history.*

Wilkinson goes on to argue that even if Paglia is correct in saying that philosophy is no longer as culturally central as it once was, the reality is that 'nothing that used to be culturally central is as culturally central as it once was because we've got a more polyglot decentralized culture'. In fact, according to him, the fact that philosophers aren't being interviewed … means that philosophy is more or less invisible to Camille Paglia, despite the fact that it is flourishing by any historical standard, and despite the fact that women, such as Martha Nussbaum and Christine Korsgaard, are at the absolute top of the game (Wilkinson, 2005). He concludes that the reason why academic philosophy is insufficiently engaged with the public, and appears not to hold a more privileged place in the fragmented popular consciousness, is due to straightforward institutional reasons: academia as it is presently constituted does reward a kind of bloodless scholasticism. Thus while accepting that direct engagement with current policy debates and cultural concerns would make philosophy better appreciated, failure to do this is a long, long way from the claim that philosophy is a dead genre (Wilkinson, 2005).

Gaile Pohlhaus (2015) and Louise Antony (2012), however, criticize and raise questions as to the tenability of 'differences in intuition' contributing to the demographic gender imbalance found in academic philosophy. Pohlhaus (pp. 2–4) submits that emphasizing differences may in some cases compound rather than alleviate philosophy's lack of demographic diversity. She argues that the way so-called gender (and cultural) 'differences' are understood by some experimental philosophers is not at all compatible with feminist projects, including those feminist projects that take seriously differences in social position (differences between women and men, as well as differences among women). In fact, for her, how and why so-called gender (and cultural) 'differences' are deployed by these experimental philosophers is not only incompatible with, but also seriously antithetical to, feminist philosophical concerns. Antony (2012, pp. 243–249) questions the degree to which the methodologies purporting to find gender differences are rigorously scientific and raises the possibility that talk of 'different voices' might do more harm than good insofar as it may inadvertently (but no less powerfully) contribute to the more rigorously empirically demonstrated phenomena of *implicit bias* and *stereotype threat* (pp. 233–236). Given the evidence, Antony cautions, we ought to take a 'perfect storm' approach to questions of diversity in philosophy, identifying and analyzing the ways in which forms of discrimination might converge, interact, and intensify within the discipline (pp. 250–251).

Antony, indeed, stresses that the strategy of positing of gender differences to account for the underrepresentation of women is not in itself, and should not be taken to be, a misogynistic or anti-feminist position. At the same time, she also stresses, it must be recognized that even if the gender-difference point is used to argue for the accommodation rather than the correction of women, even if the blame is to be laid on the discipline, the claim of differences in intuition (the 'different voices' model) is still committed to the antecedent existence of *intrinsic* gender differences (Antony, 2012, p. 229).

But Antony argues that 'one need not posit substantive intrinsic differences between men and women in order to explain the demographics in philosophy' (p. 230). She rather posits the 'perfect storm' alternative to account for gender disparity in philosophy. According to *The Oxford Dictionary*, a 'perfect storm' is, literally, 'a particularly violent storm arising from a rare combination of adverse meteorological factors' or, figuratively, 'an especially bad situation caused by a combination of unfavourable circumstances.' The perfect storm model explains women's low representation within philosophy as a kind of interaction effect among familiar kinds of sex discrimination that are operative throughout society, but that take on particular forms and force as they converge within the academic institution of philosophy.

Virginia Valian (1999) had, before Antony, ignored the different intuition argument in explaining gender disparity in philosophy. She rather latched onto the term 'implicit bias', by which is meant the attitudes or stereotypes that affect our understanding, actions and decisions in an unconscious manner; that is, when we have attitudes to people or associate stereotypes with them without our conscious knowledge, we are victims of implicit bias. Valian argues that much of our interpersonal interaction is mediated by 'gender schemas', sets of largely unconscious beliefs about men and women that condition our perceptions and shape our normative expectations (pp. 149–152). It is important to note that gender schematic thinking and acting, by the way, is not itself gendered: it is as operative in women as it is in men (Antony, 2012, p. 230) However, conflicts between gender schematic norms of femininity, on the one hand, and characteristics held to be necessary for success in academia, on the other, can result in women's work being neglected or undervalued, with predictable consequences for women's careers. Such conflicts, Valian argues, are present and operative in many different academic disciplines. They generate, in Antony's terminology, a kind of ongoing tropical storm within academia. Valian points out that the effects of gender schematic thinking can interact with, and can be intensified by, other factors. For example, women who work in areas where women are thought to be less able than men frequently suffer something called 'stereotype threat', a kind of self-stigmatizing anxiety that has been shown to degrade individuals' performance in a variety of tasks. Women's overall depressed performance can then confirm the original stereotype and reinforce gender schematic thinking.

## Implicit bias and stereotype threat

Jennifer Saul (2013a), Helen Beebee and Jenny Saul (2011), Sally Haslanger (2008), Carole Lee and Christian Schunn (2011, pp. 352–373), and Jesse Prinz (2007), as if justifying Valian, in one form or the other, argue that if we accept that the paucity of women in philosophy is as a result of difference in intuition or rationality, this does not on its own show that there is a problem to be addressed by philosophers. It could be, Saul ('Implicit Bias, Stereotype Threat and Women') argues, that women just don't like (or aren't good at) the sorts of reasoning philosophers engage in or the sorts of problems philosophers discuss, either as a result of their innate nature or as a result of their socialization. According to her, if either of these is the case, then it's far from clear that *philosophers* should feel the need to do anything about women in philosophy. Yet, she is persuaded that these hypotheses are very difficult to adequately study, and so difficult to decisively rule out; but the danger in accepting this, according to Saul, is that it warrants jumping to the conclusion that 'since we don't *know* that these hypotheses are false, we shouldn't try to do anything about women in philosophy'. In her exact words: 'some move from this to the thought that we shouldn't try to do anything about women in philosophy because we don't know that these hypotheses are false'.

To avert this danger, as it were, Saul is intensely persuaded to bring into prominent relief that women's marginalization in philosophy, as she puts it, 'women's progress in philosophy', is impeded by the presence of two well-supported psychological phenomena – 'implicit bias and stereotype threat'.

Beginning with implicit bias, The Perception Institute in explaining the meaning of the term writes:

> [T]houghts and feelings are 'implicit' if we are unaware of them or mistaken about their nature. We have a bias when, rather than being neutral, we have a preference for (or aversion to) a person or group of people. Thus, we use the term 'implicit bias' to describe when we have attitudes towards people or associate stereotypes with them without our conscious knowledge.
>
> (https://perception.org/research/implicit-bias/)

The Kirwan Institute (2015) gives a fuller explanation of the term in its 2015 review of the term implicit bias. According to this review, implicit bias, also known as implicit social cognition, refers to the 'attitudes or stereotypes that affect our understanding, actions, and decisions in an unconscious manner'. These biases, it is elaborated, encompass both favorable and unfavorable assessments; they are activated involuntarily and without an individual's awareness or intentional control. They reside deep in the subconscious, and are different from known biases that individuals may choose to conceal for the purposes of social and/or political correctness. It is also highlighted that implicit biases are not accessible through introspection and that the implicit associations we harbor in our subconscious cause us to have feelings and attitudes about other people based on characteristics such as race, ethnicity, age, and appearance. These associations develop over the course of a lifetime beginning at a very early age through exposure to direct and indirect messages. In addition to early life experiences, the media and news programming are oft-cited origins of implicit associations (Kirwan Institute, 2015).

Saul, as already adumbrated, has written variously on implicit bias with particular focus on women underrepresentation in philosophy. She defines implicit bias as 'unconscious, automatic tendencies to associate certain traits with members of particular social groups, in ways that lead to some very disturbing errors' (Saul, 2013a, p. 244). This means that implicit bias predisposes people to judge members of stigmatized groups more negatively, in a whole host of ways. They are 'unconscious biases that affect the way we perceive, evaluate, or interact with people from the groups that our biases "target"' (Saul, 2013b, p. 40). It is emphasized that recent psychological research shows that most people – even those who explicitly and sincerely avow egalitarian views – hold 'implicit biases' against such groups as blacks, women, gay people, and so on, based on unconscious stereotypes of these groups (Beebee and Saul, 2011, p. 12). These biases are extremely widespread, and found both in members of the stigmatized groups and in those who are consciously highly egalitarian. Steinpreis et al. (1999) and Vedantam (2005) echo that even members of the 'targeted' group are susceptible to implicit bias; for example, women as well as men are biased against women.

Generally, however, some of the characteristics of implicit biases have been outlined as follows:

- Implicit biases are pervasive. Everyone possesses them, even people with avowed commitments to impartiality such as judges.
- Implicit and explicit biases are related but distinct mental constructs. They are not mutually exclusive and may even reinforce each other.
- The implicit associations we hold do not necessarily align with our declared beliefs or even reflect stances we would explicitly endorse.
- We generally tend to hold implicit biases that favor our own ingroup, though research has shown that we can still hold implicit biases against our ingroup.
- Implicit biases are malleable. Our brains are incredibly complex, and the implicit associations that we have formed can be gradually unlearned through a variety of debiasing techniques.

(Kirwan Institute, 2015)

These biases, it is pointed out, manifest in, for example, association tasks asking subjects to pair positive and negative adjectives with black or white faces: most are much speedier to match black faces with negative adjectives than with positive ones. They are also manifest in behavior: studies have shown that those with anti-black implicit biases are less friendly to black experimenters and more likely to classify an ambiguous object in a black person's hand as a gun while classifying it as harmless in a white person's hand. But focusing on women's underrepresentation in philosophy, Saul canvasses that implicit biases affect the way we perceive (for instance) the quality of a woman's work, leading us to evaluate it more negatively than it deserves (Saul, 2013b, p. 40).

Saul posits that academics are clearly affected by implicit bias, even if (as seems likely) explicit commitments to egalitarianism are widespread. Jo Handelsman (2016) and Sarah Laskey (2016) corroborate this claim. According to Handelsman, 'Most people intend to be fair, if you ask them, "When you do this evaluation, are you planning to be fair?" they will 100 percent say yes'. Regrettably, she observes that 'most scientists carry these unconscious, implicit prejudices and biases that warp their evaluation of people or the work that they do' (Handelsman, 2016, pp. 4–7). Laskey highlights that scientists in particular claim, 'we're trained to be objective, so the bias studies don't apply to us'. But she interjects: 'if we take a look at the data it turns out this applies to everyone'; in essence, no one is immune to it (Laskey, 2016). Saul sums up the point by debunking any assumption as to philosophers not being prone to implicit bias. As she puts it 'I have sometimes heard it suggested that philosophers would not be subject to implicit bias against stigmatized social groups, due to their greater ability to be objective' (Saul, 2013b, p. 43). Citing Uhlmann and Cohen (2007), she demonstrates that research, however, show that people systematically overestimate their own ability to be objective. Even more importantly, it turns out that being primed with objectivity (e.g. asked to tick a box rating one's own objectivity) increases susceptibility to gender bias in job applicant evaluation (Uhlmann and Cohen, 2007).

The import, for her, is that philosophers may be *especially* subject to implicit biases, rather than especially immune from them. She also sees no reason to any claim that philosophers are unlikely to hold the same sorts of views of women in philosophy as the public at large. Noting that scientists, even women scientists, share the same sorts of biases about women in science that others do (Steinpreis et. al., 1999; Vedantam, 2005), she posits that it is reasonable to suppose that philosophers share the same sorts of biases about women (Saul, 2013b, pp. 43–45).

To demonstrate how implicit bias accounts for women's underrepresentation in philosophy, Saul first takes the case of journal submissions; she cites a study by Budden et al. that reported a 33 percent increase in representation of female authors in *Behavioral Ecology* in the four years that followed the adoption of double-blind review by the journal, which is supposed to suggest that there is gender bias favoring male authors. In an earlier article she discussed prestige bias and cites what she considers a now-classic study by Peters and Ceci (1982) where previously published papers were sent to the top psychology journals that had published them, but with false names and non-prestigious affiliations. Only 8 percent detected that the papers had already been sub-mitted, and 89 percent were rejected, citing serious methodological errors (and not the one they should have cited – plagiarism) (see Ceci and Peters, 2014, pp. 1–4). Saul argues that this makes it clear that institutional affiliation has a dramatic effect on the judgments made by reviewers (either positively, negatively, or both). These are experts in their field, making judgments about their area of expertise – psychological methodology – and yet they are making dramatically different judgments depending on the social group to which authors belong (member of prestigious vs. non-prestigious psychology department) (Saul, 2012, p. 245). Her intention in positing prestige bias no doubt is to show how pervasive implicit bias is generally.

Next, she takes the case of curriculum vitae and stresses that it is well established that the presence of a male or female name on a curriculum vitae has a strong effect on how that curriculum vitae is evaluated (Saul, 2013b, p. 41). This, she points out, is true both inside and outside academia; but nevertheless interjects that, philosophers have not specifically been studied, noting that, however, those academics who she claims are most likely to be aware of the existence of unconscious psychological processes – psychologists – exhibit just this bias. In Steinpreis et al.'s US study, 238 academic psychologists (118 male, 120 female) evaluated a curriculum vitae randomly assigned a male or a female name. Both male and female participants gave the male applicant better evaluations for teaching, research, and service experience and were more likely to hire the male than the female applicant. She also cites Moss-Racusin et al., 2012, a study in which it is alleged that faculty participants rated the same CV as more competent and hireable, and deserving of a higher salary if a male name was at the top of it. They were also more willing to mentor the males. These effects were equally strong for both male and female evaluators, of all ages. They were also shown to correlate with preexisting 'subtle' biases against women.

What data like these, she remarks, seem to show is that people – including academics, together with those with explicit egalitarian beliefs, as well as those who are themselves women – more readily associate the sorts of traits valued in CVs and in articles with men than with women. The point is further canvassed that research indicates that traits like originality, excellence, leadership, and intellectual ability seem to be more readily associated with men than with women (Valian, 1999). The effect of implicit bias thus is that women's work is being wrongly judged to be of lower quality than it actually is. This will lead to talented women philosophers not being encouraged to continue, not getting grants, not getting jobs, not getting promoted, and not getting their work read, hence the paucity of women in philosophy.

Neven Sesardic and Rafael De Clercq (2014), however, have responded to the epistemic validity of the claims of Helen Beebee, Jennifer Saul, Sally Haslanger, Carole Lee, Christian Schunn, and Jesse Prinz on implicit bias argument by underscoring that, contrary to their claims, the overall information available does not support the leap from gender disparity to discrimination hypothesis. As they put it:

> Obviously, in the absence of additional evidence, mere information about percentages is insufficient to prove 'bias and partiality': the percentage of women among philosophy professors (or among the recent hires) being much lower than 50 percent does *not*, in itself, imply that there is a bias against women in the hiring process. It may even be that the process is actually biased against men.
>
> (Sesardic and De Clercq, 2014)

To establish even a prima facie case for anti-woman hiring bias, it would be necessary, they argue, to first compare the percentage of women among the job *applicants* with the percentage of women among job *recipients*. Only if the latter percentage is lower than the former is there prima facie evidence for hiring discrimination against women. They cite Andrew Irvine (1996, pp. 255–292), who compared exactly these percentages in the Canadian academic job market over a 20-year period ending in 1996, and according to his estimations, the percentage of female job recipients was on the whole higher than the percentage of female job applicants, which led him to conclude that 'if systemic discrimination is occurring within contemporary university hiring, it is more likely to be occurring in favor of, rather than against, women' (p. 261). Doreen Kimura (2002, pp. 27–31) in her survey of 36 schools and departments, corroborates Irvine's finding: of the three most recent hires to fill positions in each school or department studied, women represented 29 percent of the total number of applicants, but 41 percent of all individuals hired. Clive Seligman's data on academic hiring at the University of Western Ontario from 1991/1992 to 1998/1999, inspired the following conclusion:

> Over the 8 years, on average: 5.4% of female applicants were appointed compared to 2.9% of male applicants; 21.7% of female applicants were interviewed compared to 15% of male applicants; and 24.9% of female applicants who were interviewed were hired whereas 19.2% of men who were interviewed were appointed. Again, the results in each of the years are remarkably consistent. Women had almost twice the chance of being hired as did men.
>
> (Seligman, 2001)

Similarly, two surveys of major research universities commissioned by the U.S. Congress to assess gender differences in the careers of science, engineering, and mathematics faculty – the area with the highest underrepresentation of women – focussed on almost 500 departments and more than 1,800 faculty members. They reported that among those interviewed for tenure-track or tenured positions, the percentage of women interviewed was higher than the percentage of women who applied for those positions, and that tenure-track women in all disciplines received a percentage of first offers that was greater than their overall percentage in the interview pool. The situation was the same with tenured positions in all disciplines except biology (National Research Council, 2010). So we find a pattern according to which there are more women, percentage-wise, at a later stage than at an earlier stage throughout the hiring process – which is exactly the opposite of what one would expect if there were discrimination against women as encapsulated in the implicit bias hypothesis. The apt question then is, why are there fewer women than men at the application stage in the first place? Could this be a result of discrimination? It could, but evidence is needed to support this hypothesis. Moreover, assuming that the situation is really so inhospitable for women in the academic job market, it would be odd if women were first discouraged from applying for academic jobs, only to be favored over men once they submit an application. There is room here for different explanations, including a theory that does not posit discrimination.

Stereotype threat is reputedly 'a well established psychological phenomenon' (Saul, 2015) and supported by 'a well-established body of research in psychology' (Saul, 2013b; see also Antony, 2012, p. 232), and is the twin of implicit bias in accounting for why

> women's progress in philosophy is impeded rather differently. Instead of affecting the way that members of a stigmatized group are *perceived or evaluated*, stereotype threat affects the way that members of that group

actually *perform*. Simply, stereotype threat refers to being at risk of confirming, as a self-characteristic, a negative stereotype about one's social group.

(Steele and Aronson, 1995, pp. 797–811)

The term 'stereotype threat' was first used by Steele and Aronson (1995), who showed in several experiments that Black college freshmen and sophomores performed more poorly on standardized tests than White students when their race was emphasized. When race was not emphasized, however, Black students performed better than and equivalent to White students. The results showed that performance in academic contexts can be harmed by the awareness that one's behavior might be viewed through the lens of racial stereotypes. In general, the conditions that produce stereotype threat are ones in which a highlighted stereotype implicates the self through association with a relevant social category (Marx and Stapel, 2006, pp. 243–254; Marx et al., 2005, pp. 432–446). When one views oneself in terms of a salient group membership (e.g. 'I am a woman', 'women are not expected to be good at math', and 'this is a difficult math test'), performance can be undermined because of concerns about possibly confirming negative stereotypes about one's group. Thus, situations that increase the salience of the stereotyped group identity can increase vulnerability to stereotype threat.

Notably, stereotype threat occurs when members of a group underperform as a result of (a) their consciousness of a negative stereotype related to their membership in said group, and (b) a desire not to conform to that stereotype. This means stereotype threat refers to a situation in which subjects tend to underperform on a given task because they are afraid of confirming a negative public stereotype about their group. In essence, victims of stereotype threat underperform on the relevant tasks because they are unconsciously preoccupied by fears of confirming the stereotypes about their group – so preoccupied that they show elevated heart rate and blood pressure (Steele, 2010, pp. 119–120, 149). According to Saul (2013b, pp. 41–42), the effect of stereotype threat, rather tragically, is strongest with those most committed to doing well in the area in question. Victims of stereotype threat are often, though not always, unaware of what is happening. Saul further elucidates that the effects of stereotype threat are dramatic. When in a threat-provoking situation, Blacks perform worse than Whites on standardized tests; girls perform worse than boys in maths; White people perform worse than Blacks at sports (Steele 2010). But when the threat is removed, performance from the stigmatized group improves dramatically – often to the point of equality. Stereotype threat is likely to be provoked where one is from a group that is negatively stigmatized in a certain context, one is in that context, and one's group membership is made salient.

The question now is: how is philosophy stereotyped? Remarkably, even feminist philosophers admit that there is no direct empirical research on stereotypes about gender and philosophy, nevertheless, Beebee and Saul

(2011, p. 12) posit that there is good reason to believe that philosophy is stereotyped as male. Saul (2013b, p. 43) says that feminist philosophers have long argued that there is a tradition in philosophy of associating reason, objectivity, and philosophical thought with maleness; and emotion, subjectivity, and the non-philosophical with femaleness (see, e.g. Haslanger, 2008). In fact, Sally Haslanger writes:

> As feminist philosophers have been arguing for decades, the familiar dichotomies with which Anglophone philosophy defines itself map neatly onto gender dichotomies – rational/emotional, objective/subjective, mind/ body; ideals of philosophy – penetrating, seminal, and rigorous; and what we do – attack, target, and demolish an opponent, all of which frame philosophy as masculine and in opposition to the feminine.
>
> (2008, p. 213)

In *The Stone* (2013), Haslanger further canvasses that philosophy is stereotyped as male, and that women philosophers often suffer from stereotype threat quite frequently. As she puts it,

> Many of us have had the experience of sitting on an airplane and being asked by the person in the next seat, 'What do you do?'
> It is a moment of uncertainty: what to say? There are risks if you reply, 'I'm a philosopher,' for you may then have the neighbor expounding 'their philosophy' … . One time, a male friend of mine got the enthusiastic response, 'Oh, you're a philosopher? Tell me some of your sayings!' However, when I've tried the 'I'm a philosopher' reply, it has prompted laughter. Once when I queried why the laughter, the response was, 'I think of philosophers as old men with beards, and you're definitely not that! You're too young and attractive to be a philosopher.' I'm sure he intended this as a compliment. But I stopped giving the answer 'I'm a philosopher.'
>
> (Haslanger, 2013)

Rae Langton (2013) depicts this vividly in her 'emblematic image of the philosopher': 'that stern, gray-bearded man – a 'serious, high-minded Dumbledore', which according to her creates a stereotype threat for any thinker who looks less white or male. Her claim is that women and blacks may underperform because they don't feel like 'proper' philosophers.

Samir Chopra (2012), expressing her agreement with Saul that philosophy is stereotyped as male, bandies what she (Chopra) dubbed the Dickhead Theory. The heart of the Dickhead Theory (DT) is that philosophy is stereotypically male because of its aggressive style of argument. This might include, for example, displaying hostility – by words, tone of voice or body language – towards a speaker or audience in a seminar (or a class discussion) whom one thinks has failed to grasp a point or adequately address an objection, or pursuing a point well past the stage where it is obvious that the speaker has no adequate response. In an email to Saul, Chopra submits:

> One of the biggest problems is that philosophy is treated like a contact sport: an argument is a contest, a chance to knock your opponent down, to utterly destroy him. Look at the way male philosophers report on question-and-answer sessions at colloquia: 'Oh, X just wiped the floor with Y; X just totally devastated Y's objection' and so on. Look at the hostility with which questioners confront speakers, or the bristling tone of most philosophy discussions. Are they doing philosophy or are they working out deep neuroses? I find all of this extremely distasteful and diligently avoid most philosophy talks simply because I cannot stand – pardon my French – all the dick-waving.
>
> (Chopra, 2012)

Chopra is emphasizing that philosophy is structured around the construction, analysis and defense of arguments, and that as such, it is an adversarial discipline; the kind of aggressive language attached to the art and practice of argumentation in philosophy is construed as offensive hence the argot 'dick-waving'. Helen Beebee, in 'Women and Deviance in Philosophy', includes a section titled 'The seminar as a philosophical battleground', which argues for the DT much more carefully and thoughtfully, and in much more temperate language. At the end of the section Bebee concludes:

> The hard question remains, of course: do women in fact, in general – or perhaps just more often than their male colleagues – find the aggressive and competitive atmosphere that is often present in the philosophy seminar uncongenial, independently of any effect it may have via stereotype threat? I do not know the answer to that question. I myself do not enjoy being on the receiving end of aggressive and competitive behavior, and … do not feel in the least bit demeaned by that confession. On the contrary: on my own personal list of thick moral concepts, these both fall under 'vice' rather than 'virtue'. I cannot, of course, speak for others. But my point here has been that there are grounds for thinking that such an atmosphere is alienating for women – and hence good reasons attempting to change the atmosphere of the seminar room when it is aggressive or competitive – whatever the answer to the hard question; so it is one that we can simply allow to lapse. The role of such an atmosphere in the pursuit of truth is, at best, neutral; at worst, it runs the risk of putting women off philosophy – thereby reinforcing the stereotype that philosophy is a man's world.
>
> (Beebee, 2013, p. 16)

Related philosophers' standard metaphors for what goes on in the seminar room are those of competition, fighting and battle (Rooney, 2010). People win and lose arguments, shoot down points, go for the jugular, fight their corner, take no prisoners, don't pull their punches, and so on. This all falls squarely in the 'stereotypically male' category. The point here is not that women are somehow less able to cope when aggressive behavior is aimed at them, and so should be treated more gently than men. It is rather that aggressive behavior, whoever it is aimed at, can heighten women's feeling that they do not belong by reinforcing the masculine nature of the environment within which they study and work. Importantly, for philosophers, being one of only a few women in a roomful of men is sufficient to make one's group membership salient. If philosophy is also stereotyped as male, as seems likely, women philosophers are likely to suffer from stereotype threat quite frequently. This will lead women to underperform at all career stages, including crucially high-stress moments like job interviews.

Although Saul, Beebee, Haslanger, Langton, Chopra and other feminist philosophers are persuaded that philosophy is stereotyped as male, yet they, as indeed most feminist philosophers, admit that psychologists have not studied philosophers' stereotypes of philosophy. Nevertheless they are too ready to interject that they have extensively studied stereotypes of mathematics. And that mathematics is strongly stereotyped as male (e.g. Nosek et al., 2002; Saul, 2013b); and for them it seems reasonable to suppose that anglophone philosophy, with its heavy use of logic, will inherit this stereotype. In fact, even if not all anglophone philosophy makes heavy use of logic, Saul argues that logical competence is generally viewed as a near-necessary condition for success in the field: logic courses, she stresses, are widely required of both undergraduate and postgraduate philosophy students (Saul, 2013b, p. 43).

## The problematic of the question of women's marginalization in African philosophy

In the foregoing, it is clear that philosophy is globally marginalized. Regrettably, the situation in Africa speaks of multi-jeopardy. First, Africa as a continent is marginalized by philosophy. This is rooted in the intentional attempt to rationalize Africans out of humanity (Uduma 2014, p. 127). In this respect, we note that Eurocentric scholars and missionaries mutilated history and concocted a false image of Africans which they presented as the substantive African identity; an identity that presents the African as pre-logical, barbaric and as such incapable of philosophic thoughts. This identity was foisted and consolidated on humanity, including Africans, and intellectually accepted as the true African identity for over four centuries. Consequently, while the racist Eurocentric description of the African makes it impossible for one to suggest that there can be anything like African philosophy, the enslavement, balk-anization, colonization, and the introduction of a Western-oriented formal education into Africa further dehumanized, traumatized and alienated Africans from their culture. This means that philosophy isn't white just because of the aristocracy of color or because only white men can afford the 'luxury' to talk about *meaningless things* rather than things that matter; it is white because, as Molefi Kete Asante (2004) puts it, the principal position in the academies of the Western world, including the universities and academies of Africa, is that

> Philosophy is the highest discipline.
> All other disciplines are derived from philosophy.
> Philosophy is the creation of the Greeks.
> The Greeks are white,
> Therefore, whites are the creators of philosophy.

The above reasoning privileges the Greeks as the originators of philosophy, the highest of the sciences. But Asante (2004) argues that there is a serious problem with this line of reasoning. According to him, the information is false because as far as scholarship can reveal, the origin of the word 'philosophy' is not in the Greek language. He admits that although it comes into English from the Greek, according to dictionaries on Greek etymology, the origin of the word is unknown. He explains that the origin of *sophia* is clearly in the African language, *Mdu Ntr*, the language of ancient Egypt, where the word *seba*, meaning 'the wise' appears first in 2052 BC in the tomb of Antef I, long before the existence of Greece or Greek. He further says that 'the word became "Sebo" in Coptic and "Sophia" in Greek. As to the meaning of philosopher, the lover of wisdom, that is, precisely what is meant by "Seba," the Wise, in ancient tomb writings of the Egyptians'. Asante (2004), however, notes and lampoons the hypocrisy of the 'whites': other people and cultures may contribute thoughts, like the Chinese, Confucius, but thoughts are not philosophy; only the Greeks can contribute philosophy. The African people may have religion and myths, but not philosophy.

Indeed, Europeans naturally tended to suspect the intellectual capabilities of the African. All sorts of theories were propounded, including what was known as phrenology, a quasi-scientific idea that sought to relate the size and shape of the skull to the level of intelligence among the races (Uduma, 2015, p. 53). Needless to say, the Europeans concluded that the rather low position of the Black man's forehead was a clear evidence of defective intellect. According to Uduma (2015, p. 53), the belief was very well known in the eighteenth century, and William Blake (1793) was clearly referring to this racist invention when he wrote 'O African! Black African! (go, winged thought, widen his forehead)'. However, the most outrageous opinion on the subject of intelligence came from an otherwise famous and respected philosopher, David Hume. In a clearly racist footnote in his essay, 'Of National Characters' (1753), Hume writes:

> I am apt to suspect the Negroes and in general all the other species of men (for there are four or five different kinds) to be naturally inferior to the whites. There never was a civilized nation of any other complexion

than white, nor even any individual eminent either in action or speculation. No ingenious manufactures amongst them, no arts, no sciences. On the other hand, the most rude and barbarous of the whites, such as the ancient GERMANS, the present TARTARS, have still something eminent about them, in their valour, form of government, or some other particular. Such a uniform and constant difference could not happen, in so many countries and ages, if nature had not made an original distinction betwixt these breeds of men. Not to mention our colonies, there are Negroes slaves dispersed all over EUROPE, of which none ever discovered any symptoms of ingenuity; tho' low people, without education, will start up amongst us, and distinguish themselves in every profession. In JAMAICA indeed they talk of one Negro as a man of parts and learning; but 'tis likely he is admired for very slender accomplishments, like a parrot, who speaks a few words plainly.

It is remarkable that during the last years of his life, Hume worked at correcting his works for a final and definitive edition which was published posthumously in 1777. In doing this, there is little doubt that he was stung by his critics (including Beattie) and he responded by revising the first two sentences of the footnote. Hume's editors, Thomas Hill Green and Thomas Hodge Grose, failed to include the revision. The missing revision, which has been recently discovered and published, makes a significant difference to the attitude conveyed by Hume's statement (Uduma, 2015, p. 54). Although the rest of the footnote remained unchanged from the original, Hume revised the opening two lines: 'I am apt to suspect the Negroes to be naturally inferior to whites. There scarcely ever was a civilized nation of that complexion, nor even any individual eminent either in action or speculation.'

For sure, the fact that Hume even revised the footnote proves that he did seriously reconsider the racist implications of his position. But his response was to abandon a polygenetic position and focus his attack solely on Blacks, singling them out as an inferior group within the human family (Uduma, 2015, p. 54).

Even today, after the great debate on its existence, African philosophy still remains a contested genre. Many Eurocentrists are only willing to admit it with the qualifier 'ethno', thus designating it as ethno-philosophy. African philosophy, in this context, is at best seen as not so much an area or topic within philosophy as it is a set of culturally original questions about the full range of philosophical issues. Indeed, as Janz points out, more often than not questions put by non-Africans about African philosophy's existence have amounted to an implicit dismissal of Africa, as those questions come with the presumption that there is no philosophy in Africa, and the onus is on those who claim there is to prove it. And it is unarguable that except for some Africans, the admittance of African philosophy as a genre is often with askance or either merely tendentious or at best tolerated.

Yet even in philosophy departments in African universities the curriculum is grossly skewed toward Western philosophy. The history of philosophy taught in these departments does not only hail the Greeks as its originators but is indeed largely the history of Western philosophy. Yes, we have discussed and elaborated on the stolen legacies or the African origin of Greek philosophy, but it has not only remained a moot point – indeed the curricula of philosophy departments in African universities betray our hesitancy on this fact – but we unconsciously still take recourse to the Greeks as making the first attempt to provide a comprehensive account of the origin and nature of the world based on observation and reasoning, that is, the first to abandon reliance on magic, superstition, religion, tradition, or authority in answering questions about the basic makeup of things and the nature of the world and of reality (Uduma, forthcoming). It is incredible that what it takes to be a graduate of philosophy in our universities in Africa is merely the regurgitation of Western philosophy. There are indeed no historical African figures studied in philosophy in African universities; the first set of professional philosophers of African descent were not united in developing African philosophy and even up till today there is no sustainable effort to decolonize the philosophy curriculum. The African undergraduate studying philosophy in an African University often finds no difference in the curriculum taught in Western universities. For sure, the problem of language and written documents are good excuses, but they are only sign-posts of our hesitancy. We must have a starting point and it must begin with decolonizing the curriculum of our African universities; African thoughts, ideas and perspectives must take center stage in the curriculum of philosophy programmes in African universities instead of being a mere addendum or appendix to the curriculum as we have it today. Johnbosco Nwogbo (2017) rightly laments:

> 'African Philosophy' treats thought by African scholars as a curiosity, and as potentially not sufficiently philosophical to be included in discussions of 'normal' philosophy. These students observe that African thought should be at the centre of philosophy done on the African continent, and that if this were the case, there would be no need to cordon off a segment of thought on the continent and call it 'African philosophy'. Philosophy done and taught in Africa ought to speak to the African experience, and the African way of being. Philosophy that does this should not be cordoned off into the title 'African philosophy' and treated as a strange phenomenon.
>
> As some philosophy students see it, it is no longer politically, and even morally, acceptable for African students to be taught philosophy exactly as they would be taught it in a European university, disregarding, in effect, the epistemic position out of which we are supposed to function. To many of these students, the subject-matter that has been termed 'African Philosophy', which they consider, not without reason, a token addition to the curriculum, is misplaced in Africa.

In effect, the present situation whereby in most of our universities in Africa the course content on African philosophy is less than 10 percent of the course requirements for graduation is totally both inapt and illogical just as it is neocolonialist. The tragedy is that the African graduate of philosophy is alienated from his immediate experience and environment, and if a discipline does not bear any relevance to its immediate environment and beneficiaries it is unjustified to expect policy makers and government to waste money on such otiose discipline(s). Edwin Etieyibo (2015) thus voices the 'moral obligations' on philosophy departments in universities in Africa to Africanize their philosophy curricula. Using Miranda Fricker's notion of 'epistemic injustice', he argues that 'an epistemic injustice is committed against individuals and groups when the curriculum is neither representative enough of their perspectives and experiences nor robustly speaks to them'. He thus sums his presentation, and plausibly so, by advocating that our curricula must 'speak to (our) students in a way they presently do not.

## In lieu of a conclusion

The question of women's marginalization in African philosophy is a knotty and complex one because it has an Ariadneian thread that indexes so many questions that definitely levitate above the gender disparity buzz in feminist scholarship. First, it, in a sense, invites the question of the marginalization of the discipline of philosophy generally. Second, African philosophy is a marginalized genre. Third, the Western philosophical tradition marginalizes women, and it is this that forms the curricula of the philosophy programmes in universities in Africa, with the result that the curricula do not speak to the African experience, world-view or perspective. In essence, philosophy as taught today in Africa seems just too white and male for post-colonial Africa. Alex Dunn (2014), in explaining what we mean by philosophy is white and male, goes beyond the obvious rather racist and sexist denotation of the expression to give it a connotative interpretation. In his blog post, 'By Definition, Philosophy Is for White Men', Dunn takes up a very different aspect of Peter Unger's treatment of everything that *has* any clear connection to the empirical world as 'not philosophy'. Basically, Unger says that Bertrand Russell wasn't really doing philosophy when he was arguing for peace, that Tim Maudlin is doing 'adulterated' philosophy in doing empirically based philosophy of physics, etc. For Unger, *philosophy proper* is 'what analytic philosophers do' and he contends that analytic philosophy has almost entirely been dominated by 'concretely empty ideas', ideas that do not make a difference to how things are with concrete reality (see Unger, 2014).

Arvan (2014), however, remarks that although Unger thinks analytic philosophy is empty, he (Unger) is, whether he recognizes it or not, playing into a perniciously exclusionary conception of what counts as 'philosophy'. The problem, very roughly, is this: for Unger, *philosophy* is basically an inquiry that has *nothing to do with the concrete world* – the world in which people suffer from war, poverty, injustice, discrimination, etc., the implication being it is a discipline by and for white men to talk about *meaningless things* rather than things that matter to non-whites, non-men, etc. (in *The Philosopher's Cocoon*, Arvan, 2014). The point is elaborated that if we go through the different sub-fields of philosophy, *the more relevant to real life* the sub-field is, the *less* prestige the area seems to have. The most prestigious areas, Unger insists, are such areas as Metaphysics, Epistemology, Philosophy of Language, Philosophy of Science (physics, etc.), Logic, and Meta-Ethics; while the least prestigious areas include Applied Ethics, Feminist Philosophy, Critical Race Theory, etc. Further, he says, it's really no wonder our field is dominated by white men. Our discipline has basically taken the areas of philosophy that are *as far removed as possible* from the daily experiences of injustice, exclusion, etc., that non-white/non-males experience and given those areas the greatest prestige, whereas the areas that speak most directly *to the interests and experience* of non-white/non-males are given far less prestige, and often derided publicly and privately. Finally, he adds, if we look at areas that deal with justice, etc., the most prestigious figures – Rawls, Nozick, etc, – have tended to be those who focus on *ideal theory* (or describing perfectly just social-political systems), all but ignoring *nonideal theory* (the area of social-political philosophy that deals with injustice).

This scenario indicates why the restructuring and decolonization of the curricula of philosophy program in African universities are desiderata. It is only such a restructuring that would invest relevance to African philosophy, and ultimately eliminate philosophy's dominance by an 'aristocracy of sex'.

## Note

1 For detailed discussion, see M. E. Waithe (ed.), *A History of Women Philosophers*, volume I. Dordrecht: Kluwer Academic Publishers, 1987.

## References

Adleberg, T., M. Thompson and E. Nahmias (2014). 'Do Men and Women Have Different Philosophical Intuitions? Further Data'. *Philosophical Psychology*. doi:10.1080/09515089.2013.878834.

Agarwal, B. (1994). *A Field of One's Own: Gender and Land Rights in South Asia*. Cambridge: Cambridge University Press.

Alcoff, L. M. (2013). 'What's Wrong with Philosophy?' *The Stone Opinionator*, 3 September. Available at opinionator@nytimes.com.

Antony, L. (2012). 'Different Voices or Perfect Storm: Why Are There so Few Women in Philosophy?' *Journal of Social Philosophy* 43 (3), 227–255.

Arvan, M. (2014). 'Analytic Philosophy, Continental Philosophy, and Natural Philosophy'. *The Philosopher's Cocoon*. Available at http://philosopherscocoon.typepad.com/blog/2014/06/analytic-philosophy-continental-philosophy-and-natural-philosophy.html

Asante, M. K. (2004). 'An African Origin of Philosophy: Myth or Reality?' Available at www.asante.net/articles/26/afrocentricity/.

Baier, A. (1985). 'Cartesian Persons', in *Postures of the Mind: Essays on Mind and Morals*. Minneapolis, MN: University of Minnesota Press.

Beebee, H. (2013). 'Women and Deviance in Philosophy', in Hutchison, K. and Jenkins, F. (eds), *Women in Philosophy: What Needs to Change?* Oxford: Oxford University Press, pp. 61–80.

Beebee, H. and Saul, J. (2011). *Women in Philosophy in the UK* , British Philosophical *Association and the Society for Women in Philosophy UK*, Available at http://bit.ly/td1PoA.

Blake, W. (1793). 'O African! Black African Go, Winged Thought, Widen His Forehead', in *A Song of Liberty: Marriage of Heaven and Hell* (c. 1790–1793).

Bowell, T. (2015). 'The Problem(S) of Women in Philosophy: Reflections on the Practice of Feminism in Philosophy from Contemporary Aotearoa/New Zealand'. *Women's Studies Journal* 29 (2), 4–21. Available at www.wsanz.org.nz/.

Buckwalter, W. and Stich, S. (2014). 'Gender and Philosophical Intuition', in Knobe, J. and Nichols, S. (eds), *Experimental Philosophy*, vol. 2. New York: Oxford University Press.

Buckwalter, W. and Stich, S. (2010). 'Gender and Philosophical Intuition: Why Are There so Few Women in Philosophy?' Talk given at the Society for Philosophy and Psychology, Portland.

Budden, A., Tregenza, T., Arrssen, L., Koricheva, J., Leimu, R. and Lortie, C. (2008). 'Double-Blind Review Favours Increased Representation of Female Authors'. *Trends in Ecology and Evolution* 23 (1), 4–6.

Calhoun, C. (2009). 'The Undergraduate Pipeline Problem'. *Hypatia* 24 (2), 216–223.

Ceci, S. J. and Peters, D. P. (2014). 'The Peters and Ceci Study of Journal Publications'. *The Winnower*, 6 May. Available at https://thewinnower.com/discussions/7-the-peters-ceci-study-of-journal-publications.

Chopra, S. (2012). 'On the Lack of Women in Philosophy: The Dickhead Theory'. Available at https://samirchopra.com/2012/12/07/on-the-lack-of-women-in-philosophy-the-dickhead-theory/.

Collins, P. H. (2008). *Black Feminist Thought: Knowledge, Consciousness, and the Politics of Empowerment*. New York: Routledge.

Correll, S. and Bernard, S. (2007). 'Getting a Job: Is There a Motherhood Penalty?' *American Journal of Sociology* 112, 1297–1338.

Dickason, A. (1976). 'Anatomy and Destiny: The Role of Biology in Plato's Views of Women', in Gould, C. C. and Wartofsky, M. W. (eds), *Women and Philosophy: Toward a Theory of Liberation*. New York: G. P. Putnam's Sons.

Dotson, K. (2011). 'Tracking Epistemic Violence, Tracking Practices of Silencing'. *Hypatia* 26(2), 236–257.

Dunn, A. (2014). 'By Definition, Philosophy Is for White Men'. Available at https://not.subtle.com/by-definition-philosophy-is-for-white-men.

Einstein, A. 'Collected quotes from Albert Einstein (14 March 1879 – 18 April 1955)' Culled from https://twitter.com/EinsteinBOT.

Etieyibo, E. (2015). 'Africanizing the Philosophy Curricula in Universities in Africa'. *ArtAfrica*, 3 November. Available at https://artsouthafrica.com/220-news-articles-2013/2538-africanizing-the-philosophy-curricula-in-universities-in-africa-by-edwin-etieyibo.html.

Gilligan, C. (1982). *In a Different Voice*. Cambridge, MA: Harvard University Press.

Goddard, E. (2008). *Improving the Position of Women in the Philosophy Profession*. Available at http://aap.org.au/women/reports/index.html#Ausreports.

Handelsman, J. (2016). 'The Fallacy of Fairness: Confronting Bias in Academic Science'. Featured Seminar in the Achieving Gender Equity in Science series. 8 March. Johns Hopkins University Mason Hall Auditorium, Baltimore, Maryland.

Haslanger, S. (2008). 'Changing the Ideology and Culture of Philosophy: Not by Reason (Alone)'. *Hypatia* 23 (2), 210–223.

Haslanger, S. (2013). 'Women in Philosophy? Do the Math'. *The Stone*. https://opiniona tor.blog.nytimes.com/2013/09/02/women-in-philosophy-do-the-math/.

Hegel, G. W. (2001). *Philosophy of Right* [1820]. Translated by S. W. Dyde Kitchener. Kitchener, ON: Batoche Books, para. 166, pp. 144–145.

Heyes, C. (2007). *Self-Transformations: Foucault, Ethics, and Normalized Bodies*. New York: Oxford University Press.

Hume, D. (1854). 'Of National Characters', in *The Philosophical Works of David Hume*, cited in Eric Morton, 'Race and Racism in the works of David Hume', *Journal of African Philosophy* 1 (1) (2002).

Hutchison, K. and Jenkins, F. (eds) (2013). *Women in Philosophy: What Needs to Change?* Oxford: Oxford University Press.

'Implicit Bias'. Available at https://perception.org/research/implicit-bias/.

Kirwan Institute. (2015). 'Implicit Bias'. Available at kirwaninstitute.osu.edu, Research.

Irvine, A. D. (1996). 'Jack and Jill and Employment Equity'. *Dialogue* 35, 255–292.

Kalnická, Z. (2010). 'Dislocating Women from Philosophy: Five Strategies'. *Clepsydra* 9, 143–157. Available at www.bdigital.unal.edu.co/50629/1/dislocatingwomen.pdf.

Kant, I. (1960). *Observations on the Feeling of the Beautiful and Sublime*. Berkeley, CA: University of California Press.

Kant, I. (1994). 'On the Distinction between the Beautiful and the Sublime'. In M. Mahowald (ed.), *Philosophy of Woman: An Anthology of Classic to Contemporary Concepts*. 3rd edn. Indianapolis, IN: Hackett.

Kimura, D. (2002). 'Sex Differences in the Brain Defining Men'. *Scientific American*. Available at www.ucd.ie/artspgs/langimp/genderbrain.pdf.

Langton, R. (2013). 'Disappearing Women'. *The Stone*. Available at https://opiniona tor.blogs.nytimes.com/2013/09/04/the-disappearing-women/?_r=0.

Laskey, S. (2016). 'The Uncomfortable Truth about Implicit Bias in Academic Science'. *Biomedical Odyssey*. Available at https://biomedicalodyssey.blogs.hopkinsmedicine.org/ 2016/02/the-uncomfortable-truth-about-implicit-bias-in-academic-science/.

Lee, C. J. and Schunn, C. D. (2011). 'Social Biases and Solutions for Procedural Objectivity'. *Hypatia* 26 (2), 352–373.

Leivesley, A. (2014). 'Why Philosophy Is Still Relevant – and Has Useful Applications'. *Huffington Post*. Available at www.huffingtonpost.co.uk/alexander-leivesley/philosophy is-still-relevant_b_5187952.html.

Marx, D. M. and Stapel, D. A. (2006). 'Distinguishing Stereotype Threat from Priming Effects: On the Role of the Social Self and Threat-based Concerns'. *Journal of Personality and Social Psychology* 91 (2), 243–254.

Marx, D. M., Stapel, D. A. and Muller, D. (2005). 'We Can Do It: The Interplay of Construal Orientation and Social Comparisons Under Threat'. *Journal of Personality and Social Psychology* 88 (3), 432–446. doi:10.1037/0022-3514.88.3.432.

Modrak, D. K. (1978). 'Philosophy and Women in Antiquity'. *Rice University Studies*, Winter.

Moss-Racusin, C. A., Dovidio, J. F., Brescoll, V. L., Graham, M. J. and Handelsman, J. (2012). 'Science Faculty's Subtle Gender Biases Favor Male Students'. *Proceedings of the National Academy of Sciences* 109 (41), 16474–16479.

Moulton, J. (1993). 'A Paradigm of Philosophy: The Adversary Method', in Harding, S. and Hintikka, M. B. (eds), *Discovering Reality* (pp. 149–164). Hingham, MA: Reidel.

National Research Council. (2010). *Gender Differences at Critical Transitions in the Careers of Science, Engineering, and Mathematics Faculty.* Washington, DC: National Academies Press.

Nosek, B., Banaji, M., and Greenwald, J. (2002). 'Math = Male, Me = Female, Therefore Math & Me'. *Journal of Personality and Social Psychology* 83, 44–59.

Nussbaum, M. C. (2017). 'Hilary Putnam (1926–2016)'. *Huffington Post.* Available at www.huffingtonpost.com/martha-c-nussbaum/hilary-putnam-1926-2016_b_9457774.html.

Nwogbo, J. (2017). 'South Africa: Decolonising African Philosophy – What the Curriculum Should Look Like'. *The Journalist*, 11 April. Available at www.thejournalist.org.za/spotlight/decolonising-african-philosophy-what-the-curriculum-should-look-like.

O'Neill, E. (1998). 'Disappearing Ink: Early Modern Women Philosophers and Their Fate in History', in Kourany, J. (ed.), *Philosophy in a Feminist Voice: Critiques and Reconstructions* (pp. 17–62). Princeton, NJ: Princeton University Press.

*Oxford Dictionaries.* 'Perfect Storm'. Available at http://oxforddictionaries.com/definition/perfect+storm.

Paglia, C. (2005). 'Ten Great Female Philosophers: The Thinking Woman's Women'. *Independent.* Available at www.independent.co.uk/news/uk.

Pohlhaus, G., Jr. (2015). 'Different Voices, Perfect Storms, and Asking Grandma What She Thinks: Situating Experimental Philosophy in Relation to Feminist Philosophy'. *Feminist Philosophy Quarterly* 1 (1), article 3. Available at http://ir.lib.uwo.ca/fpq/vol1/iss1/3.

Prinz, J. (2007). *The Emotional Construction of Morals*, Oxford: Oxford University Press.

Rini, A. (2013). 'Models and Values: Why Did New Zealand Philosophy Departments Stop Hiring Women Philosophers?' In Hutchinson, K. and Jenkins, F. (eds), *Women in Philosophy: What Needs to Change?* (pp. 127–142). New York: Oxford University Press.

Rooney, P. (2010). 'Philosophy, Adversarial Argumentation, and Embattled Reason'. *Informal Logic* 30, 203–234.

Russell, B. (n.d.). 'The Value of Philosophy'. Philosophy home page, available at www.philosophy.lander.edu/intro/russell.shtm.

Saul, J. (2012). 'Rankings of Quality and Rankings of Reputation: Problems for Both from Implicit Bias'. *Journal of Social Philosophy* 43 (3).

Saul, J. (2013a). 'Scepticism and Implicit Bias'. *Disputatio* 5 (37), 243–263.

Saul, J. (2013b). 'Implicit Bias, Stereotype Threat and Women in Philosophy', in Hutchinson, K. and Jenkins, F. (eds), *Women in Philosophy: What Needs to Change?* New York: Oxford University Press. Available at http://philosophy.fas.nyu.edu/docs/CP/6039/SaulIBStereotype ThreatWIP.pdf.

Saul, J. (2015). 'Women in Philosophy'. *The Philosophers' Magazine Online.* Available at www.philosophersmag.com/index.php/reflections/9-women-in-philosophy.

Seligman, C. (2001). 'Summary of Recruitment Activity for All Full-Time Faculty at the University of Western Ontario by Sex and Year'. Available at www.safs.ca/ap ril2001/recruitment.html.

Sesardic, N. and De Clercq, R. (2014). 'Women in Philosophy: Problems with the Discrimination Hypothesis', in *Feminist Philosophers.* Available at https://feministp hilosophers.wordpress.com/2014/12/11/problems-with-problems-with-the-discriminat ion-hypothesis/.

Steele, C. (2010). *Whistling Vivaldi: And Other Clues to How Stereotypes Affect Us.* New York: Norton.

Steele, C. M. and Aronson, J. (1995). 'Stereotype Threat and the Intellectual Test of African Americans'. *Journal of Personality and Social Psychology* 69 (5), 797–811.

Steinpreis, R., Anders, K. and Ritzke, D. (1999). 'The Impact of Gender on the Review of the Curricula Vitae of Job Applicants and Tenure Candidates: A National Empirical Study'. *Sex Roles* 41 (7/8), 509–528.

Stewart, B. D. and Payne, B. K. (2008). 'Bringing Automatic Stereotyping Under Control: Implementation Intentions as Efficient Means of Thought Control'. *Personality and Social Psychology Bulletin* 34, 1332–1345.

Superson, A. (2002). 'Sexism in the Classroom', in Superson, A. and Cudd, A. *Theorizing Backlash: Philosophical Reflections on Resistance to Feminism* (pp. 201–213). Oxford: Rowman and Littlefield.

Tuana, N. (1992). *Woman and the History of Philosophy.* New York: Paragon Press.

Uduma, U. O. (2014). 'The Question of the 'African' in African Philosophy: In Search of a Criterion for the Africanness of a Philosophy'. *Filosofia Theoretica: Journal of African Philosophy, Culture and Religions* 3 (1), 127–146.

Uduma, U. O. (2015). 'Beyond Irredentism and Jingoism: Reflections on the Nature of Logic and the Quest for (an) African Logic'. 7th Inaugural Lecture, Ebonyi State University, Abakaliki, 28 May.

Uduma, U. O. (forthcoming). *A Companion to Philosophy.*

Uhlmann, E. and Cohen, G. (2007). '"I Think It, Therefore It's True': Effects of Self-Perceived Objectivity on Hiring Discrimination'. *Organizational Behavior and Human Decision Processes,* 104, 207–223. Available online at www.sciencedirect.com.

Unger, P. (2014). *Empty Ideas: A Critique of Analytic Philosophy.* New York: Oxford University Press.

Valian, V. (1999). *Why So Slow? The Advancement of Women.* Cambridge, MA: MIT Press.

Vedantam, S. (2005). 'See No Bias'. *Washington Post,* 21 January. Available at www. washingtonPost.com/wp-dyn/articles/A27067-2005Jan21.html.

Vest, C. (2002). 'Introductory Comments', in Hopkins, N., *A Study on the Status of Women Faculty in Science at MIT.* AIP Conference Proceedings 628 (103). doi:10.1063/1.1505288.

Waithe, M. E. (ed.) (1987). *A History of Women Philosophers, Volume I.* Dordrecht: Kluwer Academic.

Waldman, K. (2013). 'What Is Philosophy's Problem with Women?' *The Slate,* 9 September. Available at www.slate.com/blogs/xxfactor/2013_/09/09/philosophyhas_a_wo man_problem_let_s_try_to_figure_out_why.html.

Wenneras, C. and Wold, A. (1997). 'Nepotism and Sexism in Peer Review'. *Nature* 387 (6631), 341–343.

Whitbeck, C. (1976). 'Theories of Sex Difference', in Gould, C. C. and Wartofsky, M. W. (eds), *Women and Philosophy: Toward a Theory of Liberation* (pp. 54–80). New York: G. P. Putnam's Sons.

Wilkinson, W. (2005). 'Paglia v. Philosophy'. *The Fly Bottle*. Available at www.willwilkinson.net/flybottle/2005/07/14/paglia-v-philosophy/.

Williams, J. (2015). 'Who Cares What Colour Philosophers Are?' *Spiked*. Available at www.spiked-online.com/newsite/article/who-cares-what-colour-philosophers-are/17034#.WUnTz9wo_IU.

# Index

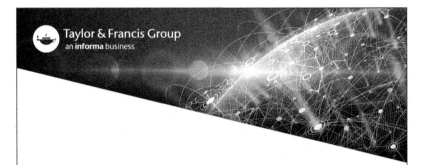